Musician–Teacher Collaborations

Musician–Teacher Collaborations: Altering the Chord explores the dynamics between musicians and teachers within educational settings, illustrating how new musical worlds are discovered and accessed through music-in-education initiatives. An international array of scholars from eleven countries present leading debates and issues—both theoretical and empirical—in order to identify and expand upon key questions: How are visiting musicians perceived by various stakeholders? What opportunities and challenges do musicians bring to educational spaces? Why are such initiatives often seen as "saving" children, music, and education?

The text is organized into three parts:

- **Critical Insights** presents new theoretical frameworks and concepts, providing alternative perspectives on musician–teacher collaboration.
- **Crossing Boundaries** addresses the challenges faced by visiting musicians and teaching artists in educational contexts while discussing the contributions of such music-in-education initiatives.
- **Working Towards Partnership** tackles some dominant narratives and perspectives in the field through a series of empirically based chapters discussing musician–teacher collaboration as a field of tension.

In twenty chapters, *Musician–Teacher Collaborations* offers critical insights into the pedagogical role music plays within educational frameworks. The geographical diversity of its contributors ensures varied and context-specific arguments while also speaking to the larger issues at play. When musicians and teachers collaborate, one is in the space of the other and vice versa. *Musician–Teacher Collaborations* analyzes the complex ways in which these spaces are inevitably altered.

Catharina Christophersen is Professor of Music Education at Western Norway University of Applied Sciences, Bergen, Norway.

Ailbhe Kenny is Lecturer of Music Education at Mary Immaculate College, University of Limerick, Ireland.

Musician–Teacher Collaborations
Altering the Chord

Edited by **Catharina Christophersen**
Western Norway University of Applied Sciences

and

Ailbhe Kenny
Mary Immaculate College, University of Limerick

NEW YORK AND LONDON

First published 2018
by Routledge
711 Third Avenue, New York, NY 10017

and by Routledge
2 Park Square, Milton Park, Abingdon, Oxon, OX14 4RN

Routledge is an imprint of the Taylor & Francis Group, an informa business

© 2018 Taylor & Francis

The right of Catharina Christophersen and Ailbhe Kenny to be identified as the author of the editorial material, and of the authors for their individual chapters, has been asserted in accordance with sections 77 and 78 of the Copyright, Designs and Patents Act 1988.

All rights reserved. No part of this book may be reprinted or reproduced or utilised in any form or by any electronic, mechanical, or other means, now known or hereafter invented, including photocopying and recording, or in any information storage or retrieval system, without permission in writing from the publishers.

Trademark notice: Product or corporate names may be trademarks or registered trademarks, and are used only for identification and explanation without intent to infringe.

Library of Congress Cataloging-in-Publication Data
Names: Christophersen, Catharina, editor. | Kenny, Ailbhe, editor.
Title: Musician-teacher collaborations : altering the chord / edited by Catharina Christophersen and Ailbhe Kenny.
Description: New York : Routledge, 2018. | Includes index.
Identifiers: LCCN 2017034838 (print) | LCCN 2017037327 (ebook) | ISBN 9781315208756 (ebook) | ISBN 9781138631595 (hardback) | ISBN 9781138631601 (pbk.)
Subjects: LCSH: Music—Instruction and study. | Teaching teams. | Composition (Music)—Collaboration.
Classification: LCC MT1 (ebook) | LCC MT1 .M987377 2018 (print) | DDC 780.71—dc23
LC record available at https://lccn.loc.gov/2017034838

ISBN: 978-1-138-63159-5 (hbk)
ISBN: 978-1-138-63160-1 (pbk)
ISBN: 978-1-315-20875-6 (ebk)

Typeset in Minion Pro
by Apex CoVantage, LLC

Contents

Foreword: Collaborative Journeys Across Pedagogical Cultures: Attunement and the Interplay of Knowing and Unknowing   ix
LIORA BRESLER

Preface   xvii

Introduction   1

1 Musical Alterations: Possibilities for Musician–Teacher Collaborations   3
AILBHE KENNY AND CATHARINA CHRISTOPHERSEN

Part I
Critical Insights   13

2 When Collaborations Go Beyond Teachers and Musicians Alone: Frame and Stakeholder Analysis as Tools for Arts Advocacy   15
HILDEGARD C. FROEHLICH

3 Teacher–Musician Collaborations on the Move: From Performance Appreciation to Dialogue   27
KARI HOLDHUS

4 Musicians as Musician–Teacher Collaborators: Towards Punk Pedagogical Perspectives   39
GARETH DYLAN SMITH

5 Role Expectations and Role Conflicts within Collaborative Composing Projects   50
CHRISTIAN ROLLE, VERENA WEIDNER, JULIA WEBER, AND MATTHIAS SCHLOTHFELDT

vi • Contents

6 Thwarting the Authority of Purpose: Epistemic
Responsibility within Collaborations ... 62
CATHY BENEDICT

Part II
Crossing Boundaries ... 71

7 SongPump: Developing a Composing Pedagogy
in Finnish Schools Through Collaboration
Between Professional Songwriters and
Music Teachers ... 73
HEIDI PARTTI AND LAURI VÄKEVÄ

8 Teaching Cantonese Opera in Hong Kong Schools:
Interaction and Collaboration Between Music
Teachers and Artists ... 85
BO-WAH LEUNG

9 Intending to Leave a Deep Impression: Challenges
of the Performance Event in Schools ... 96
CECILIA K. HULTBERG

10 The Complete Musician: The Formation
of the Professional Musician ... 108
JUNE BOYCE-TILLMAN

11 An Urban Arts Partnership: Teaching Artists and
the Classroom Teachers Who Collaborate
with Them ... 121
HAROLD F. ABELES

12 Dialogues between Teachers and Musicians
in Creative Music-Making Collaborations ... 133
RANDI MARGRETHE EIDSAA

13 Abigail's Story: The Perspective of the Professor/
iPadist/Teaching Artist ... 146
CLINT RANDLES

Part III
Working Towards Partnership   157

14 "Ideal Relationships": Reconceptualizing Partnership in the Music Classroom Using the Smallian Theory of Musicking   159
JULIA PARTINGTON

15 Nurturing on the Go? A Story of Nomadic Partnership   171
KATHARINE KRESEK

16 Musician–Teacher Collaborations in Composing Contemporary Music in Secondary Schools   180
VICTORIA KINSELLA, MARTIN FAUTLEY, AND NANCY EVANS

17 "I'm Just the Bass Player in Their Band": Dissolving Artistic and Educational Dichotomies in Music Education   193
LARS BRINCK

18 Small Composers: Creating Musical Meaning in a Community of Practice   204
SVEN-ERIK HOLGERSEN, PETER BRUUN, AND METTE TJAGVAD

19 Equal Temperament: Coteaching as a Mechanism for Musician–Teacher Collaboration   217
MARITA KERIN AND COLETTE MURPHY

Conclusion   231

20 Alteration, Disruption, or Reharmonization? Pathways for Musician–Teacher Collaborations   233
CATHARINA CHRISTOPHERSEN AND AILBHE KENNY

List of Contributors   245

Index   249

Foreword

Collaborative Journeys Across Pedagogical Cultures: Attunement and the Interplay of Knowing and Unknowing[1]

Collaborations provide opportunities to create something bigger than ourselves, and through the creative-collaborative processes, become *more*. As in all relationships, collaborations are a double-edged sword: They can also limit, resulting in becoming less. It is with this acknowledgement that I have approached collaborations as a musician and as a researcher. In the latter role, I examined others' collaborations in schools and cultural centers and have also been an "insider," collaborating with others on research projects. Navigating positions, traveling long analytic and emotional distances in relation to collaborative action, has highlighted the nuanced interplay of knowing and unknowing that is part of a deeply collaborative mind-set.

Initially trained as a solo pianist, I discovered nearly forty years ago the vitality and power of collaboration in chamber music. Chamber music expanded my repertoire and transformed my entire experience of music-making. I still recall vividly the intensive work on Beethoven's Piano Trio Op 11 in the Bayreuth youth chamber music festival in preparation for a concert recorded by German radio and the deep bonding it generated with violinist Dinah and cellist Thilo. This experience was quite different from our spontaneous, "one-shot" sight reading with no anticipated outcome except the joy of creating music. Sight readings followed the festival's breakfasts as we checked with our meal mates about who played what instrument, then looked for sheet music. There was a casual, light-hearted quality to this kind of mutual engagement. Still, in both sequential and one-shot collaborative music-making, it was the attunement among players that made it memorable (or not). This attunement, I believe, is key for all collaborations. Cultivated rather than taught, it takes a concentrated presence of ear, body, and mind creating a meaningful interplay between individual and group. Attunement takes an *open* listening to what the other players bring to the encounter, a willingness to shape and be shaped. It draws on the knowledge and skills each of us possesses, and at the same time, requires "letting go" of control.

These earlier musical experiences have formed the ways I think about the big and small collaborative processes that make a good life—good conversations, good parenting, good research projects, and good classrooms where teachers collaborate with students. In each of these encounters, our own individual voices and actions become part of something bigger. The chamber music encounters of Bayreuth, like the university courses I teach or my research projects, are spaces dedicated to communal oeuvres for student participation (in teaching) and for creating a product geared to public presentation (in music and research). Different collaborative circumstances assume different leadership positions: Performing in chamber music is generally egalitarian, whereas the roles of teaching or directing a research project entail outlining a vision and the active elicitation of others' voices. Still, I found music ensembles to be a useful metaphor in my role as a Principal Investigator leading a group of research assistants (Bresler et al. 1996). The creation of an "interpretive zone" felt similar to chamber music work, where each researcher's voice, distinct yet complementary, contributed uniquely to the texture of the process and product. In both music and research making, there were shared (typically implicit) expectations about the desired nature and quality of the outcome.

It is the absence of shared expectations that can hinder collaborations among participants enculturated in communities with different value systems, goals, and identities, as I found in my research in schools. One memorable example in a study initiated by the Getty Center/College Board was a project on integrating arts with the academic curriculum in five high schools representing different parts of the United States (Bresler 2002). Requiring collaborative work with teachers from diverse disciplines and with museum staff, those successful collaborations provided special structures dedicated to regular discussions of the curriculum. There, academic and arts teachers reconsidered and negotiated assumptions about contents, pedagogies, learning spaces, and the relationships between schooling and the arts world. As in the systematic rehearsals of chamber music, the imminent audience of students for the carefully prepared formal and operational curricula was an important presence throughout these collaborative processes.

The makeup of participants and their professional identities, specific values, and commitments shape the dynamics of interaction. Semester-long collaborations between visual art teachers and teaching artists in schools (Bresler et al. 2000) were quite different from occasional encounters between teachers and performing artists in the schools (Bresler et al. 1997) and in performing arts centers (Bresler 2010). The lack of awareness of each other's assumptions, disciplinary traditions, axioms, and priorities reminded me at times of systemic therapy and family dynamics identified, for example, by therapist Virginia Satir (1983) or the discrepant communication style between men and women identified by linguist Deborah Tannen (1991, 1996). The challenge of creating a collaborative style that embraces all participants is very real. It requires awareness and sensitive listening to what is said (the explicit), as well as to what is not said (the implicit and the null) and attention to ongoing negotiations within specifically designed structures to be able to work through these differences.

Contextualizing Educational Collaborations: A Quiet Evolution

Although collaboration has existed among humans since the early activities of hunting wooly mammoths and gathering crops, the scholarly attention to its processes and significance is relatively recent. In his discussion of culture more than forty years ago, Clifford Geertz refers to Susanne Langer's notion of *grande idée*—certain ideas that burst upon the intellectual landscape with extraordinary force. Promising to resolve many fundamental problems at once, these ideas become the conceptual center point around which a comprehensive system of analysis can be built (Geertz 1973, 3). I regard collaboration as such an example of the grande idée concept, with roots in twentieth-century psychology, anthropology, and sociology and the recognition of the necessary (and ever-present) need for collaboration in educational settings during the past fifteen years.

This burst of research literature had to overcome conventional ways that were codified in educational theory and practice. In the context of schooling, collaboration defies the common enculturation of teachers as single rulers of their classrooms. In secondary and tertiary education, it goes against the structural "siloed" culture of disciplines. In the art worlds of music and dance, collaboration among participants breaches the values of uniqueness, individuality, and competition (Löytönen 2016). If the nineteenth century's worldview is associated with extraordinary genius and the twentieth century with the rational scholar and scientist, the post-modern sensitivity of the late twentieth century and early twenty-first century—with its emphasis on processes and acknowledgement of context—has facilitated inquiry into collaboration. The work of pioneering early twentieth-century harbingers, Russians Lev Vygotsky and Mikail Bakhtin, introduced relationship as compared to the isolated individual. Vygotsky, writing in the 1930s (but discovered in the West almost half a century later when the world was ready for the idea) introduced the notion of the shared nature of learning in his ground-breaking *zone of proximal development* (Vygotsky 1978). Bakhtin's concept of *heteroglossia* and polyphony of voices (Bakhtin, 1981), initially within the context of a novel, affected the ways we think of human activity. The emphasis on connection over isolation (Gergen 2015) laid the foundations for social constructionism. Kenneth Gergen's notion of the *relational self* (Gergen 1991; McNamee and Gergen 1999) develops a social conception of the person. The world of the mind, Gergen argues, emerges from participation in the social world. Gergen claims that "there is no *me* and *you* until there is *us*" (2015, 104). The notion of "us," I suggest, requires attunement similar to the mind-set I described in chamber music.

Some examples of recent publications serve to contextualize this present volume and its contributions. The area of creativity has looked to interdisciplinarity and collaboration as ways of thinking "outside the box." Miell and Littleton (2004), for example, draw on a sociocultural approach to understanding collaborative creativity across a wide range of domains, from music composition and school-based creative writing and art, to fashion design, theater production, and business. Assuming that creativity is a fundamentally social process, the authors examine the cultural, institutional, and interpersonal contexts that sustain such activity, investigating the role of cultural tools and technologies in supporting collaborative creativity.

The work of Keith Sawyer and his notions of "group genius" (2007), grounded in improvisational drama, have provided useful frameworks for arts educators. If drama is acknowledged to be an inherently collaborative discipline, classical music (occupying a central place in twentieth-century music education research) has centered on either individual solo practices or orchestra, the latter characterized by cooperation and uniformity. The attention to *attunement* as a special mind-set makes collaboration a different type of endeavor, as compared, for example, to the more procedural nature of cooperation or the seemingly rational, emotion-free associations of deliberation (e.g. Schwab 1969; Walker 1990). Attunement, I suggest, implies connection and responsiveness, invoking Buber's *I and Thou*, rather than traditional organizational lenses.[2]

Music aesthetician Claire Detels' plea (1999) for softer boundaries across music disciplines with the implied need for collaboration signaled, I believe, a discipline that was lagging behind other arts disciplines. Yet the next decade or two witnessed a proliferation of scholarship and field-based research on collaboration in music education. In this collaborative turn, the Nordic countries have made remarkable contributions.

Helena Gaunt and Heidi Westerlund's volume on collaborative learning in higher music education (Gaunt and Westerlund 2013) conceptualizes collaboration as a powerful way to deal with current challenges in a changing world. The work on improvisation in teacher education conducted in Stord/Haugesund University College (e.g. Holdhus et al. 2016) recognizes collaboration as key to dynamic, vital pedagogies.

Arts education literature includes some fine examples of knowledge production emerging out of collaborative projects among school teachers. Dance educator Teija Löytönen's study of fifteen dance teachers and three principals of dance schools in Helsinki (Löytönen 2016) and music educator Cecilia Björk's study of five music teachers in rural Finland (Björk 2016) center on professional knowledge intimately woven with the social and emotional aspects of the work. Löytönen and Björk have skillfully initiated and facilitated unique and productive collaborative spaces for dance and music teachers. The rich descriptions of conversations and group dynamics convey the power of teachers' close listening to each other, where complex and sensitive professional dilemmas are shared and attended to with depth, respect, and care.

The range of emotions experienced in collaborative work, compellingly alluded to in both the Löytönen and Björk studies, is the focus of dance researchers Leena Rouhiainen and Soili Hämäläinen (2013). Rouhiainen and Hämäläinen observe the experiences of a dance pedagogy student in a dance-making process involving a cross-artistic group of students in the performing arts, highlighting emotional challenges and insights identified by the student.

Still, the potential of collaboration to limit, resulting in "becoming less," is common enough. There is much to learn from what is missing in educational projects that do not provide for conditions that support collaborative work. Catharina Christophersen (2013), investigating The Cultural Rucksack, a national program for arts and culture in Norwegian schools, portrays a series of dilemmas, challenges, and tensions in teachers' statements and actions, indicating their lack of influence over the artistic program. Although teachers were pleased that students and teachers were able to enjoy professional arts and culture at school, theirs was more of an accompanying role, where they were positioned as artists' helpers, students' guards, or mediators between artists and students. Similarly, Holdhus and Espeland (2013) examine the nature of music education provided by The Cultural Rucksack, the rationale and philosophy that the music programs bring to schooling, and the kinds of challenges that these events represent for the artists as well as the teachers involved. Holdhus and Espeland argue that neither education nor visiting arts programs seem to have adjusted their practices to recent trends in Western performance practices and aesthetics, nor to an educational practice building sufficiently on a pedagogy of relations. Whether it is artists visiting schools (Bresler et al. 1997; Christophersen 2013; Holdhus and Espeland 2013) or school groups attending performing arts centers as part of youth performances (Bresler 2010), the discrepancy of goals and shared practices between members of those distinct institutions makes for limited educational opportunities. Like chamber music, collaborative work requires time and commitment, typically not part of institutional structures and traditions.

Opening Space for New Knowledge

Reading the thick descriptions of successful and less successful collaborative projects testifies to the interplay between knowing and unknowing. Unknowing requires a willingness to hold one's expertise and beliefs within a space that allows an encounter with others' knowledge. Genuine listening, as I learned in my chamber music experiences and, later, in the conduct of observations and interviewing, calls for laying aside one's knowing. My use of unknowing is similar to Suzuki Roshi's notion of *beginner's mind* (Suzuki 1970). Unknowing involves an *awareness* of one's existing knowledge, rather than tightly grasping it. The "opening" process is characterized by a spacious interest in others' perspectives (Bresler 2015), where the self subsides to allow for new experiences. Unknowing is distinct from ignorance—the latter is devoid of awareness or openness, and therefore self-maintains a lack of knowledge.

These studies of collaboration between teachers and musicians offer a rich array of cases, artistic activities (composing, improvising, performing), musical genres (from pop and punk to Cantonese opera), and settings (classrooms, public chamber music halls, cathedrals). The diverse types of collaboration are embedded in specific micro, meso, and macro contexts; across cultural traditions; and between or within individual personalities. Issues of dynamics in education, power, and control are shown to operate within given institutional structures and communicative styles.

Reading this collection, we are sensitized to the questions of "what is good collaboration?" and "what is collaboration good for?" We begin to recognize where differences are and what kinds of structures can facilitate possibilities of diversity. Through collaborative reading along with creative action, we can draw on diverse types of knowing and unknowing to augment the broadest range of educational possibilities and practices.

Liora Bresler
University of Illinois at Urbana-Champaign

Notes

1 Many thanks to Betsy Hearne for reading the paper and for her insightful comments.
2 The area of jazz improvisation also implies attunement, see, for example, Berliner (1994), and the discussion of communities of musical practices by Kenny (2014, 2016).

References

Bakhtin, Mikail M. 1981. *The Dialogic Imagination: 4 Essays*. Translated by Michael Holquist and Caryl Emerson and edited by Michael Holquist. Austin, TX: University of Texas Press.

Berliner, Paul. 1994. *Thinking in Jazz: The Infinite Art of Improvisation*. Chicago: University of Chicago Press.

Björk, Cecilia. 2016. "In Search of Good Relationships to Music: Understanding Aspiration and Challenge in Developing Music School Teacher Practices." PhD diss., Åbo Akademi University, Åbo.

Bresler, Liora. 2002. "Out of the Trenches: The Joys (and Risks) of Cross-Disciplinary Collaborations." *Bulletin of the Council for Research in Music Education*, 152 (Spring), 17–39.

Bresler, Liora. 2010. "Teachers as Audiences: Exploring Educational and Musical Values in Youth Performances." *Journal of New Music Research*, 39 (2), 135–45.

Bresler, Liora. 2015. "The Polyphonic Texture of a Collaborative Book: Personal and Communal Intersections." In *Beyond Methods: Lessons from the Arts to Qualitative Research*, edited by Liora Bresler, 1–15. Malmö: Lund University. Accessed June 27, 2017, http://mhm.lu.se/sites(mhm.lu.se/files/perspectives_in_music10.ped

Bresler, Liora, Lizanne DeStefano, Rhoda Feldman, and Smita Garg. 2000. "Artists-in-Residence in Public Schools: Issues in Curriculum, Integration, Impact." *Visual Arts Research*, 26 (1), 13–29.

Bresler, Liora, Judith D. Wasser, and Nancy Hertzog. 1997. "Casey at the Bat: A Hybrid Genre of Two Worlds." *Research in Drama Education: The Journal of Applied Theatre and Performance*, 2 (1), 87–106.

Bresler, Liora, Judith D. Wasser, Nancy Hertzog, and Mary Lemons. 1996. "Beyond the Lone Ranger Researcher: Team Work in Qualitative Research." *Research Studies in Music Education*, 7 (1), 13–27.

Buber, Martin. 1971. *I and Thou*. New York: Simon and Schuster.

Christophersen, Catharina. 2013. "Helper Guard or Mediator? Teachers' Space for Action in The Cultural Rucksack, a Norwegian National Program for Arts and Culture in Schools." *International Journal of Education & the Arts*, 14 (SI 1.11). Accessed May 24, 2017, www.ijea.org/v14si.

Detels, Claire. 1999. *Soft Boundaries: Re-Visioning the Arts and Aesthetics in American Education*. Westport, CT: Bergin & Garvey.

Gaunt, Helena, and Heidi Westerlund. 2013. *Collaborative Learning in Higher Music Education*. London: Ashgate.

Geertz, Clifford. 1973. *The Interpretation of Cultures*. New York: Basic Books.

Gergen, Kenneth J. 1991. *The Saturated Self*. New York: Basic Books.
Gergen, Kenneth J. 2015. *An Invitation to Social Construction*, 3rd edition. Los Angeles, CA: Sage.
Holdhus, Kari, and Magne Espeland. 2013. "The Visiting Artist in Schools: Arts Based or School Based Practices?" *International Journal of Education & the Arts*, 14 (SI 1.10). Accessed June 15, 2015, www.ijea.org/v14si1/.
Holdhus, Kari, Sissel Høisæter, Kjellfrid Mæland, Vigdis Vangsnes, Knut Steinar Engelsen, Magne Espeland, and Åsmund Espeland. 2016. "Improvisation in Teaching and Education—Roots and Applications." *Cogent Education*, 3 (1). Accessed June 27, 2017, doi: 10.1080/2331 186X.2016.1204142
Kenny, Ailbhe. 2014. "Collaborative Creativity Within a Jazz Ensemble as a Musical and Social Practice." *Thinking Skills and Creativity*, 13 (September 2008), 1–8.
Kenny, Ailbhe. 2016. *Communities of Musical Practice*. Abingdon: Routledge.
Löytönen, Teija. 2016. "Collaborative Inquiry in a Socially Shared Contextual Frame: Striving Towards Sensible Knowledge Creation on Dance Education." *Teachers College Record*, 118 (2), 1–38.
McNamee, Sheila, and Kenneth J. Gergen. 1999. *Relational Responsibility: Resources for Sustainable Dialogue*. Thousand Oaks, CA: Sage.
Miell, Dorothy, and Karen Littleton, eds. 2014. *Collaborative Creativity: Contemporary Perspectives*. London: Free Association Books.
Rouhiainen, Leena, and Soili Hämäläinen. 2013. "Emotions and Feelings in a Collaborative Dance-Making Process." *International Journal of Education & the Arts*, 14 (6). Accessed June 15, 2017, www.ijea.org/v14n6/.
Satir, Virginia. 1983. *Conjoint Family Therapy*. Palo Alto, CA: Science and Behavior Books.
Sawyer, Keith. 2007. *Group Genius: The Creative Power of Collaboration*. New York: Basic Books.
Schwab, Joseph J. 1969. *College Curriculum and Student Protest*. Chicago: University of Chicago Press.
Suzuki, Shunryu. 1970. *Zen Mind, Beginner's Mind*. Edited by Trudy Dixon. New York: Weatherhill.
Tannen, Deborah. 1991. *You Just Don't Understand: Women and Men in Conversation*. New York: Ballantine Books.
Tannen, Deborah. 1996. *Gender and Discourse*. London: Oxford University Press.
Vygotsky, Lev. 1978. *Mind in Society: The Development of Higher Psychological Processes*. Cambridge, MA: Harvard University Press.
Walker, Decker F. 1990. *Fundamentals of Curriculum*. New York: Harcourt Brace Jovanovich.

Preface

Like many good editorial collaborations, this one began over coffee in New York. Both visiting scholars at Teachers College, Columbia University at the time, Ailbhe from Ireland and Catharina from Norway, sought out a cozy spot around the corner to meet up. During that afternoon, we discovered that we not only had mutual academic interests, but that we had also both done recent research on arts-in-education initiatives. In the many discussions we touched upon that afternoon, a few issues in particular stood out. Why are so many music initiatives in schools, delivered from outside the system, seen as "saving" children/music/education? When put forward as "collaborations," just how collaborative are they? Why do we continually hear and read about the transformative power of such visiting arts initiatives when music delivered by teachers inside the system is questioned, scorned, and, at times, ridiculed? What are the different perspectives and approaches to musician–teacher collaborations internationally? How can we challenge the prevailing discourse and move the work of musician–teacher collaborations forward? And so, over a polka dot tablecloth, the idea for this book was conceived.

Following the line of our discussion in a New York coffee shop, this book offers a systematic critical exploration of musician–teacher collaborations within educational contexts. The chapters in this volume have been selected from a large pool of submissions following an open call internationally. Drawn from ten countries, across twenty chapters, both theoretical and empirical writings are put forward specifically on the topic of musician–teacher collaboration. The geographical spread of the chapters aims to provide varied and context-specific arguments, while, of course, also speaking to the macro issues at stake. More specifically, the chapters offer openings, pose questions, suggest approaches, and point to potential pathways for musician–teacher collaborations of the future.

The chapters of the book have been divided into three parts. In the first part, titled "Critical Insights," new theoretical frameworks and concepts are brought to the table, providing alternative perspectives on musician–teacher collaboration. The chapters in the second part of the book, "Crossing Boundaries," present challenges for visiting musicians/teaching artists in educational contexts, as well as a discussion about what such music-in-education initiatives contribute. The third part of the book, "Working Towards Partnership," tackles some dominant narratives and perspectives in the field through a series of empirically based chapters discussing musician–teacher collaboration as a field of tension. This last section concludes with a reflective offering to draw connections between the chapters and drive the conversation forward for musician–teacher collaboration. Thus, through both research and practice perspectives in the book, the complexities of music-in-education collaborations are problematized and discussed.

The title of the book, we hope, invites further pondering and questioning. An altered chord used in a piece of music typically is employed to change the character or color of the sound. Thus, the musical piece is unsettled in some way, perhaps leading to surprise or tension in its disruption. We thought this was a most interesting way to think about musicians collaborating with teachers within educational spaces: One is in the space of the other and vice versa, and so that space is inevitably altered. Akin to the change of notes played in a chord, these "alterations" create new spaces to inhabit, negotiate, and work within.

The creation of new spaces is not limited to musician–teacher collaborations, but also applies to the collaborative efforts preceding the publication of this book. We, the editors, would like to express our sincere thanks to the authors for contributing their chapters to this volume: Thank you for entering our space and letting us enter your space, thus together creating new insights and perspectives.

Introduction

1

Musical Alterations: Possibilities for Musician–Teacher Collaborations

AILBHE KENNY AND CATHARINA CHRISTOPHERSEN

Introduction

An altered chord is often used to change the character or color of a piece of music. This lowering or raising to a neighboring pitch typically functions as a means to unsettle, to create an element of surprise, to add tension, or to increase interest in its disrupted diatonic chord progression. In choosing the subtitle for the book, *Altering the Chord*, this notion of disruption appeared to problematize musician–teacher collaboration as a form of music education. As such, a musician entering an educational setting "alters" the space, potentially adding elements of surprise, tension, and/or interest. These "alterations" can, of course, be hugely advantageous to schools, teachers, children, young people, and broader communities, as well as to the musicians themselves. Whether live performance, song writing, traditional opera, creative composition, or innovative music technologies, new musical worlds can be discovered and accessed through such music-in-education initiatives.

Too often, however, such initiatives within education tend toward "victory narratives." These dominant discourses ascribe the success of music-in-education initiatives to musicians' presence and artistic abilities alone, thus ignoring what musical cultures, expertise, and knowledge already exist within these settings prior to the intervention. This is perhaps due to a perceived (or real) need to serve greater political agendas, satisfy multiple stakeholders, create employment opportunities, and attract increased funding. Or perhaps it is due to a lack of criticality in the overall aims, functions, and inherent values of such projects that are often presented as a "magic bullet" for music education. There is much to consider. This book offers a systematic critical exploration of musician–teacher collaborations. Contemporary international perspectives, both theoretical and empirical, explore the possibilities and pathways of such initiatives to open up discussion and debate about musician–teacher collaborations.

Setting the Scene

The terms "arts-in-education" and therefore "music-in-education" have become a dominant feature of arts, music, and educational discourse. Internationally, musicians, arts organizations, and institutions have progressively positioned themselves as having a role to play within educational contexts and "outreach" initiatives. For example, large-scale programs continue to develop at Carnegie Hall, The Berlin Philharmonic, Opera Australia, and the British Broadcasting Corporation (BBC), to name but a few. In particular, "collaboration," "partnership," and the "teaching artist" as policy choices have gained increased popularity as a means of delivering arts-in-education (EC 2011; UNESCO 2006, 2010). Multiple benefits of such initiatives, both intrinsic and extrinsic to arts education, have been widely reported (Bamford 2006; Burnaford et al. 2001; Colley et al. 2012; Deasy and Stevenson 2005; Downing et al. 2007; Fiske 1999; Hallam et al. 2010; Irwin et al. 2005; Kenny 2009, 2010, 2011; Woolf 2004).

Tensions often arise, however, around remits and responsibilities within arts-in-education initiatives. In particular, debates about the role of visiting artists in schools abound (Christophersen 2013, 2015; Egan 2005; Eisner 2002; Holdhus and Espeland 2013; Jeffery 2005; Kenny 2010; Kenny and Morrissey 2016; Wyse and Spendlove 2007; Wolf 2008). Through an examination of the government-supported Norwegian "Cultural Rucksack" program, there was evidence of a prevailing *doxa* amongst teachers and artists that the program was "good" with the result that the class teacher often took on a peripheral, if not marginalized, role in the program (Christophersen 2013, 2015). Similarly, in studies of the "Creative Partnerships" program in the United Kingdom, difficulties emerged with conflicting expectations and identities between artists and teachers (Griffiths and Woolf 2009; Wyse and Spendlove 2007). Such issues raise important questions regarding visiting artists in educational contexts. Specific to visiting musicians in classrooms as a means of delivering music education, some researchers have questioned its ideological origins, aims, and approaches (Bowman 2007; Christophersen 2015), though to a limited degree.

Internationally, interventions by artists in schools tend to be initiated or led by arts and cultural organizations. For instance, the "Cultural Rucksack" program in Norway stemmed from "various cultural programs for children and young people" (Christophersen et al. 2015, 11), "Creative Partnerships" (2002–2011) in the United Kingdom was an Arts Council of England initiative, and Canada's "Learning Through the Arts" initiative was developed by the Royal Conservatory of Music, Toronto (Kind et al. 2007). Where such music-in-education initiatives are government funded—many such initiatives are profiled in this book—issues of balancing artistic aims with governmental social, cultural, economic, or political remits often arise. Furedi (2004, 98) warns, "Governments throughout history have attempted to mobilize the arts to further political ends." Conflicts exist within such social agendas for the arts where Buckingham and Jones argue (2001, 13):

> [T]here is a danger that "creativity" and "culture" will come to be seen as magic ingredients that will somehow automatically transform education, and bring about broader forms of social and economic regeneration, in and of themselves.

This is not to say that additional benefits outside of artistic or creative outcomes are not advantageous, but overemphasis on the value of music to serve political agendas could, in practice, lead to music-in-education being viewed as "icing on the cake" (Laycock 2008, 64).

Towards "Collaboration"

Successful arts and music-in-education programs are now widely recognized as requiring a collaborative, long-term approach (Bamford and Glinkowski 2010; Kenny 2010; Kenny and Morrissey 2016; Wolf 2008; Kind et al. 2007). Wolf contends, "In the best of partnerships, teachers and artists become colleagues, collaborating on projects that will encourage creativity based on the expertise of all involved and focused on the children's talents and needs" (2008, 90). This laudable aim for a collegial approach raises important questions regarding musician–teacher collaborations as potential sites for oppositional relationships at one end of the continuum or transformative practice at the other end.

The term "collaboration" is a contested one. The collection of chapters in this book alone attests to the multiple lenses and definitions one could ascribe to the term. An interpersonal psychological focus, for instance, sees "collaboration" as transactional through human interaction. For Vygotsky (1962; Vygotsky and Cole 1978), learning through social interaction is embedded within social events, as "situated action" within a "zone of proximal development." This view allows for varying levels of expertise and skills within collaborations where apprenticeship or peer learning is encouraged. Sociocultural theorist Jerome Bruner extends this "scaffolding" and "mediational" approach to learning that is context specific within a "community of mutual learners" (1996, 24). A "communities of practice" framework (Lave and Wenger 1991; Wenger 1998) builds on such theories again where members within communities are seen to learn through a social process of peripheral participation. Within music contexts, a "communities of musical practice" framework (Kenny 2016) furthers the argument that musical and social interaction are interrelated when people come together to make music. Therefore, if learning occurs from and with others, as members of communities, the assumption is that within musician–teacher collaborations, collective knowledge through dialogic practice will be key to transformative practice.

Moran and John-Steiner emphasize the transformational nature of collaboration as (2004, 11), "an intricate blending of skills, temperaments, effort and sometimes personalities to realize a shared vision of something new and useful." Maxine Greene also presents convincing arguments in this regard (Greene 1995, 2001). Greene, building on the work of Dewey and Vygotsky, argues for knowledge to be constructed through experience in partnerships—through creating relational pedagogic spaces for transformation. Liora Bresler similarly comments on the collaborative nature of artist-teacher partnerships, allowing for potential "transformative practice zones" (Bresler 2002). This book seeks to investigate the collaborations where such "zones" might occur and examine the conditions necessary to facilitate pedagogic and professional transformation. Musician–teacher collaborations then can create exciting opportunities for both musicians and teachers to challenge, develop, and potentially transform their practices to ultimately benefit the children and young people they teach. Kaplan reminds us (2014, 175), "Collaboration is profound because the demands of a sharable pedagogy challenge us to devise those practices that will implement a common experience. Collaboration leads to, indeed it thrives on, variety."

Research carried out by the two editors in Norway and Ireland, respectively, offer some interesting insights into the notion of collaboration. It was found that due to the compulsory nature of the Norwegian "Cultural Rucksack" program, often involving once-off artist interventions in schools, that this has resulted in a lack of ownership amongst teachers (Christophersen 2013; Christophersen et al. 2015). Christophersen argues that although this program was "originally intended as a collaborative effort between the fields of culture and education", it has become about "giving external specialists access to children during school hours" (2013, 14). The Cultural Rucksack program is, however, currently undergoing reorganization in order to increase the educational influence over the program. An Irish report on teacher–artist partnerships (Kenny and Morrissey 2016) highlights the importance of shared professional development for artists and teachers: "The partners journeyed together in their learning, respected each other's varied inputs, shared experiences, valued differing strengths and invested in relationship-building" (2016, 86). The most successful collaborations occurred where both parties meaningfully invested over a sustained period of time, but also where a high level of local and national support was given.

These studies reveal that effective musician–teacher collaborations within educational settings do not occur in a vacuum. Collaborations are highly dependent on open communication, shared extensive planning, flexibility, ongoing support, and cooperation (Abeles 2004; Abeles et al. 2002; Bamford and Glinkowski 2010; Cape UK 2009; Colley et al. 2012; Galton 2008; Holdhus and Espeland 2013; Myers and Brooks 2002). Thus, a collaborative model for music-in-education initiatives moves us towards a view of the musician as "partner" in the classroom, but one where "caution is needed therefore to ensure that artists involved with schools are not seen as a replacement for the teacher but rather an additional support and resource" (Kenny 2010, 163). As partners, recognition of the teacher's knowledge and perspectives needs to be identified as equally important as the musician's. At their best, the collaboration facilitates professional learning as a reciprocal act between musician and teacher. As Wolf asserts, "for partnerships to be truly collaborative, the stream of learning must flow both ways" (2008, 93).

Musician/Teacher Dichotomies

The discourses surrounding music-in-education initiatives tend to dichotomize musician and teacher. There is often a perception that the former brings "authenticity" and specialist expertise to the musical experience, whereas the latter serves as an educational guide or, at worst, a "guard" over behavior management (Christophersen 2013). Laycock (2008) identifies one major source of conflict within such collaborations as a clash between child-centered approaches and art form–centered approaches to delivering arts education. Formal educational settings are perceived as typically conservative environments, whereas perceptions of musicians' working lives tend towards notions of freedom and liberalism. Indeed, even amongst children, differences can be noted between "school" music and music delivered by someone "outside" the system (Kenny 2014a, 405):

> [T]he children recognised the musical practice in the project as being distinct from musical practices in school . . . Clara comments "school has boring music and this music is cool". The element of this music practice being "fun" and school music being "boring" was something which was significant.

This echoes with the oft-claimed disconnect between formal and informal music education (Allsup 2003; Burnard et al. 2008; Green 2002; Jorgenson 2003). Yet learning music formally and informally often occur simultaneously in practice (Espeland 2010; Finney and Philpott 2010; Folkestad 2006; Kenny 2016; Veblen 2012). Rather than being in tension with each other, then, musician–teacher collaborations may offer new possibilities to act as a bridge between formal and informal musical learning.

Akin to the formal/informal divide, musician/teacher dichotomies have also been recognized as unhelpful and inaccurate (Bennett and Stanberg 2008). These roles and identities are, of course, often overlapping and interrelated. Kind et al. (2007) contends that within the teacher–artist collaboration, both teacher and artist learning needs should be attended to, all the time taking account of the relational nature of these needs, "as artists and teachers work together, both influence each other and shape each other's experiences, teaching and artistic practices. Learning is not unidirectional moving from artists to teachers, or even from teachers to artists" (841). It has been well researched that teachers' beliefs about the arts, prior experience of the arts, and self-efficacy in teaching the arts has important consequences for how it is taught in schools (Collanus et al. 2012; Greene 1995; Kenny 2014b; Kenny et al. 2015; Pitfield 2012; Sefton-Green et al. 2011; Winters 2012). In developing models of musician–teacher collaboration, opportunities for teachers to connect or reconnect with music as an art form is as important therefore as its connection to the children and young people in order to build capacity and maximize impact into the future. Equally, opportunities for the musicians to reflect and challenge their views of education through collaboration will also influence their teaching approaches, as well as the discourse about collaboration projects in general.

Aim and Plan of the Book

This book explores the field of musician–teacher collaboration within educational settings through international snapshots of leading debates and issues. There has been little systematic critical exploration of this topic, and teacher/educational perspectives are particularly lacking in the research literature. The twenty chapters herein contribute contemporary perspectives from across ten countries that explore and problematize existing discourses that surround musician–teacher collaborations. Thus, both the theoretical and empirically based chapters present varied insights to further debates, development, and research in this field.

The book is divided into three parts. In Part I, "Critical Perspectives," chapters with distinct theoretical frameworks ranging from relational aesthetics, punk pedagogy, performativity, social systems theory, cultural sociology to symbolic interactionism provide points of departure for scholarly critique on musician–teacher collaboration. Hildegard Froehlich begins by employing elements of frame and stakeholder analyses to examine the relationship between educators, artists, the public, and policy makers. Froehlich calls us to question "the stakes" from the outset of collaborations in order to benefit the most important stakeholders involved—the learners. Chapter 3 critiques the traditional school concert in its sender–receiver orientation and lack of contextual consideration. Kari Holdhus proposes an alternative form that is relational and dialogic and that moves towards actual musician–teacher collaboration. Gareth Dylan Smith in Chapter 4 explores the potential of punk pedagogical approaches within the field of musician–teacher collaboration. He argues for a more flexible and multifaceted view of musicians that looks beyond the notion of celebrity. Christian Rolle, Matthias Schlothfeldt, Julia Weber, and Verena Weidner (Chapter 5) report on a German project for composers to provide input in educational contexts. Using Luhmann's social systems theory, the chapter problematizes role definitions, expectations, and conflicts within collaborative composing endeavors. In the last chapter of this section, Cathy Benedict (Chapter 6) questions the very purpose of education, advocating for the merits of epistemic responsibility to guide our practices. Echoing Froehlich's opening arguments in Chapter 2, she contends that for any meaningful collaboration to occur there needs to first be a challenge to the primacy of purpose of that collaboration.

Part II of the book, "Crossing Boundaries," presents chapters based on empirical research to explore the challenges of the visiting "expert" (musician/teaching artist) within educational contexts. The first three chapters deal with specific projects in schools, namely, pop music composing in Finland, Cantonese opera in Hong Kong, and chamber music in Sweden. Heidi Partti and Lauri Väkevä (Chapter 7) argue that the Finnish composing project exemplifies ways to help teachers facilitate creative collaborations beyond musical genres, and Bo-Wah Leung (Chapter 8) reports on different musician/teacher roles and collaboration modes taken in a genre-specific study. Cecilia Hultberg in Chapter 9 uses a cultural-psychological lens to investigate how musicians and teachers might facilitate students to have moving experiences at music performance events. June Boyce-Tillman (Chapter 10) and Harold Abeles (Chapter 11) focus their writings on examining the multifaceted challenges for professional musicians/teaching artists in schools and how to prepare them to work in educational contexts from differing U.K. and U.S. perspectives. Randi Eidsaa in Chapter 12 focuses on the role of dialogue between musicians and teachers within Norwegian collaborations through case studies of verbal interactions. The final chapter in this section (Chapter 13) takes a look at one student and teacher/musician/researcher story of music-making on an iPad in the United States. Clint Randles here highlights the potential of technologically mediated music-making for people with special needs.

The final part of the book, "Working Towards Partnership," challenges some dominant narratives and seeks new pathways for musician–teacher collaboration. Drawing on Smallian theory, Julia Partington begins by seeking an alternative model of musician–teacher collaboration rooted in the mutual exploration of "ideal relationships" through "musicking." Katie Kresek in Chapter 15 offers her distinct U.S. perspective on collaboration where she highlights the challenge of "nomadic conditions" for teaching artists as they navigate demands from multiple institutions to highly individualized partnerships with classroom teachers. Chapter 16 focuses on the relationship between composers, teachers, and pupils but this time in a Birmingham secondary school composing project. In this contribution, Martin Fautley, Victoria Kinsella, and Nancy Evans explore notions of expertise, roles, and expectations, as well as differences between learning and doing. Chapters 17 and 18 further probe musician–teacher dichotomies using a "community of practice" framework for their studies. Lars Brinck (Chapter 17) offers a space for recognizing both musicians' pedagogical resources and teachers' artistic resources, and Peter Bruun, Mette Tjagvad, and Sven-Erik Holgersen (Chapter 18) examine professional collaboration as a field of tension between these very distinct pedagogical and artistic intentions. In Marita Kerin and Collette Murphy's chapter (Chapter 19) the learning from a coteaching mixed-methods study is offered to identify different levels of reciprocal professional development for furthering collaborations.

The book finishes with a reflective offering from the editors to make connections among the various chapters and drive the conversation forward for musician–teacher collaborations. Christophersen and Kenny call for a rethinking and reimagining of musician–teacher collaboration in order to address key challenges for future pathways in this field. Drawing from the contributions by international scholars, Chapter 20 raises pertinent questions to inform research, policy, and practice, as well as stimulate debate about existing rhetorics that surround musician–teacher collaborations.

References

Abeles, Harold. 2004. "The Effect of Three Orchestra/School Partnerships on Students' Interest in Instrumental Music Instruction." *Journal of Research in Music Education*, 52, 248–63.

Abeles, Harold, Mary Hafeli, Robert Horowitz, and Judith Burton. 2002. "The Evaluation of Arts Partnerships and Learning in and Through the Arts." In *The New Handbook of Research on Music Teaching and Learning*, edited by Richard Colwell and Carol Richardson, 931–40. New York: Oxford University Press.

Allsup, Randall Everett. 2003. "Mutual Learning and Democratic Action in Instrumental Music Education." *Journal of Research in Music Education*, 51 (24), 24–37.

Bamford, Anne. 2006. *The Wow Factor: Global Research Compendium on the Impact of the Arts in Education*. New York: Waxmann Munster.

Bamford, Anne, and Paul Glinkowski. 2010. *Wow, It's Music Next: Impact Evaluation of Wider Opportunities in Music at Key Stage 2*. London: Federation of Music Services.

Bennett, Dawn, and Andrea Stanberg. 2008. "Musicians as Teachers: Fostering a Positive View." In *Inside, Outside, Downside Up: Conservatoire Training and Musicians' Work*, edited by Dawn Bennett and Micheal Hannan, 11–22. Perth: Black Swan Press.

Bowman, Wayne. 2007. "Who Is the 'We'? Rethinking Professionalism in Music Education." *Action, Criticism, and Theory for Music Education*, 6 (4), 109–31.

Bresler, Liora. 2002. "Out of the Trenches: The Joys (and Risks) of Cross-Disciplinary Collaborations." *Council of Research in Music Education*, 152, 17–39.

Bruner, Jerome S. 1996. *The Culture of Education*. Cambridge, MA: Harvard University Press.

Buckingham, David, and Ken Jones. 2001. "New Labour's Cultural Turn: Some Tensions in Contemporary Educational and Cultural Policy." *Journal of Education Policy*, 16 (1), 1–14.

Burnaford, Gail, Arnold Aprill, and Cynthia Weiss. 2001. *Renaissance in the Classroom: Arts Integration and Meaningful Learning*. Mahwah, NJ: Lawrence Erlbaum Associates.

Burnard, Pamela, Steve Dillon, Gabriel Rusinek, and Eva Saether. 2008. "Inclusive Pedagogies in Music Education: A Comparative Study of Music Teachers' Perspectives from Four Countries." *International Journal of Music Education*, 26 (2), 109–26.

Cape UK. 2009. *The Teacher Artist Partnership Programme (TAPP) Model*. Leeds. www.capeuk.org/assets/files/CapeUK_TAPP_01(1).pdf

Christophersen, Catharina. 2013. "Helper, Guard or Mediator? Teachers' Space for Action in The Cultural Rucksack, a Norwegian National Program for Arts and Culture in School." *International Journal of Education & the Arts*, 14 (SI 1.11). Accessed June 11, 2017, www.ijea.org/v14si1/.

Christophersen, Catharina. 2015. "Changes and Challenges in Music Education: Reflections on a Norwegian Arts-in-Education Programme." *Music Education Research*, 17 (4), 364–80.

Christophersen, Catharina, Jan Kåre Breivik, Anne D. Homme, and Lise H. Rykkja. 2015. *The Cultural Rucksack: A National Programme for Arts and Culture in Norwegian Schools*. Oslo: Arts Council of Norway.

Collanus, Miia, Seija Kairavuori, and Sinikka Rusanen. 2012. "The Identities of an Art Educator: Comparing Discourses in Three Teacher Education Programmes in Finland." *International Journal of Education Through Art*, 8 (1), 7–21.

Colley, Bernadette, Randi M. Eidsaa, Ailbhe Kenny, and Bo-Wah Leung. 2012. "Creativity in Partnership Practices." In *The Oxford Handbook of Music Education*, edited by Gary McPherson and Graham Welch, vol. 2, 408–26. Oxford: Oxford University Press.

Deasy, Richard J., and Lauren M. Stevenson. 2005. *Third Space: When Learning Matters*. Washington, DC: AEP Publications.

Downing, Dick, Pippa Lord, Megan Jones, Kerry Martin, and Iain Springate. 2007. *Study of Creative Partnerships' Local Sharing of Practice and Learning*. Slough: NFER.

EC. 2011. European Commission. "Creative Europe—a New Framework Programme for the Cultural and Creative Sectors (2014–2020)."

Egan, Kieran. 2005. *An Imaginative Approach to Teaching*. San Francisco, CA: Jossey Bass.

Eisner, Elliott. 2002. *The Arts and the Creation of Mind*. New Haven, CT: Yale University Press.

Espeland, Magne. 2010. "Dichotomies in Music Education—Real or Unreal?" *Music Education Research*, 12 (2), 129–39.

Finney, John, and Chris Philpott. 2010. "Informal Learning and Meta-Pedagogy in Initial Teacher Education in England." *British Journal of Music Education*, 27 (1), 7–19.

Fiske, Edward B. 1999. *Champions of Change: The Impact of the Arts on Learning*. Washington, DC: Arts Education Partnership.

Folkestad, Göran. 2006. "Formal and Informal Learning Situations or Practices vs Formal and Informal Ways of Learning." *British Journal of Music Education*, 23 (2), 135–45.

Furedi, Frank. 2004. *Where Have all the Intellectuals Gone? Confronting 21st Century Philistinism*. London: Continuum.

Galton, Maurice. 2008. *Creative Practitioners in Schools and Classrooms. Final Report of the Project: The Pedagogy of Creative Practitioners in Schools*. Cambridge: University of Cambridge.

Green, Lucy. 2002. *How Popular Musicians Learn*. Hants: Ashgate.

Greene, Maxine. 1995. *Releasing the Imagination: Essays on Education, the Arts, and Social Change*. San Francisco, CA: Jossey-Bass.

Greene, Maxine. 2001. *Variations on a Blue Guitar: The Lincoln Center Institute Lectures on Aesthetic Education*. New York: Teachers College Press.

Griffiths, Morweena, and Felicity Woolf. 2009. "The Nottingham Apprenticeship Model: Schools in Partnership with Artists and Creative Practitioners." *British Educational Research Journal*, 35 (4), 557–74.

Hallam, Susan, Andrea Creech, Katherine Shave, and Maria Varvarigou. 2010. *Report from the LSO on Track Evaluation: September 2009–August 2010*. London: University of London, Institute of Education.

Holdhus, Kari, and Magne Espeland. 2013. "The Visiting Artist in Schools: Arts Based or School Based Practices?" *International Journal of Education & the Arts*, 14 (SI 1.10). Accessed October 20, 2013, www.ijea.org/v14si1/.

Irwin, Rita L., Sylvia Kind, Kit Grauer, and Alex F. de Cosson. 2005. "Integration as Embodied Knowing." In *Interdisciplinary Art Education Builds Bridges to Connect Disciplines & Cultures*, edited by Mary Stokrocki, 44–59. Reston, VA: National Art Education Association.

Jeffery, Graham. 2005. *The Creative College: Building a Successful Learning Culture in the Arts*. Straffordshire: Trentham Books.

Jorgenson, Estelle. 2003. *Transforming Music Education*. Bloomington, IN: Indiana University Press.

Kaplan, Andy. 2014. "Editor's Introduction: Collaboration as Opportunity." *Schools: Studies in Education*, 11 (2), 173–9.

Kenny, Ailbhe. 2009. *Knowing the Score: Local Authorities and Music*. Dublin: St. Patricks College, Wexford Co. Council, Sligo County Council.

Kenny Ailbhe. 2010. "Too Cool for School? Musicians as Partners in Education." *Irish Educational Studies*, 29 (2), 153–66.

Kenny, Ailbhe. 2011. "Mapping the Context: Insights and Issues from Local Government Development of Music Communities." *British Journal of Music Education*, 28 (2), 213–26.
Kenny, Ailbhe. 2014a. "Practice Through Partnership: Examining the Theoretical Framework and Development of a 'Community of Musical Practice.'" *International Journal of Music Education*, 32 (4), 396–408.
Kenny, Ailbhe. 2014b. "Sound Connections for Institutional Practice: Cultivating 'Collaborative Creativity' Through Group Composition." In *Developing Creativities in Higher Music Education: International Perspectives and Practices*, edited by Pamela Burnard, 469–92. Oxon: Routledge.
Kenny, Ailbhe. 2016. *Communities of Musical Practice*. Abingdon: Routledge.
Kenny, Ailbhe, Michael Finneran, and Eamonn Mitchell. 2015. "Becoming an Educator in and Through the Arts: Forming and Informing Emerging Teachers' Professional Identity." *Teaching and Teacher Education*, 49, 159–67.
Kenny, Ailbhe, and Dorothy Morrissey. 2016. *Exploring Teacher-Artist Partnership as a Model of CPD for Supporting and Enhancing Arts Education in Ireland*. Dublin: Association of Teachers/Education Centres in Ireland, Department of Education and Skills, Department of Arts, Heritage and Gaeltacht.
Kind, Sylvia, Alex de Casson, Rita Irwin, and Kit Grauer. 2007. "Artist-Teacher Partnerships in Learning: The in/Between Spaces of Artist-Teacher Professional Development." *Canadian Journal of Education*, 30 (3), 839–64.
Lave, Jean, and Etienne Wenger. 1991. *Situated Learning: Legitimate Peripheral Participation*. Cambridge: Cambridge University Press.
Laycock, Jolyon, ed. 2008. *Enabling the Creators: Arts and Cultural Management and the Challenge of Social Inclusion*. Oxford: European Arts Management Project in Association with Oxford Brookes University.
Moran, Seana, and John-Steiner, Vera. 2004. "How Collaboration in Creative Work Impacts Identity and Motivation." In *Collaborative Creativity: Contemporary Perspectives*, edited by Dorothy Miell and Karen Littleton, 11–25. London: Free Association.
Myers, David E., and Arthur C. Brooks. 2002. "Policy Issues in Connecting Music Education with Arts Education." In *The New Handbook of Research on Music Teaching and Learning*, edited by Richard Colwell and Carol Richardson, 909–30. New York: Oxford University Press.
Pitfield, Maggie. 2012. "Transforming Subject Knowledge: Drama Student Teachers and the Pursuit of Pedagogical Content Knowledge." *Research in Drama Education: The Journal of Applied Theatre and Performance*, 17 (3), 425–42.
Sefton-Green, Julian, Pat Thomson, Ken Jones, and Liora Bresler. 2011. *The Routledge International Handbook of Creative Learning*. London: Routledge.
UNESCO. 2006. United Nations Educational, Scientific, and Cultural Organization. *Road Map for Arts Education: The World Conference on Arts Education, Building Creative Capacities for the 21st Century*. Lisbon: UNESCO.
UNESCO. 2010. United Nations Educational, Scientific, and Cultural Organization. *The Seoul Agenda: Goals for the Development of Arts Education*. Lisbon: UNESCO.
Veblen, Kari K. 2012. "Adult Music Learning in Formal, Nonformal, and Informal Contexts." In *The Oxford Handbook of Music Education*, edited by Graham Welsh and Gary McPherson, 243–25. New York: Oxford University Press.
Vygotsky, Lev S. 1962. *Thought and Language*. Cambridge, MA: Massachusetts Institute of Technology, Wiley.
Vygotsky, Lev S., and Michael E. Cole. 1978. *Mind in Society: The Development of Higher Psychological Processes*. Cambridge, MA: Harvard University Press.
Wenger, Etienne. 1998. *Communities of Practice: Learning, Meaning, and Identity*. Cambridge: Cambridge University Press.
Winters, Mandy. 2012. "The Challenges of Teaching Composing." *British Journal of Music Education*, 29 (1), 19–24.
Wolf, Shelby A. 2008. "The Mysteries of Creative Partnerships." *Journal of Teacher Education*, 59 (1), 89–102.
Woolf, Felicity. 2004. *Partnerships for Learning: A Guide to Evaluating Arts Education Projects*, 2nd edition. London: Arts Council England. Accessed September 10, 2010, www.artscouncil.org.uk/media/uploads/documents/
Wyse, Dominic, and David Spendlove. 2007. "Partners in Creativity: Action Research and Creative Partnerships." *Education 3–13*, 35 (2), 181–91.

Part I
Critical Insights

2
When Collaborations Go Beyond Teachers and Musicians Alone: Frame and Stakeholder Analysis as Tools for Arts Advocacy[1]

HILDEGARD C. FROEHLICH

Introduction

Collaborative efforts among various constituents engaged in seeking to strengthen the place of music schooling as a part of compulsory schooling constitute situated actions, which might benefit the discourse if critically examined. Focusing on situations in which music educators act as one special-interest group among many stakeholders, the chapter introduces elements of frame and stakeholder analyses as a research tool for unpacking the at times rather tenuous relationship between and among educators, artists, the public, and policy makers. Such active involvement in learning to understand "otherness," it is argued, could benefit engagements in interdisciplinary collaborations of all kinds, but might especially strengthen research on arts advocacy and policy work.

Setting the Scene

The parent association of an elementary school in a rural area of the Midwest United States has urged the principal to assure that at least as much instructional time is allotted for the visual arts as is already allotted for music. To accomplish that goal, the principal asks the music specialist to let go of 35 percent of instruction time per week per class to make such rebalancing possible. Most immediately, the music teacher's reaction is one of resistance. His program is a strong one, and he would like to keep it that way. However, upon considering his situation in the bigger picture of what's best for the students, best for a sense of collegiality between him and the art specialist, and best for his own relationship with the principal, he realizes that working with the art teacher might be his wisest pathway. Together, the colleagues come up with a rotation plan of instruction that culminates in a winter program in which both art and music are publicly presented in the form of painted scenes that depict seasonal songs performed by the children. The performance program includes handwritten notations of the songs similar to what the children have seen in reproductions of medieval musical manuscripts. Brief written essays on the history of musical notation accompany the song displays. The project turns out to be the beginning of many programmatic collaborations thereafter. In terms borrowed from interactionist theories, of which frame and stakeholder analyses are a part, the music teacher opted for embracing a stake favored by others rather than himself.

Collaborative efforts among all sorts of groups and communities, not just those shared by music and art teachers or teachers and professional musician-artists, are generally considered a desirable as well as necessary part in strengthening, if not affirming, the place of music schooling as an educational goal for all school-aged children. But calls for cooperation and collaboration in the arts and arts education also occur when public funding of educational programs becomes an issue and budget cuts threaten the place of the arts in a curriculum. It is in those moments that special-interest groups in the arts and education often seek to strengthen their collective political power by proposing collaborations among music teachers and teachers in the visual arts and/or drama, professional artists/musicians and educators, or similar special-interest groupings.

An example from the United States that may illustrate the successful collaboration between different interest groups to solidify the place of music in the curriculum is that of a project known as the *Mississippi Blues Trail Curriculum*, an 18-lesson sequence that explored "Mississippi History through the lens of the Mississippi Blues Trail" (Washington Post/Associated Press 2014). With the help of blues scholar Scott Barretta, music educator Mark Malone designed the curriculum, drawing from research about "people, places and events significant in developing the local music." This information had become available as the result of the construction of highway markers along Highway 61, also known as the Blues Highway. The curriculum's core learning objectives evolved around "Music, Meaning, Cotton, Transportation, Civil Rights and Media." The program was pilot tested at Tunica Elementary School (Tunica, Mississippi, near Highway 61), where the students (mostly fourth graders, that is, generally nine- to ten-year-olds) learned rhythm and blues chord patterns, wrote blues songs about themselves and their surroundings, and studied poetry on past and present travails of growing cotton. The importance of the program was agreed upon by several interest groups (representatives from the Mississippi arts commission, state education board, school administrators and board members, parent association, social studies and music faculty). Without knowing the details of all negotiations involved, the story of the *Mississippi Blues Trail Curriculum* may nonetheless serve as an example of how a diverse group of stakeholders became collaborators, finding common ground in the process of articulating and implementing a reportedly successful model curriculum for a particular locality in the United States (for further information, go to https://www.howtolearn.com/2014/01/social-studies-with-the-mississippi-blues-trail-curriculum/).

Common to nearly all collaborative projects are the time and effort necessary to debate and negotiate goals and objectives, as well as methods of implementation among those groups who have a stake in reaching their envisioned goals. Differences in viewpoints, artistic preferences, and educational priorities require dialogue, especially with "other"-minded colleagues in the arts, education, and governmental agencies. It takes political know-how and negotiating skills to make sure that all groups stay "on board" throughout the process of distilling one common purpose from a variety of individual interests, preferences, and values. In such situations, which the (U.S.) National Association for Music Education (formerly known as MENC) refers to as "[thinking] beyond the bubbles" (NAfME 2014), tensions can and do arise because of often-conflicting professional identities, disagreements about funding priorities, and diverse aesthetic predilections (Caust 2003; Christophersen 2015; Christophersen et al. 2015; Garnham 2005; Kenny and Morrissey 2016; Kenny 2010). Although everyone may be well intentioned to find the best solution to a specific challenge, each potential collaborator also brings to the project her own interests and preferences that derive from personal history and biography, her expertise with an artistic medium, and cultural as well as creative biases. These interests and biases color and shape the stakes that are brought to the collaboration and that, if not clearly articulated, can lead to unwanted discord among all collaborators during all phases of a project, from its planning to—once implemented—its evaluation.

Any situation in which differences in viewpoints, artistic preferences, and educational priorities must be identified and sorted out would bring together what Goffman (1974/1986, 8) called "situated perspectives." In particular, participants in dialogues with "other"-minded colleagues in the arts, education, and governmental agencies bring those situated perspectives to bear on decisions with consequences for later actions. This chapter makes the case that researching and fully understanding the perspectives each collaborating participant brings to an envisioned project might be key to the success of such a project. In such larger collaborative undertakings as the *Mississippi Blues Curriculum* described earlier, no one perspective may be assumed to be self-evident or remain unchallenged. In fact, one might assume that the larger a project and the more groups of individuals are involved in the decision making, the more special interests, often competing, tend to be embedded in a complex system of individually held artistic and social values, group norms, and power hierarchies that determine a particular group's stated or assumed goals (Frey 2003; Heclo 1978; Reed et al. 2009). Thus, whether the pathway is that of professional musicians collaborating with music teachers, general educators with licensed school music educators, or music teachers with their visual arts, drama, or science colleagues, knowing what stakes each participant brings to the table should be considered an essential component in articulating a project's goals, implementing them, and assessing their overall benefit for the students. However, not only educational and artistic values are in question, but communal and social benefits as well (Baumgartner and Jones 2002; Benham 2011; Torgerson 2003; Vennix 1996).

In this chapter, two analytic tools—frame and stakeholder analysis—are proposed as ways for identifying what different groups of individuals bring to the table in light of larger, overriding goals. Those goals may be about what teachers and musicians value when collaborating with each other in a local school, what several schools cooperating with each other wish to accomplish for the benefit of the entire community, or what elected and appointed representatives of special-interest groups hope to achieve when seeking to advance the course of school music through public activism and political action.

Frame analysis, developed by Erving Goffman (1974/1986), is rooted in symbolic interactionism, a pragmatic social theory that originated in the United States in the early twentieth century. Frames are the meanings individuals bring to their interactions with others (Brooks 2007; Edgley 2003; Goffman 1981a; Reynolds and Herman-Kinney 2003). Fully understanding those meanings can strengthen purposeful discourse. Stakeholder analysis, first mentioned in organizational and management literature during the 1970s and 1980s, examines relationships between individuals (Brugha and Varvaskovszky 2000; Reed et al. 2009). In the looking glass of interactionism, "stakes" are valued focal points in a person's perception of the world and, thus, interactions with others. When these become the factual givens that determine the success of all subsequent phases in collaborations of all kinds, knowledge about the stakes that individuals bring to a discourse is not a "necessary evil" but a "necessity" (Kavaratzis 2012, 7).

Frame Analysis

Each person's perceived reality becomes, in Erving Goffman's (1974/1986) terms, a "frame." It is the set of concepts and perspectives present in individuals, groups, and societies that result from lived experiences and that guide observable actions. To understand *framing* as it shapes any interaction, one needs to ask (with Gregory Bateson), "what is really going on here?" The types of framings Goffman considered were frame fabrications, keying, frame breaks, misframing, and . . . frame disputes" (Goffman 1974, 497–498). Of those terms, *keying* (perhaps the least self-explanatory) is defined as "the set of conventions by which a given activity, one already meaningful in terms of some primary framework, is transformed into something patterned on this activity but seen by the participants to be quite something else" (ibid 44). Goffman also suggested that "mode" might have been a better term than "key" (ibid 44), alluding to the fact that when dialoguing participants are "keyed" to the urgency of an issue, they actually are in different "modes." An example of applying the meaning of keying to the *Mississippi Curriculum* project might be what each participant harbored as the concept of "music" before the project began. Whereas one participant, possibly the social studies teacher, may have had the singing of seasonal songs in mind, the music teacher's primary framework might have been her full knowledge of what a traditional fourth-grade skill set in music was expected to be. At first, these notions likely guided both participants' deliberations. Eventually, however, the "key" to the shared framework was that of the blues as the glue that held the curricular activities together.

Frame fabrication, "the intentional effort of one or more individuals to manage activity so that a party of one or more others will be induced to have a false belief about what it is that is going on" (Goffman 1974, 83), is possibly the least easily detected but the most manipulated form of discourse. One speaker's intentions are not what they appear to be or what the speaker purports them to mean. Fabrication means to intentionally be vague about the context in which an activity is planned. Here, an example might be the ambiguity found in many arts policy statements to generically endorse or mandate instruction in music and the fine arts in a curriculum (see, for example, Arts Education Partnership 2014). Although possibly sufficient for policy makers taking action by voting for or against such a proposed legislation, the rather vague wording is likely less helpful when school administrators, practicing teachers, and artists seek to implement the policy in the context of a particular school curriculum. An intentionally vague wording early on in the process can run the risk of weakening the effect of the legislation later.

Unlike frame fabrications, *frame breaks* and *misframing* are not necessarily intentional but can happen as the result of unforeseen circumstances and/or misused or misunderstood terminologies. The latter may be the case when definitions of terms are assumed rather than spelled out or when terms in one geopolitical setting do not match with their meaning in another. The latter may occur, for example, when the often-heard European reference to "Didaktik" and "Bildung," two essential terms in the German tradition of music education philosophies but not necessarily meaning the same in their Anglo-American usage, may and can lead to breakdowns in communication across international groups of arts advocates.

Misframing easily brings about *frame disputes*, a phenomenon similar to what many years ago Walter Gallie (1956, 97) called "essentially contested concepts" (see also Gallie 1955; Miles 2012). The meanings of seemingly well-understood and shared terms and concepts are at first assumed, but differences in interpretation and definition become clear as the discourse unfolds. Such may be the case when words like "musical," "beautiful," "democratic," "education," or "artistic" enter a conversation. Although it is easy to refer to the terms themselves, it is less clear whether everyone agrees on their specific meaning. Thus, whereas leaders in one special-interest group may frame the discourse in a particular way to make information agreeable to all group members, the nature of the discourse changes when each participant adds or even superimposes his or her own frame in the process (D'Angelo and Kypers 2010; see also Entman 1993, 2007; Gamson and Modigliani 1989; Heimovics et al. 1993; Kuypers 2006). It is easy to hypothesize that the more groups seek to collaborate with each other, the more likely frame disputes arise, a risk that results from the desire to reach out to other special-interest groups for input and participation. In such situations where collaborations require the cooperation between local-level private interest groups and state as well as national political-legislative representatives, it may not be uncommon that such tangible, quantifiable benefits as academic progress, functional literacy, the development of social skills, a productive citizenry, and economic growth through the arts are cited more frequently by all collaborators than seemingly idealistic, intangible quality-of-life issues that are believed to be furthered by the acquisition of musical skills and knowledge (Bladh and Heimonen 2007; Dryzek 1990/1994, 2006; Gutmann and Thompson 2004). The much-acclaimed "Mozart effect" could be considered the source of frame disputes as well (see Bastian 2000; Rauscher et al. 1993; Newman et al. 1995; Steele et al. 1999).

Stakeholder Analysis

The center of stakeholder analysis is—as the name suggests—one stakeholder in his or her standing among other stakeholders. A stakeholder as unit of analysis can be "individuals, groups and organizations" (Brugha and Varvaskovszky 2000, 239). This means that stakeholder analysis can take place at the macro as well as the micro and meso levels of study. The question guiding such analyses is situated in asking who holds power over whom and why; in most basic terms, "who's in, and why?" (Reed et al. 2009, 1933). This question is about "stakeholder representation, legitimacy, participation, power, and knowledge," almost always leading to further queries that include (Reed et al. 2009, 1934):

> How can diverse stakeholders be adequately represented? How can the relative interest and influence of different stakeholders be taken into account? And if stakeholders are defined by the issues that are being investigated, then who defines these issues?

The first issue in any form of collaboration may well be that of representation: Who is part of the project? Who was involved at its beginning, and who remained in it throughout? Collaborations between teachers and musicians alone may be easier to assess in that regard than projects involving multiple groups of decision makers (for example, parents, school administrators, and/ or political leaders). At the same time, however, outreach programs and arts advocacy projects might actually be in greater need for such analyses than teacher–artist collaborations at the micro level of one particular school. Just in terms of representation and legitimacy alone, the selection process of those participating in a national project would require ascertaining whether participation was voluntary or decreed and whether the participants were appointed or elected. And were all "players" in the project equally informed of its purpose and did they all actually share a belief in its urgency? In short, stakeholder analyses could play an important part in determining who among multiple collaborators (for example, program directors, teachers, musician-artists, school administrators, teachers, and curriculum experts) would be considered most responsible for the seeming success of a project in terms of goal setting, implementation, and evaluation.

Different approaches to stakeholder analysis exist, among them the *descriptive*, the *normative*, and the *instrumental*. The descriptive analysis simply reports the relationship between all stakeholders and the objective at hand. Kennon et al. (2009) suggest the distinction between influential and important stakeholders, calling influential those individuals who have power over an organization; important stakeholders are those who have power over project implementation. But one might also argue that holding the role as implementer without having been a stakeholder at the planning stage can diminish the implementer's effectiveness. Thus, although the distinction between influential and important stakeholders may be politically expedient, it may also create uneven power relationships, the study of which would be useful in the context of existing collaborations among musicians and teachers (Christophersen 2015; Christophersen et al. 2015; Kenny and Morrissey 2016; Kenny 2010), music teachers and classroom teachers (Randall 2012), and other projects currently (and reportedly) in planning stages (Dalton 2016).

Normative stakeholder analyses aim at solving a common problem based on reason, consensus, and cooperation. This approach responds to Jürgen Habermas' (1984/1987) theory of communicative action and rationality. It is a model for a form of participatory democracy that, when applied to education, would turn both teachers and students into one community of learners. Clearly, such a perspective presents a radically different model from what presently appears to be the custom in most schools, colleges, and universities of most industrialized nations. Applied to music and education, then, a normative stakeholder discourse would be that everyone in the conversation is being heard and valued equally. The power among stakeholders would be uniformly distributed. Normative discourse of this kind sometimes runs the risk of being construed by some critics as "too much talk, not enough action," because much time tends to be spent on sorting out differences in perceptions and personal preferences.

The *instrumental* stakeholder aims to win an argument in order to expedite the envisioned outcome (for more, see Reed et al. 2009). Perhaps that model resembles many advocacy groups of today that are institutionally bound and often hierarchically structured. Because of a stakeholder's particular position as administrative or legislative liaison, one stake is given more value than another, thus leading to the assumption of there being a single "winner." Needless to say, critical theorists/pedagogues in particular would consider the instrumental stakeholder approach antithetical to any system of discursive democratic principles. In the latter, political decisions as well as policies should be based on consensus-driven (normative) rather than power-driven (instrumental) rationality (see Dryzek 1990/1994, 2006).

Whether a potential or actual collaborator is seen by others as an instrumental rather than a normative stakeholder requires contextual knowledge that allows exploration of the frames of experience each stakeholder brings to the advocacy table. For instance, a musician-artist who aspires to let her teaching be guided by the vision of being or becoming a professional conductor may be viewed by other stakeholders outside of music as a somewhat autocratic, and possibly an insufficiently student-centered, instrumental stakeholder. Musically trained observers, however, might recognize the teacher's intent and condone it as normative conduct. On the other hand, a teacher-educator who allows his pupils to explore music of their own choice, asks for discussion on repertoire choices, and places emphasis on verbal explorations and written essays about personal music preferences may be eyed critically by his professional performer-colleagues. Similarly, what is a convincing argument for music teachers may not be so for school administrators. Musician-artists may not share in what policy makers and politicians favor. Successful collaborations therefore should take into account those differences, identified as frames and stakes, respectively, throughout all phases of a project.

In summary, differences in perceptions (frames) and envisioned purposes (stakes) set the boundaries among the group(s) involved in planning an advocacy project, implementing its phases, and evaluating those. In all phases, therefore, questioning established assumptions about valued knowledge and skills in music should become a matter of course. In addition, researchers and scholars in the arts, education, and arts policy should not shy away from probing what any one group of representatives has embraced as valued knowledge before (see also Benham 2011; Kos 2010; Markusen and Gadwa 2010). With such research in hand, both frame and stakeholder analyses can provide explicit guidelines for homing in on joint foci of attention by all collaborating partners prior to the time that irrevocable decisions are being made or individual players begin to feel left out of the decision-making process. A formidable challenge in all forms of stakeholder discourse lies in identifying the stakes first and separating them from the personas of the stakeholders, whether the latter are paid performers, scholars, lobbyists, teachers, first-grade pupils, or college students.

Applications Not Only to Matters of Arts Advocacy

If the assumption of like-mindedness among participants in any collaborative project is proactively questioned and examined by means of frame and stakeholder analyses, any "chord alterations" (see Chapter 1) stand a chance of being purposeful and intentional. Without such research, however, numerous chord alterations may remain unprepared, out of context, and, thus, without purpose. What, then, might be the specific implications of both analytical approaches for collaborations of the kind described throughout this entire book? How can such analyses improve or strengthen various forms of collaborations among musicians and teachers, teachers of different subject matter expertise, administrators and artists, and/or teacher–artists and policy makers in educational contexts and beyond?

From a research perspective, providing descriptive data about differences in perceptions (frames) and envisioned purposes (stakes) would be beneficial in seeing the boundaries among the group(s) involved in planning a project, implementing its phases, and evaluating those. Frame analytical data would focus on the verbal discourse among project participants, identifying possible conflicts created by ambiguities in and misunderstandings among speakers. Descriptive stakeholder analytic data would go beyond the study of verbal discourse and include interpersonal nonverbal interactions among individuals and the groups to which an individual most immediately connects. From such descriptive data about frames and stakes would follow the second step, the determination as to whether normative or instrumental interactions prevail among collaborating partnerships.

It is a hypothesis worth exploring whether, politically, the instrumental stakeholder model might be the most expedient and functional one in use. Ultimately, however, and in keeping with the hope for normative rather than instrumental discourse in arts education for the twenty-first century, it should be the goal of all collaborators to view each other as stakeholders of equal stature and to accept all stakes as carrying equal weight. It is about valuing and accepting the stakes that different music(k)ers hold in their respective roles as lifelong participants in performance, instruction, arts advocacy, and scholarship.[2] The question "why don't they see things the way I do?" might turn into "what do I hear that I have overlooked or am unaware of?" "How can I change my own language to be understood by those with unlike experiences?" "What is at stake for my counterpart?" "Where do I agree, where do I disagree and why, and where are points of possible consensus?" And "which of the identified stakes holds the greatest promise of turning 'others' into visions of 'us'?" Such queries, similarly asked by experienced teachers almost daily, might also become guiding principles in project(s) in which collaborations with seemingly other-minded colleagues and participants are called for. This is a challenge in line with principles of transformative pedagogies, in which the ultimate beneficiaries are hoped to be the learners, that is, the students (see, among others, Aróstegui et al. 2004; Bladh and Heimonen 2007; O'Neill 2012; Regelski 2016; Schmidt 2005). Therefore, the most important stakeholders in arts education of all kinds might be the learners—active collaborators in planning, implementing, and evaluating projects of benefit to all.

Notes

1 Parts of the content in this chapter were first published in Froehlich (2015).
2 The bracketed spelling of music(k)er refers to the combined usage of Small's (1997, 1998) *musicking* and Elliott (1995) and Elliott and Silverman's (2015) *musicing*. The term *music(k)ing* connotes "the complex nature of what it means to take part, in any capacity, in a musical performance, whether by performing, by listening, by rehearsing, or practicing, by providing material for performance (what is called composing) or by dancing. Varying degrees of consciousness, knowledge, and thought by those who participate impact how such communicative acts are explored, affirmed, and celebrated and/or judged either aesthetically, socially, or both according to criteria formed within the community of music(k)ers themselves" (Froehlich 2015, 107–8).

References

Aróstegui, José Luis, Robert Stake, and Helen Simons. 2004. "Music Education for the 21st Century: Epistemology and Ontology as Bases for Student Aesthetic Education." *Education Policy Analysis Archives*, 12 (54), 1–16.

Arts Education Partnership. 2014. "A Snapshot of State Policies for Arts Education." March. Accessed January 16, 2017, www.aep-arts.org/wp-content/uploads/2014/03/A-Snapshot-of-State-Policies-for-Arts-Education.pdf.

Bastian, Hans-Günther. 2000. "Musikerziehung und ihre Wirkung." In *Eine Langzeitstudie an Berliner Grundschulen*. Mainz: Schott Musik International. The Impact of Music(Education): A Longitudinal Study at Elementary Schools in Berlin].

Baumgartner, Frank R., and Bryan D. Jones, eds. 2002. *Policy Dynamics*. Chicago: University of Chicago Press.

Benham, John L. 2011. *Music Advocacy: Moving from Survival to Vision*. Published in Partnership with MENC: The National Association for Music Education. Lanham, MD: Rowman & Littlefield.

Bladh, Stephan, and Marja Heimonen. 2007. "Music Education and Deliberative Democracy." *Action, Criticism and Theory for Music Education*, 6 (1). www.maydaygroup.org/ACT/v6n1/Bladh_Heimonen6_1.pdf.

Brooks, JoAnn M. 2007. "Understanding Virtuality: Contributions from Goffman's Frame Analysis." In *Virtuality and Virtualization*, edited by Kevin Crowston, Sandra Sieber, and Eleanor Wynn, 201–13. IFIP International Federation for Information Processing, Vol. 236. Boston, MA: Springer.

Brugha, Ruariri, and Zsuzsa Varvaskovszky. 2000. "Stakeholder Analysis: A Review." *Health Policy and Planning*, 15 (3), 239–46.

Caust, Jo. 2003. "Putting the 'Art' Back into Arts Policy Making: How Arts Policy Has Been 'Captured' by the Economists and the Marketers." *International Journal of Cultural Policy*, 9 (1), 51–63.

Christophersen, Catharina. 2015. "Changes and Challenges in Music Education: Reflections on a Norwegian Arts-in-Education Programme." *Music Education Research*, 17 (4), 364–80.

Christophersen, Catharina, Jan-Kare Breivik, Anne Homme, and Lise Rykkja. 2015. *The Cultural Rucksack: A National Programme for Arts and Culture in Norwegian Schools*. Bergen: Fagbokforlaget.

Dalton, Lucy. 2016. "Teaching Together: International Collaboration." *Musical Futures Guest Blog*. Accessed January 8, 2017, www.musicalfutures.org/musical-futures- blog/teaching- together-international-collaboration.

D'Angelo, Paul, and Jim A. Kypers. 2010. *Doing News Framing Analysis: Empirical and Theoretical Perspectives*. New York and London: Routledge.

Dryzek, John S. 1990/1994. *Discursive Democracy: Politics, Policy, and Political Science*. Cambridge: Cambridge University Press.

Dryzek, John S. 2006. *Deliberative Global Politics: Discourse and Democracy in a Divided World*. Cambridge: Polity.

Edgley, Charles. (2003). "The dramaturgical genre." In *Handbook of Symbolic Interactionism* (Larry T. Reynolds and Nancy J. Herman-Kinney, editors). Lamham: Rowman & Littlefield, 141–172.

Elliott, David J. 1995. *Music Matters: A New Philosophy of Music Education*. New York and Oxford: Oxford University Press.

Elliott, David J., and Marissa Silverman. 2015. *Music Matters: A New Philosophy of Music Education*, 2nd edition. Oxford and New York: Oxford University Press.
Entman, Robert M. 1993. "Framing: Toward Clarification of a Fractured Paradigm." *Journal of Communication*, 43 (4), 51–8.
Entman, Robert M. 2007. "Framing Bias: Media in the Distribution of Power." *Journal of Communication*, 57 (1), 163–73.
Frey, Bruno S. (2003). *Arts and Economics. Analysis and Cultural Policy* (2nd edition). Berlin-Heidelberg-New York: Springer-Verlag.
Froehlich, Hildegard C. 2015. *A Social Theory for Music Education: Symbolic Interactionism in Music Learning and Teaching*. Lewiston, NY: The Edwin Mellen Press.
Gallie, Walter B. 1955. "Essentially Contested Concepts." *Proceedings of the Aristotelian Society* New Series, 56, 167–98. www.jstor.org/stable/4544562.
Gallie, Walter B. 1956. "Art as an Essentially Contested Concept." *The Philosophical Quarterly*, 6 (23), 97–114.
Gamson, William A., and Andre Modigliani. 1989. "Media Discourse and Public Opinion on Nuclear Power: A Constructionist Approach." *American Journal of Sociology*, 95 (1), 1–37.
Garnham, Nicholas. 2005. "From Cultural to Creative Industries. An Analysis of the Implications of the 'Creative Industries' Approach to Arts and Media Policy Making in the United Kingdom." *International Journal of Cultural Policy*, 11 (1), 15–29.
Goffman, Erving. 1974. *Frame Analysis: An Essay on the Organization of Experience*. Cambridge, MA: Harvard University Press. 1986 Reprint with a foreword by Kenneth M. Berger. Boston, MA: Northwestern University Press, in arrangement with Harper & Row.
Goffman, Erving (1981). *Forms of Talk*. Philadelphia: University of Pennsylvania Press.
Gutmann, Amy, and Dennis Thompson (2004). *Why Deliberative Democracy?* Princeton, NJ: Princeton University Press.
Habermas, Jürgen. 1984/1987. *The Theory of Communicative Action*, Vols. 1 and 2. Introduction and Translation by Thomas McCarthy. Boston, MA: Beacon Press.
Heclo, Hugh. 1978. "Issue Networks and the Executive Establishment." In *The New American Political System*, 1st edition, edited by Anthony King, 87–107, 115–24. Washington, DC: American Enterprise Institute. Also in Daniel C. McCool. 1995. *Public Policy Theories, Models, and Concepts: An Anthology*, 268–87. Prentice Hall.
Heimovics, Richard D., Robert D. Herman, and Carole L. Jurkiewicz Coughlin. 1993. "Executive Leadership and Resource Dependence in Nonprofit Organizations: A Frame Analysis." *Public Administration Review*, 53 (5), 419–27.
Kavaratzis, Mihalis (2012). "From 'necessary evil' to necessity: stakeholders' involvement in place branding." *Journal of Place Management and Development*, 5 (1) 7–19.
Kennon, Nicole, Peter Howden, and Meredith Hartley. 2009. "Who Really Matters? A Stakeholder Analysis Tool" [online]. *Extension Farming Systems Journal*, 5 (2), 9–17. Accessed June 18, 2016, http://search.informit.com.au/documentSummary;dn=733413362842369;res=IELHSS>ISSN: 1833-203X.
Kenny Ailbhe. 2010. "Too Cool for School? Musicians as Partners in Education." *Irish Educational Studies*, 29 (2), 153–66.
Kenny, Ailbhe, and Dorothy Morrissey. 2016. *Exploring Teacher-Artist Partnership as a Model of CPD for Supporting & Enhancing Arts Education in Ireland: A Research Report*. Dublin: Association of Teachers/Education Centres in Ireland, Department of Education and Skills, Department of Arts, Heritage and Gaeltacht.
Kuypers, Janet (2006). "Dreams." *Writing and Images from a Chicago Art Show plus Assorted Dreams Poems*. Retrieved from http://books.google.com/books?hl=en&lr=&id=5fj4mwra_00C&oi=fnd&pg=PA4&dq=+++Kuypers,+2006+music&ots=ffA_gzDlAr&sig=C5Oykg1k42tBe39LFDW9OObpi64#v=onepage&q&f=false.
Kos, Ronald P., Jr. 2010. "Developing Capacity for Change: A Policy Analysis for the Music Education Profession." *Arts Education Policy Review*, 111 (3), 97–104.
Markusen, Ann, and Anne Gadwa. 2010. "Arts and Culture in Urban or Regional Planning: A Review and Research Agenda." *Journal of Planning Education and Research*, 29 (3), 379–91.
Miles, Samantha. 2012. "Stakeholder: Essentially Contested or Just Confused?" *Journal of Business Ethics*, 108 (3), 285–98.
National Association for Music Education. 2014. "Why Music? Music Helps Educate the Whole Child." Accessed January 10, 2017, www.nafme.org/wp-content/files/2014/08/BroaderMindedInsert.pdf.

Newman, Joan, John H. Rosenbach, Kathryn L. Burns, Brian C. Latimer, Helen R. Matocha, and Elaine Rosenthal Vogt. 1995. "An Experimental Test of 'the Mozart Effect: Does Listening to His Music Improve Spatial Ability?" *Perceptual and Motor Skills*, 81 (3, Supplement), 1379–87.

O'Neill, Susan A. 2012. "Becoming a Music Learner: Towards a Theory of Transformative Music Engagement." In *The Oxford Handbook of Music Education*, Vol. 1, edited by Gary E. McPherson and Graham F. Welch, 163–86. Oxford and New York: Oxford University Press.

Randall, Mac. 2012. "Putting Music and Classroom Teachers Side by Side: A Growing Utah Program Brings an Integrated Arts Education Approach to Elementary Schools and Universities." *Teaching Music* (October), 52. Accessed January 8, 2017, http://wccnafme.weebly.com/uploads/1/2/9/1/12915361/teaching_music_october_2012_51-60.pdf

Rauscher, Frances H., Gordon L. Shaw, and Katherine N. Ky. 1993. "Music and Spatial Task Performance." *Nature*, 365 (6447), 611.

Reed, Mark S., Anil Graves, Norman Dandy, Helena Posthumus, Klaus Hubacek, Joe Morris, Christina Prell, Claire H. Quinn, and Lindsay C. Stringer. 2009. "Who's in and Why? A Typology of Stakeholder Analysis Methods for Natural Resource Management." *Journal of Environmental Management*, 90 (5), 1933–49.

Regelski, Thomas A. 2016. *A Brief Introduction to a Philosophy of Music and Music Education as Social Praxis*. New York and London: Routledge.

Reynolds, Larry T., and Nancy J. Herman-Kinney. 2003. "General Introduction." In *Handbook of Symbolic Interactionism*, edited by Larry T. Reynolds and Nancy J. Herman-Kinney, 3–12. Lanham, MD: Rowman & Littlefield.

Schmidt, Patrick. 2005. "Music Education as Transformative Practice: Creating New Frameworks for Learning Music Through a Freirian Perspective." *Visions of Research in Music Education*, 6 (1), 1–14. Accessed January 10, 2017, www.rider.edu/~vrme.

Small, Christopher. 1997. "Musicking: A Ritual in Social Space." In *On the Sociology of Music Education*, edited by Roger R. Rideout, 1–12. Proceedings of the Symposium for Music Education, University of Oklahoma School of Music, April 1995, Norman, OK: School of Music, University of Oklahoma.

Small, Christopher. 1998. *Musicking: The Meanings of Performing and Listening*. Hanover, NH: University Press of New England.

Steele, Kenneth M., Simone Dalla Bella, Isabelle Peretz, Tracey Dunlop, Lloyd A. Dawe, G. Keith Humphrey, Roberta A. Shannon, Johnny L. Kirby Jr, and C. G. Olmstead. 1999. "Prelude or Requiem for the 'Mozart Effect'?" *Nature*, 400 (6747, Scientific Correspondence), 826–7.

Torgerson, Douglas. 2003. "Democracy Through Policy Discourse." In *Deliberative Policy Analysis: Understanding Governance in the Network Society*, edited by Maarten A. Hajer and Hendriks Wagenaar, 113–38. Cambridge: Cambridge University Press.

Vennix, Jac A. M. 1996. *Group Model Building: Facilitating Team Learning Using System Dynamics*. Chichester: J. Wiley.

The Washington Post/Associated Press. 2014. "The Blues Can Be More than a Music Lesson." January 12. Accessed March 3, 2014, www.washingtonpost.com/lifestyle/kidspost/the-blues-can-be-more-than-a-music-lesson/2014/01/10/1a08c1d2-71e8-11e3-9389-09ef9944065e_story.html

3
Teacher–Musician Collaborations on the Move: From Performance Appreciation to Dialogue

KARI HOLDHUS

Introduction

[R]estore continuity between the refined and intensified forms of experience that are works of art and the everyday events, doings, and sufferings that are recognized to constitute experience.

—(Dewey 1934, 2)

A number of writers point out that it should be a goal to perceive aesthetic subjects (for example, music, arts and crafts, dance, drama) as the root of the school system instead of treating them as add-ons (Aulin-Gråhamn et al. 2004; Bamford 2012; Espeland et al. 2013). This then also should be the case for the practices of visiting artists and professional concert performances in schools. In this chapter, I argue that visiting artists' practices must be school led and school based, which can be achieved by fostering respectful and equity-based teacher–artist partnerships built on the school's institutional and pedagogical functions (Bresler 2002; Booth 2009; Heggedal 2013).

Throughout this text, I focus on the necessity of dialogic teacher–musician collaborations in school concert visits. Previous research (Breivik and Christophersen 2013) has noted that true collaboration is difficult when artists hold the power to define their visiting practices. In the following reflections on this topic, I point out possible paths towards collaboration by underlining common features as well as productive differences between teachers and musicians.

The chapter starts with a description of the current rationale for visiting musicians in schools based on research within the Norwegian context (Holdhus and Espeland 2013) and continues with an outline of a dialogic, contemporary, and heteronomic practice that can be used as an alternative to school concert visits. This proposal is followed by an argument for a greater degree of ownership among teachers and pupils regarding visiting musician practices.

Many reflections in this chapter will necessarily concern the arts and its integration into schools in a general sense. Many contemporary discussions about the arts that can be explored in the context of music stem from other artistic subjects. Thus, the term "arts" is used when the text refers to a broader artistic context than only music. "Music" is used when applying broader artistic or pedagogic phenomena to music, as well as when musical content and form are the direct object of the text. As the text evolves, the term "school concert visit" changes to "visiting musical events" to illustrate the necessary differentiation of these forms.

Point of Departure

The immediate background for this chapter is my monograph *Star experiences or gym hall aesthetics?—A study of quality conceptions in visiting concert programs at school*[1] (Holdhus 2014) and other research on similar topics (Bjørnsen 2011; Borgen and Brandt 2006; Breivik and Christophersen 2013; Digranes 2009). The monograph discusses how the artistic power of definition frames and shapes relations between musicians and schools.

In Norway, the professional concert organization, "Concerts Norway," employs freelance musicians to produce and play concerts in schools, framed by an effective touring scheme. The organization's goals are for every child to attend two concerts a year and for children to be exposed to a variety of genres during their time at school (Concerts Norway 2017).[2] With 630,000 pupils in compulsory state schooling, this system generates 1,260,000 "tickets" a year, and the number of performances each year varies between 8,000 and 9,000. The main rationale of the practice is a democratic one: Every child, regardless of their geographical, religious, sociocultural, or economic background, should have access to professionally performed live music. However, schools, teachers, or pupils do not have a say during the production, performance, or evaluation of these concerts. Thus, although the Norwegian visiting concert practice can be seen as a democratic way of distributing live music, it lacks democratizing functions (Bjørnsen 2011).

Throughout the Western world, there is a long tradition of visiting artists at schools, often mentioned in connection with "arts integration in schools" (Grumet et al. 2015, 268; UNESCO 2006). Some of these practices are explicitly intended to be collaborative, like "Creative Partnerships" (2012) and teaching artists (Booth 2009), and many stem from the educational programs of arts institutions that offer long- or short-term artist engagements within schools. Concerts Norway is connected to the Blackboard Music Project (2017), a European forum focused on visiting music practices hosted by Jeunesses Musicales International (2017) and financed by Creative Europe (European Union 2017).

Background: "State of the Art"

The results of my previous study suggest that musicians view school concert visits as arts experiences that have little to do with school. The musicians

I interviewed seemed to view themselves as artists who have the right to control the content and form of concerts. Interestingly, not only the musicians but also the teachers participating in my study perceive the existing intervention and transmission approach as the right one (Holdhus 2014). The teacher–musician relationship can be seen as symbolic violence, which is characterized by domination. According to Bourdieu and Wacquant (1992) neither the dominant nor the dominated party in a symbolic violent relationship is conscious of the violence. The objective power relations are hidden, and power is provided through misrecognition. In this type of situation, all parties approve of the symbolic violence because no one perceives it as violence, except as a relational law of nature. All implicated parties, including the dominated ones, who unconsciously support the continuation of existing power relations, see the dominant culture as legitimate. Pre-reflexive acceptance emerges because the dominated group has internalized the power structures. According to common school concert visit practice, the musicians define quality and teachers approve these definitions, thus diminishing their own professional knowledge and skills and deeming them irrelevant to the quality of concerts (Christophersen 2013; Holdhus 2014).

In my study, the participating musicians were often set in their views about music and concerts, creating a sender–receiver relationship between them and their audience (Holdhus 2014). According to many of the musicians, as learning is tied to accountability regimes and the "three Rs" (reading, writing, and (a)rithmetic), they served as missionaries for the arts as an alternative to learning, which they saw as a disciplinary and nonaesthetic phenomenon (Digranes 2009; Holdhus 2014). Thus, many of these musicians denied pedagogy and learning as elements of aesthetic experiences (Holdhus 2014).

The rationale for this stance is work oriented. Within this view, artistic work is seen as a subject with an inherent message that speaks directly to the heart and emerges free of all learning processes and cultural contexts (Bowman 2007; DeNora 2000; Goehr 2007). This rationale can derive from genius-aesthetic views, which are of ancient Western origin (Kris and Kurz 1981). According to myth and common interpretations of Kant's highly complex work, genius is given by God and requires no education. Music is seen as divine, and therefore an explanation or pedagogy is not needed for the art to reach man's heart (Kant 1987).

The musicians participating in my study also largely viewed pupils as aesthetic and creative beings that are inherently suited to understand music (Valberg 2011). In some musicians' view, the child and the musician formed a team, fighting against what they perceived to be oppression of creativity by the teacher and school (Digranes 2009; Holdhus 2014). As a consequence, the teacher becomes superfluous, and collaboration is reduced to a practical event in which the teacher facilitates the musician's intervention (Christophersen 2013).

How to engage teachers in school concert visits has been debated for years. Until now, teachers and pupils have not been granted ownership by building on their competencies and thoughts. There are, however, signs that the previously described practice of musical intervention is about to change in Norway (Holdhus and Espeland 2013). Within the fields of visual arts and theater, contemporary artists and researchers have started to approach schools in a more inclusive way (Heggedal 2013; O'Neill and Wilson 2010). The sender–receiver-based music performances for students in Norway are due to change because of a major reorganization of the Norwegian visiting artist program, The Cultural Rucksack. However, musicians worry that school contextualization will push the concerts into something strongly curricular (Ørstavik 2016).

Contemporary Art Forms and Schools

An array of contemporary and heteronomic art forms can inform visiting musicians in schools, including relational art (Bourriaud 2002),[3] performative art (Fischer-Lichte 2008),[4] dialogical art (Kester 2004), and different combinations of practice and theory, like collaborative art, community music, or socially engaged art. In alignment with Bishop (2012), I choose to relate these flourishing art forms, referring to them as *participatory art*. Participatory art can be visual art, theater, performance art, or music, but they all cherish audience participation.

In participatory art, the audience is often invited into a frame created by the artist, and within this frame, participants act, react, and interact with each other and the artist (Thygesen 2009). The school context adds complexity to this picture because schools involve learning and *Bildung*.[5] Additionally, teachers have knowledge about their pupils and ways to deal with aesthetic enterprises, which should be incorporated into participatory art. A concert in a school context thus needs to be approached in a more context-specific manner than many other performative events that involve a relationship between the artist and participants. This is due to the teacher's role, responsibility, and power within the school context (Holdhus 2015).

Dialogic Art

When searching for artistic approaches and philosophies to fulfill the need for contextualization and school ownership, *dialogic art* can be a starting point. This is mainly because dialogic artistic practices acknowledge joint production processes that involve the artist as well as participants. Dialogical artistic practices are grounded in the politically active art practices of the 1960s (Lacy 1995) and in Hal Foster's (1995) significant essay "The Artist as Ethnographer," which addresses problems that occur when artists' understanding of audience situations is insufficient to formulate an artistic base that includes the participants.

Foster (1995) claims that whereas ethnographers and anthropologists problematize and reflect on their roles and functions in an effort to make processes transparent, artists are still relatively unaware of art's function in social contexts (for example, in schools).

Kester (2004) claims that there is a need for an aesthetic exchange in which the artist's beliefs are challenged through collaboration with the audience on a work. The audience's situation and the artwork's physical context are considered production factors. To more thoroughly contextualize and appropriate their art, as Foster (1995) encourages, dialogical musicians in schools must search for contextual significance through performance ethnography (Denzin 2003). The school as an artistic venue is composed of both professional adults, who are responsible for pupils' learning, and pupils, who encounter the school's agendas through their musical ways of being (for example, through play, intersubjectivity, listening, creation) and socioemotional competence and agency (Bjørkvold 1992). The musician thus might need to research and immerse himself or herself into the life-worlds, learning strategies, and competencies of both groups in order to contribute to a truly contextualized process and performance.

Kester (2004) argues that dialogical art practices should be performative to such an extent that both the artist's and the participants' identities in the artwork are produced through social meetings. The performativity of dialogic art, however, is not the performativity of theater because the dialogical artist is no different from the other participants in the project. Kester claims that conventional art is usually produced in isolation from the audience and is based on the artist's nonresearched beliefs about the audience (Kester 2004, 92). When such works reach their audience, the audience is not offered the possibility to give feedback that can lead to modification of the work. That is why Kester claims that there is a need for aesthetic exchanges in which the artist's beliefs are challenged through collaboration with the audience; this allows dialogic meetings to occur during production. Artist(s), audience, and context are thus the three poles that produce the artwork through dialogue.

Figure 3.1 suggests that artwork is created on four equal poles that function dialogically. According to this model, context and musical material contribute to the creation of artwork as well. Notably, the artwork is placed in the middle of the model, perhaps to point out its centrality as an artifact. A significant feature of dialogic and relational art practices is that newness is no longer required; in fact, the artistic/musical material can be chosen or composed by the actors because what is interesting is what happens to it through collaboration and participation (Bourriaud 2002). According to Bourriaud (2002), who described different participatory art forms as "relational aesthetics," the real artwork lies in the interaction that occurs, not in the material as such. The fourth pole, context, significantly contributes to the work, especially for school concert visits, due to the complexity of the school's societal and institutional habits and the cultural and educational diversity of those at the school.

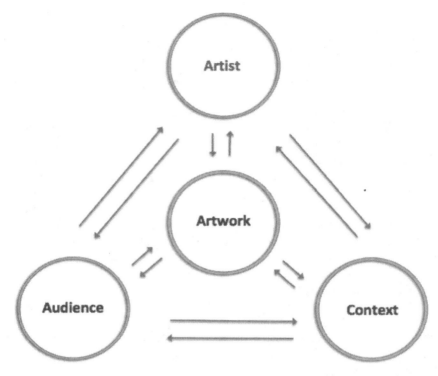

Figure 3.1 A socially interactive model of art practice by Steven Willats (approx. 1970)
(Kester 2004, 92; Willats 2017)[6]

The power structure of a dialogic artwork is intended to be equal, but Kester (2004) problematizes discrepancies in the language and social background of different participants as obstacles to an equal collaboration. Within schools, the age and knowledge bases of different collaborators will differ greatly; for instance, the collaboration may involve six-year-olds, experienced teachers, and awarded artists. Kester's critics claim that equality between participants in an artistic process cannot exist when the participants are socially and intellectually diverse and that concealing this fact would be an ethical pitfall (Bishop 2012). However, according to Kester, musicians', teachers', and pupils' contributions should be perceived as equal and an artwork should emerge from consensus. At a school, there must be equity and respect between the teacher and pupil, though the teacher still has a duty to lead an education process that enhances pupils' understanding of the world (Biesta 2013), which conflicts with the goal of equal contribution. Likewise, it could be counterproductive for a musician to not utilize her practical musical and production skills throughout the process. Thus, one can think of the three participating groups as representatives of different features in a dialogic constellation. For instance, pupils' contributions will be derived from their unique perspectives as children and pupils in a specific context and time and may, for example, include contemporary digital and/or pop culture topics (Juncker 2013).

Kester's desire for consensus must be addressed. Tensions between teachers and musicians are usually perceived as a threat to visiting musicians' practice, but one could also identify possibilities arising from these tensions (Borgdorff 2012). Achieving consensus among teachers, musicians, and pupils can be productive but might jeopardize both the pedagogical and artistic possibilities of musical visits because "unease, discomfort or frustration, along with fear, contradiction, exhilaration and absurdity—can be crucial to any work's artistic impact" (Bishop 2012, 26). In pedagogy, "aporia," a state of constant doubt and bafflement, is desired because one of the major functions of contemporary education is to teach pupils to understand the world as multifaceted and complex (Mayo 2004). According to contemporary pedagogy scholars, pupils should be trained to cope with problems that aren't necessarily solvable and relationships that aren't necessarily positive (Bingham and Sidorkin 2004). In an environment acknowledging complexity and contradiction, such as shared leadership between teachers and musicians, contributing to dialogical musical processes may help pupils achieve those goals. Highlighting consensus in relational practices might hide the importance of leadership, which, according to Bishop (2012) and Rancière (2009), is contestable, because, as Rancière (2009) claims, many participatory art forms are suited to manipulate groups of participants; the artist lets people believe they can decide for themselves during an experience, whereas, in fact, they silently are led to certain political, aesthetic, or educational decisions. Within dramaturgy, one can find specific techniques to manipulate audiences, such as seduction or provocation (Thygesen 2009). Ranciére (2009) argues against manipulations unless they are made explicit to participants. There might be tempting pedagogical or artistic reasons for manipulating audiences, but Rancière (2009) claims manipulative techniques challenge the very nature of aesthetic practices. Along with Dewey (1934), Rancière has an underlying respect for the participant's, or "viewer's," intelligence and right to interpret and handle an artistic situation. Thus, he purports, it would be fairer to tell pupils what one is aiming for and then leave it to them to find ways to create a meaningful relation to the work or activity in question (Ruitenberg 2011). Actors facilitating participatory musical events should constantly scrutinize and reflect upon their agendas throughout the processes and the creation of products.

Traditionally, aesthetic forms fall into two categories. A heteronomy-aesthetic approach treats art as intrinsically interwoven into the everyday lives and learning of human beings (Dewey 1934), whereas its counterpoint, autonomy-aesthetic art, views art as separate from culture, context, and participation. However, Rasmussen (2015) warns about the dangers of creating a dichotomy between "either mere art or mere life" (127). Heteronomy in art, though, can be seen as fundamentally different from the autonomy-aesthetic approach. Whereas autonomy-aesthetic approaches state that artworks have intrinsic meaning and can yield experiences that are free from contextual influences (Hanslick 1854), heteronomy-aesthetic art is planned to interweave into, participate in, and influence its societal and cultural context.

The school concert visit is heteronomic because schools are pedagogical institutions and thus everything that happens there is directed toward pupils' learning and *Bildung* (Bresler 2002). According to Bresler, all events at school will inevitably be colored by this context. Rasmussen (2015) clearly values heteronomy, arguing that "[c]ontextual considerations, such as site, audience, participants, and materials are part of aesthetic considerations of producing powerful aesthetic experiences" (124). How concerts in schools can be better integrated or contextualized is a core question, and acceptance of a visiting musical event's heteronomic stance, and hence their connection to the field of education, can be part of the answer.

To music educators, heteronomy fits well with the theory of "musicking" discussed by Small (2011), a term that he defines as "to music." This is a broad definition comprising every human action related to music, not only performing or listening. For instance, writing a chapter on musical collaboration is "musicking" according to this definition.

Ownership and Engagement

In the previous section, I suggested participatory and dialogic ways to conduct visiting musical events in schools as a means to achieve deep contextualization and school anchoring. For such processes to reach their full potential, one must strive for a more even power balance among all participants. This power balance, however, cannot be achieved unless there are equal opportunities for ownership and engagement within the musical enterprise in question.

To achieve psychological ownership, an object must feel like "mine" or "ours" (Pierce et al. 2003). According to Pierce, Kostova, and Dirks, ownership is constructed in the following way: We gain control over the object, learn to know it, and invest in it. In order to learn to know the object, we must have some feelings for it and be allowed to change it; ownership enables us to adjust the object for our needs. When people feel ownership of a social unit or object, they will develop a kind of citizen behavior that contributes to the development of the social unit. Another sign of ownership behavior is willingness to sacrifice something personal and take risks to support the ownership. Owners develop a defense instinct, care for their object or field, and take responsibility for it. Within dialogic music practices, this is demonstrated by discussing and relying on the teacher's wishes regarding content and/or the pupil's wishes regarding bodily participation.

Examples of how power is balanced in teacher–musician collaborations can be found in the rationale for "teaching artists," a widespread phenomenon throughout North America. In his book *The Music Teaching Artist's Bible*, Booth (2009) claims "The first and most important thing that school professionals want from musicians is *respect*" (130). Further, he urges all musicians to spend time in schools in order to better understand teachers' and pupils' everyday lives, thus adding to Foster's (1995) view of the artist as ethnographer. According to Booth (2009), musicians must appreciate where the power in the school lies (with teachers and administrators) and connect to the curriculum. For me, ownership seems to be more evenly distributed within the presented "teaching artist" rationale than through the intervention practice described in my research (Holdhus 2014).

Aside from mutual ownership, what are the prerequisites of fruitful teacher–musician collaboration? First, there must be interdisciplinary knowledge; musicians need knowledge of teachers and schools, and vice versa. The literature on artist–teacher relations states that such collaborations are complex: on the one hand, rewarding, and on the other, full of conflict and dilemmas. In a report from the Teaching Artists Research Project (Rabkin et al. 2011), the artist–teacher relationship is called a "partnership dance" (110). The report recognizes that these relationships involve a learning spiral consisting of several steps. The first is "TAs and teachers asking each other questions about their intentions and aspirations for the work they will do together" (Rabkin et al. 2011, 111). The next step is to construct the classroom as a safe community of learners that respects every voice and agrees on rules and working habits (Rabkin et al. 2011). The third step is what Rabkin et al. (2011) calls "careful attention to the language of arts" (111), meaning that artists teach artistic techniques, forms, and ways of working in order to enhance and enrich creative processes. To me, this means attending to the artistic side of the enterprise, or the pole "work" seen in Kester and Willats' model earlier (Kester 2004, 92). These three steps are constantly reflected on and discussed by pupils, teachers, and artists and the spiral ends where it began—by revisiting the initial goals for the project in question.

Through repeated interdisciplinary meetings, the participants' prior values and behaviors might transform into joint values. According to Wenger (1998), the emergence of joint values and ownership is what creates a learning fellowship. The differences between the teacher and musician may not be huge, but because they are from two different disciplines, they will need to conduct encounters as described by Buber (1970): with a great amount of openness towards the other and a reciprocal agreement to take the other's perspective (Rommetveit 1974).

Closing Comments

This chapter's main argument is that visiting musicians and teachers should strive to build creative and interdisciplinary communities for visiting musical events for and with pupils in order to contribute to the deep contextualization of visiting musicians in schools. Evenly distributed ownership and ethical participant dialogues should ground this interdisciplinarity.

Applying dialogic musical practices in schools will produce different results than the more common sender–receiver-based concerts. However, as pointed out in this chapter's discussion of heteronomy, contextualization does not necessarily lead to nonaesthetic products. It is my belief that neither teachers nor musicians will need to change so much that their original discursive identity is threatened. However, there is a possibility that respective identities might be redefined through collaborative practice (Brown 2017, 73–9).

In the end, I think there is, and perhaps always should be, a tension between the arts and school because they are different societal institutions (Berger and Luckmann 1967). School represents enculturalization and learning, whereas some aspects of the arts aim for the opposite. The arts can be subversive and produce an "otherness" (Lehmann 2013), or an alternative to the methods of schooling that are taken for granted.

Schools' welcoming of visiting musicians can be seen as a hallmark of deep democracy in education; the schools must be ready to invite critical and multifaceted voices to contribute to its institutional, pedagogical, and democratic functions. I believe that professional and ethical contextualization of visiting artists can help schools achieve this state.

Notes

1 The title is translated from Norwegian.
2 Concerts Norway will be phased out by 2018 and replaced with a new organization, Art for Young People in Norway (AYAN). More information can be found at the following site: www.kulturtanken.no/a-new-mandate/?rq=English.
3 Bourriaud's arguments are that art lies in human interaction and its social context and that art is a situation in which the audience creates a community.
4 Fischer-Lichte's main contribution to the literature is the autopoetical feedback loop theory, which is a theory of presence. In a performative event, the audience and artist shape the event together according to the situation, which will never be the same twice. Audience agency and bodily actions shape the situation.
5 *Bildung* is German for education or formation and refers to the German tradition of self-cultivation (as related to the German for creation, image, shape), wherein philosophy and education are linked in a manner that refers to a process of both personal and cultural maturation (Wikipedia: Bildung).
6 A version of the figure is printed in Kester's book and labeled "Courtesy of the artist." It doesn't seem to be printed elsewhere. I refer, though, to Willats' home page for further contextualization.

References

Aulin-Gråhamn, Lena, Magnus Persson, and Jan Thavenius. 2004. *Skolan och den radikala estetiken*. Malmö: Studentlitteratur.
Bamford, Anne. 2012. *Arts and Cultural Education in Norway*. Bodø: Nasjonalt senter for kunst og kultur i opplæringen.
Berger, Peter L., and Thomas Luckmann. 1967. *The Social Construction of Reality: A Treatise in the Sociology of Knowledge*. New York: Doubleday.
Biesta, Gert. 2013. *The Beautiful Risk of Education*. Boulder, CO: Paradigm.

Bingham, Charles, and Alexander M. Sidorkin, eds. 2004. *No Education Without Relation.* New York: Peter Lang.
Bishop, Claire. 2012. *Artificial Hells: Participatory Art and the Politics of Spectatorship.* London: Verso Books.
Bjørkvold, Jon Roar. 1992. *The Muse Within: Creativity and Communication, Song and Play Through Childhood to Maturity.* New York: Harper Collins.
Bjørnsen, Egil. 2011. *Norwegian Cultural Policy: A Civilising Mission?* Kristiansand: Agderforskning.
Booth, Eric. 2009. *The Music Teaching Artist's Bible: Becoming a Virtuoso Educator.* Oxford: Oxford University Press.
Borgdorff, Henk. 2012. *The Conflict of the Faculties: Perspectives on Artistic Research and Academia.* Leiden: Leiden University Press.
Borgen, Jorunn Spord, and Synnøve S. Brandt. 2006. *Ekstraordinært Eller Selvfølgelig? Evaluering Av Den Kulturelle Skolesekken i Grunnskolen.* Oslo: NIFU STEP.
Bourdieu, Pierre, and Loïc J. D. Wacquant. 1992. *An Invitation to Reflexive Sociology.* Cambridge: Polity Press.
Bourriaud, Nicolas. 2002. *Relational Aesthetics.* Dijon, France: Presses du réel.
Bowman, Wayne. 2007. "Who Is the 'We'? Rethinking Professionalism in Music Education." *Action, Criticism, and Theory for Music Education,* 6 (4), 109-31.
Breivik, Jan Kåre, and Catharina Christophersen. 2013. *Den Kulturelle Skolesekken.* Oslo: Kulturrådet.
Bresler, Liora. 2002. "School Art as a Hybrid Genre: Institutional Contexts for Art Curriculum." In *The Arts in Children's Lives,* edited by Liora Bresler and Christine Marmé Thompson, 169-83. Dordrecht, The Netherlands: Kluwer Academic Publishers.
Brown, Neil C. M. 2017. *Studies in Philosophical Realism in Art, Design and Education.* Switzerland: Springer.
Buber, Martin. 1970. *I and Thou.* New York: Charles Scribner's Sons.
Christophersen, Catharina. 2013. "Helper, Guard or Mediator? Teachers' Space for Action in *The Cultural Rucksack,* a Norwegian National Program for Arts and Culture in Schools." *International Journal of Education & the Arts,* 14 (SI 1.11). Accessed January 25, 2017, www.ijea.org/v14si1/.
Concerts Norway. 2017. "Web Page, English." Accessed January 25, 2017, www.rikskonsertene.no/english/children/.
Creative Partnerships. 2012. Accessed January 25, 2017, http://creative-partnerships.com.
DeNora, Tia. 2000. *Music in Everyday Life.* Cambridge: Cambridge University Press.
Denzin, Norman K. 2003. *Performance Ethnography: Critical Pedagogy and the Politics of Culture.* Thousand Oaks, CA: Sage.
Dewey, John. 1934. *Art as Experience.* New York: Penguin.
Digranes, Ingvild. 2009. *Den Kulturelle Skulesekken: Narratives and Myths of Educational Practice in DKS Projects Within the Subject Art and Crafts.* Oslo: The Oslo School of Architecture and Design.
Espeland, Magne, Thomas Arnesen, Ingrid Grønsdal, Asle Holthe, Kjetil Sømoe, Hege Wergedahl, and Helga Aadland. 2013. "Skolefagsundersøkelsen 2011: Praktiske og estetiske fag påbarnesteget i norsk grunnskule." HSH rapport No. 7, Høgskolen Stord/Haugesund, Stord.
European Union. 2017. "Creative Europe Programmes." Accessed January 25, 2017, https://ec.europa.eu/programmes/creative-europe/.
Fischer-Lichte, Erika. 2008. *The Transformative Power of Performance: A New Aesthetics.* London: Routledge.
Foster, Hal. 1995. "The Artist as Ethnographer?" In *The Traffic in Culture: Refiguring Art and Anthropology,* edited by George E. Marcus and Fred R. Myers, 302-9. Berkeley, CA: University of California Press.
Goehr, Lydia. 2007. *The Imaginary Museum of Musical Works: An Essay in the Philosophy of Music.* New York: Oxford University Press.
Grumet, Madeleine R., Deborah Randolph, and Faye Stanley. 2015. "Arts Integration." In *The Routledge International Handbook of the Arts and Education,* edited by Mike Fleming, Liora Bresler, and John O'Toole, 268-79. Abingdon: Routledge.
Hanslick, Edward. 1854. *Vom Musikalisch-Schönen: Ein Beitrag Zur Revision Der Ästhetik Der Tonkunst.* Darmstadt: Wissenschaftliche Buchgesellschaft.
Heggedal, Katrine. 2013. "Strukturer Til Fremme Av Kvalitet? En Polemisk Kronikk Om Kunstnerisk Kvalitet Og Organisering Av Den Kulturelle Skolesekken." *Periskop.* Accessed January 25, 2017, www.periskop.no/strukturer-til-fremme-av-kvalitet/

Holdhus, Kari. 2014. *Stjerneopplevelser Eller Gymsalsestetikk? En Studie Av Kvalitetsoppfatninger i Skolekonsertpraksiser (Star Experiences or Gym Hall Aesthetics?—a Study of Quality Conceptions in Visiting Concert Programs at School)*. København: Aarhus Universitet.
Holdhus, Kari. 2015. "Skolekonserter-Relasjonelle Kunstdidaktiske Praksiser?" *Studia Musicologica Norvegica*, 39 (1), 87–105.
Holdhus, Kari, and Magne Espeland. 2013. "The Visiting Artist in Schools: Arts Based or School Based Practices?" *International Journal of Education & the Arts*, 14 (SI 1.10).
Jeunesses Musicales International. 2017. "Young Audiences Music." Accessed January 25, 2017, http://jmi.net/programs/yam.
Juncker, Beth. 2013. *Børn Og Kultur i Norden: Nordiske Forskningsperspektiver i Dialog*. København: Bin-Norden.
Kant, Immanuel 1987. *Critique of Judgment*. Indianapolis: Hackett Publishing.
Kester, Grant H. 2004. *Conversation Pieces: Community and Communication in Modern Art*. Berkeley, CA: University of California Press.
Kris, Ernst, and Otto Kurz. 1981. *Legend, Myth, and Magic in the Image of the Artist: A Historical Experiment*. New Haven, CT: Yale University Press.
Lacy, Suzanne. 1995. *Mapping the Terrain: New Genre Public Art*. Seattle: Bay Press.
Lehmann, Niels. 2013. "En Mangfoldighed Af Andethedserfaringer: Om Æstetik på Flere Måder." *Tidsskrift for Boerne-Og Ungdomskultur*, 57, 25–36.
Mayo, Chris. 2004. "Relations are Difficult." In *No Education Without Relation*, edited by Charles Bingham and Alexander M. Sidorkin, 121–36. New York: Peter Lang.
O'Neill, Paul, and Mick Wilson. 2010. *Curating and the Educational Turn*. Amsterdam: de Appel Arts Centre.
Ørstavik, Maren. 2016. "Nye Kulturtanken Kan Gi Mindre Jobb for Musikere." *Ballade*. Accessed January 25, 2017, www.ballade.no/sak/nye-kulturtanken-kan-gi-mindre-jobb-for-musikere/
Pierce, Jon L., Tatiana Kostova, and Kurt T. Dirks. 2003. "The State of Psychological Ownership: Integrating and Extending a Century of Research." *Review of General Psychology*, 7 (1), 84–107.
Rabkin, Nick, Michael Reynolds, Eric Christopher Hedberg, and Justin Selby. 2011. *Teaching Artists and the Future of Education: A Report on the Teaching Artist Research Project: Executive Summary*. Chicago: NORC at the University of Chicago.
Rancière, Jean-Jacques. 2009. *The Emancipated Spectator*. New York: Verso.
Rasmussen, Bjørn. 2015. "The Absent Recognition of Heteronomous Arts Education." In *The Routledge International Handbook of the Arts and Education*, edited by Mike Fleming, Liora Bresler, and John O'Toole, 106–28. Abingdon: Routledge.
Rommetveit, Ragnar. 1974. *On Message Structure*. Hoboken, NJ: Wiley.
Ruitenberg, Claudia W. 2011. "Art, Politics, and the Pedagogical Relation." *Studies in Philosophy and Education* 30(2): 211–223.
Small, Christopher. 2011. *Musicking: The Meanings of Performing and Listening*. Middletown: Wesleyan University Press.
Thygesen, Mads. 2009. "Interaktion Og Iscenesættelse." *Peripeti: Tidsskrift for Dramaturgiske Studier*, 11(1), 5–17.
UNESCO. 2006. *Road Map for Arts Education*. Paris: UNESCO.
Valberg, Tony. 2011. *En Relasjonell Musikkestetikk: Barn på Orkesterselskapenes Konserter*, Vol. nr 97. Göteborg: Musikhögskolan, Göteborgs Universitet.
Wenger, Etienne. 1998. *Communities of Practice: Learning, Meaning, and Identity*. Cambridge: Cambridge University Press.
Willats, Stephen. 2017. "Homepage." Accessed January 25, 2017, http://stephenwillats.com/context/

4

Musicians as Musician–Teacher Collaborators: Towards Punk Pedagogical Perspectives

GARETH DYLAN SMITH

Introduction

In the film *School of Rock*, the disgruntled, energetic music teacher character, Mr. S., jokes over lunch with other staff, saying that, having failed an audition to play for the Polish Philharmonic, "I just decided to give up on myself and become a teacher, because those that can't *do*, teach . . . am I right?" (Rudin and Linklater 2003). His comment is met with awkward laughter from the other staff, who recognize that teachers are sometimes seen as failed professionals in other domains. Mr. S. is an impoverished guitarist, teaching under false pretenses primarily to make rent money, having been kicked out of his rock band. He finds during the film that teaching is actually in many ways more rewarding than only pursuing his fading dream of rock stardom, and in the final scenes he sets up his own music school. *Mr. Holland's Opus* (Field et al. 1995) is a more deliberate parable, in which the protagonist is a composer who discovers how a fulfilling, complex life as a high school teacher and father leads to neglect of his work as a composer. At the end of the thirty-year arc of that film's narrative, the piece of music that Mr. Holland has been trying to write since the start of the film is performed by current and former students. His "opus," then, is both the musical composition and, moreover, his impactful life's work as a school music teacher.

Musicians or Teachers

The view of teachers as unsuccessful musicians, although widespread, is not ubiquitous nor upheld by evidence. It simultaneously celebrates the notion of the professional or career musician (Hallam and Gaunt 2012; Rowley et al. 2015; Smith 2013) while downplaying the work of musicians as teachers. This discourse is reinforced in popular public consciousness by legislation and attitudes from governments seen across education sectors internationally, where teachers are increasingly distrusted, held accountable to and, moreover, punishable by measures of evaluation that include performance-related pay, teaching

39

to learning outcomes and for test results, and the resultant widespread, general disincentivizing of actual *teaching* (Allsup 2015). Professional musicians, on the other hand, are celebrated for their contribution to cultural life. Teaching is often perceived as "just something that musicians do" rather than as a career or job in itself (Froehlich and Smith 2017). However, musicians collaborate with teachers, communities, and institutions *as* teachers far more than *with* teachers; the Musicians' Union in the UK finds that a high proportion of musicians in the country work in education; the union characterizes them as "musicians who teach" (Musicians' Union 2016) rather than solely as "teachers."

A few words concerning this author's positionality may help to situate this chapter in the context of the book. I think of myself as a musician and a teacher, as my professional and personal lives are both characterized by a great deal of activity in music-making and teaching. In my current position as a lecturer in an institution of higher music education, my identity and authority in the role, and thus my ability to impact the musicking successes of my students, derive from the necessity to maintain legitimacy and authenticity as a musician and a teacher. There is also increasing national governmental pressure bearing down on the higher education sector in the UK where I work, to ensure that lecturers are "professional," credentialed educators, as well as being highly competent in their areas of expertise.

It is problematic to perpetuate the false binary of teaching expertise and/or musicianship. More needs to be done, for instance, to help undergraduate music students see that earning their degree is not the end of their professionalization process. In England, where degrees (in music and most other subjects) can be supplemented by a year of teacher training in order for candidates to achieve "Qualified Teacher Status," the duality of "musician" and "music teacher" is perhaps less rigid than in a system such as in the United States where undergraduates choose to earn degrees *either* in music education (as teachers) *or* in music (as musicians). As Kenny points out, there are often particular challenges in "teacher education programs where tensions exist between developing students' own creativity and the institutional demands of fostering creative pedagogical approaches for classroom teaching" (2014, 293). Nonetheless, it is abundantly clear to many who have exited from education systems and who continue to seek fulfillment in their adult lives that musicking and teaching are not mutually exclusive. Allowing students to envision and contentedly realize multiple identities in a lifetime—simultaneously and in succession—is a responsibility that weighs heavily on institutions of higher music learning (Laycock 2008), where musician–teacher faculty are responsible for preparing student musicians for increasingly diverse careers that are very likely to include working as teachers and with teachers in diverse educational and community settings (Bennett 2008, 2013; Creech and Papageorgi 2014). It is difficult to reconcile this, though, with ever-stronger emphases on vocationalism (Parkinson 2017a; Parkinson and Smith 2015).

This chapter explores the notion of musician–teacher collaborations from the perspective of musicians who *are* teachers (or teachers who *are* musicians). "Teacher" and "musician" roles are viewed as frequently necessarily interwoven and inseparable—viewing musicians as collaboratively fulfilling roles as teachers, rather than working as "musicians" in collaboration with others identifying as "teachers" (Bennett and Stanberg 2008). People who identify as musicians frequently teach, and recognizing one's role as either teacher or musician does not negate one's role as the other or as occupying any numerous other positions. After exploring various pieces of the puzzle that parses people into particular and polarized positions, the chapter briefly explores the potentiality of punk pedagogical approaches and concludes by summarizing benefits of viewing the term "musician" as less exclusive, more flexible, and multifaceted. I have noted elsewhere that "Neoliberalism, and the institutions, attitudes, and systems that it effects and affects are . . . instruments of a symbolic violence that penetrates and has an impact upon all aspects of our experience in the world" (Smith 2015, 65), including in music education. This chapter advocates moving away from, and proposing a punk resistance to, the individualist, hypersubjectivist values pervasive in many contemporary societies and their institutions of music-making and learning. Casting career musicians as (only) musicians and (therefore) not also teachers breeds tension and competition, whereas a collaborative level playing field acknowledges multifacetedness and nurtures democratic, mutually beneficial cooperation.

Musicians and Teachers

Regardless of how musicians are perceived, or how they may perceive themselves, musicians' labor frequently includes more than the obviously or "purely" musical, as they may teach in schools, colleges, universities, and a diverse range of community settings (Helfter and Ilari 2015; Higgins 2012). Evidence from musicians consistently disputes the consensus perpetuated throughout society; the UK Musicians' Union (2012, 3) finds that "musicians are experienced, qualified and multi-skilled." Musicians' diverse work has been described in terms of numerous musical creativities (Burnard 2012, 2013; Smith and Gillett 2015; Teague and Smith 2015) that include entrepreneurial activity, collaborative and solo writing, performing and production, and the envisioning and management of "boundaryless" careers. Arthur et al. (2005, 178) note that "people who exhibit boundaryless career behavior report considerably higher levels of career success"; however this is construed by the individuals in question. Menger (1999) and Hewison (2014) highlight the centrality of entrepreneur-like behavior in the lives and careers of self-employed musicians, traits identified as typical of musicians' income streams over hundreds of years (Weber 2004). Cartwright also points to the centrality of this modus operandi, coining the term "orchestration" to describe the careful balancing of multiple threads within networks of contacts comprising the web that supports musicians' multifaceted lives (Cartwright and Smith 2013; Cartwright et al. 2015).

Froehlich and Smith (2017) discuss the conflicting and complementary identities that manifest as musicians train to become school music teachers and as teachers progress through careers as musicians and teachers. A musician's increasing voluntary and compulsory commitments over a lifetime to various organizations and individuals raise issues of professionalism and professionalization in relation to remuneration for one's work and obligations to ensembles, schools, family, and career (Gaunt and Papageorgi 2010; Hallam and Gaunt 2012), meaning that defining success as a musician can be complicated due to the plethora of people—including the individual musician—judging "success" according to different criteria (Kirschner 1998; Smith 2013). It is incumbent on those teaching in higher education to ensure that students and graduates embrace careers and personal agency that include the possibility of being a teacher—as part of being a musician (Burnard and Haddon 2015).

Musicians manage and maintain the importance of making music and make time for making music in increasingly busy and complex adult lives, even when their day-to-day work and family patterns may seem to make music-making next to impossible. This dedication can be explained in terms of identity realization and a eudaimonic commitment to pursuit of one's self-evident purpose in life (Smith 2016) and has been characterized by Stebbins as "serious leisure" or "devotee work" (2014, 4). There is increased momentum to emphasize the value of viewing music-making as valuable in the lives of people as a leisure activity, unfettered and untroubled by monetary or employment concerns—what Mantie and Smith (2016, 3) refer to as "avocational involvement with music as an integral part of the human condition." Such a viewpoint—conceptualizing everyone as musicians and disrupting the us-and-them hierarchy—contains democratizing potential (Keil 1987; Mantie 2016), but also risks threatening the societal and economic value of musicians. This work also forms part of a growing body of literature exploring the vast range of activities, roles, and identities occupied and enacted by contemporary musicians (see for example Cottrell 2004; Cremata et al. 2016).

The idea that musicians are a special, mythical class of people has been deliberately and profitably perpetuated by such institutions as the record industry and its supporting mainstream media, along with publishing companies. The Romantic notion of the lone genius composer (Beethoven, Wagner, Liszt), performer (Paganini, Buddy Rich, Steve Vai), collective genius (the Beatles, Queen, or N.W.A.), or artistic phenomenon (David Bowie, Björk, Frank Zappa) tends to create in the minds and "collective consciousness" a sense of *musicians* and *not-musicians*. Most people, including most teachers, fall squarely into the latter group, creating a power relationship in collaborative settings, whereby teachers' pedagogical knowledge can be undervalued in the presence of mystical musical mastery. This hierarchy and bifurcation are preserved by musicians and the institutions that serve and create them (conservatoires, universities, talent shows) in order to preserve the special status accorded (by) musicians and in order to sell to nonmusicians the special things that musicians do and make (recordings, concerts, etc.). However, as the music industry that grew up in the twentieth century—marketing physical products and selling an allegedly elite group of especially popular musicians to passively consuming masses (Adorno and Bernstein 2001; Scruton 2000)—has dissolved (Cartwright et al. 2015), music-making and distribution appear to occur in more (albeit not wholly) democratic ways (Bell 2015). Institutions of higher music learning are advocating and developing musicians for a more socially orientated musicianship, more deeply rooted in collective musicking and community-focused ideals, than has traditionally been the case. Simultaneously, agendas and program aims at these institutions align with government ideals and policy foci that are often highly instrumental and employment or industry focused (Parkinson 2017a). This leads to increasingly complex, competing authenticities for musicians, institutions of higher music learning, and the public and communities with whom and within which they work (Parkinson and Smith 2015): Just who are the "musicians" and who are the "teachers"?

Musicians as Teachers: A Punk Pedagogical Perspective

Higher music education faces an existential crisis, and those of us working in it have much with which to grapple (Hebert et al. 2017). Challenges for the sector include the fact that universities in the current climate are viewed (and increasingly funded and rewarded) primarily as vocational training centers in a competitive international market economy (Parkinson 2017a), although others view the UK higher education sector as insufficiently marketized and focusing too little on preparing graduates for employment (Harniess 2017). In a discussion around empowering students in higher education spaces by acknowledging and enabling individual and collective agency through making music, Niknafs and Przybylski (2017) refer to Tuan's (1977) conceptualization of turning places into liminal spaces with potential to foment transformative change. Parkinson and Smith (2015, 118) contend that the higher music education community "has an opportunity and a responsibility in this moment to move iteratively and mindfully towards an epistemology of authenticity in its institutionalized beliefs and practices." Such an orientation would create and require space for discussion around, for instance, what it means to be authentically musical, authentically educated, or to have an authentic career. This type of approach is increasingly being identified in scholarship as "punk pedagogy" (Smith et al. 2017).

Conceptions of teachers and musicians fit into a wider view of the music-educational-industrial "ecosystem" that comprises, sustains, and surrounds us all (Bennett 2015, 30). This ecosystem includes schools, colleges, universities, community music groups, and what has ubiquitously, yet ambiguously, been referred to as the "music industry"—a constellation of connections and collaborators so broad and multifarious (Jones 2017) that Williamson et al. (2011) suggest it might more helpfully be construed as the music *industries*—which has changed to be almost unrecognizable in recent years (International Federation of the Phonographic Industry 2017). Established music industry structures have collapsed in the past decade, and the industries continue to reshape and restructure (Cartwright et al. 2013; Parkinson et al. 2015) with no new stasis clearly forthcoming. Musicians are increasingly cast as collaborative entrepreneurs (Bennett 2013; Hewison 2014; Smith 2015), creating and negotiating interdisciplinary networks for mutual benefit and value exchange—approaches characterized by a do-it-yourself (DIY) punk ethos (Harniess 2017; O'Dair and Beavan 2017; Smith and Gillett 2015).

Discussing punk pedagogies in practice, Dines notes, "the porous nature of punk means that it can draw upon the multifarious to create identity and meaning. It can draw upon a plethora of ideas and beliefs to supplement its core" (2015, 22). Punks often thus ally themselves with anarchist ideals of disrupting and replacing hierarchies of power, seeking to replace these with systems that emphasize nurturing individual freedom and responsibility to a mutually defined collective. As Torrez states, punk pedagogy embodies an attitude whereby "individuals take on personal responsibility (anarchist *agency* in the face of capitalist *structuralism*) by rejecting their privileged places in society and working in solidarity with those forced on the fringes. By doing so, we strike to undo hegemonic macrostructures" (2012, 135). As Erico Malatesta has noted, anarchism means "freedom for everybody . . . with the only limit of equal freedom for others" (1993, 53). In Stirner's words, "only freedom is equality" (2005, 20). These ideals are similar to those of community music settings where musician–teacher facilitators embrace "unconditional hospitality" for all participants (Higgins 2012, 143), echoing the imperative in arts partnership programs with schools that those involved acknowledge and embrace one another's expertise and abilities (Woolf 2004).

Niknafs and Przybylski (2017, 421) explain the need for "de-institutionalizing space" in places of higher learning, in keeping with anarchist pedagogues, Kaltefleiter and Nocella (2012, 203), who exhort collaborative efforts between staff and students in educational institutions to create "a resistance culture wherein individuals question the ways in which members of society come to internalize and to believe the ideologies" upon which our knowledge and understanding are founded. In institutions of higher music education, the embrace by entrepreneurial music educators of anarchist and punk pedagogical approaches could help to challenge unconsciously perpetuated normative understandings of what it means to be a musician, a teacher, and a member of society. These approaches also could inform perspectives on teacher training and music teacher education. A punk pedagogical approach rests on dedication to and embrace of an ethos. Because learning any role or combination of roles is an iterative, developmental process, it is reassuring to consider that "changing society anarchically through learning . . . is a process of 'becoming anarchist' that necessarily eludes any final resolution" (Antliff 2012, 328); punk embraces the pedagogies of perpetual DIY music-teacher-entrepreneurs.

Punk, and more particularly punk pedagogies, may offer constructive (if perhaps simultaneously *de*structive) ways through and out of the mire of lies, self-indulgence, and self-centeredness that threaten to overwhelm and undermine democratic societies, helping to halt humanity's hastening descent into violent and totalizing national and international systems of governance (Giroux 2017). Musician–teachers adopting a punk pedagogical ethos have the opportunity to instill in students, in and through music classroom experiences, the key twenty-first-century attribute of resilience in these difficult times (Kallio 2017). Having the courage of one's convictions as a punk pedagogue and facing up to the destabilizing and inhumane conditions in which people increasingly live and work, by challenging them through engaging students in critical discussion, we can empower and enable those in teachers' care to lead meaningful and agentive lives (Teles and Guerra 2017).

Conclusions

To return to a key point underpinning the argument in this chapter: It is highly valuable to understand the ways in which musicians collaborate *as* teachers (notwithstanding the tremendous value also in apprehending how musicians collaborate *with* teachers). There is, for instance, dissonance between music colleges' presentation of "success" as a musician and the examples they see every day in their lecturers, tutors, and PhD advisors—individuals who, in addition to performing and composing, work as teachers in higher education and in diverse community and studio settings, exemplifying the variegated nature of musicians' work. Being "a musician" does not rule out being a teacher; often working as the latter is a vital, integral part of being the former (Abeles et al. 2010; Burnard 2012; Higgins 2012; Pitts 2012; Rainbow 1996; Vasconcelos 2015). It is arguably incumbent on all musicians (and those who train, teach, coach, and mentor them) to acknowledge musicians' work as teachers, including how they influence younger or less experienced musicians through performances, recordings, magazine columns, blogs, social media, and interviews. Learners ascribe pedagogic authority to people like whom they aspire to be—John Bonham, Franz Liszt, Taylor Swift, Kendrick Lamar, Bob Dylan, Carole King, Beyoncé. All musicians, therefore, are in effect *already* engaged in the education and enculturation of others; Bourdieu and Passeron termed this ascription of educational value to others "pedagogic authority" (1977, 19). By embracing an ethos that draws on punk sensibilities, it is possible for musicians to own and to speak from this platform of pedagogic authority without defaulting to the hierarchical career and occupational stratification to which we have become used (Higgins 2012, 50–1), but which instinctively we know is inaccurate. By embracing "anarchist *agency*" (Torrez 2012, 135), we strike to undo "hegemonic macrostructures" that, for instance, lead to the celebration of musicians and the denigration of the work and role of the teachers. Illich (1970, 19) writes of a need for "separating learning from social control"; understanding pedagogic authority from a punk pedagogical perspective offers a means to this end.

There is work to do in higher music education and music education more broadly in managing the expectations of students, not in ways that threaten to undermine their aspirations or destabilize the value they perceive in being musical or in pursuing excellence in musical performance, writing or production, etc., but rather in supporting students to adopt broad definitions of what it means to be a musician and empowering them with the agency to become whom they can (Kallio 2017). If we consider an interrelated ecosystem of symbiotic, codependent, interrelated, and nonhierarchical skills and attributes that can all be developed in nonexclusive ways across lifetimes, this may help to disrupt the binary, allowing musicians to be understood as and valued for occupying the range of occupational niches that they do, including multivariate teaching roles in community, studio, higher education, and school settings. As Parkinson (2017b) advises, punk pedagogy is potentially enabling for educators (and students) as a "mythological tool, encapsulating and ennobling their ethical frameworks and validating their responses to the pressures of academic life in a troublesome higher education climate."

References

Abeles, Hal, Colleen Conway, and Lori A. Custodero. 2010. "Framing a Professional Life: Music Teacher Development Through Collaboration and Leadership." In *Critical Issues in Music Education: Contemporary Theory and Practice*, edited by Harold F. Abeles and Lori A. Custodero, 303–20. New York: Oxford University Press.

Adorno, Theodor W., and Jay M. Bernstein. 2001. *The Culture Industry: Selected Essays on Mass Culture*. Hove: Psychology Press.

Allsup, Randall E. 2015. "The Eclipse of a Higher Education or Problems Preparing Artists in a Mercantile World." *Music Education Research*, 17 (3), 251–61.

Antliff, Allan. 2012. "Afterword: Let the Riots Begin." In *Anarchist Pedagogies: Collective Actions, Theories, and Critical Reflections on Education*, edited by Robert H. Haworth, 326–8. Oakland, CA: PM Press.

Arthur, Michael B., Svetlana N. Khapova, and Celeste P. M. Wilderom. 2005. "Career Success in a Boundaryless Career World." *Journal of Organizational Behavior*, 26, 177–202.

Bell, Adam P. 2015. "DAW Democracy? The Dearth of Diversity in 'Playing the Studio.'" *Journal of Music, Technology and Education*, 8 (2), 129–46.

Bennett, Dawn E. 2008. *Understanding the Classical Music Profession: The Past, the Present and Strategies for the Future*. Farnham: Ashgate.

Bennett, Dawn E. 2013. "The Role of Career Creativities in Developing Identity and Becoming Expert Selves." In *Developing Musical Creativities in Higher Music Education: International Perspectives and Practices*, edited by Pamela Burnard, 234–44. New York: Routledge.

Bennett, Dawn E., and Andrea Stanberg. 2008. "Musicians as Teachers: Fostering a Positive View." In *Inside, Outside, Downside Up: Conservatoire Training and Musicians' Work*, edited by Dawn Bennett and Michael Francis Hannan, 11–22. Perth: Black Swan Press.

Bennett, Toby. 2015. *Learning the Music Business: Evaluating the 'Vocational Turn' in Music Industry Education*. London: UK Music.
Bourdieu, Pierre, and Jean-Claude Passeron. 1977. *Reproduction in Education, Society and Culture*. London: Sage Publications.
Burnard, Pamela. 2012. *Musical Creativities in Practice*. Oxford: Oxford University Press.
Burnard, Pamela. 2013. "A Spectrum of Musical Creativities and Particularities of Practice." In *Developing Musical Creativities in Higher Music Education: International Perspectives and Practices*, edited by Pamela Burnard, 77–86. New York: Routledge.
Burnard, Pamela, and Elizabeth Haddon. 2015. *Activating Diverse Musical Creativities: Teaching and Learning in Higher Music Education*. London: Bloomsbury.
Cartwright, Philip A., Alex Gillett, and Gareth D. Smith. 2015. "Valuing Networks for Emerging Musicians." In *Les tendances technico-économiques de la valeur*, edited by Valérie Lejeune, 129–60. Paris: l'Harmattan.
Cartwright, Phillp A., and Gareth D. Smith. 2013. "Innovation and Value in Networks for Emerging Musicians." In *Strategies and Communications for Innovations: An Integrative Management View for Companies and Networks*, edited by Nicole Pfeffermann, Tim Marshall, and Leitizia Mortara, 437–45. New York: Springer.
Cottrell, Stephen. 2004. *Professional Music-Making in London: Ethnography and Experience*. Aldershot: Ashgate.
Creech, Andrea, and Ioulia Papageorgi. 2014. "Concepts of Ideal Musicians and Teachers: Ideal Selves and Possible Selves." In *Advanced Musical Perfrmance: Investigations in Higher Education Learning*, edited by Ioulia Papageorgi and Graham Welch, 99–114. Farmham: Ashgate.
Cremata, Radio, Joseph Pignato, Bryan Powell, and Gareth D. Smith. 2016. "Let's Take This Outside: Flash Study Analysis and the Music Learning Profiles Project." *Action, Criticism, and Theory for Music Education*, 15 (5), 51–80.
Dines, Micheal. 2015. "Learning Through Resistance: Contextualisation, Creation and Incorporation of a 'Punk Pedagogy.'" *Journal of Pedagogical Development*, 5 (3), 20–31.
Field, Ted, Robert W. Cort, Michael Nolin, and Patrick Sheane Duncan (Producers) and Stephen Herek (Director). 1995. *Mr. Holland's Opus* [motion picture]. United States: Hollywood Pictures.
Froehlich, Hildegard, and Gareth Dylan Smith. 2017. *Sociology for Music Teachers: Practical Applications*. New York, NY: Routledge.
Gaunt, Helen, and Ioulia Papageorgi. 2010. "Music in Universities and Conservatoires." In *Music Education in the 21st Century in the United Kingdom: Achievements, Analysis and Aspirations*, edited by Susan Hallam and Andrea Creech, 260–78. London: Institute of Education.
Giroux, Henry A. 2017. "Democracy in Exile and the Curse of Totalitarianism." Accessed March 4, 2017, www.counterpunch.org/2017/01/31/democracy-in-exile-and-the-curse-of-totalitarianism/
Hallam, Susan, and Helena Gaunt. 2012. *Preparing for Success: A Practical Guide for Young Musicians*. London: Institute of Education.
Harniess, Warrick. 2017. "Punk Entrepreneurship: Overcoming Obstacles to Employability in the UK's Higher Education Pseudo-Market." In *Punk Pedagogies: Music, Culture and Learning*, edited by Gareth Dylan Smith, Mike Dines, and Tom Parkinson, 57–72. New York: Routledge.
Hebert, David, Joseph Abramo, and Gareth Dylan Smith. 2017. "Sociological Issues in Popular Music Education." In *The Routledge Research Companion to Popular Music Education*, edited by Gareth D. Smith, Zack Moir, Matt Brennan, Shara Rambarran, and Phil Kirkman, 451–78. Abingdon: Routledge.
Helfter, Susan, and Beatriz Ilari. 2015. "Activating Empathic Creativity in Musicking Through University-Community Partnerships." In *Activating Diverse Musical Creativities: Teaching and Learning in Higher Music Education*, edited by Pamela Burnard and Elizabeth Haddon, 137–58. London: Bloomsbury.
Hewison, Robert. 2014. *Cultural Capital: The Rise and Fall of Creative Britain*. London: Verso.
Higgins, Lee. 2012. *Community Music: In Theory and in Practice*. New York: Oxford University Press.
Illich, Ivan. 1970. *Deschooling Society*. London: Marion Boyars.
IFPI. 2017. Global Music Report 2017: Annual State of the Industry. London: IFPI.
International Federation of the Phonographic Industry. 2014. "IFPI Digital Music Report: Lighting Up New Markets." Accessed October 6, 2016, www.ifpi.org/downloads/Digital-Music-Report-2014.pdf

Jones, Michael. 2017. "Teaching Music Industry in Challenging Times: Addressing the Neoliberal Employability Agenda in Higher Education at a Time of Music-Industrial Turbulence." In *The Routledge Research Companion to Popular Music Education*, edited by Gareth D. Smith, Zack Moir, Matt Brennan, Shara Rambarran, and Phil Kirkman, 341–4. Abingdon: Routledge.

Kallio, Alexis A. 2017. "Give Violence a Chance: Emancipation and Escape in/from School Music Education." In *Punk Pedagogies: Music, Culture and Learning*, edited by Gareth Dylan Smith, Mike Dines, and Tom Parkinson, 156–170. New York: Routledge.

Kaltefleiter, Caroline K., and Athnoy J. Nocella II. 2012. "Anarchy in the Academy: Staying True to Anarchism as an Academic-Activist." In *Anarchist Pedagogies: Collective Actions, Theories, and Critical Reflections on Education*, edited by Robert H. Haworth, 200–16. Oakland, CA: PM Press.

Keil, Charles. 1987. "Participatory Discrepancies and the Power of Music." *Cultural Anthropology*, 2 (3), 275–83.

Kenny, Ailbhe. 2014. "Sound Connections for Institutional Practice: Cultivating 'Collaborative Creativity' Through Group Composition." In *Developing Creativities in Higher Music Education: International Practices and Perspectives*, edited by Pamela Burnard, 293–304. New York: Routledge.

Kirschner, Tony. 1998. "Studying Rock: Towards a Materialist Ethnography." In *Mapping the Beat: Popular Music and Contemporary Theory*, edited by Thomas Swiss, John Sloop, and Andrew Herman, 247–68. Oxford: Blackwell.

Laycock, Jolyon, ed. 2008. *Enabling the Creators: Arts and Cultural Management and the Challenge of Social Inclusion*. Oxford: European Arts Management Project in Association with Oxford Brookes University.

Malatesta, Errico. 1993. *Errico Malatesta: His Life and Ideas*, 3rd ed., V. Richards (Ed.). London: Freedom Press.

Mantie, Roger. 2016. "Leisure Grooves: An Open Letter to Charles Keil." In *The Oxford Handbook of Music Making and Leisure*, edited by Roger Mantie and Gareth D. Smith, 619–38. New York: Oxford University Press.

Mantie, Roger, and Gareth D. Smith. 2016. "Grasping the Jellyfish of Music Making and Leisure." In *The Oxford Handbook of Music Making and Leisure*, edited by Roger Mantie and Gareth D. Smith, 3–12. New York: Oxford University Press.

Menger, Pierre-Michel. 1999. "Artistic Labor Markets and Careers." *Annual Review of Sociology*, 25, 541–74.

Musicians' Union. 2012. *The Working Musician*. London: DHA Communications.

Musicians' Union. 2016. "Contract: Private Teaching." Accessed April 14, 2017, www.musiciansunion.org.uk/Files/Contracts/Teaching/T1-Contract-Private-Teaching.

Niknafs, Nasim, and Liz Przybylski. 2017. "Popular Music and (R)Evolution of the Classroom Space: Occupy Wall Street in the Music School." In *The Routledge Research Companion to Popular Music Education*, edited by Gareth D. Smith, Zack Moir, Matt Brennan, Shara Rambarran, and Phil Kirkman, 412–24. Abingdon: Routledge.

O'Dair, Marcus, and Zukeila Beavan. 2017. "Just Go and Do It: A Blockchain Technology 'Live Project' for Nascent Music Entrepreneurs." In *Punk Pedagogies: Music, Culture and Learning*, edited by Gareth Dylan Smith, Mike Dines, and Tom Parkinson, 73–88. New York: Routledge.

Parkinson, Tom. 2017a. "Dilemmas of Purpose in Higher Popular Music Education: A Critical Portrait of an Academic Field." *Journal of Popular Music Education*, 1 (2), 133–50.

Parkinson, Tom. 2017b. "Being Punk in Higher Education: Subcultural Strategies for Academic Practice." In *Punk Pedagogies: Music, Culture and Learning*, edited by Gareth Dylan Smith, Mike Dines, and Tom Parkinson, 173–90. New York: Routledge.

Parkinson, Tom, Mark Hunter, Kimberly Campanello, Mike Dines, and Gareth D. Smith. 2015. *Understanding Small Music Venues: A Report by the Music Venues Trust*. London: Music Venues Trust.

Parkinson, Tom, and Gareth D. Smith. 2015. "Towards an Epistemology of Authenticity in Higher Popular Music Education." *Action, Criticism, and Theory for Music Education*, 4 (1), 93–127.

Pitts, Stephanie. 2012. *Chances and Choices: Exploring the Impact of Music Education*. New York: Oxford University Press.

Rainbow, Burnarr. 1996. "Onward from Butler: School Music 1945–1985." In *Teaching Music*, edited by Gary Spruce, 9–20. London: Routledge.

Rowley, Jennifer, Dawn E. Bennett, and Peter Dunbar-Hall. 2015. "Creative Teaching with Performing Arts Students: Developing Career Creativities Through the Use of ePortfolios for Career Awareness and Resilience." In *Activating Diverse Musical Creativities: Teaching and Learning in Higher Music Education*, edited by Pamela Burnard and Elizabeth Haddon, 241–60. London: Bloomsbury.

Rudin, Scott. (Producer) and Richard Linklater (Director). 2003. *School of Rock* [motion picture]. United States: Paramount Pictures.

Scruton, Roger. 2000. *An Intelligent Person's Guide to Modern Culture*. South Bend, IN: St. Augustine's Press.

Smith, Gareth D. 2013. "Seeking 'Success' in Popular Music." *Music Education Research International*, 6, 26–37.

Smith, Gareth D. 2015. "Neoliberalism and Symbolic Violence in Higher Music Education." In *Giving Voice to Democracy: Diversity and Social Justice in the Music Classroom*, edited by Lisa DeLorenzo, 65–84. New York: Routledge.

Smith, Gareth D. 2016. "(Un)Popular Music Making and Eudaimonia." In *The Oxford Handbook of Music Making and Leisure*, edited by Roger Mantie and Gareth D. Smith, 151–70. New York: Oxford University Press.

Smith, Gareth D., Mike Dines, and Tom Parkinson. 2017. "Punk Pedagogies: Perspectives on Practices." In *Punk Pedagogies: Music, Culture and Learning*, edited by Gareth Dylan Smith, Mike Dines, and Tom Parkinson, 1–10. New York: Routledge.

Smith, Gareth D., and Alex Gillett. 2015. "Creativities, Innovation and Networks in Garage Punk Rock: A Case Study of the Eruptörs." *Artivate: A Journal of Entrepreneurship in the Arts*, 4 (1), 9–24.

Stebbins, Robert A. 2014. *Careers in Serious Leisure: From Dabbler to Devotee in Search of Fulfillment*. New York: Palgrave Macmillan.

Stirner, Max. 2005. "False Principles of Our Education." In *No Gods, No Masters: An Anthology of Anarchism*, edited by Daniel Guérin, 17–20. Oakland, CA: AK Press.

Teague, Adele, and Gareth D. Smith. 2015. "Portfolio Careers and Work-Life Balance Among Musicians: An Initial Study into Implications for Higher Music Education." *British Journal of Music Education*, 32 (2), 177–95.

Teles, Tiago S., and Paula Guerra. 2017. "From Punk Ethics to the Pedagogy of the *Bad Kids*: Core Values and Social Liberation." In *Punk Pedagogies: Music, Culture and Learning*, edited by Gareth Dylan Smith, Mike Dines, and Tom Parkinson, 210–24. New York: Routledge.

Torrez, Estrella. 2012. "Punk Pedagogy: Education for Liberation and Love." In *Punkademics: The Basement Show in the Ivory Tower*, edited by Zack Furness, 131–42. Brooklyn, NY: Minor Compositions.

Tuan, Yi-Fu. 1977. *Space and Place: The Perspective of Experience*. Minneapolis, MN: University of Minnesota Press.

Vasconcelos, António A. 2015. "Being a Composer in an Age of Uncertainties, Risks Diffuse Creativity: Learning, Career and Creativities." In *Activating Diverse Musical Creativities: Teaching and Learning in Higher Music Education*, edited by Pamela Burnard and Elizabeth Haddon, 177–202. London: Bloomsbury.

Weber, William. 2004. "The Musician as Entrepreneur and Opportunist, 1700–1914." In *The Musician as Entrepreneur, 1700–1914: Managers, Charlatans, and Idealists*, edited by William Weber, 3–21. Bloomington, IN: Indiana University Press.

Williamson, John, Martin Cloonan, and Simon Frith. 2011. "Having an Impact? Academics, the Music Industries and the Problem of Knowledge." *International Journal of Cultural Policy*, 17 (5), 459–74.

Woolf, Felicity. 2004. *Partnerships for Learning: A Guide to Evaluating Arts Education Projects*, 2nd edition. London, UK: Arts Council England. Accessed September 10, 2010, www.artscouncil.org.uk/media/uploads/documents/.

5
Role Expectations and Role Conflicts within Collaborative Composing Projects

CHRISTIAN ROLLE, VERENA WEIDNER, JULIA WEBER, AND MATTHIAS SCHLOTHFELDT

Introduction

Within recent years composing music with children and young people has increasingly become an important educational field of practice, even in the German-speaking countries. In many cases, professional composers run workshops in cooperation with educators. Such collaborations are promising but at the same time challenging for the parties involved. Funded by the German Ministry of Education and Research, the project KOMPAED[1] (www.kompaed.de) is devoted to the development of a program of continuing education for professional composers with a focus on composition pedagogy in order to help them to interact appropriately in educational situations. This was and still is accompanied by research, starting with a needs analysis and an exploration of the composers' personal belief systems concerning arts and education, and continuing with an evaluation of the impact of the developed program of support. The authors of this chapter are members of the KOMPAED project group, whereby some of us are more involved in the program of continuing education itself and others are occupied with the attendant research issues. In this chapter, we will not focus on the training program but rather on the research.

Findings indicate that some of the major challenges with composing projects in educational settings are associated with ambiguously defined roles and role conflicts. This may not come as a surprise to some readers; however, we were somewhat astonished to observe how difficult it is to address these issues or, more so, to develop an alternative understanding of the respective roles. In the following discussion, we try to explain the strong role expectations and the emerging, almost insoluble, role conflicts against the theoretical background of Niklas Luhmann's sociological systems theory (Luhmann 1989, 2012/13). We have chosen this theoretical framework because we assume that there are deep-seated structural problems—call them discursive tensions—responsible for many challenges in collaborative composing projects.

Challenges

In Germany, the Response tradition is of particular significance. This model for composing projects in schools was imported from England, where members of the *London Sinfonietta* began educational work under this label in 1983 (see for example Ruffer 1988 or Winterson 1994). Supported by Gillian Moore, Richard McNicol, and others, similar projects started in Berlin in 1988 and in Frankfurt am Main in 1990. Through the participation of members of *Ensemble Modern*, Response is still alive in the Frankfurt region (Müller-Hornbach 2011). The aim of performing musicians or composers conducting workshops with students was to foster the interest of young listeners in experiencing art music through active engagement (Olson 2009, 35). In the 1990s the Schleswig-Holstein Musik Festival, together with Hans Werner Henze, took over the idea, and soon other German major cities followed. In Austria *Klangnetze* started its work, and today we have many collaborative composing projects through the German-speaking countries under various names like *Meet the Composer* in Essen (see Schlothfeldt 2011, 180–1), *Klangradar 3000* in Northern Germany, and *Querklang* in Berlin.

Common across the projects mentioned is that a performing musician or a composer visits a school several times over a sustained period in order to work with students and encourage and support them in composing. In most cases this project model leads to a performance, either in the school environment or in the local concert hall. As our needs analysis and evaluations of past projects indicate, collaborative composing projects may suffer from the involved artists' lack of educational skills.[2] However, KOMPAED's efforts to help composers develop the necessary skills have revealed some fundamental problems that have something to do with deep-seated convictions of the parties involved. There is good reason to believe that the various parties involved have different objectives. Apart from their wish to earn money, many of the artists aim to spark interest in New Music; the cooperating teachers often have broader music educational objectives; and the students may have expectations that do not meet the intentions of either of the other parties involved (see for example Handschick 2012; Wieneke 2016; Schatt 2009).

For understandable reasons, a cooperating organization such as a concert hall or an orchestra may be interested in developing young audiences (Mandel 2012). If not only students, teachers, and musicians are involved, but also teachers and students from music academies (see Schlothfeldt 2009, 2011; Schatt 2009; Müller-Hornbach 2011), the complexity increases. In many cases the teacher and the visiting composer might have different ideas concerning their own and the students' roles. A music teacher who sincerely wants to support the students by offering concrete suggestions such as "What do you think about a minor key?" or "Try to inverse the melody" might exasperate a composer who intended to intervene only by request and who may want to answer by asking in a Socratic manner in order to offer room for the students' own ideas (see also Reese 2003).[3] Moreover, in many cases, teachers and musicians might have differing views about the learning processes that take place, even if they agree about the overall objectives of the joint composing project.

It is not just that these discrepancies exist. It is even difficult to address them. To put it in Foucauldian terms (Foucault 1969, 1977), the disparate views seem to be governed by the discursive formation of education, on the one hand, and the discursive field of aesthetics, on the other hand. However, in this article we will not analyze the resulting tensions employing discourse theory, but will instead adopt some distinctions and concepts from sociological systems theory (see Luhmann 1989, 2000, 2012/13), hoping this allows for further clarification. To put it in Niklas Luhmann's terms, the educational system does not harmonize with the art system (Weidner 2015).

Looking at the Interviews Through Luhmann's Eyes

As a theoretical background we will use some major assumptions from Niklas Luhmann's sociological systems theory (see Luhmann 1989, 2000, 2012/13; Luhmann and Schorr 2000). Unlike many other societal theories—and in this way more similar to discourse theories—Luhmann's theories do not focus on people and their behavior to explain relevant processes within society, but rather on communicative structures.

With respect to his societal theory, Luhmann concentrates on communication systems such as science, economics, education, or arts. He points out diverse functions and expectations that are important within each of the fields, identifying a characteristic binary code for each system. Whereas the scientific system, for example, uses the code true/false to order its operations, the economic system follows the code paying/not paying. For investigating role changes and role conflicts in the context of our projects, this theoretical background has been helpful because it allows us to distinguish between the social contexts which people are involved in and the individuals themselves. From this perspective, we do not necessarily refer to the individual composer (who visits a school) when we speak of "the artist," and we do not refer to the individual teacher (who is working at a school) when we talk about "the educator." Yet we are able to describe differing role assignments and conflicting role expectations as results of institutional and situational conditions in order to grasp the complexity of the functional relationships.

In addition to these basic assumptions from Luhmann's systems theory we will take up his distinction between two types of communication: a stable one—such as in science, legal rights, or economy—and a rather unstable one—such as in art or in the communication of love:

> Other media take pride in being not technicizable, and they see this not as a deficit but as a particular quality. This is the case with love and with

art. It is not by chance that in these two cases, the general is stressed in the particular—in love in the special subject, in art in the special object.
(Luhmann 2012/13, 220)

This differentiation is not as well known as other theoretical tools of Luhmann's theory complex, but when used within societal analysis it helps to figure out diverse communication strategies without being restricted to a particular code or a single function. Applying it to an aspect of educational communication (see Weidner 2015, 81–2), we can consider a certain vicinity between the composer's dealing with works of art and his or her wish to support individuals in developing their own composing.

In the following analysis we draw on different interview data sources collected as part of the formative evaluation of the KOMPAED training. Using the first set of data we had the goal of developing a training program based on an analysis of the challenges that had emerged in composition projects. For this purpose we interviewed two project organizers, two teachers, and six composers who had been chosen by selective expert sampling. The second set of data was collected during the training program and consisted of five case analyses of composers participating in the training. The five composers, chosen through diversity sampling, were interviewed three times during the 8-month program. The first interview tackled their general ideas and beliefs about composition pedagogy; in the second and third interviews they were asked to reflect upon their own projects. The transcribed interviews were analyzed against the theoretical background of Luhmann's systems theory.

The Relational Triangle

In collaborative composing projects that take place in schools, we are dealing with at least three parties that are characterized by different role assignments and different role expectations. We will examine two relations within the triangle, composer–teacher–student, namely composer–student and composer–teacher. The relation student–teacher could not be investigated within our project; due to our focus on the role of the composer, we did not collect any data in this field.

Composer–Student

When asked about the educational activities of symphony orchestras and concert halls during a collaborative school project (see Egeler-Wittman 2013, 87), the German composer Markus Hechtle remarked that he thought there might soon be more music educators than musicians. This seemed to him to be undesirable. Hechtle's remark can be seen as an indicator to what the sociologist Niklas Luhmann has described as "resonance problems" of social functional systems (see Luhmann 1989, 15–21). Although the composer has worked in the field of music education by composing for student ensembles, he obviously does not consider himself an educator. On the contrary, he wants to disassociate himself from professional music educators. We frequently observe this concern in the context of arts education where artists are involved. In the field of composition pedagogy, there is paradoxically a certain skepticism and several reservations against teaching composition (Hickey 2012, 7). This cannot only be explained by the legacy of the concept of the artistic genius (Kaschub and Smith 2009, 8–11); it is explained more precisely by reference to the education system as having two conflicting functions:

> In a certain sense, [since the end of 18th century] the school was the unity of two functions that could no longer be integrated in pedagogical reflection, namely, the function of education and the function of social selection—whether for further education or economic employment. As an educator, the teacher considered himself responsible only for training and education; as a representative of the school, he practiced selection with the judgments that he communicated.
> (Luhmann 2012/13, 238)

This means that a conflict arises within the education system between the aim of educating children and young people in the right way (the educational function governed by the code transmittable/nontransmittable) and the necessity to grade (the selection function governed by the code better/worse [see Luhmann 2002, 73; see also Luhmann and Schorr 2000]).[4]

Artists' reservations towards pedagogical programs may primarily concern the selection function and the school as an institution. Indeed, institutional requirements in many cases seem to obstruct, if not destruct, educational efforts. From the perspective of composition pedagogy, it might not be appropriate to assess students' compositions. It appears not to be the best way to teach a defined group of children at a designated time for a certain period. When composing projects take place at schools, it is necessary to continue to supervise the students even if classroom disruptions hamper the successful continuation of the composing process. Music teachers usually meet these challenges (see Christophersen 2013). However, this does not lead to their recognition as musicians and arts educators on an equal footing.

If one has a closer look at what might be expected from composers in collaborative projects, it does not seem to be clear whether they are in demand as actual composers. The organizer of an education program describes the cooperation partners she prefers to work with in collaborative composing projects as versatile practitioners rather than specialized artists, "I have already worked with people who studied composition, but [. . .] in these contexts I often work with people that stick out like a sore thumb."[5] Their exact formal education seems secondary. Her underlying concept of a composer is shown when she stresses that the artists she works with are "not unworldly people, where you have the impression they lock themselves up in a closet and draw music notes on pieces of paper." Despite her skepticism towards the presumed habitus of composers, the organizer is interested in a particular "artistic approach and in helping children to develop a special attitude" which is where composers come into play because, as the organizer reckons, "they are better at doing this [. . .] better than educators for example, [. . .] because composers always have this attitude." Apparently, although she argued in one moment for working with people who do different things and do not compose the whole day, shortly thereafter she argued for working with people who have a certain attitude typical of composers. This can be taken as an example of the contrast between art and education. In this kind of argumentation, art is more likely to be attributed to composers as a professional or even an innate characteristic.

Some connections can be made between the educational challenges that the participants of the KOMPAED training describe and these contradictory expectations of an organizer. One composer, for example, expresses the tension she feels when deciding how open she should keep the composition process or to what extent she should directly intervene. For example, she suggested at some point to the students to leave out the beat that they had used throughout their whole composition. Looking back she considered the suggestion "a very strong influence that I actually did not want to give." But she also admitted that the students did not make use of the open setting the way she had intended. The more open she kept the process, "the more conventional the results were" from her point of view. On the one hand she preferred to hold back completely, and even considered suggestions and alternative solutions an inappropriate influence on the process. On the other hand she did not know how to deal with the fact that the musical product, which the students created without her intervention, did not fulfill her artistic standards.

This also shows that the composers sometimes have difficulties appreciating students' works if they seem to be too conventional. It raises the question of whether, or to what extent, originality and novelty can serve as criteria for the quality of students' compositions. Maud Hickey and Scott D. Lipscomb, however, claim that "Our music teaching culture tends to favor the 'safe' side" (2006, 97)—which suggests and confirms that issues of assessment are a significant cause for conflict between the education system and the art system.

Furthermore, the interviews reveal that composers sometimes feel the need to differentiate between the students' composing and a "real" or "serious" form of art. This correlates to the aesthetic discourses at music academies and universities where the composers themselves have been educated. In the underlying discourse, composing is not something that everybody can do (see for example Berkeley 2001, 123–24). Connected to this is the issue of whether composing is teachable at all and the question of whether children's music inventions should be called "compositions."

Different "versions" of the relationship between art and school (Liebau 2009) may be instructive in clarifying these "attitudes" and "approaches." First, Eckart Liebau states that the school is a dominant institution that encodes every action that takes place in its context as pedagogical. Second, he raises the fundamental question of whether something like free art at school could exist at all (ibid 53). He then juxtaposes a "school of art" and an "art of school." Although art's autonomy is a prerequisite in the school of art, it only serves the learner's autonomy. The art of school, on the other hand, results from artistic goals and reasons. Thus its goal isn't education (in the sense of personal growth or the German term *Bildung*[6]) but art itself.

The radical and "noneducational" character of Liebau's perspective is apparent in his considerations concerning which values should guide a "school-art" (see also Bresler 2002). The main focus, he claims, should be on the success of the work of art. The artist's aesthetic interest is crucial, and pedagogy becomes a means to this end (ibid). Thus, students become integrated in the art; they become artists participating in the artistic process (ibid). From our point of view, this idea is of interest to composition pedagogy because it allows us to analyze the implications of some partially hidden opinions.

Furthermore, by separating an art-of-school perspective from a school-of-art perspective, it is possible to describe the maxims, implicit or explicit, more generally in the context of composition pedagogy. This includes, among others, the idea of *responding* to students' compositions verbally or sonically and, in doing so, to pursue premises such as:

> Get to know students' music well before offering critiques./ Encourage students to find solutions to musical problems on their own./ Help students discover how other composers may have addressed problems similar to ones they are having.
>
> (Reese 2003, 216)

These examples are mostly centered on the students' interests and their development as composers (see also Kenny 2014). According to Liebau this should be regarded as a "school of art," where the artistic activity is guided and motivated by pedagogy. A contrast with this might be an idea implied in the context of the *Response* model: Assuming that the initiative is taken by a composer with her or his professional work of art, this implies that students respond to it. Although this response can be pedagogically motivated, it suggests a process with an artistic coding in Luhmann's terms.

Besides other interpretations, this polarization offers an opportunity to clarify the role of the composers involved. If they were inspired by the idea of complete freedom for the students' composing, their role would be closer to a facilitator who supports the students finding of and realization of their individual interests. Thus, the most important professional skill would be "being able to step aside," and their specific competence as composers would come into play when they asked the right questions based on experience and their broad musical vision. On the contrary, if they were inspired by the idea of contributing to the setting with their artistic profile, their most important skill would be "presenting their own ideas," which could inevitably lead to the limitation of the students' freedom.

Composer–Teacher

Analyzing composers' expectations relating to the teachers involved in the projects, it becomes clear that the composers expected different teachers than those they found. Many positive descriptions of their individual partners indicated this.

One composer, for example, emphasized that the teacher was young, not yet very established in the school, and open minded. Another composer noticed that his partner "strangely enough is very familiar with the computer software" that he used. Furthermore he noticed that she wanted to do something new and was looking especially for New Music. How he described these aspects can be interpreted as an indication that it was not normal for him for teachers to know how to handle sequencer software, to look for something new, and like to teach New Music in the classroom. The suspected gap between his expectations and his experience became even clearer when he spoke of his responsibility towards teachers—and here he spoke of teachers in general—when he said that he had "to convince them why New Music is necessary." Although the experience showed something else, the general expectations reinforced that to him this experience is an exception.

Furthermore, the needs analysis shows that the music teacher sometimes remains a "hidden expert." One composer, who is well experienced in working at schools, stated that the role of the teacher is:

> really only about being present . . . They participate more actively in the organization: How do the students get to the concert? How do the instruments get there? But they don't play a part in supervising the [students'] composing. [If they do] that often has counterproductive effects.

At some points in the interviews, an educational dimension was added, for example, by saying that a teacher's role is one of "observer" and only there "to control the discipline." Occasionally we found statements that illustrated why this silent partnership can be essential for composers. One composer was surprised and alarmed that the teacher worked with the students on their composition in his absence. The composer had focused on New Music as the goal of composing projects in schools, and the teacher was not aware of this goal or did not know how to achieve it in the way the composer had intended. So it "turned into a rondo then—which contradicts completely [his] own aesthetics."

According to Magne Espeland, the "view of the status of the artist/musician as superior to that of the music educator has been around for a long time" because his "'burning artistic impulse' . . . to a large extent, compensate[s] for the lack of educational skills" (Espeland 2010, 136, referring to MacPherson 1915, 37). Although shared experiences in collaborative projects in recent years may have—as Espeland suggests—increased mutual respect, the artist/teacher dichotomy still exists in the discourse: The composer often presumes the role of the artistic expert, whereas the cooperating teacher remains responsible solely for smooth functioning of the (nonartistic and noneducational) framework. Catharina Christophersen (2013) suggests that this relationship is problematic. She compares the behavior of teachers who have the role of "helper" or "guard" with the way these teachers are evaluated by other participants in the projects. There were very negative attributions that describe teachers as uninvolved because they "disturb the performance by actively silencing the students" (Christophersen 2013, 4). It seems likely that a teacher who is only active in the background without participating in the artistic processes can easily be interpreted as disinterested and indifferent. The question remains how to develop an approach to team teaching that allows the teacher to take on both responsibilities—that is, providing the composer with good working conditions in the classroom, as well as contributing to artistic and educational issues.

Conclusions and Unanswered Questions

In summary, we can identify some interconnections between certain groups of people and their functions in contextual relation to each other: The role of artistic expert is more likely to be attributed to composers than to educators. Teachers are often described as nonartistic supporters, acting more often as organizers.

Furthermore we can see that the role expectations attributed to the different groups of people involved are often unclear, sometimes even contradictory. This applies to composers, who are expected on the one hand to be versatile and flexible in their interactions within the educational context, and on the other hand to constantly maintain a certain artistic attitude and standard. However it also applies to teachers, who are expected to not overstep the boundary into the artistic process, yet are often criticized for being seemingly disinterested and uninvolved.

Ambiguous role definitions seem to lead to tensions in the educational process. This pertains to the question of whether—and to which extent—composers should intervene in the composing process by giving aesthetically motivated impulses or whether they should instead hold back and let the process develop with as little guidance as possible. It also pertains to the effectiveness of teamwork when preformed beliefs (concerning the abilities or predispositions of teachers, for example) determine the project development more than the actual interactions between the partners.

Several perspectives on collaborative projects remain uninvestigated at this point. How would two partners in different roles—a teacher and a composer—describe the same project? Would they reveal contradictory or similar perceptions? Are there blind spots in the roles of the different partners? How would the students in a collaborative project evaluate the teacher–composer team? How would they observe their interactions and their different roles?

During collaborative projects the relationship between teachers and students changes, in contrast to that of the usual classroom setting. Because a teacher is occupied during a project more with organizational duties and educational assessment than with musical issues, we assume that this influences the way students perceive their teacher and their music lessons in general. The relation student–teacher was not a focus of KOMPAED. Therefore, we can only make assumptions and point to future research while taking existent literature (for example Fautley 2004) into consideration.

The question remains: Which conclusions can be drawn on a more practical level and, specifically, which conclusions can be made about the KOMPAED training? It seems advisable to introduce issues concerning team teaching into the discussions and to bring teachers and composers together for some of the training modules (see for example Kenny and Morrissey 2016).

Above all, it remains open how the aforementioned observations about collaboration within composing projects would change if composition pedagogy were a regular component of the music education programs at universities (see for example. Kaschub and Smith 2013; Smith 2014). It could be expected that the relational triangle would change significantly if future music teachers had significantly more experience in composing, and certainly if future composers had more experience in teaching.[7]

Notes

1 KOMPÄD is an acronym for Kompositionspädagogik. The project is jointly realized by Cologne University, Jeunesses Musicales Germany, the University of Music in Saarbruecken, Folkwang University of the Arts in Essen, and Erfurt University. In an 8-month program KOMPAED provides workshops and seminars with various experts and a form of on-the-job-training. The participating composers develop and direct their own educational projects that can take place in schools or music schools or can be conducted independently from any institution. During the entire course of these projects they are individually coached by members of the project team and by experienced educators.
2 This can also be seen in other evaluation results, as, for example, an evaluation of response projects of London Sinfonietta in the 1990s (Winterson 1994) or of composing projects in four schools in Essen/Germany (see Schatt 2009).
3 Isolde Malmberg made another observation by pointing out that artists' interventions are more goal and product oriented (they contribute new ideas, are more likely to evaluate the aesthetic quality of students' products, and orient the work process more toward the performance) (Malmberg 2012, 430).

4 "One of the most important system effects [...] is the possibility of a second-coding of the whole system, which follows the scheme better/worse. The education itself cannot be fully judged with regard to the code transmittable/non-transmittable, and this doesn't mean any indication for the assessment of its successes" (Luhmann 2002, 73).
5 All quotations have been translated from the original German by the authors for the purposes of this chapter.
6 The Enlightenment conception of Bildung as a process of self-formation, particularly through the arts, is still an important reference point in continental European debates and in reflections about music education (see Nielsen 2007). Although an equivalent English term does not exist, John Dewey's ideas concerning a kind of liberating educative experience and its role for personal growth show many similarities (see Dewey 1938; Rolle 1999, 37–55).
7 We thank Lesley Olson for not only proofreading but also commenting and helping us to improve our article, even though she cannot be held responsible for any errors of appraisal.

References

Berkeley, Rebecca. 2001. "Why is Teaching Composing so Challenging? A Survey of Classroom Observation and Teachers' Opinions." *British Journal of Music Education*, 18 (2), 119–38.
Bresler, Liora. 2002. "School Art as a Hybrid Genre: Institutional Contexts for Art Curriculum." In *The Arts in Children's Lives: Context, Culture, and Curriculum*, edited by Liora Bresler and Christine M. Thompson, 169–84. New York: Kluwer.
Christophersen, Catharina. 2013. "Helper, Guard or Mediator? Teachers' Space for Action in The Cultural Rucksack, a Norwegian National Program for Arts and Culture in Schools." *International Journal of Education & the Arts*, 14 (SI 1.11). Accessed October 17, 2016, www.ijea.org/v14si1/v14si1-11.pdf
Dewey, John. 1938. *Experience & Education*. New York: Kappa Delta Pi.
Egeler-Wittmann, Silke. 2013. *Face to Face: Jugendliche erarbeiten und performen gemeinsam mit Profimusikern zeitgenössische Musik*. Mainz: Schott.
Espeland, Magne. 2010. "Dichotomies in Music Education—Real or Unreal?" *Music Education Research*, 12 (2), 129–39.
Fautley, Martin. 2004. "Teacher Intervention Strategies in the Composing Processes of Lower Secondary School Students." *International Journal of Music Education*, 22 (3), 201–18.
Foucault, Michel. 1969. *L'Archéologie du savoir*. Paris: Gallimard. (English as *Archaeology of Knowledge*. Translated by M. Sheridan Smith. New York: Routledge, 1989).
Foucault, Michel. 1977. "The Confession of the Flesh." Interview. In *Power/Knowledge: Selected Interviews and Other Writings*, edited by Colin Gordon, 1980. New York: Pantheon Books.
Handschick, Matthias. 2012. "Visionen und Realitäten—Schüler-Kompositionsprojekte zwischen Kunstanspruch und Klischeeproduktion. Eine kritische Reflexion des Schüler-Kompositionsprojekts *SWR-Klangvisionen* mit Helmut Lachenmann, Sylvain Cambreling und dem SWR Sinfonieorchester Freiburg und Baden-Baden." In *neues hören und sehen ... und vermitteln. Pädagogische Modelle und Reflexionen zur Neuen Musik*, edited by Michael Dartsch, Sigrid Konrad, and Christian Rolle, 115–31. Regensburg: ConBrio.
Hickey, Maud. 2012. *Music Outside the Lines. Ideas for Composing in the K–12 Classrooms*. Oxford: Oxford University Press.
Hickey, Maud, and Scott D. Lipscomb. 2006. "How Different Is Good? How Good Is Different? The Assessment of Children's Creative Musical Thinking." In *Musical Creativity: Multidisciplinary Research in Theory and Practice*, edited by Irène Deliège and Geraint A. Wiggins. Hove: Psychology Press.
Kaschub, Michele, and Janice Smith. 2009. *Minds on Music: Composition for Creative and Critical Thinking*. Lanham, MD: Rowman & Littlefield Education.
Kaschub, Michele, and Janice Smith. 2013. *Composing Our Future: Preparing Music Educators to Teach Composition*. Oxford: Oxford University Press.
Kenny, Ailbhe. 2014. "Sound Connections for Institutional Practice: Cultivating 'Collaborative Creativity' Through Group Composition." In *Developing Creativities in Higher Music Education: International Perspectives and Practices*, edited by Pamela Burnard, 293–304. London and New York: Routledge.
Kenny, Ailbhe, and Dorothy Morrissey. 2016. *Exploring Teacher-Artist Partnership as a Model of CPD for Supporting and Enhancing Arts Education in Ireland*. Dublin: Association of

Teachers/Education Centres in Ireland, Department of Education and Skills, Department of Arts, Heritage and Gaeltacht.
Liebau, Eckart. 2009. "Die Kunst der Schule." In *Curriculum des Unwägbaren. II. Die Musen als Mägde: Von der Veränderung der Künste in der Schule*, edited by Johannes Bilstein and Winfried Kneip, 43–58. Oberhausen: Athena.
Luhmann, Niklas. 1989. *Ecological Communication*. Translated by John Bednartz Jr. Chicago: University of Chicago Press.
Luhmann, Niklas. 2000. *Art as a Social System*. Translated by Eva M. Knodt. Stanford, CA: Stanford University Press.
Luhmann, Niklas. 2002. *Das Erziehungssystem der Gesellschaft*. Berlin: Suhrkamp.
Luhmann, Niklas. 2012/13. *Theory of Society*. Translated by Rhodes Barrett. Stanford, CA: Stanford University Press, 2 vols.
Luhmann, Niklas, and Karl Eberhard Schorr. 2000. *Problems of Reflection in the System of Education*. Translated by Rebecca A. Neuwirth. Berghahn: Waxmann.
MacPherson, Stewart. 1915. *The Musical Education of the Child*. London: Joseph Williams.
Malmberg, Isolde. 2012. *Projektmethode und Musikunterricht: Didaktisch-methodische Perspektiven der Projektmethode für Lehr-und Lernprozesse im Musikunterricht*. Münster: LIT Verlag.
Mandel, Birgit. 2012. "Kulturvermittlung, Kulturmanagement und Audience Development als Strategien für Kulturelle Bildung." In *Handbuch Kulturelle Bildung*, edited by Hildegard Bockhorst, Vanessa-Isabelle Reinwand-Weiss, and Wolfgang Zacharias, 279–83. München: kopaed:
Müller-Hornbach, Gerhard. 2011. "Kompositionspädagogik und 'Response' an der Hochschule für Musik und Darstellende Kunst Frankfurt am Main." In *Komponieren mit Schülern*, edited by Benjamin Lang and Philipp Vandré, 163–73. Regensburg: ConBrio.
Nielsen, Frede. 2007. "Music (and Arts) Education from the Point of View of Didaktik and Bildung." In *International Handbook of Research in Arts Education*, edited by Liora Bresler, 265–85. Dordrecht, The Netherlands: Springer.
Olson, Lesley. 2009. "On Response Projects and Responses to It." In *Unser Faust—Meet the Composer: Ein Kompositionsprojekt an Essener Schulen*, edited by Peter W. Schatt, 35–46. Regensburg: ConBrio.
Reese, Sam. 2003. "Responding to Student Compositions." In *Why and How to Teach Music Composition: A New Horizon for Music Education*, edited by Maud Hickey, 211–32. Reston: MENC.
Rolle, Christian. 1999. *Musikalisch-Ästhetische Bildung: Über die Bedeutung ästhetischer Erfahrung für musikalische Bildungsprozesse*. Kassel: Bosse.
Ruffer, David. 1988. "The London Sinfonietta Education Programme—an Analysis of an Interface Between the Professional Artist and Music in Education." *British Journal of Music Education*, 5 (1), 45–54.
Schatt, Peter W., ed. 2009. *Unser Faust—Meet the Composer. Ein Kompositionsprojekt an Essener Schulen. Bericht—Evaluation—Dokumentation*. Regensburg: ConBrio.
Schlothfeldt, Matthias. 2009. *Komponieren im Unterricht*. Hildesheim: Olms.
Schlothfeldt, Matthias. 2011. "Kompositionspädagogik an der Folkwang Universität der Künste Essen." In *Komponieren mit Schülern*, edited by Benjamin Lang and Philipp Vandré, 175–82. Regensburg: ConBrio.
Smith, Janice P. 2014. "Musical Creativities in the Practice of Composition Pedagogy: Releasing the Muse in Current and Future teachers." In *Developing Creativities in Higher Music Education: International Perspectives and Practices*, edited by Pamela Burnard, 139–50. London and New York: Routledge.
Weidner, Verena. 2015. *Musikpädagogik und Musiktheorie: Systemtheoretische Beobachtungen einer problematischen Beziehung*. Münster: Waxmann.
Wieneke, Julia. 2016. *Zeitgenössische Musik vermitteln in Kompositionsprojekten an Schulen*. Hildesheim: Olms.
Winterson, Julia. 1994. "An Evaluation of the Effects of London Sinfonietta Education Projects on Their Participants."*British Journal of Music Education*, 11 (2), 129–41.

6
Thwarting the Authority of Purpose: Epistemic Responsibility within Collaborations

CATHY BENEDICT

Introduction

What is the purpose of education? This is a question so pervasive it borders on the mundane. Worded this way, the question has no descriptor (music) preceding education; perhaps suggesting two separate questions detached from each other, neither one influencing the other. But, of course, this is indeed *the* question, sans modifier, that should guide our practice. I am not suggesting one shouldn't concern oneself with the purpose of an education in music. I am suggesting, however, that larger epistemological questions precede this egocentric focus. And although it may seem clear that the purpose of education should be at the center of the debate, too often *purpose* is linked to knowledge *gains*, where acquisition is an end so worthy as to squander the merits of any examination of means.

This chapter suggests, that although powerful, the topic or question of the musician–teacher collaboration is the wrong one with which to begin. It is wrong in that it denies the grappling with and pondering of one of the basic, fundamental existential questions. What does it mean to know, how do we come to know, and what is the purpose of knowing?

In the following, I advocate for the merits of epistemic responsibility in the context of a public educative context, arguing it to be an impactful and meaningful way to challenge the primacy of *purpose in any collaboration*, whether poet/language arts or musician–teacher. This does not obviate the necessity of content decisions or accountability, but it does propose engagements with teaching and learning where "our responsibility is not just a moral quality we happen to possess or have learnt through experience, but a way of approaching our communicative interactions, a stance towards credibility and credulity that is shared" (Origgi 2008, 36). The focus of this chapter, then, will be to ask questions and raise points that transcend the musician–teacher collaboration, which is merely one confluence of many that may, I will suggest, serve only to produce "incessant noise" (Arendt 2005, 262).

Personal Epistemology

Teachers invite people into their classes for multiple reasons; this is certainly not the purview of music classes. The children's book author, invited into the reading circle, might be there to talk about the process she goes through as she engages in her writing. Perhaps she is an author the children have grown up reading, and by her presence children are presented with a role model to whom they might aspire. Entrepreneurs, athletics, civil servants, all might be brought into the classroom to engage with the students. Each had a humble beginning, perhaps just as the students might; they've worked their way up through the system and now have arrived to share their wisdom. "Here is a famous/successful (fill in the blank) in my class, surely I can grow up and be just like her!" "If he can do it, so can I!" The provision of these models reflects both hope and a "why not try anything" attitude: wizardry, magic, anything is possible! However, as Freire (1994) points out "hope is an ontological need" and that hope, although "necessary . . . [is] not enough" (8). Thus, without a conscious awareness of one's personal epistemology, "try anything" as a pedagogical strategy and hope as a belief in the magical will probably not call us to attend to (for instance) whether support systems exist (including societal and ideological discourses) that make this wizardry happen. Indeed, providing these models without interrogating systems of oppression, including cultural capital and cultural codes, teachers "abdicat[e] their duty to teach" (Delpit 1995, 31). All of which either falls somewhere on the continuum of, at best, naïveté or, at worst, neo-progressive pedagogies that serve as a "mechanism of social control" (Giroux 1984, 31).

Epistemology resides both in the philosophical (the nature of knowing) and psychological (how one comes to know). When we consider the psychological development of personal epistemology and epistemological beliefs, Hofer and Pintrich (1997, 88) describe this as:

> how individuals come to know, the theories and beliefs they hold about knowing, and the way such epistemological premises are a part of and an influence on the cognitive processes of thinking and reasoning.

Personal epistemology, then, not only influences the choices we make in our day-to-day decisions but also those decisions within the context of public education. Within the personal epistemology literature there is discussion as to whether there are "linkages . . . to other constructs in cognition and motivation" and even what "dimensions [personal epistemology] encompasses" (Hofer and Pintrich 1997, 89). Important for this chapter, then, are the questions of domain specificity of personal [musicianship] epistemology and "how such beliefs might connect to [musical] disciplinary beliefs" (ibid). More to the point, however, is how coercively influential a "shared view of cognition and knowing" might be when we consider responsibility and moral commitment to the purpose of the educative process (Hofer 2008, 17).

Authority

Authority is such a part of schooling that the concept often takes on the perception of *rightness*, of common sense. Authority as rightness is not, however, Arendt's (1958) conceptualization in which common sense as action is made in relation with the world. Rather, commonsensical views of what is already *known* and therefore *right* construct authority and establish it as a pervasive marker of not just schooling, but, as we shall see, many collaborative practices as well. In these spaces content predicates and preempts engagement (and thinking), and thus the authority of what is already known prevents us from interrogating the complications of what is said to be known, which detracts alternative epistemic perspectives, and—in a vicious cycle—compresses what it means *to know*.

From primary music classrooms to higher education, faculties of music, language, and actions continually vie for, dismiss, and even ignore the complexities of epistemic authority, interrogating or reifying what (and who) counts. As such, the possibility of relativism threatens (Code 2006), and in these muddied educational waters certainty appears in the form of purpose. The notion of *purpose*, mercurial and continually shaped by ideological winds, has been argued and contested throughout the history of public schooling. Yet capricious (and vague) as purpose may be, it continues to provide safer and more secure ground than grappling with contentions and dynamic understandings that emerge from socioeconomic tensions; racial challenges; and personal, social, and cultural ways of knowing. For this context, then, bringing in role models to collaborate with the vague purpose of demonstrating to students how "musicians" do "it" provides a purposeful enough goal without really having to interrogate questions such as who benefits (the students, the teachers, the collaborators) and why.

This indicates that, as a form of action, teaching lies within the epistemological space of responsibility crafted as one in which both the balance of accountability and curricular goals are explicitly addressed with and not for students. Research suggests "the variety of contexts within which epistemic beliefs are held, employed, and articulated" (Gottlieb and Mandel Leadership Institute 2007, 6) are as important as research into models of epistemic development. Recognizing that multiple epistemological paradigms exist, including conditions (Kitcher 1990) and contexts that are cultural (Gottlieb and Mandel Leadership Institute 2007), communicative (Origgi 2008), and place-based (Gruenewald 2003), the purpose of education must move from finality of content toward education *as* an epistemological responsibility. Nothing, then, would be sacrosanct or "known." Givens such as "student-centered" and "inquiry-based" learning, "cooperative learning," and collaborations must be examined and interrogated as slogans through which the "ambiguity of language [not only] serves a political function—it obscures different and possible social interests" (Popkewitz 1980), again such as who stands to gain and to what end. And, in this case, whose epistemic rights?

To think through collaboration (and thus purpose) grounded in epistemology, I pose questions to assist *framing capacity*. The notion behind a *framing capacity* functions within the reasoning that "one must maximize as much as possible the multiplication of small narratives" (Lyotard and Thébaud 1996, 59). In music education, Higgins (2008) provides examples of how these multiple small narratives and ways of knowing are present in community music practices and how they are essential to their "productivity" and democratic nature. Tensions such as clashing unarticulated goals between teacher/collaborator/learner, what learning and knowing is or even looks like, or even space/time constraints mismatched and even at odds philosophically (epistemologically) could provide fertile ground for discussion and growth if framed as such. Veloso and Carvalho (2012) show how children construct quite complex ways of being creative, highlighting that imagination depends on playing with multiple accounts or viewpoints. Here, as in myriad other research, framing is a complex capacity for sense making and remaking, helping to re-evaluate what we might have previously considered to be normative and common sense: collaborations.

Collaborations

Collaborations between public education and professional musicians are the backbone of any self-respecting symphonic orchestra. The Cincinnati Symphony Orchestra, New York Philharmonic, Berliner Philharmoniker, the Chicago Symphony, and LA Phil (to name a few) all support education programs. One might posit that the LA Phil takes this one step further in its extensive El Sistema–inspired program, wherein the "LA Phil and its community partners provide free instruments, intensive music training, and academic support to students from underserved neighborhoods, empowering them to become **vital citizens, leaders**, and **agents of change**" (bold in text) (as of June 2017, www.laphil.com/education/yola).

Setting aside the LA Phil for one moment, orchestras such as those mentioned have multiple purposes for their education programs, but above all, their purpose is to bring Western classical music into the lives of children. The New York Philharmonic and their Philharmonic Teaching Artists, for instance:

> use major orchestral repertoire to teach students, their teachers, and parents how to listen, perform and compose, preparing them to hear concerts in their own school and at the Philharmonic and establishing music as an essential element of the classroom and of the school community.
> (as of June 2017, http://nyphil.org/education/learning-communities/philharmonic-schools)

The Cincinnati Symphony Orchestra "leverage(s) live music performance and instrumental coaching to supplement your students' learning in an up close and personal environment" (as of June 2017, www.cincinnatisymphony.org/community-plus-learning/for-educators/musicians-in-schools). The embedded assumption as to what constitutes learning (and the purpose of learning) remains unclear. Whether this choice is deliberate is also unclear. One might interpret these mission statements as ways to build audiences, or perhaps more cynically conclude they have been mandated by funding sources to create education and outreach programs. What is clear in both these mission statements is 1) outside experts can accomplish something others cannot and 2) the purpose of an education in music is inextricably tied to a traditional classical model. Frustratingly, the purpose for both the orchestras and the public schools that welcome these projects remains vague, assumed, and rarely interrogated.

At the other end of the spectrum, whether a symphonic organization can *empower* anyone is an extreme example of purpose. Although not belittling or even dismissing purposes that encompass social change and justice, these extremes highlight differing (contrasting?) epistemological beliefs at work. Do, or should, all epistemological premises count equally? Is there a "natural" authority in differing epistemic perspectives? What are the epistemic rights and duties of students and teachers? Do pedagogical strategies such as collaborations and cooperative learning afford space for epistemic agency (Duarte 2001)?

These are not easy questions, nor should they be. However, to enter these questions we must first return to epistemology as it resides in philosophy and the nature of knowing.

Epistemological Premises

Collaborations are engagements that occur between. Between what may seem obvious—in this context, musician/learner, musician/student, musician/teacher. Agreeing in this moment that what constitutes a musician is someone with a certain set of skills that is invited in, what matters more here is what constitutes learner, student, and, indeed, teacher. Biesta (2010) asks us to consider the "subjects of teaching." He is, in this context, referring to students and how we might "call" them. He presents three ways of referencing: learner, student, and finally, speaker. The learner is constructed as someone who lacks, and thus in need of someone who knows, who has arrived. Using Rancière's pedagogical goal (purpose) of liberty and emancipation, Biesta underscores the importance of "taking the authority of educator out of the picture so that education dissolves into learning" (2010, 544). Thus, the one "who can" prevents and stands in the way of the appearance of a space in which all would be able to speak without fear or constraints of not knowing. For Biesta, then, "emancipatory education can therefore be characterized as education that starts from the assumption that all students can speak—or to be more precise: that all students can *already* speak" (2010, 549).

According to Biesta, it isn't just that all epistemological premises count equally. His purpose is liberation from transactions: the student as the consumer of knowledge created outside herself, the musician or organization as the provider of this knowledge, and what is learned as a commodity (2004, 58). This then implies that in the case of collaborations, everyone involved, including the students, must grapple with the discursive practices that both shape and act against epistemic responsibilities. Which would mean that discussions as to what (and ways of) learning(s) and knowing(s) may be gained (or thwarted) when someone from the outside comes into a space that has been attended to by both the teacher and students. Conversations that focused on epistemological concerns (whether named epistemological or not) would necessarily move beyond the simple purpose of the collaboration to grappling with the importance of how one comes to "know" something and what knowing might mean in the moment of the collaboration, as well as once the collaboration has concluded. These conversations are easier to facilitate than one might think. Simply making a slight switch in one's language by asking what one "thinks" one knows rather than a definitive stance as to what is known opens up the space for mutual perspectives, and, indeed, theories, to be interrogated.

In the seminal piece, "Division of Cognitive Labor," Kitcher (1990, 7) addressing the sciences and scientific growth, asks the following:

> Does the sophisticated work in [the] history of science not reveal to us that there are numerous cases in which equally reasonable people may disagree about the merits of rival theories, perhaps because they have different ideas about the significance of different problems or about the appropriate criteria for solving those problems?

Kitcher is speaking to how members of the scientific community, as singular researchers, do not or cannot possibly study all areas of science (thus the division of labor). This diversity of epistemological beliefs and pursuits is constructive as cognitive diversity prevents "uniformity of opinion" (ibid 9), which leads toward a blindness of possibilities that occur when differing ways of thinking clash and diverge in new directions. On the other hand, Muldoon examines "an economic approach to the division of cognitive labor" (2013, 118) and warns that although diversity is integral to opening new spaces of knowing, unfortunately, particular reward systems (dictated by discursive formations) often prescribe what epistemic projects count and are deemed important, even worthy. Perhaps one way to place the "rival theories" argument in the context of collaborations is the epistemic project of what counts as literacy. The classroom music teacher may believe that one is not musically literate unless one can read and write Western classical notation. The collaborator, on the other hand, has an epistemological stance that has been constructed by her experiences in free improvisation. She has come to understand that notation is only one way of "knowing" and, more often than not, a Western-centric way of knowing. Perhaps, being "literate" for her has more to do with a collaboration based on deep listening and responding in the moment. These epistemological differences are precisely the moments that offer new ways of considering and constructing heretofore unimagined possibilities for musical literacy. Yet without recognizing the economic discourse and questioning the "who stands to gain, what, and why rewards system," potentially rich and rewarding discussion as to what is literacy in the twenty-first century goes by, and little is done to challenge or interrogate discursive formations that reward a status quo intent on reproducing free market behaviors.

Social Epistemology

Earlier in this chapter the issue of domain specificity of personal epistemology was raised and "how such beliefs might connect to disciplinary beliefs" (Hofer and Pintrich 1997, 89). Although personal epistemology plays a large role in curricular and pedagogical decisions, the point I would now like to explore are those ways personal epistemology is constructed by disciplinary beliefs. Take, for example, the music teacher who believes literacy is connected to note reading and writing. It is most likely that this teacher was raised in the Western classical tradition where repertoire dictates musical decisions, including processes of development and evaluatory criteria. The collaborator, on the other hand, whose personal epistemological beliefs are grounded in her experiences of free improvisation, is not anchored in a discipline defined by singular practices. Her disciplinary beliefs are more likely grounded in broader philosophical views that understand education to be something other than a series of transactions (Biesta 2004).

Psychological models suggest we come to know by engaging with others, by communicating with others. Broncano (2008, 11) expounds on this by differentiating between instrumental knowledge (how to, for instance) and knowledge dependent on "explicit epistemic intentions of transmitting and *sharing* knowledge" (italics added). The former suggests that construction of shared trust for musicians (and by extension music educators) steeped in the Western classical tradition is very much shaped by the musical experiences that come to be valued and replicated through skill development and repertoire. The "normativity" of this creates, as Broncano writes, "epistemic rights and duties to the participants" (ibid 11). Therefore, one cannot be a classical musician, or in the case of our classroom teacher, even a musician, without taking on the obligation to reproduce paradigmatic knowings grounded in the Western classical tradition. In the context of uninterrogated collaborations, rights and duties might result in the reification of particular musics and ways of coming to know how to produce those musics. The latter, on the other hand, suggests a level of shared trust must be involved in embracing and welcoming that which we cannot control or predict. This has little to do with possessing knowledge and everything to do with seeing "learning as a reaction to a disturbance, as an attempt to reorganize or reintegrate as a result of disintegration" (Biesta 2004, 62). And, indeed, it is possible, of course, to challenge the authority of normativity. "Musicians," teachers, students, all collaborators, are epistemic agents; all have the ethical duty to "think what [they] are doing" (Arendt 1958, 5). Unfortunately, too often the rewards, and even punishments (in the discursive guise of accountability), go far in prohibiting and disavowing collaborations that fuel chaotic learning environments in which epistemological "rights" might be reimagined, indeed, improvised.

Final Thoughts

For Arendt, common sense is made in relation with the world. Not the world of music, but the world writ large. Returning to the premise that epistemic responsibility transcends purpose, the pedagogical implications raised by Arendt's thinking in this context are manifold. Indeed, Arendt believes we distinguish ourselves, our distinctness, through speech and action in the plurality (disturbances) of all others. However, Arendt also understood the necessity of thinking alone as the condition under which subjectivity and judgment are made possible. She also warned how easy it is to dismiss the necessary conditions for this space. Collaborations may not be the optimal space for students to contemplate and think alone. Indeed, Duarte suggests these kinds of collaborative models may be "creating conditions of 'nonthinking'" (2001, 202). If we consider the problematic "rights and duties" discussed earlier as reifying a paradigm of replication, then the uncontested authority of collaborations may thwart that which leads students toward independence and emancipation. As Biesta reminds us, "all students can *already* speak" (2010, 549). Rather than simply "learning from each other," recognizing each other as epistemic agents might move us (musicians, teachers, students) to "negotiate[ing] epistemic standards through conversation" (Origgi 2008, 35). These conversations are dependent on a "space of appearance" (Arendt 1958, 200) where we are seen and heard by others. Clearly this is a fragile space, one that is dependent on being willing to forgo epistemological certainty and confront a constructed social epistemology.

It might not always be practical to image collaborations transcending stated or even the unstated purpose of product as tangible proof. Performance of any kind is product; it does not, however, need to be a commodity used in exchange for imagined social capital. The educative space is not contested turf for the emergence of winners and losers. It is a space of responsibility where we are present to all, continually reorganizing what it means to know. Epistemic responsibility moves in multiple directions, not linear, not sequentially. The questions to whom and to what we are responsible force recognition of authority in all its discursive guises. We do well to consider Arendt's "incessant noise" (2005, 262) as that which covers to what we should be attending before embracing collaboration as normative. Epistemological possibilities abound; responsibility resides in our refusal to reinscribe authority.

References

Arendt, Hannah. 1958. *The Human Condition*. Chicago: University of Chicago Press.
Arendt, Hannah. 2005. *The Promise of Politics*. New York: Schocken.
Biesta, Gert. 2004. "Against Learning. Reclaiming a Language for Education in an Age of Learning." *Nordisk Pedagogik*, 23, 54–66.
Biesta, Gert. 2010. "Learner, Student, Speaker: Why It Matters How We Call Those We Teach." *Educational Philosophy and Theory*, 42 (5–6), 540–52.
Broncano, Fernando. 2008. "Trusting Others: The Epistemological Authority of Testimony." *THEORIA.Revista de Teoría, Historia y Fundamentos de la Ciencia*, 23 (1), 11–22.
Code, Lorraine. 2006. *Ecological Thinking: The Politics of Epistemic Location*. New York: Oxford University Press.
Delpit, Lisa. 1995. *Other People's Children: Cultural Conflict in the Classroom*. New York: The New Press.
Duarte, Eduardo M. 2001. "The Eclipse of Thinking: An Arendtian Critique of Cooperative Learning." In *Hannah Arendt and Education, Renewing Our Common World*, edited by Mordechai Gordon, 201–24. Oxford: Westview Press.
Freire, Paulo. 1994. *Pedagogy of Hope*. Translated by Robert R. Barr. New York: Continuum.
Giroux, Henry A. 1984. *Ideology, Culture, and the Process of Schooling*. Philadelphia, PA: Temple University Press.
Gottlieb, Eli, and Mandel Leadership Institute. 2007. "Learning How to Believe: Epistemic Development in Cultural Context." *The Journal of the Learning Sciences*, 16 (1), 5–35.
Gruenewald, David. 2003. "Foundations of Place: A Multidisciplinary Framework for Place-Conscious Education." *American Educational Research Journal*, 40 (3), 619–54.
Higgins, Lee. 2008. "The Creative Music Workshop: Event, Facilitation, Gift." *International Journal of Music Education*, 26 (4), 326–38.
Hofer, Barbara K. 2008. "Personal Epistemology and Culture." In *Knowing, Knowledge and Beliefs: Epistemological Studies Across Diverse Cultures*, edited by Myint Swe Khine, 3–22. Netherlands: Springer.
Hofer, Barbara K., and Paul R. Pintrich. 1997. "The Development of Epistemological Theories: Beliefs About Knowledge and Knowing and Their Relation to Learning." *Review of Educational Research*, 67 (1), 88–140.
Kitcher, Phillip. 1990. "The Division of Cognitive Labor." *The Journal of Philosophy*, 87 (1), 5–22.
Lyotard, Jean Francois, and Jean-Loup Thébaud. 1996. *Just Gaming*. Minneapolis, MN: University of Minnesota Press.
Muldoon, Ryan. 2013. "Diversity and the Division of Cognitive Labor." *Philosophy Compass*, 8 (2), 117–25.
Origgi, Gloria. 2008. "Trust, Authority and Epistemic Responsibility." *Theoria*, 23 (61), 35–44.
Popkewitz, Thomas. 1980. "Global Education as a Slogan System." *Curriculum Inquiry*, 10 (3), 303–16.
Veloso, Ana Luísa, and Sara Carvalho. 2012. "Musical Composition as a Way of Learning: Emotion and the Situated Self." In *Musical Creativity: Insights from Music Education Research*, edited by Oscar Odena, 73–91. Surrey: Ashgate.

Part II
Crossing Boundaries

7

SongPump: Developing a Composing Pedagogy in Finnish Schools Through Collaboration Between Professional Songwriters and Music Teachers[1]

HEIDI PARTTI AND LAURI VÄKEVÄ

Introduction

Based on recent research reports, one could argue that creative music-making activities have not established a central role in Finnish music classrooms. According to the National Assessment of Learning Outcomes in Music (Juntunen 2011), composing is only occasionally taught in Finnish basic education (grades 1–9). In addition, a recent nationwide survey indicates that as much as three out of four music teachers feel that they have not been equipped with adequate tools and skills for teaching composing during their studies (Partti 2016).[2] Facilitating group-based composing and collaborative creativity in heterogeneous classrooms is perceived as especially challenging. Yet previous curriculum documents (e.g. Finnish National Board of Education 1970, 2004), as well as the recently introduced National Core Curriculum for Basic Education (Finnish National Board of Education 2014), indicate that the creative production of music should be taught to all pupils at all grades. The most recent core curriculum further emphasizes creative collaboration as a central learning approach in music, as well as in other school subjects (ibid).

In this chapter, we examine questions related to teaching creative music-making in schools. What could be the role of a professional composer or songwriter in music education? What would the introduction of such professionals into the classrooms require from the teachers? We examine these questions through the case of a recent developmental project that brought professional composers into music classrooms in Finnish comprehensive and upper secondary schools. The project, called BiisiPumppu [SongPump], was organized by the Finnish Composers' Copyright Society (Teosto) during the academic year of 2013–14. In the project, teachers collaborated with professional songwriters, lyricists, musicians, and music producers to instruct pupils in how to create their own pieces of music.[3] The BiisiPumppu project thus exemplifies collaborative efforts between teachers, composers, and schools that may open new avenues for more participatory music education in a variety of musical-aesthetic contexts. Based on a case study conducted by the first author of this chapter, we will discuss themes pertaining to how the project succeeded, how the stakeholders benefited from the effort, and what kinds of development ideas emerged in terms of music pedagogy. We will also address some critical aspects of the project, suggesting ways in which similar initiatives can better take into account the specific characteristics of school music in the future.

Supporting Multiple Creativities

Creativity has been a central concern in the field of music education for decades (e.g. Burnard 2006, 2012; Paynter 1970; Webster 1996, 2002). In addition to the artistic processes and outcomes, creativity can be discussed in terms of learning. From this standpoint, one can learn in more or less creative ways, although the judgment of what can be considered creative in the musical learning process appears to be culturally, specific and contextual.

If we accept Burnard's (2012) view that there is not only one kind of musical creativity but, rather, multiple creativities, we may pay attention to the differences in the ways in which our students create music. Thus, depending on the context, producing musical remixes in the digital domain could be understood as a creative activity as much as writing songs with a guitar or composing with a pen and paper. Moreover, there might not be a clear boundary between musical creativity and creativity in other artistic domains. The digital arts, in particular, tend to support hybrid creativities bridging conventional understandings of what the artworks are and how they should be produced (Hugill 2008; Michielse 2015; Väkevä 2010, 2012). Considering the aforementioned conditions may lead one to question whether it is possible to teach musical creativity in the first place. If we do not settle for psychological explanations for creativity as an individual characteristic lying within the human mind, but instead look for social interaction and mediated activity between an individual and environment as its clues (e.g. Hakkarainen 2013; Kenny 2014; Sawyer 2007), it seems reasonable to expect that teachers can have an impact on how creativity is developed in their pupils. On the one hand, the teacher could be considered a specific conveyer of skills and knowledge who, for instance, instructs her pupils in the craft of songwriting; on the other hand, she could be viewed as a general facilitator of the culture of creativity, aiming to, for example, promote overall attitudes favorable to artistic creation in the classroom (Muhonen 2016). Again, the division seems to be more a matter of perspective than of degree. Furthermore, learning contexts are always composed of a wide variety of situational factors, including the pupil's cultural background, her current interests, the curricular goals relevant for her stage of development, and the teacher's aesthetic preferences. The music teacher's excellence in teaching creativity seems to be dependent on her ability to recognize its different manifestations in diverse domains of musical practices and her aptitude to support these manifestations in educationally relevant contexts.

Composing Pedagogy in Finnish Music Education

Ojala and Väkevä (2013) have observed that there is a historical emphasis on performance-based studies in the Finnish music education system and that composing has been traditionally seen as an art that only a minority of students are expected to be capable of or interested in learning. Although projects have been tailored to advance Finnish composing pedagogy at every level of the educational system (ibid), it appears that Finnish music teachers do not generally get much training in composing pedagogy, regardless of how many years they dedicate to studying music education. Exceptions seem to be based on the teacher's own interest and her willingness to study composing outside the training programs (Partti 2016).

Even if reproductive learning practices are usually associated with classical music studies, the lack of a composing pedagogy in music teacher preparation does not seem to be genre specific. Popular music became an integral part of Finnish classroom music in the 1980s, and popular music styles and genres still play a major role in how Finnish pupils are introduced to music in schools, especially in higher grades (Kallio and Väkevä 2017; Muukkonen 2010; Väkevä 2006; Westerlund 2006). This is also reflected in the music teacher training programs, which frequently offer courses in popular music and popular music pedagogy. Although popular music pedagogy in Finland and elsewhere has emphasized the differences in how popular music and other musical genres are learned (Green 2001, 2008; Rodriguez 2003), it seems that such musics are most often rehearsed for performances utilizing ready-made sources, such as school music textbook arrangements or transcriptions. As Finnish music teachers themselves report (Partti 2016), there is a lack of pre-service and in-service training programs and available resources for creative music-making pedagogy.[4] Yet the National Core Curriculum for Basic Education (Finnish National Board of Education 2014) expects that teachers teach for creative cooperation in musical environments and instructs teachers to support the students' productive efforts as one basis for assessment.

The Case of BiisiPumppu

The BiisiPumppu [SongPump] project was organized by the Finnish Composers' Copyright Society (Teosto), whose primary interest was to draw attention to composing and promote songwriting as a hobby, or even as a career choice, for children and young people. Although the BiisiPumppu project was specifically designed for schools, its main priority was not to develop composing pedagogy, but rather to increase the quantity and quality of Finnish songwriting

(Teosto 2013). In order to inspire new songwriters—the possible future customers of Teosto—the project was designed as a collaborative effort bringing together schools and some of the most eminent Finnish composers.

The BiisiPumppu project took place in twelve schools around Finland during the academic year 2013–14. Schools could apply to participate in the project, which was free of charge for them. Teosto's aim was to choose primary, lower secondary, and upper secondary schools that varied in size and location as well as in curricular aims and expectations. Each school was assigned a pair of professional musicians—most often a lyricist along with a composer. Eighteen professional musicians in total were involved in the project.

The data of this case study consist of individual interviews of eight teachers and four composers who participated in the BiisiPumppu project. The interviews were carried out by the first author between January and March 2015. In addition to the interviews, the data consist of five journals kept by the participating teachers during the BiisiPumppu project.[5] The journals provide an interesting insight into the process and into situations that the teachers had perhaps forgotten by the time of the interviews. The journals were also used to generate interview questions and as a source for stimulated recall interviews. The aim of the data analysis was to investigate questions related to composing pedagogy in schools. The interviews and teacher journals were analyzed by "identifying, analysing, and reporting patterns (themes) within data," as well as interpreting "various aspects of the research topic" (Braun and Clarke 2006, 79). This thematic analysis was partly based on an analysis reported in a book on the project (Partti and Ahola 2016).

In addition to the interviews and journals, plenty of other project-related material was available, such as recordings and notations of the pupils' songs made during the project and newspaper articles and television interviews. This material was not included in the data analysis, but was used to corroborate findings and to introduce new perspectives of interpretation.

Promoting Musical Creativity Through Composer/Teacher Partnerships

BiisiPumppu was designed by Teosto along with a steering group that consisted of music educators and other professionals working in the field. The main purpose was to inspire pupils to create and share their own musical ideas and to encourage and equip teachers to find new ways of introducing composing in music classrooms. The implementation of the project varied significantly due to the participating teachers' different levels of expertise and confidence in teaching creative music-making. In some schools, the composers would lead the activities while the teacher would adopt the role of a supporter (see also Christophersen 2013), who would provide guidance in pupils' creative processes but also actively learn new skills in composing. In other schools, the teacher would have a clearer vision and plan for the project, and the composers would work alongside her by helping pupils to refine their ideas. In each school the teacher and visiting composers would work as a team from the planning stage to the end of the project, and pupils would compose music in groups.

Unlocking the Process of Composing

The twelve schools participating in BiisiPumppu differed from each other not only in size and location, but also in terms of teachers' and pupils' previous experiences in creative music-making. In some classrooms, composing had been a part of music teaching for some time, and the role of the visiting composers was to assist the pupils in developing their creative ideas by providing practical suggestions and advice.

For instance, in one upper secondary school where songwriting had already been an integral part of music teaching, the music teacher designed a songwriting camp which took place on school premises over a weekend. Prior to the weekend, the work had already begun in Finnish-language classes, where a professional lyricist had visited to relate her working methods and to give students guidance. After working on the lyrics for a couple of weeks, the music teacher would pair off the students who had written the lyrics with those who would compose the music. During Saturday and Sunday, the school would be transformed into a large "hit factory" where the lyricist–composer teams would work on their songs with the help of their music teacher and the professional composers.

> We worked from 10am to 6pm on both days. The school was empty, with a number of classrooms available. This allowed us to distribute instruments around the school so that each team could work in their own space. The teams would work on their own for a while, after which [the composers] would wander around to help the teams to further work on their songs. By the end of the first day, every team had produced a demo version of their song, which we would listen to and comment on as a group. Based on the received ideas for development, the work continued on the following day.
>
> (Teacher A)

In other schools the project was the first step taken into the world of creative music-making. In contrast to the schools where pupils were already comfortable with the idea of composing their own songs, and thus ready to be challenged to further develop their ideas, pupils with no prior experience in composing seemed to be surprised, even somewhat anxious, when introduced to the opportunity to produce their own musical thoughts.

A music subject teacher working in a primary school in Eastern Finland recalls doubts expressed by her pupils when she told them about the upcoming project. According to the teacher, the pupils had been worried about not knowing how to make their own songs. It seems that, in the pupils' minds, composing music required a special talent that would allow one to "come up with a hit song in one go" (Teacher B). This kind of reaction was not uncommon among other BiisiPumppu participants. Many teachers had encountered their pupils' reservations, even concerns, in the early days of the project. A journal entry by teachers of a primary school in the metropolitan area of Helsinki illustrates these attitudes:

> Some of the pupils were not that excited [when they heard about the project], because they felt that the content of the project (making one's own songs) was distant and too difficult. One reason for confusion was also related to the fact that songwriting was a completely new and unfamiliar activity for many pupils, something that they did not have any practical knowledge about.
> (School 1 Journal, September 24, 2013)

Soon after the project started, however, the initial worries vanished. The teachers emphasized the importance of meeting "a real professional" (Teacher B) in allowing pupils to get closer to a world that would otherwise seem unattainable. One teacher describes a lesson, during which the visiting lyricist took the students on a step-by-step tour into the anatomy of one of her songs. Although the teacher had already tried to explain to his students that writing a song is a process, the opportunity to witness the progress of a well-known song from early drafts into a completed recording had finally helped to get the message across, "Undoubtedly, the greatest learning outcome was to see that... even professionals need to rework their ideas and make multiple versions [of their songs]" (Teacher A).

In addition to providing a model of "ways of being a composer" (Barrett 2006, 210), the composers seem to have adopted the more general role of a facilitator of creativity by making deliberate efforts to scaffold pupils' composing processes. Composing would often take place in small groups, and sometimes as one big group, where pupils would take the lead in sharing their creative ideas and commenting on those of others. The division of responsibilities between the teacher and composers was determined by the teacher's expertise in composing pedagogy, but also, and importantly, by the visiting composer's confidence in working with young people. Although some composers considered it crucial that the teacher would be in charge (see Webb 2005), others seem to have been more confident in adopting a fluid division of roles. The division of roles also varied according to schools, as one of the composers explains:

> The two primary schools [I visited] significantly differed from each other. In one school, I was mostly an observer while the teacher would direct the activities. This teacher had a very hands-on approach to teaching, and

a strong personality ... While in another school [my colleague] and I had the responsibility to plan and lead the lessons ... We visited three classrooms in that school, a few times each. During the first visit, we would introduce ourselves, our plans for the sessions, and so forth. The next time we would begin by giving the pupils ideas to get started in writing as well as some concrete writing assignments—a kind of raw material to muck around in their collaborative process of making a classroom song, which they all wanted to make. The pupils then kept on working on the lyrics of the song until the next session, during which we [the visitors] participated and helped in composing the song.

(Composer B)

The composer–teacher teams could be understood to have worked as responsive guides (Viilo et al. 2011, 54) who seek to empower and equip pupils to find their own voice through musical explorations and peer support. The need to challenge myths related to what composing is and who can be a composer seemed to be on the agenda of both the teachers and visitors. Each of the interviewed composers emphasized their intent to unlock the process of composing. Although they were often introduced to and perceived by the pupils as "celebrities," they appear to have adopted the role of a facilitator who encourages youngsters to get started and aims to demystify the art of composing. One composer repeatedly mentions the importance of openness and transparency:

I wanted to show the kids how songs are born in reality. I didn't want to go and fiddle with the songs somewhere out-of-sight, but to make them then and there, together. In this way, the kids would see that there was nothing wondrous taking place—but all of a sudden we would have an audible song!

(Composer A)

Another composer recalls telling the pupils that they should not feel discouraged if they struggled in writing songs, as the only way to get better is by practicing. He also highlights the importance of revealing the different stages of recording and producing. According to him, schools would do well if they invited pupils to witness the process of a hit song from its early drafts to the final product, as this kind of understanding would further demystify composing, particularly in the context of popular music.

A Leap into the Unknown

Both the teachers and the composers highlighted the importance of leaving the framework of the project as broad as possible. Pupils were not hurried to come up with songs. The main goal was to provide everyone with an opportunity to experience the process of creating and sharing musical ideas. BiisiPumppu challenged the participants to find their place in a new kind of setting. The pupils were not only rehearsing how to collaborate creatively. The visiting composers also had to find a way to apply their skills in a school context. As for teachers, conducting an open-ended project in collaboration with someone they were not familiar with required open-mindedness and flexibility, as is illustrated in a comment by a classroom teacher working in a southeastern primary school:

> The project forced one to look for creative solutions, as there was no set model available for the teaching ... As a teacher, you needed enough courage to try something that you had not done before. Instead of staying safely in your comfort zone, anything could happen once you set out to compose with the students. It was a leap into the unknown!
>
> (Teacher C)

The teacher continues by pointing out the possibilities offered by the kind of situation in which no one could hold on to familiar templates:

> Maybe this was exactly the feature that made room for creativity and freed both children and adults to invent. Everything could not be planned and considered beforehand. Instead, one had to come up with suitable solutions to different situations ... It looks like the BiisiPumppu project took us to the very core of creativity.
>
> (Teacher C)

Such broad-minded attitudes towards possibilities, opened up by collaboration with the visiting composers, are evident throughout the teachers' stories. Rather than assuming a protective attitude toward their classroom activities or their own expert status, teachers underline the positive potential of receiving composers outside of school contexts. As a music subject teacher working in an upper secondary school states:

> I have worked long enough to know my own limitations. If there is someone who dares and cares to join in, it is not a threat [to my professionalism], but an opportunity, for sure.
>
> (Teacher A)

Although some of the teachers admit to having wondered what the professional composers would think about when they witnessed music-making activities in schools, the pride of one's own pedagogical skills eventually overcame the feelings of nervousness:

> But then I thought: let them [the visiting composers] think whatever they like, this is how we do things here. To me it is really valuable that in

our classroom everybody—not just some specific, chosen group—does something and rehearses playing in a band, for instance. That is something I am proud of and something I wanted to show to the musicians as well.

(Teacher E)

It seems that the participating teachers perceive their professionalism as a social journey that can be shared with other experts, in and out of school. This kind of understanding of the construction of expertise as a learning partnership, rather than merely an individual effort (see Riel and Polin 2004; Wenger 1998), can enable teachers to surpass their previous level of expertise by utilizing each other's expertise as a learning resource.

Discussion

In this chapter, we have explored collaborative efforts between music teachers and professional musicians in promoting musical creativity. Our exploration proceeded through the case study of BiisiPumppu, a Finnish classroom composing pedagogy project. The project raises interesting questions regarding the possibilities and challenges of introducing professional composers to school music lessons. Specifically, it inspires discussion of the variety of roles that music teachers and visiting artists can step into when participating in such projects.

At best, the composers not only provided models of how to create original music, but also contributed in facilitating the creative culture in the school. Yet the need for teachers with a clear vision of educational aims to coordinate the learning environments seems evident (see, e.g. Mota 2014). Regardless of whether the teachers would have a visible role in guiding the composing activities during the composer's visits or not, all of them had been making plans and prepared their pupils weeks prior to the visits. This kind of pedagogical leadership calls for flexibility and resourcefulness from the teacher—inventiveness to fit the visits into busy school days, willingness to work along with other teachers to integrate composing as part of the learning, knowledge of how to team up the pupils in constructive ways, capacity to provide them with encouragement and emotional support for the creative processes in heterogeneous groups, and even commitment to work on weekends to provide access to the premises.

The composers had not been trained as music teachers, and some of them reported feelings of uneasiness in facing the pupils. Thus, it seems that a mutual clarity regarding the respective roles of the collaborators is an imperative in such projects. Projects like BiisiPumppu may offer indispensable opportunities for joint enterprises to advance educational development. However, most often these enterprises take place within such a limited period of time that the growth of learning partnerships seems to be somewhat restricted (Hart et al. 2011; Wenger 1998). The collaborators' ability to work as colleagues

(Wolf 2008) by utilizing each other's expertise and experience as their learning resource thus becomes a central denominator of the successful composer/teacher partnership.

One could ask: How does cooperation with such interest groups as Teosto frame the collaboration between teachers and professional composers? In this project, the focus of composing was on songwriting, which was due to Teosto's interest in supporting the training of future copyright holders. However, according to the National Core Curriculum, Finnish classroom music education should be committed to a wide variety of musical approaches (Finnish National Board of Education 2014). In addition, one can ask whether compulsory education is the appropriate context for music instruction organized along with professional and economic interests, even when the interests are shared by the teacher.

It could also be interesting to compare notions of quality in connection to such projects. Are the criteria for quality drawn from those of the music industry or from the goals of music education—or both? Although BiisiPumppu proves that constructive results can be obtained by pairing music teachers with composers in contexts where the teachers generally lack previous preparation in composing pedagogy, it also raises critical questions about whose criteria should be used when assessing the creative work of the students. Is the quality of a project to be determined on the basis of the musical products? Or should it also be assessed on the basis of the learning process by taking into account the ways a "shared motivation, shared purpose, [and] solidarity based on shared values" (Renshaw 2013, 239) between the participants is facilitated? Perhaps too tight a focus on the creative product implies the danger of guiding the teacher's attention away from the learning process and its creativity, or rather, from the variety of creativities afforded by musical learning processes in different contexts (see also Burnard 2012; Kaschub and Smith 2009; Ojala and Väkevä 2013).

All in all, the BiisiPumppu project indicates that there are a variety of ways to facilitate creativity by introducing composing workshops in schools. While paying attention to the concerns mentioned earlier, a long-term goal could be to introduce such practices to everyday schoolwork, where composers could provide their expertise, but on the conditions established by the curriculum and mediated by the teacher's pedagogical tact.

Notes

1 This research has been undertaken as part of the ArtsEqual project funded by the Academy of Finland's Strategic Research Council from its Equality in Society program (project no. 293199).
2 In Finnish comprehensive schools, music at the primary level (grades 1 to 6) is taught most often by classroom teachers who may or may not have specialized in music during their studies. At the lower secondary school (grades 7 to 9) and upper secondary school (grades 10 to 12) levels, music is usually taught by qualified music subject teachers, who are professional music pedagogues with a master's degree in Music Education. It seems likely that teachers who hold no

formal music teacher qualification especially lack the competencies to support creative music-making. It should also be noted that Finnish municipalities and schools are allowed to write their own individual curricula based on the national core curriculum; thus, there might be differences in emphasis on creative musical production in different regions and schools.

3 The participating musicians referred to themselves by different definitions, including a composer, songwriter, lyricist, and music producer. For the sake of clarity, they are in this chapter referred to as composers.

4 The first national initiative for in-service training in composing pedagogy (SÄPE) was launched at the time of the writing of this chapter in October 2016.

5 The interviews were conducted and the teacher journals written in Finnish. The direct quotations in this chapter were translated into English by the first author.

References

Barrett, Margaret. 2006. "Creative Collaboration: An 'Eminence' Study of Teaching and Learning in Music Composition." *Psychology of Music*, 34 (2), 195–218.
Braun, Virginia, and Victoria Clarke. 2006. "Using Thematic Analysis in Psychology." *Qualitative Research in Psychology*, 3 (2), 77–101.
Burnard, Pamela. 2006. "Reflecting on the Creativity Agenda in Education." *Cambridge Journal of Education*, 36 (3), 313–18.
Burnard, Pamela. 2012. *Musical Creativities in Practice*. Oxford: Oxford University Press.
Christophersen, Catharina. 2013. "Helper, Guard or Mediator? Teachers' Space for Action in The Cultural Rucksack, a Norwegian National Program for Arts and Culture in Schools." *International Journal of Education and the Arts*, 14. Accessed January 16, 2017, www.ijea.org/v14si1/.
Finnish National Board of Education. 1970. *Peruskoulun opetussuunnitelmakomitean mietintö I. Opetussuunnitelman perusteet*. Helsinki: Komiteanmietintö.
Finnish National Board of Education. 2004. *Peruskoulun opetussuunnitelman perusteet*. Helsinki: Opetushallitus.
Finnish National Board of Education. 2014. *Perusopetuksen opetussuunnitelman perusteet*. Helsinki: Opetushallitus.
Green, Lucy. 2001. *How Popular Musicians Learn: A Way Ahead for Music Education*. Hampshire: Ashgate.
Green, Lucy. 2008. *Music, Informal Learning and the School: A New Classroom Pedagogy*. Aldershot: Ashgate.
Hakkarainen, Kai. 2013. "Mapping the Research Ground: Expertise, Collective Creativity and Shared Knowledge Practices." In *Collaborative Learning in Higher Music Education*, edited by Helena Gaunt and Heidi Westerlund, 13–26. Surrey: Ashgate.
Hart, Angie, Alex Ntung, Juliet Millican, Ceri Davies, Etienne Wenger, Howard Rosing, and Jenny Pearce. 2011. *Community—University Partnerships Through Communities of Practice*. Brighton: Connected Communities. Accessed February 2, 2017, http://eprints.brighton.ac.uk/14336/1/UoB%20CC%20discussion%20paper.pdf
Hugill, Andrew. 2008. *The Digital Musician*. New York: Routledge.
Juntunen, Marja-Leena. 2011. "Musiikki." In *Perusopetuksen musiikin, kuvataiteen ja käsityön oppimistulosten arviointi 9. Vuosiluokalla*, edited by Sirkka Laitinen, Antti Hilmola, and Marja-Leena Juntunen, 36–94. Helsinki: Opetushallitus.
Kallio, Alexis A., and Lauri Väkevä. 2017. "Inclusive Music Education?" In *Popular Music in the Nordic Countries: Transnational Dynamics in the Early 21st Century*, edited by Antti-Ville Kärjä and Fabian Holt. Oxford: Oxford University Press.
Kaschub, Michele, and Janice Smith. 2009. *Minds on Music: Composition for Creative and Critical Thinking*. Lanham, MD: Rowman & Littlefield.
Kenny, Ailbhe. 2014. "Sound Connections for Institutional Practice: Cultivating 'Collaborative Creativity' Through Group Composition". In *Developing Creativities in Higher Music Education: International Perspectives and Practices*, edited by Pamela Burnard, 469–93. Oxford: Routledge.
Michielse, Maarten. 2015. "Remix, Cover, Mash: Remediating Phonographic-Oral Practice Online." PhD diss., Maastricht University.
Mota, Graca. 2014. "Thorns and Joys in Creative Collaboration: A Project with Music Education and Visual Arts Students." In *Collaborative Creative Thought and Practice in Music*, edited by Margaret S. Barrett, 221–38. Surrey: Ashgate.

Muhonen, Sari. 2016. "Songcrafting Practice: A Teacher Inquiry into the Potential to Support Collaborative Creation and Creative Agency Within School Music Education." PhD diss., Sibelius Academy, Studia Musica 67, Helsinki.
Muukkonen, Minna. 2010. "Monipuolisuuden eetos: Musiikin aineenopettajat artikuloimassa työnsä käytäntöjä." PhD diss., Sibelius-Akatemia, Studia Musica 42.
Ojala, Juha, and Lauri Väkevä. 2013. "Säveltäminen luovana ja merkityksellisenä toimintana." In *Säveltäjäksi kasvattaminen: Pedagogisia näkökulmia musiikin luovaan tekijyyteen*, edited by Juha Ojala and Lauri Väkevä, 10–22. Helsinki: Opetushallitus.
Partti, Heidi. 2016. "Muuttuva muusikkous koulun musiikinopetuksessa." *The Finnish Journal of Music Education*, 19 (1), 8–28.
Partti, Heidi, and Anu Ahola. 2016. *Säveltäjyyden jäljillä: Musiikintekijät tulevaisuuden koulussa.* Helsinki: Sibelius-Akatemia.
Paynter, John. 1970. *Sound and Silence: Classroom Projects in Creative Music (Resources of Music).* Cambridge: Cambridge University Press.
Renshaw, Peter. 2013. "Collaborative Learning: A Catalyst for Organizational Development in Higher Music Education." In *Collaborative Learning in Higher Music Education*, edited by Helena Gaunt and Heidi Westerlund, 237–46. Surrey: Ashgate.
Riel, Margaret, and Linda Polin. 2004. "Online Learning Communities: Common Ground and Critical Differences in Designing Technical Environments." In *Designing for Virtual Communities in the Service of Learning*, edited by Sasha Barab, Rob Kling, and James H. Gray, 16–50. New York: Cambridge University Press.
Rodriguez, Carlos Xavier, ed. 2003. *Bridging the Gap: Popular Music and Music Education.* Reston: MENC.
Sawyer, Keith. 2007. *Group Genius: The Creative Power of Collaboration.* New York: Basic Books.
Teosto. 2013. "Koulujen BiisiPumppu -pilottiprojekti: projektisuunnitelma." An unpublished project plan of the BiisiPumppu project, October 22.
Väkevä, Lauri. 2006. "Teaching Popular Music in Finland: What's Up, What's Ahead?" *International Journal of Music Education*, 24 (2), 126–31.
Väkevä, Lauri. 2010. "Garage Band or GarageBand®? Remixing Musical Futures." *British Journal of Music Education*, 27 (1), 59–70.
Väkevä, Lauri. 2012. "Digital Artistry and Mediation: (Re)mixing Music Education." *National Society for the Study of Education*, 111 (1), 177–95.
Viilo, Marjut, Pirita Seitamaa-Hakkarainen, and Kari Hakkarainen. 2011. "Supporting the Technology-Enhanced Collaborative Inquiry and Design Project: A Teacher's Reflections on Practices." *Teachers and Teaching: Theory and Practice*, 17 (1), 51–72.
Webb, Rosemary. 2005. "Leading Teaching and Learning in the Primary School: From 'Educative Leadership' to 'Pedagogical Leadership.'" *Educational Management Administration and Leadership*, 33 (1), 69–91.
Webster, Peter. 1996. "Creativity as Creative Thinking." In *Teaching Music*, edited by Gary Spruce, 81–91. London: Routledge.
Webster, Peter. 2002. "Creative Thinking in Music: Advancing a Model." In *Creativity and Music Education*, edited by Timothy Sullivan and Lee Willingham, 16–34. Toronto: Canadian Music Educators' Association.
Wenger, Etienne. 1998. *Communities of Practice: Learning, Meaning, and Identity.* Cambridge: Cambridge University Press.
Westerlund, Heidi. 2006. "Garage Rock Bands: A Future Model for Developing Musical Expertise?" *International Journal of Music Education*, 24 (2), 119–25.
Wolf, Shelby A. 2008. "The Mysteries of Creative Partnerships." *Journal of Teacher Education*, 59 (1), 89–102.

8
Teaching Cantonese Opera in Hong Kong Schools: Interaction and Collaboration Between Music Teachers and Artists

BO-WAH LEUNG

Background

Since 1997 when Hong Kong was returned to China, how to create a Chinese national identity has been an issue in the field of school education in Hong Kong. Including Cantonese opera in the school-based music curriculum in Hong Kong schools has been encouraged for more than a decade to promote Chinese and local culture (Curriculum Development Council 2003; Curriculum Development Council and Hong Kong Examination and Assessment Authority 2007). However, research reveals that teachers are lacking in both confidence and competence in teaching such a genre due to their frame of mind, developed from their Western-music orientation (Leung 2014). Most music teacher education programs in Hong Kong traditionally focus on teaching Western music and Chinese music is rarely mentioned (Leung 2015). Under such circumstances, the author initiated a government-granted project to link up music teachers with professional artists of Cantonese opera to coteach in music classes. Based on observations and interviews, this chapter reports the different roles taken by music teachers and artists and four kinds of collaboration modes undertaken by the participants. I will discuss the relevant issues related to teacher–artist collaboration in a broad sense so that the findings of this specific study not only relate to a specific context of teaching and learning, but also relate to overall challenges of such collaboration to provoke further research and discussion.

Teaching Cantonese Opera in Schools

Cantonese opera is one of the approximately 400 Chinese opera genres that is popular in south China. Due to the wide global audience, Cantonese opera has been included in the Intangible Cultural Heritage list of UNESCO in 2009. Cantonese opera requires artists to be competent in singing, reciting, acting, movement, and martial arts in order to perform the integrated arts on stage

(Chan 1991; Ng 2015). Because Cantonese opera contains strong Chinese cultural and philosophical ideology, it is considered that teaching Cantonese opera in schools would be effective in nurturing Chinese culture among Hong Kong students (Ng et al. 2009; Ng et al. 2010).

Cantonese opera has been identified as a core element of the school music curriculum by the Education Bureau. In 2003 the official music curriculum guide of Hong Kong was published to provide a guideline for school music teachers to design their school-based music curriculum. Music teachers are encouraged to include Cantonese opera as a Chinese opera genre in their music curriculum (e.g. see Tang and Leung 2012). Furthermore, the new Hong Kong Diploma of Education Examination (HKDSE) was introduced in 2012 as a public examination for all senior secondary school graduates to enter into the university. In this examination, music is one of the electives that candidates may select (Leung 2015). The music examination possesses three compulsory papers and one elective paper. As a compulsory paper, paper one—Listening—requires all candidates to respond to questions about Classical music, Chinese instrumental music, Cantopop music, and Cantonese operatic music. In summary, Cantonese opera has been included as a core element of Chinese music that should be taught in both primary and secondary schools.

Teaching Cantonese opera in schools may imply some issues with regard to the learning motivation of students. Leung and Leung (2010) investigated the learning motivation of both primary and secondary students using a questionnaire survey based on the self-efficacy theory (Bandura 1995, 1997) and expectancy-value theory (Wigfield and Eccles 2000). The questionnaire survey was done twice, before and after eight weeks of teacher–artist collaborative teaching in Cantonese opera in schools. Furthermore, semi-structured interviews with teachers and focus group interviews with students were used to further understand how students perceive the learning of Cantonese opera. A total of 354 primary students and 342 junior secondary students responded to the questionnaires. Findings reveal that after learning, primary students had significantly increased their self-efficacy, expectancy, intrinsic value, attainment value, and perceived difficulty, whereas secondary students had significantly increased their perceived difficulty. Interviews with both students and teachers reveal that primary students tend to be more receptive because they have no previous stereotype of the genre, whereas secondary students tend not to prefer Cantonese opera due to their social identity perhaps conflicting with the traditional image of the genre.

Researching Partnership Teaching of Cantonese Opera

Supported by the Quality Education Fund of the Education Bureau, the author implemented a three-year project on collaborative teaching of Cantonese opera with local artists and school music teachers from 2009 to 2012 (Leung 2013). This chapter reports part of the findings of this study as the foundation for further discussion of teacher–artist collaboration. A total of 54 primary and secondary schools, 180 school music teachers, 12 Cantonese opera artists, and more than 6,000 students participated in this project. During the project the author visited most of the schools to observe class teaching and to conduct interviews with the artists and teachers. The objectives of this project were to:

1. Develop students' skills in singing, reciting, and movement of Cantonese opera
2. Develop students' competence of performing and appraising Cantonese opera
3. Raise the learning motivation and interest of students in Cantonese opera
4. Develop students' national identity through understanding the genre and Chinese culture

In this project the learning content was developed collaboratively by the artists and teachers. In general, most of the participating schools included the following:

1. Singing and reciting: Artists and/or teachers designed learning tasks of singing and speeches in Cantonese opera.
2. Virtual movement: Artists and/or teachers selected movement from daily life for learning.
3. Fighting: Students learned dancelike fighting with spears and swords.
4. Demonstration: Teachers and artists demonstrated all of the first three tasks during classes for students' experience and understanding.

The author employed a nonparticipant observation method (Smart, Peggs and Burridge 2013) by sitting at the back of the classrooms and taking video recordings. After recording the author repeatedly reviewed the video recordings to identify characteristics of teaching and learning behaviors between the artist and the teacher. Before teaching, the school music teacher connected with the artist in order to collaboratively develop the teaching scheme and plan. Teachers also undertook eighteen hours of Cantonese opera workshops in knowledge, theories, singing, and reciting skills of Cantonese opera before the implementation of the project. The workshops equipped the teachers with a basic understanding of Cantonese opera in order to strengthen their confidence and motivation for learning and teaching the genre.

Roles of Teachers and Artists

After reviewing the observation notes and video recording clips, roles and modes of collaboration, as well as the roles of artists and teachers during the collaborative teaching, are identified (Leung 2013). There were five roles for teachers in the classroom within the partnership mode. First, the music teacher was the director of teaching content. Although the artist knew about Cantonese opera much more than the teacher, the teacher had to fulfill his or her duty to select appropriate content for students, to establish appropriate learning goals, to arrange the content into different lessons, and to design and document the teaching and learning through teaching plans and schemes. Furthermore, the teacher acted as an administrator by communicating with and inviting the artist to school for a meeting and to complete the teaching design. Within this task, the teacher was the core member, whereas the artist appeared to be passive, providing only professional recommendations to assist the teacher to complete the task.

The findings also point to another major role of the teacher, namely, to manage the classroom. The teacher had to observe the students' behavior and consider their learning motivation in order to keep the class in a positive learning atmosphere so that the artist might focus on teaching. In addition, the teacher had to ensure the planned content was completed within the class time with appropriate pacing. He or she might have had to communicate with the artist in order to speed up the pace. The third role that the teacher undertook was the director of the class. Because teachers were more experienced in delivering learning content and pedagogical discourse than the artists, they often took the lead to address issues with content. Fourth, teachers undertook the responsibility of encouraging students to learn. Because the teacher might not have been familiar with the learning content, sometimes she or he might have learned with the students and provided a positive atmosphere to encourage students to learn. Finally, the teacher sometimes supplemented the artists' teaching. When the artist was not capable of providing a detailed and understandable verbal explanation, the teacher would take a "translator's role" to interpret what the artist has said.

There are three different roles that the artists may undertake during collaborative teaching as identified in this research. First, the artist acted as a professional artist in class who assisted the teachers to teach the genre. She or he often demonstrated as a supplement to the teacher's verbal explanations and descriptions. In addition, when the teacher did not provide sufficient and accurate description of knowledge, the artist supplemented for the teacher. Second, sometimes the artist might direct the class in transmitting knowledge and skills. When the teacher was not confident enough in teaching the genre, the artist always had to undertake a more directed role in initiating the whole lesson. Finally, the artist also acted as a partner in the teaching collaboration with a more equal contribution in teaching. She or he might respond to the teacher's request and provide all kinds of support during class.

Four Teacher–Artist Collaborative Modes

As observed, four teacher–artist collaborative modes in teaching Cantonese opera in school were identified (Leung 2013). The first one was titled "teacher-centered with artist as assistant." This was the most common mode.

The teacher was responsible for delivering the teaching and learning content through PowerPoint presentations, "chalk and talk," and audio-video recording presentations. The teacher proactively explained the concepts and knowledge about the genre and normally started and ended the lessons. The artist undertook the role of assisting the teacher, who sat aside waiting for the teacher's request for help and demonstration. She or he might provide necessary supplementary knowledge and demonstrate singing and instrument playing when necessary. Sometimes she or he might have to make revisions or correct the teacher's inaccurate descriptions about Cantonese opera. Vignette 1 demonstrates a scene with such a teaching mode as an example:

Vignette 1

It is a Primary Four class. The teacher is teaching the class to sing a piece of Cantonese operatic song. The teacher shows the lyrics with the rhythm symbols and teaches the students to count each of the four beats with specific hand signs while singing. When the class is singing, the artist walks close to individual students and reminds some of them to sit straight and pay attention to the lower abdomen in order to maintain proper breathing. She walks to a student who sings out of tune and points to her own ear in order to remind the student to listen closely to himself when singing because the student sounds out of tune.

"Artist-centered with teacher as assistant" is the second mode. In this mode the artist was the center of the class while the teacher acted as a teaching assistant. Because the artist is generally strong in skills, whereas the teacher might be knowledgeable rather than skillful in the art form, when teaching some skills to the class rather than appraising and providing conceptual understanding, it was more likely that the artist took the initiative to teach. She or he might employ the learning and teaching approaches from their own learning experiences in teaching and demonstrating. The artist might also plan the teaching and learning activities that they believe to be effective. In such a mode the teacher acted as a class monitor and assisted the artist to teach. Vignette 2 is another example:

Vignette 2

The artist starts the class by inviting six Primary Five students to learn how to play the spear. She stood before the students and demonstrates the movement of her hands in order to brandish the spear. She first holds the spear with her left hand and brandishes, then stops and requests the students to imitate. When the students complete this movement, the artist holds the spear with her right hand to brandish again and stops. Again, she requests the students to imitate, and the students do. The artist repeats this procedure twice and requests the students to practice the movement by themselves repeatedly. She then goes to observe each and every student closely and provides guidance. When she finds a student who could not complete the movement smoothly, she teaches her again. The music teacher is sitting aside and observes the teaching process.

The third mode was named "collaborative mode with parallel participation." In this mode the teacher and the artist collaboratively discuss different issues of Cantonese opera. For example, when teaching the percussion patterns, some students were invited to practice on the instruments. The teacher could not simultaneously teach all the students to play the instruments; thus the artist helped to teach the students. Vignette 3 is an example:

Vignette 3

In a Primary Four classroom, the artist invites three students to come out to learn to play a specific percussion pattern, which is to accompany a specific singing excerpt. The three students are holding a pair of small cymbals, a gong, and two woodblocks. When the artist talks to these three students, the teacher talks to the whole class about the instruments and encourages the class to pay attention to those three students playing percussion. Afterwards, the teacher asks the whole class to recite the rhythmic pattern. Right after the recitation, the three students play the rhythmic pattern to echo the whole class. The music teacher comments that two of the three students were not playing accurately and asks them to play again.

The final mode of collaborative teaching was the "teacher-as-student mode." This was the least common but most interesting mode amongst all videotaped classes. In such a mode the teacher learns with the students, without providing any instruction to the class. When the teacher was lacking knowledge in some specific topics and the teacher was highly motivated, she or he would learn with the students in order to show his or her learning passion to encourage students to learn. This mode was usually employed in teaching some movements that the students may find difficult to learn. When the learning task was difficult, this mode was the most encouraging. Vignette 4 provides an example:

Vignette 4

The classroom is a dance room with a Primary Five class. The teacher starts with a short speech telling students that they are going to learn a set of movements accompanying singing in a Cantonese opera setting. The artist, teacher and all students are standing; all of them are wearing a pair of long sleeves, which is a necessary costume for the movements. There is a big mirror on one side of the dance room. The artist and the teacher stand in front of the class and they all face the mirror. The artist starts to demonstrate the movements with verbal explanation. During the explanation the teacher imitates the movements of the artist while all students are listening to the artist. There is accompanying music playing; the artist does the movement and sings with the music. The teacher also sings to the music accompaniment while moving. After the demonstration of the whole set of movements, the artist requests the class to do the movement simultaneously with the artist. Afterwards the artist requests the students to get into groups of two and repeat the movement by watching each other's movements. The artist and the teacher then sing the song to accompany students' movements.

Reflection and Challenges

To a certain extent, this project has achieved success. Some of the music teachers in Hong Kong have started to encounter Cantonese opera through their own learning experiences as well as teaching collaboratively with artists. Some of the participating teachers have changed their perception and preference towards Cantonese opera. It was evident that some teachers in the same study changed their personal attitude and frame of mind that learning and teaching Cantonese opera was boring and difficult (Leung 2014). As reported, some of them even learned the genre with the students during class. This indicates that the direct interaction with the genre and the artist brings teachers new challenges and stimulation, which may refresh their artistic and teaching lives. As artists and teachers work together, both influence each other and shape each other's experiences, teaching, and artistic practices. Learning is not unidirectional, moving from artists to teachers, or even from teachers to artists; the participating artists have also expanded their perspective in terms of teaching (Catterall and Waldorf 1999; Kenny and Morrissey 2016; Kind et al. 2007). Some of the artists were also involved in teaching Cantonese opera in cocurricular activities offered in schools. However, the students were limited to those who were highly motivated, but the main aim was to train future artists through the training of skills. Music lessons in the school curriculum are in a different context with an overall educational aim of expanding students' musical experience in general education (Bowman 2012). Some artists have started to reconsider that introducing Cantonese opera in school is actually an advocative activity that may nurture future audiences. In this sense, the collaboration between teacher and artist is successful.

Although the project seems to be successful in introducing Cantonese opera as a local Chinese traditional art form to schools, how to sustain the teaching and learning of Cantonese opera in schools remains a question. There is no continuous funding from the government to support such collaboration. Without the assistance of the artists, most music teachers may go back to their own comfort zone and focus on Western music. Sustainability is a major problem, which is shared by other studies such as Hanley (2003). This could happen in not only the case of teaching and learning Cantonese opera in Hong Kong, but also other art forms in other regions. In order to provide a solution to the problem, an understanding of the shortfalls of teacher–artist collaboration is necessary. The following discussion is raised from the current study, but the issues may be found in other art forms in other regions.

Some teachers may rely totally on the artist in teaching, designing, and preparing teaching materials and regard the artist as a "temporary teaching assistant." This is a common problem that happens in those schools where the teachers do not value the educational significance of teaching the arts in schools. Some teachers may miss the opportunity to learn the genre with the artist. They merely regard the opportunity as an occasional offer by external organizations or by the government. During the whole process, they have not developed a new concept about the music genre or a reflection on the issue of reviewing and updating the content of a school music curriculum. Those teachers tend not to make changes in their professional careers. In such cases, the aims cannot be achieved.

On the other hand, the participating artists may find difficulties with pedagogy because they are inexperienced in delivering teaching in a classroom context. "Teaching artist" is a concept found in some developed countries where artists focus on teaching alongside their rich experience in art making (e.g. see Risner and Anderson 2014). How to develop artists' knowledge and skills in pedagogy is another main issue. As observed in the classes in this study, it seems that most artists are not capable of managing the classroom. They tend to employ traditional teaching practices applied by their former teachers rather than considering modern pedagogy. According to a study in the United States, teaching artists in dance and theater tend to receive sufficient training in their subject but insufficient training in arts education pedagogy (Anderson and Risner 2012), whereas some teaching artists have undertaken pedagogy courses to enhance their competence in teaching (Saraniero 2009). Teaching artists should develop curriculum planning skills, professional development skills, and an ability to collaborate with teachers and other artists in order to become "master teaching artists" who are capable of teaching students, teachers, and other adults and mentoring other artists (Shepherd 2007). In general, teaching artists do not have a formal pathway in their professional development in teaching. They have to explore different channels provided by the community and/or the government. This relies on how much the government or community values the notion of hiring teaching artists in schools.

With collaborative teaching between teachers and artists, students' perception towards the identity of the teacher and the artist may be confused. The study reveals that students tend to prefer the artists to the teachers in teaching. On the other hand, artists tend to treat the students on a more equal status rather than in a formal student–teacher relationship (Burnard and Swann 2010). Consequently, students tend to regard the artist as a "friend" rather than a "teacher." According to my observations of teaching in those participating schools, the relationship between students and artist in the classroom seems to be rather friendly. In Hong Kong, school education is affected, to a certain extent, by Chinese culture, which appreciates and expects students to obey the teacher. It is common to see that teachers in Hong Kong have to develop a sense of authority in the classroom in order to maintain good classroom management and win the students' respect and collaboration. In such circumstances, school music teachers may be situated in an unfavorable position in that students might prefer the artist's teaching where they may allow them to walk and talk freely during class time.

Traditionally, in Hong Kong, the music teacher enjoys high status and a good image as "artist" in the class, especially when the teacher is regarded as a skillful artist. When the artist enters the classroom with highly relevant artistry and skills, the students may find the teacher comparably inferior in terms of artistry. This is reasonable because the profession of arts education in schools requires diverse knowledge and skills, such as professional knowledge of education, including cultural, political, empirical, pragmatic, and conceptual knowledge (Burnard 2013) and artistic knowledge (Stephens 2013), whereas teachers' specific artistry and art making might not be comparable to professional artists. However, young students may not understand such a discrepancy; as a result of the teaching collaboration, they may underrate their teachers and prefer the teaching artists in class. This is a concern that school arts teachers might have, which hinders the involvement of teaching artists in school arts education. According to Vitale (2015), music teachers with competence in music performance have received a high level of respect from students, colleagues, parents, and even administration in schools. Music teachers might need to therefore continuously develop their artistry in order to earn the respect of students.

Music skills and knowledge of school music teachers have remained an issue for school music education and teacher education. It is evident that generalists are not competent and confident enough in teaching music because they lack specialized music knowledge and skills (Holden and Button 2006). In Hong Kong, although most music teachers are "specialists," apparently they are not competent and confident in teaching Cantonese opera due to their Western music–focused teacher education (Leung 2015). These teachers might even tend to regard those artists as temporary teachers and assistants who come to help release them from part of their teaching job. At this point, professional development of teachers is critical. In Hong Kong, most of the music teacher education programs tend to focus on Western music and Chinese music has been marginalized (Leung 2014). However, music teachers may change their musical preference from Western music to Chinese music when they are immersed in learning and teaching the genre with increased understanding and experience (Leung 2014). Thus, pre-service music teacher education programs need to further strengthen music teachers' knowledge and skills in the relevant areas so that they need not rely totally on the artists in classroom teaching. On the other hand, ample opportunities should be offered to in-service teachers for their continuous needs in learning a higher level of artistry to cope with the challenges.

In conclusion, to sustain teaching and learning of the arts in schools, totally relying on the teacher–artist collaboration is not feasible. The government should communicate well with the teacher education institutions in formulating the expectation of teaching and learning of the genre. Teacher education programs should ensure that teachers are able to perform and make art, demonstrate an understanding of the historical and cultural background of different genres, develop an appropriate attitude and value system toward the different art forms, reflect on transmitting local culture through teaching and learning arts in schools, and reflect on teacher attitudes. In-service teacher training should be continuously offered for teachers' professional development, and the government is responsible for facilitating all school teachers in pursuing these programs. Teacher–artist collaboration in teaching might be merely a transitional measure for a sustainable future.

References

Anderson, Mary Elizabeth, and Doug Risner. 2012. "A Survey of Teaching Artists in Dance and Theater: Implications for Preparation, Curriculum, and Professional Degree Programs." *Arts Education Policy Review*, 113, 1–16.

Bandura, Albert. 1995. *Self-Efficacy in Changing Society*. Cambridge: Cambridge University Press.

Bandura, Albert. 1997. *Self-Efficacy: The Exercise of Control*. New York: W. H. Freeman.

Bowman, Wayne. 2012. "Music's Place in Education." In *The Oxford Handbook of Music Education*, Vol. 1, edited by Gary McPherson and Graham F. Welch, 21–39. New York: Oxford University Press.

Burnard, Pamela. 2013. "Introduction: The Context for Professional Knowledge in Music Teacher Education." In *Professional Knowledge in Music Teacher Education*, edited by Eva Georgii-Hemming, Pamela Burnard, and Sven-Erik Holgersen, 1–15. Surrey: Ashgate.

Burnard, Pamela, and Mandy Swann. 2010. "Pupil Perceptions of Learning with Artists: A New Order of Experience?" *Thinking Skills and Creativity*, 5, 70–82.

Catterall, James, and Lynn Waldorf. 1999. "Chicago Arts Partnerships in Education: Summary Evaluation." In *Champions of Change: The Impact of the Arts on Learning*, edited by Edward Fiske, 47–62. Accessed March 23, 2017, http://artsedge.kennedy-center.org/champions/pdfs/champsreport.pdf

Chan, Sau Yan. 1991. *Improvisation in a Ritual Context: The Music of Cantonese Opera*. Hong Kong: The Chinese University Press.

Curriculum Development Council. 2003. *Arts Education Key Learning Area: Music Curriculum Guide (Primary 1—Secondary 3)*. Hong Kong: Curriculum Development Council.

Curriculum Development Council and Hong Kong Examinations and Assessment Authority. 2007. *Music Curriculum and Assessment Guide (Secondary 4–6)*. Hong Kong: Curriculum Development Council and Hong Kong Examinations and Assessment Authority.

Hanley, Betty. 2003. "The Good, the Bad, and the Ugly—Arts Partnership in Canadian Elementary Schools." *Arts Education Policy Review*, 104 (6), 11–20.

Holden, Hilary, and Stuart Button. 2006. "The Teaching of Music in the Primary School by the Non-Music Specialist." *British Journal of Music Education*, 23 (1), 23–38. doi: http://dx.doi.org/10.1017/S0265051705006728

Kenny, Ailbhe, and Dorothy Morrissey. 2016. *Exploring Teacher-Artist Partnership as a Model of CPD for Supporting and Enhancing Arts Education in Ireland*. Dublin: Association of Teachers/Education Centres in Ireland, Department of Education and Skills, Department of Arts, Heritage and Gaeltacht.

Kind, Sylvia, Alex de Coss, Rita L. Irwin, and Kit Grauer. 2007. "Artist-Teacher Partnership in Learning: The In/Between Spaces of Artist-Teacher Professional Development." *Canadian Journal of Education*, 30 (3), 839–64.

Leung, Bo-Wah. 2013. "Xianggang Zhongxiaoxue Yueju Jiaoxue Yanjiu: Jiaoshi he Yiren xiezuo he Hudong [Research of Teaching Cantonese Opera in Hong Kong Primary and Secondary Schools: Collaboration and Interaction of Teachers and Artists]." In *Jingyan Yibai Nian: Jinian Ren Jian-hui Nushi Bainian Danchen Yueju Yishu Guoji Yantaohui Lunwenji 2013* [Stunning for 100 Years: In Memory of the Hundred Years of Birth of Madam Run Jian-hui Cantonese Opera International Conference Proceedings 2013], edited by Siu-hon Wong, 770–80. Hong Kong: Chunghua Book Shop.

Leung, Bo-Wah. 2014. "Teachers' Transformation as Learning: Teaching Cantonese Opera in Hong Kong Schools with a Teacher-Artist Partnership." *International Journal of Music Education*, 32 (1), 119–31. doi: 10.1177/0255761413491174.

Leung, Bo-Wah. 2015. "Becoming Music Teachers in Hong Kong: Challenges and Opportunities." In *The Preparation of Music Teachers: A Global Perspective*, edited by Sérgio Figueiredo, José Soares, and Regina F. Schambeck, 315–43. Porto Alegre, Brazil: The National Association of Research and Post Graduate Studies in Music. www.anppom.com.br/publicacoes/selo-pmb

Leung, Bo-Wah, and Eddie C. K. Leung. 2010. "Teacher-Artist Partnership in Teaching Cantonese Opera in Hong Kong Schools: Student Transformation." *International Journal of Education and the Arts*, 11 (5). www.ijea.org/v11n5/

Ng, Wing Chung. 2015. *The Rise of Cantonese Opera*. Urbana, Chicago, IL and Springfield: University of Illinois Press.

Ng, Fung Ping Dorothy, Ling-sung Albert Chung, and Wai-ip Joseph Lam. 2009. "A Curriculum Development and Strategies of Integrating Cantonese Opera in Chinese Language Education in Hong Kong." *The International Journal of Learning*, 15 (12), 59–66.

Ng, Fung Ping Dorothy, Wai-ip Joseph Lam, and Kai-kwong Choi. 2010. "The Application of Free Web Tools to E-learning Platforms for Integrating Cantonese Opera into Hong Kong Chinese Language Education in the Era of Web 2.0." *The International Journal of Learning*, 16 (12), 67–85.

Risner, Douglas S., and Mary E. Anderson. 2014. *Hybrid Lives of Teaching Artists in Dance and Theatre Arts: A Critical Reader*. Amherst, NY: Cambria Press.

Saraniero, Patti. 2009. "Training and Preparation of Teaching Artists." *Teaching Artist Journal*, 7 (4), 236–43.

Shepherd, Barbara. 2007. "The First Teaching Artist Fellowship at Montalvo Arts Center: Identifying the Qualities of Master Teaching Artists." *Teaching Artist Journal*, 5 (4), 253–9.

Smart, Barry, Kay Peggs, and Joseph Burridge. 2013. *Observation Methods*. London: Sage.

Stephens, Jonathan. 2013. "Artistic Knowledge in Practice." In *Professional Knowledge in Music Teacher Education*, edited by Eva Georgii-Hemming, Pamela Burnard, and Sven-Erik Holgersen, 73–96. Surrey: Ashgate.

Tang, Chiu Lung, and Bo-Wah Leung. 2012. "Applying the Variation Theory in Teaching Cantonese Opera (Yueju) to Improve Learning Effectiveness." *International Journal for Lesson and Learning Studies*, 1 (3), 261–75.

Vitale, John L. 2015. "Attitudes and Perspectives of Teacher Performers on Pedagogy and Perceived Student Learning in the Elementary and Secondary School Music Classroom." *Canadian Journal of Education*, 38 (1), 1–27.

Wigfield, Allan, and Jacquelynne S. Eccles. 2000. "Expectancy-Value Theory of Achievement Motivation." *Contemporary Educational Psychology*, 25 (1), 68–81.

9
Intending to Leave a Deep Impression: Challenges of the Performance Event in Schools

CECILIA K. HULTBERG

Introduction

This chapter deals with conditions for presenting professional performances to secondary school audiences in settings they are requested to attend. At stake are settings where teachers and students meet visiting artists on the day they present a performance with music that students usually do not listen to. The discussion concerns approaches that may facilitate musicians and teachers to interact in ways that offer students opportunities to have moving experiences with the music. The chapter draws on a case study with two Swedish musicians and a teacher, all of them experienced in this field.

Contextual Background

In Sweden, music is a subject in the compulsory "grundskolan" (nine grades, age six/seven to fifteen/sixteen), approximately corresponding to primary school (grades one to six) and lower secondary school (grades seven to nine). The curriculum highlights music-making and listening; students' active participation in class ensembles is highly prioritized, which mainly implies performing popular music, especially in grades seven to nine. In these classes, music also includes discussions of music's expression in various contexts and reflection on ethnic/gender issues. In upper secondary schools (age fifteen/sixteen to eighteen/nineteen), music is voluntary; some schools provide programs with music profiles (Skolverket 2011).

The performance events addressed here are administered by regional distributers offering schools selections of performances with professional artists. Highly respected cultural organizations subsidize the events, which may give rise to the impression that these are imposed on schools, as found in Norway (Christophersen 2013; Holdhus and Espeland 2013), where the conditions resemble those in Sweden. Teachers, many of whom are interested in participating, may need to take on roles as educational guides facilitating a dialogue between musicians and students (Christophersen 2013) or refrain from participating, regarding musicians as a replacement for them (Kenny 2010, 163). The latter leaves students without expert pedagogic guidance, for which there is a great need, especially if musicians apply a strictly framing work-oriented approach in concert settings that leave aside students' and teachers' experiences and provide little space for active participation, as found by Holdhus (2015, 299).

The challenges at stake in this chapter concern adolescents, young persons in a turbulent period of life, in which they distance themselves from childhood and "create" themselves (Drotner, 1996). In this process their creation of aesthetic products, representing communicable individual expressivity, is crucial (ibid). However, claiming that media allow audiences to "understand themselves in a social, historical or maybe an existential perspective," Drotner also highlights the importance of participating as audiences in various public cultural contexts (1996, 14), in which they communicate with cultural/aesthetic products created by others.

According to the German sociologist Ziehe, the educational mission of school implies a commitment to give students access to experiences that differ from those they may have in everyday life and to leave space for follow-up reflection on different perspectives to make it a meaningful experience (2000). Likewise, Georgii-Hemming and Kvarnhall (2015, 27–44) emphasize that school should provide students with pedagogically guided opportunities to listen to music that they are not familiar with or even do *not* want to identify with. They also maintain that discussion about the music with a focus on social equality may contribute to making listening a meaningful experience (ibid 31). Regarding the performances referred to here, this highlights the challenge for musicians and teachers to relate their competencies to each other in service of the students.

Theoretical Considerations

The interactive character of learning, (implicitly) referred to earlier, is central to the theoretical framework underpinned by Vygotsky's theory of cultural history and the cultural-psychological development based on this. This perspective implies that individuals develop familiarity with a tradition by *inter*acting with cultural representatives (here, students interact with musicians and teachers) and artifacts (here, students interact with the music and/or the performance as a whole). This *intern*alization (between persons or persons and cultural artifacts) is followed by *intra*nalization (in the individual), during which individuals re-create their experiences and make these "their own," after which they may present their new, deeper understanding and *extern*alize it. Sharing the new knowledge with others implies an evaluation of its relevance to the context in question, that is, a starting point for further learning (Vygotsky 1978).

In a similar way, Dewey discusses "having an experience" (1939, 35–57), something emotionally moving that leaves a lasting impression as a whole, which other experiences may not necessarily do. His particular interest concerns *aesthetic* experiences (experiences with aesthetic artifacts), which he considers fundamental to life per se because of the emotional character and the shift between tension and relaxation. Having an aesthetic experience, repeatedly recalling it emotionally, and reflecting intellectually on its dynamic shifts, individuals may extend their areas of feeling safe, which may help them cope with new situations later in life (ibid)—an example of experience-based learning.

In line with Dewey, the English psychologist Winnicott claims that cultural experiences, whether had as active participator or as a receiver, may remain valuable personal sources for a creative approach to challenges during adult life, provided that these experiences occur in situations in which the young people feel trust and have opportunities to process their impressions. Hence, he finds it important that adult caretakers introduce young people to cultural experiences that they would not have access to otherwise (1971).

According to Vygotsky (1978), it is important to relate new tasks to an individual's zone of proximal development (ZPD) and to provide a scaffold to facilitate mastery of a task (Clark 1997, 195). This approach corresponds to Vygotsky's idea of dialogic teaching, in which both students and teachers are given mutual opportunities to learn (1934). Applied to professional school performance, musicians and teachers are challenged, first, to scaffold students' interaction with it; second, to interact with students when they are reflecting on the experiences; and third, to mutually account for each other's approaches.

A Case Study with Experienced and Engaged Participants

The case study underpinning this chapter is part of a larger project (Hultberg 2017) about the work of a small freelance company, the Opera Bureau (OB), that presents theatrical performances, mainly of baroque music. This project explores the two musician leaders' artistic considerations and ways of addressing different audiences, school audiences included. The latter are addressed here with a special focus on approaches to performances attended by a Swedish teacher and her classes. Data consist of observations of performances and interactive sessions, interviews with musicians and teachers, and documents: OB's school material and students' writings about their experiences of the performance. Earlier experiences from school performances offer a reflective lens for the participants' actions and considerations. Musicians have accepted the use of their original names; fictitious names are used for the teacher and her students. Informed consent has been obtained regarding the musicians' and the teacher's participation and the inclusion of students' writings.

Participants' Mixed Background Experiences

The OB is led by Catalina (violinist) and Christina (soprano), both specialists in baroque music. For each production, they select music they appreciate for its qualities and potential to convey emotions that may suit a storyline about a gender issue. The musicians' intention is to awaken interest in this area by means of performances that address both artistic and social concerns. With a small group of artists, they create narrative theatrical performances characterized by simplicity and equality on stage: All performers act with elaborate bodily expression, which means that the instrumentalists are actors without sheet music, making music an integral part of the performance as a whole (Hultberg 2017). From a theoretical perspective, the aim is to *present performances as artifacts* through interaction with individuals as aesthetic experiences (Dewey 1934; Vygotsky 1978).

OB productions have been selected by regional distributors, who have provided them as one-day performances that administrators in schools may order. Musicians send information about their performances to the distributers, who forward it to the schools. Catalina describes this organization as:

> a disadvantage for musician-teacher collaboration because it is difficult to get in touch with single teachers. Actually, it is not organized for collaboration. The forthcoming organization depends on the orientation of the individual producers, respectively.

To prepare for the interaction with teachers as well as for students' active participation and reflection, OB events include workshops and discussions. Christina, who provides inviting and informative material about the event, emphasizes the two-fold purpose: "It is more than merely entertainment; the gender aspect is so important that it must not be left aside before or after the performance." She further elaborates:

> We have e-mailed the school-kits to the distributors, who forwarded them to the teachers . . . Sometimes the kits are handed out to students to read on their own . . . Sometimes the teacher has gone through the introduction in a lesson, sometimes the kits haven't reached the students at all. As visiting musicians, we feel that we cannot expect teachers to spend time on the school material . . . Most teachers attend the workshops but some of them are absent, expecting us to "take care" of the class.

The musicians' experiences of teachers' participation in audience discussions vary, but on most occasions, some participating teachers address aspects they have discussed in class, initiate a theme, and encourage students to respond or follow up on students' inputs.

When visiting schools, the musicians usually meet two classes at a time in introductory workshops before the performance and a follow-up audience discussion with all participating classes. Catalina emphasizes that "it is positive to meet students 'on their home turf' but exhausting to have workshops in several classes *and* the performance on one day." When the event takes place in a concert hall, the conditions vary. On the one hand, the musicians appreciate that students are given access to settings representing public cultural life, which may, per se, be a great experience; on the other hand, in some public halls workshops *and* discussions need to be scheduled after the performance, which leaves no possibility for students and musicians to meet and interact beforehand.

The musicians' mixed experiences confirm earlier findings in different ways: The teacher, who participate in discussions and encourage students to participate as well, function as guides and facilitators, as found by Christophersen (2013). Some teachers' lack of interest in participation, as also found by Kenny (2010), may depend on lack of ownership (Christophersen 2013; Holdhus and Espeland 2013), but also on organizational gaps in the distribution of school material. The experiences also reveal *unpredictability imposed on musicians* by local conditions for carrying through the event. This has made them realize that they need to be prepared to take full responsibility for interactive sessions to provide students with access to active and reflective participation, although they would prefer to collaborate with teachers. Recognizing the limitation of their professional pedagogic competencies in terms of voice and violin tuition, they have consulted a gender pedagogue (class teacher) specializing in drama and norm critique in order to be well prepared to take students' preconditions into account. On her advice, they have also informed themselves about equality from different perspectives, about experience-based learning in terms of Dewey (1939), and about the impact of bodily posture.

Emphasizing the inclusion of the gender issue in the introduction and the follow-up, Christina highlights the OB leaders' intention to give students the opportunity to participate actively in sessions reflecting the social dimension of the performance. As referred to in the background, guided listening and reflective discussion are important to make adolescent experiences with music that they usually do not listen to meaningful for them (Georgii-Hemming and Kvarnhall 2015; Ziehe 2000). In line with this, OB leaders consider collaboration with teachers of special importance regarding the gender aspects to ensure that students' needs are accounted for.

Adolescent students' reflections are crucial to Sara, who teaches Swedish at an upper secondary school that provides programs with different profiles, music included. She introduces her students to professional school performances by integrating the content into her subjects, starting out with informative material about the performance and her own familiarity with the music. She has noticed that "many students appreciate challenging performances of high quality rather than merely entertaining ones," which is in line with her own expectations. A few weeks after the beginning of the upcoming autumn term, she is going to attend a thematic OB performance with two new music profile classes. However, due to earlier experiences, she is skeptical about "politically correct" performances:

> It is important that the performance is of high quality. This is more important than that a performance is niched to what is regarded "politically correct," like gender and minority groups in school. This, in itself, is not sufficient for a performance to be good.

She exemplifies this by referring to a thematic performance in which she found that the social theme was superficially treated and the performance was partly lacking in high quality:

> The whole was embarrassing rather than good. *Some* of the music performances were very good, for instance those of [instrumentalist]. But this is not sufficient if the whole is not. Some of my students were disappointed; they felt as if they had not been respected.

Sara's expectation, that the performance should challenge and not only entertain, is consistent with the intention of the OB leaders. According to Vygotsky (1978), this implies expectations on performers and teachers to adapt the challenge to students' preconditions (ZPD) and provide scaffolding that facilitates them to meet the challenge. Like the musicians, Sara refers to quality criteria concerning the *entire performance* as a cultural artifact, the interaction with which she expects to be meaningful for the young audience (Dewey 1934; Vygotsky 1978). To be so, she expects performers to acknowledge adolescents in a similar way as adults by presenting well-prepared performances of the music and additional content. Accordingly, her opinion is also consistent with a *situated work orientation*, as applied by the OB leaders.

Sara's interest in school concerts, in spite of mixed experiences, is consistent with findings indicating that many teachers take a positive attitude to school concerts (Christophersen 2013; Holdhus 2015). Mixed experiences have made Sara, Catalina, and Christina take action as their points of departure, separately, to provide as good conditions as possible for students' participation. According to Sara's experiences, performances ought to challenge students; in terms of Vygotsky (1978), this means that musicians are expected to account for their earlier experiences in order to adapt their interaction with the performance to their zone of proximal development. In addition, this calls for guidance and scaffolding to facilitate students to process their experiences (ibid).

Preparation for the Event

"The Courtesan and Her Love," the production mainly referred to here, is based on music by the Venetian 17th-century composer Barbara Strozzi and her contemporaries. Inspired by Strozzi's life history, it problematizes the situation of a woman who puts aside societal expectations, being an unmarried mother living in open relationships and claiming to be a composer, the latter regarded a male occupation. The OB leaders, a male theorboist and female baroque dancer, present the story musically and theatrically, with a few short spoken lines in Swedish.

Connected to the performance, OB offers introductory workshops in baroque dance led by the dancer and the instrumentalists, as well as discussions led by Christina. Participation in the workshop implies actively experiencing symbolic gestures and movements characteristic to the historical/musical context and, as such, underpinning the storyline (learning by active participation). The school kit presents an inviting teaser, synopsis, lyrics, historical background, scenographer's and costume designer's introduction, suggestions about discussion questions, and music for listening. Christina also sends suggestions on discussion questions to the producer who is going to attend the performance.

The design and content of the school kit appeal to Sara. However, she wonders about her new students' experiences with early baroque music because they have just left the compulsory school in which music to a large extent focuses on popular music:

> There are few students with a classic orientation—many of the teachers [of this upper secondary school] are specialized in jazz. Many students are not familiar with classical music except those who have chosen this orientation.

Accounting for her earlier mixed experiences, Sara designs a two-step task that implies argumentation in writing, as required in the Swedish syllabus: a letter to the ensemble about their impression of the performance, followed by a review in which students may develop their ideas (interview with Sara, written instructions to students). She informs students that she intends to send their letters to the performers and the producer.

Although teacher and musicians have not met, their preparation pathways match each other: Sara uses the school kit and music from the performance as cultural tools for introducing her students to the context; the musicians prepare for a workshop that gives students the opportunity to participate in experience-based learning (Dewey 1939) about bodily expression underpinning context and storyline. Sara designs a task, a cultural tool, by means of which she empowers her students to review the performance. Musicians invite students to discuss the performance, that is, recall their experiences with it—intrapersonally interacting with their own representations of it—while mutually learning from each other, externalizing their own experiences, and internalizing those of others (Vygotsky 1978). Sara provides preconditions for students to deepen their reflection while writing about their impressions.

The matching pathways of teacher and musicians derive from their common approach to the performance as a whole that should be more than entertainment and address something that concerns the students. This common approach also implies that the performance as a whole should challenge students to interact with it, reflect on it, and share their experiences with others.

The Event: Collaborative Moderation and Exchange of Experiences

The performance takes place in a public chamber music hall; the audience consists of classes from different schools: compulsory school, grade nine, and classes from various upper secondary school programs. For local reasons, all interactive sessions have to take place in parallel sessions directly after the performance. Accordingly, before attending the performance, there is no introductory workshop in which students, teachers, and performers can participate, no opportunity for them to interact, as planned for by Catalina and Christina. Workshops are led by instrumentalists and the baroque dancer; audience discussions are led by Christina and supported by the (female) producer to whom she had suggested discussion questions in advance.

The audience is silent and still during the performance. Afterward, there is a short break during which the audience splits in two groups, one leaving the hall for the workshop in another room, the other group staying for the audience discussion. In the spur of the moment, the producer (who recognizes Sara from previous school concerts) asks Sara to join her in a talk on stage while they are waiting for Christina to return after having changed clothes and to participate as comoderator during the discussion. Christina, who has not met Sara before, appreciates her way of addressing aspects of great concern to students and handing them over to her to respond. This gives rise to an engaging talk from the very beginning, "Sara asked me questions that sparked the conversation," from which lively audience participation develops. The appreciation is mutual; Sara finds Christina "very well-prepared for leading the discussion and addressing the students in a pedagogically good way."

Sara is also deeply impressed by the performance as a whole: "It is of top quality. Absolute top quality!" She comments analytically on presentations of single works of music and the way the ensemble integrates different arts expression in the conceptual performance, challenging audiences to reflect. However, regarding her comoderation of the audience discussion, she refers mainly to her pedagogical competencies, although she is well versed and knowledgeable in the area: "My pedagogical experience is absolutely most important!"

The local preconditions are problematic: Being seated in the public hall with classes and teachers from other schools, students may not feel safe, which is important for reflecting and sharing experiences (Dewey 1934; Winnicott 1971). Consequently, moderators are challenged to facilitate active participation for students. Relating to students' experiences (connecting to their ZPD, Vygotsky 1978), Sara sets a context with which students are at least partly familiar; thus, her initial contribution provides a scaffold (Clark 1997; Vygotsky 1978) for students to enter the discussion more comfortably. The moderators' appreciation of each other's contributions brings about a generous atmosphere for sharing experiences. In this situation, Sara is a moderator on at least equal terms with Christina, rather than a guide and facilitator (Christophersen 2013).

To Sara's students, the collaborative moderation also implies an opportunity to recall and reflect on their experiences (Dewey 1934) as preparation for the writing task. Only a few of the students with a classical music profile have participated in the writing task that was carried out while the school orchestra was on tour. In spite of this, most of the letters describe students being deeply moved by the entire performance of the music itself, the musical/bodily expressive performance, the simplicity, and the gender issue. Students with various expectations highlight the artists' respectful and challenging way of addressing the audience with a well-prepared performance integrating music, dance, and theatrical acting with symbolic gestures and attributes. However, a few students claim that the storyline was difficult to understand and the passages without music were rather dull. A few other students, who neither attended the lesson in which Sara introduced the production nor read the handout, maintain that they appreciate the music but recognize that they would probably have had stronger experiences if they had been familiar with the context of the production. Some students highlight the baroque dance workshop for contributing to a better understanding of the historical and social context in an enjoyable way.

On the one hand, the letters confirm the importance of providing guided introduction. On the other hand, the overall positive experiences of students who did take part in Sara's introduction show that this was a sufficient preparation for interacting with this performance in a meaningful way—having "an aesthetic experience" with it (Dewey 1934). This is further highlighted by letters from students attending the performance with very low expectations and who even distance themselves from baroque music and opera, here exemplified by excerpts from two of them:

Tim, who never liked opera or baroque music, looks forward to having a nap during the performance:

> But honestly, I couldn't fall asleep. I was completely stuck in the performance from the very beginning . . . In the performance the ensemble also depicts the contemporary view of women very well. That you with

four people and very little props created such a fantastic experience is extremely impressive.

Doris was disappointed by the only opera she has seen before:

> Everything indicated that it would be as hokey and incomprehensible as last time. But then began the performance and I was immediately spellbound by the music . . . The music and the dance were so wonderful and presented what happened very clearly . . . It was beautiful, imaginative, mystic, uncomfortable, and this in its simplicity.

Sara's two-step writing task aims to put students into a power position equal to that of the artists because it asks for the students' reflections and well-argued considerations. Read by the producer, they may influence the selection of future events. Once having recognized that the performance appeals to them after all, the upcoming task may also have enhanced students' attention and encouraged them to participate actively in the audience discussion. Having discussed this with Sara, Catalina and Christina included suggestions on similar tasks in their school kits (agreed to by Sara).

A Common Approach: Providing Readiness to Collaborate

The exchange of previous experiences facilitates Sara and Christina to collaborate in a fruitful way in a workshop introducing "Lovisa Ulrika," a production related to an 18th-century Swedish queen who learns what it means to hold and to lose power. Directly before the workshop, the same producer as last time suggests that Sara could participate actively in the workshop, which Christina welcomes. Christina begins as planned, showing and commenting on the effects of different bodily postures based on psychological theories about this and invites students to try out poses related to the story on themselves and on each other in small groups and to give feedback about their impressions. After a while, Sara deepens the discussion and initiates further exercises related to the huge differences in social ranking within the historical context.

Sara's role here is not clear. At first she assists Christina supporting students (Christophersen 2013), but later on, she takes action as a session leader, bringing into play a new perspective that may enhance students' understanding of the historical conditions on which the performance is based. Christina appreciates Sara's contribution, which follows the OB plan to combine students' active participation (internalization) with reflection, individually (intranalization) and in groups (externalization, Vygotsky 1978).

Sara's and the musicians' common approach to the performance as a whole and students' interaction with it provides good conditions for their spontaneous collaboration in both settings. In addition, their interest in the professional domain of each other is important. Here, Sara and Christina enter the event well prepared for participating from their different points of departure, respecting each other and leaving space for each other's mutual contributions.

Concluding Considerations: Towards a Musician–Teacher Partnership?

The present study shows the importance of teachers' and musicians' common understandings of the performance event, implying a focus on *students' meaningful interaction with a challenging performance as a whole* (interaction, individuals-cultural artifact, adapted to students' ZPD: Vygotsky 1978), as well as *their reflection on it musically and socially*, as argued for by Ziehe (2000) regarding school settings. To performers, this implies putting music interpretation into a context that concerns students—a *situated* work-oriented approach (Holdhus 2015). To teachers, it implies introducing students to the context and planning for follow-up reflection in situations in which students feel safe (Winnicott 1971). In the present study, the teacher's and the musicians' common approach and their commitment to their responsibilities allowed them to coordinate their preparation without interacting directly with each other and to develop a readiness to collaborate on equal terms in sessions connected to the performance. Thus, they acted implicitly as *partners striving towards a common goal*.

Such common understanding, the prerequisite for the positive outcome referred to in the present case study, cannot be taken for granted. Conversely, participants' earlier experiences confirm previous research showing that both teachers and musicians may not engage meaningfully with the entire performance and students' interaction with it (Christophersen 2013; Holdhus and Espeland 2013; Kenny 2010). This calls for a reconsideration of professional school performances addressing adolescent students and an agreement on the purpose. Drawing on the previous reasoning and the importance of the communicative dimension (Drotner 1996), I propose an overall general purpose as *providing good opportunities for students' meaningful interaction with a challenging performance as a whole*—with implications as described earlier.

Regarding one-day events that may need to be considered for economic reasons, a common approach in line with the proposition noted earlier may constitute a starting point for a teacher–musician partnership based on mutual respect and exchange of experiences. In the present study, such exchange brought about development of the OB school kit; this could have been achieved much earlier, though, if musicians and teachers had had the opportunity to interact directly as described earlier while preparing the events. This underlines further the need for providing preconditions for musicians and teachers to collaborate in similar partnerships related to a performance event. If this cannot be achieved, the many-sided problems characterizing one-day events with professional school performances, and the mixed experiences of these, constitute arguments to question why such should be provided at all. Because it cannot possibly be an option to refrain from presenting challenging music performances to adolescent students, devoted musicians, teachers, producers, and researchers are challenged to exchange experiences to develop a variety of fruitful practices.

References

Christophersen, Catharina. 2013. "Helper, Guard or Mediator? Teachers' Space for Action in The Cultural Rucksack, a Norwegian National Program for Arts and Culture in School." *International Journal of Education & the Arts*, 14 (SI 1.11). Accessed January 17, 2017, www.ijea.org/v14si1/.

Clark, Andy. 1997. *Being There. Putting Brain, Body, and World Together Again*. Cambridge, MA, The MIT Press, A Bradford Book.

Dewey, John. 1934. *Art as Experience*. New York: G. P. Putman's Sons.

Dewey, John. 1939. *Experience and Education*. New York: The Macmillan Company.

Drotner, Kirsten. 1996. *At Skæbe Sig-Selv* [To Create Oneself], 2nd edition. København: Gyldendahl.

Georgii-Hemming, Eva, and Victor Kvarnhall. 2015. "Music Listening and Matters of Equality in Music Education." *Swedish Journal of Music Research*, 2, 27–44.

Holdhus, Kari. 2015. "Skolekonserterna og Skolekonteksten: Mellom verkorientering og kunstdidaktikk." *Nordic Research in Music Education Yearbook*, 16, 293–314.

Holdhus, Kari, and Magne Espeland. 2013. "The Visiting Artist in Schools: Arts Based or School Based Practices?" *International Journal of Education & the Arts*, 14 (SI 1.10). Accessed January 5, 2017, www.ijea.org/v14si1/.

Hultberg, Cecilia K. 2017. "Staging Baroque Music—and Shedding Light on Timeless Gender Issues." In *Research Ethics and Artistic Freedom in Artistic Research: The Swedish Research Council's Yearbook 2017*, edited by Torbjörn Lind, 108–17. Stockholm: Vetenskapsrådet.

Kenny, Ailbhe. 2010. "Too Cool for School? Musicians as Partners in Education." *Irish Educational Studies*, 29 (2), 153–66.

Skolverket. 2011. *Musik. Kursplan i musik för grundskolan*. Stockholm: The Swedish National Agency for Education. Accessed August 31, 2016, https://www.skolverket.se/om-skolverket/publikationer/.

Vygotsky, Lev S. 1978. *Mind in Society: The Development of Higher Psychological Processes*. Cambridge, MA: Harvard University Press.

Vygotsky, Lev S. 1981/1934. *Thought and Language*. Cambridge, MA: The MIT Press.

Winnicott, Donald. 1971. *Playing and Reality*. London: Tavistock.

Ziehe, Thomas. 2000. "School and Youth—a Differential Relation: Reflections on Some Blank Areas in the Current Reform Discussions." *Young: Nordic Journal of Youth Research*, 8 (1), 54–63.

10

The Complete Musician: The Formation of the Professional Musician

JUNE BOYCE-TILLMAN

Introduction

The history of collaboration between professional musicians and teachers is peppered with examples of misunderstandings and mismatches between aims and objectives. This chapter will examine some of the reasons for these in the style of training given in conservatoire contexts—such as individualized examinations, aesthetic value systems, failure to address personal attributes, and the way organizations outside of the professional music-making world function. A model developed in the University of the Arts Helsinki will be used to analyze the competencies required for artists working outside conventional performance contexts (Hiensius and Lehikoinen 2013). This chapter will use material of autoethnographic origin, participant and nonparticipant observation, and interviews from three musician/teacher projects.

A Qualification Framework for Artists

Some of the problems with musician–teacher collaborations lie in the skills with which the respective professional trainings equip them and conflicting expectations (Laycock 2008). Hiensius and Lehikoinen (2013) identify certain key competencies necessary for working in contexts outside of the professional musical world: contextual, pedagogic, artistic/creative, research, social, project management, and marketing. Within these areas, they identify the following strands: cognitive, functional, personal, and ethical.

The first competencies are contextual, where the cognitive strand concerns knowledge of school organization, educational structures, and ethical procedures. The personal strand requires the ability to communicate comprehensibly, verbally, and in writing the relationship between needs of the school and the cultural organization/artist, including negotiations, contracts, facilitation, and evaluation processes (Hempel and Rysgaard 2013, 41). This is necessary to build trust (Reddington 2015):

The most important factor in a successful collaboration then is trust, in order to build the basis of a partnership where areas of conflict are identified and rectified as they present themselves.

The personal strand also includes personal attributes and behaviors—how to conduct oneself in particular situations (Sonvilla-Weiss 2008, 111):

> Art education evolves increasingly away from the traditional "cocoon" towards a curricula focused on critical and creative thinking, interdisciplinarity, openness to society, flexibility, contextual ability, social communicative skill and practice in a collaborative environment.

Music education in conservatoires is, in general, examined individually, limiting the ability to translate skills into other contexts, including openness and adaptability—ideally based on an interdisciplinary background. The ethical strand requires an understanding of the role of music education in the wider curriculum; values are seldom taught in musical training programs—seeing beyond its purely decorative function to its potential for personal and social transformation (Berthoin Antal 2009, 6):

> The term "value added" may at first sight appear inappropriate in connection with the arts, but we choose it consciously, in keeping with recent attempts to overcome the divide between the economic concept of "value" and the "values" in social relations.

Pedagogic competencies (Hempel and Rysgaard 2013, 47) include a variety of abilities, including designing handouts, environmental preparations, flexibility, and facilitation methods (Lehikoinen 2013, 54–5). In these projects, the functional strand concerns tailoring the materials to the needs of orate and literate musicians of various abilities and experiences, including recordings, scores, and word sheets. This takes an immense amount of consultation with school staff, which includes such needs as meal breaks, work breaks for the unionized orchestral musicians, tiredness on the part of the frail, and so on. Whereas technical music skills are well developed in professional musicians, their pedagogical functioning is seldom developed.

The artistic/musical competencies include the overall artistic design and the ability to see the world artistically and with an "inquiry-based approach and the open process" (Lehikoinen 2013, 54–5). This includes artistic perception and reflective ways of thinking and practical knowledge of the arts. The technical/musical ability of the professional musician is usually in a particular style, and asking them to enter different styles requires confidence building and new associated skills.

The research competencies involve the ability to evaluate outcomes, including knowledge about research approaches (Lehikoinen 2013, 58). These need to be there from the beginning of the creation of the piece (Schiuma 2010). The social competencies involve the ability to design the interaction process (often based on experience), including how to engender trust, self-knowledge of the cultural preconceptions and experiences of school staff, skills, and the ability to relate to different personalities (Hempel and Rysgaard 2013, 44), including group dynamics, social interaction, and communication (Lehikoinen 2013, 56).

Project management competencies involve defining challenges, targets, components, time plans, budget, flexibility in management, handling partners within a realistic time frame including paperwork, and contracts (Lehikoinen 2013, 59). Innovation needs to be undertaken by the musicians and teachers collaboratively (Miell and Littleton 2004), working with diverse ways of seeing things to generate creative sparks. Roberto Gómez de la Iglesia stresses that "diversity is not only a key source of creativity, it is also the motor required for the virtuous cycle that spirals from quality to excellence, and from excellence to difference" (Berthoin Antal 2011). Marketing competencies involve sales, negotiation skills, and communication (Lehikoinen 2013, 60). I have chosen to concentrate here on some of these competencies.

The Projects

The three projects that underpin this chapter were all initiated by cultural organizations outside of the classroom (Holdhus and Espeland 2013, 17). This raises questions around the training of teachers, which is often based in schools, being the prime base of education. Teachers need to be aware of the increasing number of outreach programs initiated by music institutions and organizations; these projects can be a way of alerting teachers to goals and developments from an artistic point of view through effective communication (Dwyer 2011).

The first project used in this chapter—initiated by Winchester University, UK—is entitled *Conflict to Chorus* and is presented from an autoethnographic perspective. This piece—composed and conducted by me and performed in Winchester Cathedral, UK, in 2015, involved:

- Different world musics traditions
- School children from Hampshire schools
- A professional orchestra
- People with diagnosed memory loss
- Pupils with profound and multiple learning difficulties (PMLD)
- Community choirs
- Notated choral parts for Winchester University choirs and soloists
- A visually impaired young singer/songwriter

The data from the second project (Boyce-Tillman et al. 2015) are taken from an evaluation report that used nonparticipant observation and interviews. The project, which was organized by a classical orchestra entitled *La Folia*, involved working with special schools towards a presentation in Salisbury Cathedral, UK. Its aims were to give a means of expression to young people with limited means of communication and to reveal these possibilities to a wider audience. It also included professional development for the professional artists involved and the school teachers. They used a wide variety of musical forms, including song writing, movement, and the visual arts. It was led by Howard Moody, conductor, composer, arranger, and instrumentalist. The team consisted of an actor, a singer and animateur, an Indian dance movement therapist, and a visual artist.

The data from the third project were collected through participant observation from a doctoral project that I supervised. This was the education program of a professional orchestra, who carried out a composition and performance training project in a music school in Greece designed to widen the experience of both students and music teachers. The final performance of the composed music was planned for a prestigious concert hall. Within the terms of the funding partnerships, it was part of the orchestral strategy for community involvement.

Contextual Competence

This is the first of the competencies seen as necessary for such projects (Hiensius and Lehikoinen 2013). This is often a weakness in collaborative projects in terms of time, space, and other organizational demands:

> There appears to be little mutual understanding between employers and music leaders about what constitutes a reasonable code of practice, especially when the time frame of the projects happened to be short.
> (Swanwick 2008, 19)

In my project, my professional skill and abilities, based on twenty-three years in educational contexts, informed my project (Tillman 1976, 1983, 1990, Boyce-Tillman 1989, 1991, 2016). This background enabled teachers in these projects to trust me. My doctoral work was on children as improvisers, which enabled me to include "holes" in the pieces for improvisation. The new aspect in *Conflict to Chorus* for me was the children with profound and multiple learning difficulties; here I was able to work collaboratively with a composer with experience in this area. Working in the university in the context of performing arts has enabled a grasp of interdisciplinarity. I am also a practicing Anglican priest, which enables me to understand the way that the sacredness of a Christian space operates; also helpful in this context was the dean of the cathedral, who shared my personal philosophy to make the space open to as many people as possible. Therefore, there were shared values among the participants.

The personal ethics and professional values are based on my concept of radical musical inclusion; this is a desire for social transformation by having people with a variety of experiences and skills come together and develop musical structures that will contain them all. Professionally there were ethical problems, particularly in the inclusion of people with a variety of needs (Yinger 2014), and this needed an immense amount of work in the area of practical risk assessment.

A central problem in this and the third project was the relative value given to the literate and the orate traditions:

> The worth and status of oral, improvised, informal or amateur music making can be eroded both explicitly . . . and in more subtle ways, by use of terminology such as high or low culture, amateur and professional musician, national, or local performer, and so on.
> (Morgan and Boyce-Tillman 2016, 57)

This has led to the valuing of the difficult (Ong 1982) so that "Students may feel proud of their composition that is actually silly for us" (Yeorgouli-Bourzoucos 2004,176).

The professional musicians needed to learn:

> new skills and expanding the meaning of concepts, often "unlearning" what was formerly believed to be true . . . Through performance, communities are finding ways of seeking truth and also recognizing its multiple faces.
> (Cohen 2008, 31)

There seems to have been little attention to the ethical aspects in the Greek project, which led to some competitive elements creeping in. The *La Folia* project, however, had paid careful attention to this area, requiring high levels of interpersonal respect and valuing the students' contributions highly, as well as challenging them cognitively, emotionally, creatively, and physically.

My functional contextual grasp has been gained over a large number of experiences of dialogue using music from the 1980s. These projects were managed by a relationship between the administrator of Foundation Music at the university and the manager at the cathedral. Even so, this relationship is not easy in relation to the liturgical activities of the cathedral.

The project in the Greek school showed the problem of a lack of contextual knowledge (Kenny 2010). Swanwick expresses the desire that musicians and teachers set up real contexts for mutual learning (Swanwick 2008, 20–1). However, in the Greek project, the school teachers felt that the orchestral musicians were unfamiliar with the general practice and philosophy of the school. This meant a failure in mutual trust. The teachers were afraid of potential assessment, the relationship with their regular work at the school, and lack of information about the time involved.

In my project, this was an essential part of the initial negotiations; it involved many school visits; in the PMLD school, it enabled me to feel the atmosphere of that school with the result that the deputy head teacher wrote:

> The level of engagement by our students was exceptional and required enormous cognitive and physical concentration to execute. The respect afforded to our students was humbling; for me the moment when two conductors, baton poised, watched and waited for our students to finish will be a lifelong image of respect.
>
> (Unpublished interview 2015)

The Demands of the Venue

My piece involved scattered choirs and instrumentalists. This demanded people taking responsibility for judging their space in the piece. For some musicians this came easily, but others found the absence of the central control of a conductor directing them problematic. The PMLD children were liable not only to play in the sections that were allocated for their improvisations, but also to make sounds at other times as well. In this case, a second composer worked with the children in the performance, improvising to incorporate the sounds into the piece.

In the *La Folia* project, there was movement around the space for both performers and audience. This led to difficulties in seeing and hearing. In the cathedral also, it was complex to fit the performance around liturgical life. Audience members saw the regular prayers interrupting the performance. In the Greek project, Dr. Yeorgouli-Bourzoucos saw the development of a democratic creative agora outside of the formal sessions as a place for improvisational exploration. Here the students subverted traditional pedagogy in their free time at lunchtime outside of formal education:

> A musical agora is not a straightforward issue; it is complex, when compared to the simplified, industrialised way education operates in general. Finally, it might need the support of teachers and education officers with much intuition and courage . . . They need to hand it over to other people, to students who will develop freely with their own individual and contextual timing and objectives.
>
> (Yeorgouli-Bourzoucos 2004, 221)

What is interesting here is that given inadequate liaison, the students themselves were able to set up their structures independent of both orchestral musicians and teachers. This could be seen as a positive outcome in that creativity was triggered within the students themselves—a formal music context generates an informal context:

> The big challenge to music educators today seems to me to be not how to produce more skilled professional musicians but how to provide that kind of social context for informal as well as formal musical interaction that leads to real development and to the musicalizing of the society as a whole.
> (Small 1998, 208)

Pedagogic Competence

In the personal strand here, the Greek project had an aim to improve the personal and cooperative skills of the school instrumental teachers:

> Improvising as freedom and as self-transformation . . . is a significant side of the nurture needed to balance the challenge of music study. Equality, joy, sense of well-being, appreciation of silence, and sense of direction are some of the social skills acquired through improvisation workshops, according to teachers with similar experiences.
> (Yeorgouli-Bourzoucos 2004, no page numbers)

The teachers did discover new personal qualities for improvising, such as childlikeness and naivety, which are very different from the critical thinking and competence promoted by the rest of the curriculum. However, some teachers felt that the orchestral musicians were not honoring the personal feelings of the students and were only concerned about the final performance in a prestigious concert hall, resulting in elitism. In the end, only the most advanced players were selected even though there were other players who might have benefitted greatly from the experience. This was in stark contrast to the *La Folia* project where prolonged involvement with the schools and extensive experience in the area made the participants very empathetic (Laurence 2008, 25).

The innovative nature of my project needed courage at a purely personal level. Its inclusive nature involved encompassing musical structures to provide a scaffold for everyone's learning (Vygotsky 1962). With very short rehearsal time in Winchester Cathedral—a place unfamiliar to them—it required a very charismatic leadership style to drive the project. Here again process overrode some more traditional approaches to the perfection of the product. In the functional strand, the pedagogic methods varied from group to group; members of the local Music Services vocal team also taught. The children with profound and multiple learning difficulties were taught by a composer who was already working with them, funded by a music project on inclusion and working with a regular teacher at the school.

In the Greek project, the teachers felt personally that they needed more time for discussion about their feelings towards the project and the relationship of these new initiatives to government initiatives or well-tried and trodden paths, especially the way they were taught in the conservatoire, which some thought imprisoned them.

Crucial in all the projects was the ability of the classical musicians to initiate and engage in improvisatory activities. The problem here is the embracing of a freedom unfamiliar in notated Western classical traditions (Csikszentmihaly 1993). In the Greek project, some of the music teachers thought that playing from a score was safer. Others saw the value of improvisation as improving their students' classical playing. Others saw the Western classical instrumentalists struggling to improvise and more traditional Hellenic instrumentalists from the orate traditions as more at ease with this.

In the functional strand, the use of drama in the *La Folia* project helped unleash improvisatory skills in music and movement. Improvisatory techniques are much more familiar to actors than to musicians trained in the Western classical tradition. These empathetic workshops provoked a very powerful song encapsulating the world of homelessness and despair, "Cold and miserable, I don't know how to ask for help . . . I want my family, I want my friends" (Boyce-Tillman et al. 2015, no page numbers).

In the *La Folia* project, there was an understanding of different creative ways of engaging with the students. In one school, teachers and/or support staff were present in all the workshops. The leader of the project planned the sessions to draw in carers and teachers, including confidence-building activities. However, carers saw their role as primarily concerned with health and well-being and were hampered by their own bad experiences of music in school. However, what did become clear to carers was the importance of nonverbal forms of communication for their children. In one of the schools, staff were encouraged to attend sessions by receiving extra payments. The usual problems were encountered of staff seeing the time as a chance to complete other projects. However, those who came undoubtedly learned new strategies.

In the Greek project, in the functional strand, the use of a circular layout of workshops played a crucial part in their success, as it was seen to represent liberation, equality, empowerment, and creativity (Boyce-Tillman 2000, 268). The teachers saw communicating with others as an important part of the workshop and enjoyed the playful approach and the openness to popular music.

Continuing Professional Development for Teachers

This functional strand was part of all of the projects, but seems to be only realized in some of them, as Christophersen found in the Norwegian Rucksack project:

> The researchers have heard tales about teachers who are uninvolved and who do not pay attention to what is happening at the performance; and of upper-secondary school teachers who do not even attend, sending their students to performances without showing up themselves. There were

also some reports of poor behaviour on the part of attending teachers at performances.

(Christophersen 2013, 4)

In the Greek project, many teachers felt they had learned new pedagogies, especially the importance of mutuality—all learning from one another. The *La Folia* project evaluation saw a need to develop some guidelines for the school staff on the level of participation required and to consider applying for the funding for this, which would contribute to the sustainability of the work:

The communication is mostly between students and artists, while the teachers stay in the background and off-center. If TCR productions first and foremost are supposed to create warm and intimate encounters between students and artists, there is not much room for the teachers.

(Christophersen 2013, 10)

This is clearly an area ripe for development.

Artistic/Creative Competence

The growth of community choirs within the UK show the rise of a new aesthetic in musicking (Small 1998, Morgan and Boyce-Tillman 2016). The classical perspective emphasizing performance, perfection, and virtuosity has been:

the standard or "taproot" aesthetic that has been recognised in music education since its inception in the mid-1800s. The second is an aesthetic for singing which stresses community building, diversity, group collaboration and relationship.

(Pascale 2005, 167)

The rise of the second value system has challenged the values engendered in many professional classical musicians:

The other crucial choice illuminated by the past involves the courage to make painful decisions about values. Which of the values that formerly served a society well can continue to be maintained under new changed circumstances?

(Diamond 2005, 522–3)

I have been taken up with the concept of radical musical inclusivity in the context of a globalizing world and the need for interhuman connection (Illman 2010; Boyce-Tillman 2011). Flexibility is required to cross these traditions, "Because much of my material is folk based, I also explain that the music is usually just a guideline or a reminder, not a set of precise instructions—a river rather than a road" (Morgan and Boyce-Tillman 2016, 60). Leaders of these projects require new skills and methods (Vella-Burrows and Hancox 2012, 16). These are much more all-embracing than the average conservatoire training in ensemble leadership.

In the cognitive strand in my project, new artistic/creative competencies were needed in the overall construction and conception of the works. I had developed ways of integrating newly composed material, existing material, improvised and dramatic elements, and audience involvement so that the works challenge existing artistic conventions. It meant rethinking the role of the lone composer that I was trained to be and developing as more of a frame builder.

One of the problems in the ethical strand in the Greek project was the meeting of the two aesthetic value systems. Some teachers were surprised at the quality of the final product; others, however, found the final product weak. They also commented on the orchestral musicians as drawing primarily on contemporary classical composers such as Boulez; those teachers who were more experienced in improvisatory traditions saw this as somewhat limiting for the students. Comments from the classical instrumental teachers reflected their own inability, already discussed, to teach improvisatory skills and the values that they ascribed to them.

In my piece, professional musicians were asked to walk while improvising. It was clear that one player was uncomfortable doing anything other than playing from a printed score. In another case, the orchestra had employed a composer to work with the children and an animateur to work with their singing. Both of these appeared to have little experience with children or community projects. The composer appeared to use the children to carry out his own ideas, and the animateur could not tailor her sessions to fit with the needs of the venue. They were too used to these competencies only in the context of a concert hall (IFFACCA 2008).

Research Competencies

I will deal with this competency only briefly. In my projects, the cognitive strand here includes years of research into the use of a variety of musics in the context of the fragmentation of contemporary society (Matarasso 2011). However, in some contexts, there is a concentration of the Western classical musical tradition, and this is what feeds into the music conservatoires in the UK where most professional musicians are trained.

Both of the other projects included a variety of musics. The *La Folia* project did this deliberately and chose musicians who were at ease moving between a variety of artistic identities. The Greek project had as one of its aims the broadening of the curriculum into a more holistic pedagogical practice—re-creating music paideia—including Western classical and Hellenic traditional instruments.

The most resourceful of the professional musicians in all the projects had expanded their personal musical horizons beyond the demands of academe/ conservatoire by informal music learning (Green 2002; Veblen 2012). The formalized individual lesson of the Western classical tradition has concentrated on classical technique with a consequent devaluing of other aspects of the musical experience (Boyce-Tillman 2016).

The functioning of the research aspect of the projects was often not seen to be part of the process but franchised out to independent evaluators—as in the *La Folia* project. However, whether or not this is done, the ability to evaluate and assess at a micro level is an integral part of the project and needs to be part of the professional musicians' tool kit (Boyce-Tillman et al. 2012). Assessment practices in the literate classical tradition may not be appropriate for projects involving orate traditions.

Summary

The three projects suggest that certain competencies are necessary for collaborative projects between musicians and teachers beyond artistic skills. These are:

- Contextual, including a grasp of organization and performance venues and their associated ethics and values
- Pedagogic, including the ability to relate to a variety of people and lead improvisatory and collaborative groups
- Artistic, including valuing diversity
- Research, including the evaluative and the reflexive

Two of these projects were led by professional musicians who worked in schools that shared their more socially-based value systems. In the Greek project, the contrasted values within the team became problematic. Conservatoire training needs to include reflection on the often-unquestioned value systems that underpin them. These three projects would suggest changes in training for both professional musicians and school teachers or further training developed that could lead to a shared realization of the power of music for personal and social transformation.

References

Berthoin Antal, Ariane. 2009. "Transforming Organisations with the Arts." TilltEurope Project Research Report, 6. Accessed June 13, 2014, https://wzb.eu/sites/default/files/u30/researchreport.pdf

Berthoin Antal, Ariane. 2011. "Managing Artistic Interventions in Organisations: A Comparative Study of Programmes in Europe." Accessed April 22, 2015, www.ssoar.info/ssoar/handle/document/26762.

Boyce-Tillman, June. 1989. "Towards a Model of Development of Children's Musical Creativity." *Canadian Music Educator*, 30 (2), 169–74.

Boyce-Tillman, June. 2000. *Constructing Musical Healing: The Wounds that Sing*. London: Jessica Kingsley.
Boyce-Tillman, June. 2011. "Making Musical Space for Peace." In *Peace and Policy Dialogue of Civilization for Global Citizenship*, Vol. 15, *Music and Solidarity: Questions of Universality, Consciousness and Connection*, edited by Felicity Laurence and Olivier Urbain, 185–201. New Brunswick, NJ and London: Transaction Publishers.
Boyce-Tillman, June. 2016. *Experiencing Music—Restoring the Spiritual, Music as Wellbeing*. Oxford: Peter Lang.
Boyce-Tillman, June, Yvon Bonenfant, Inga Bryden, Olu Taiwo, Tiago de Faria, and Rohan Brown, 2012. "PaR for the Course: Issues involved in the Development of Practice-Based Doctorates in the Performing Arts." www.heacademy.ac.uk/resources/detail/disciplines/dance-drama-music/Boyce-Tillman_2012.
Boyce-Tillman, June, Elizabeith Scott-Hall, Shirley Taylor, and David Walters. 2015. *La Folia: The Magna Songs Project: A Research-Based Evaluation of the Effectiveness of an Arts Project on the Pupils, and Its Impact on the Professional Artists and Audience*. Salisbury: La Folia.
Christophersen, Catharina. 2013. "Helper, Guard or Mediator?" Teachers' Space for Action in The Cultural Rucksack, a Norwegian National Program for Arts and Culture in School." *International Journal of Education & the Arts*, 14 (SI 1.11). Accessed January 30, 2017, www.ijea.org/v14si1/v14si1-11.pdf
Cohen, Cynthia. 2008. "Music: A Universal Language?" In *Music and Conflict Transformation: Harmonies and Dissonances in Geopolitics*, edited by Olivier Urbain, 26–39. London: I.B. Tauris.
Csikszentmihalyi, Mihaly. 1993. *The Evolving Self*. New York: Harper and Row.
Diamond, Jared. 2005. *Collapse, How Societies Choose to Fail or Survive*. London: Allen Lane.
Dwyer, M. Christine. 2011. *Reinvesting in Arts Education: Winning America's Future Through Creative School*. Washington, DC: President's Committee on the Arts and the Humanities.
Green, Lucy. 2002. *How Popular Musicians Learn*. Hants: Ashgate.
Hempel, Gerda, and Lisbeth Rysgaard. 2013. "Competencies—in Real Life." In *Training Artists for New Contexts; Competencies for New Contexts*, edited by Joost Hiensius and Kai Lehikoinen, 29–47. Helsinki: Theater Academy of the University of the Arts.
Hiensius, Joost, and Kai Lehikoinen, eds. 2013. *Training Artists for New Contexts; Competencies for New Contexts*. Helsinki: Theater Academy of the University of the Arts.
Holdhus, Kari, and Magne Espeland. 2013. "The Visiting Artist in Schools: Arts Based or School Based Practices?" *International Journal of Education & the Arts*, 14 (SI 1.10). Accessed January 30, 2017, www.ijea.org/v14si1/v14si1-10.pdf
IFFACCA. 2008. "International Federation of Arts Councils and Federal Agencies." Accessed January 30, 2017, https://ifacca.org/en/news/2008/10/17/enabling-creators-arts-and-cultural-management-and/
Illman, Ruth. 2010. "Plurality and Peace: Interreligious Dialogue in a Creative Perspective." *International Journal of Public Theology*, 4, 175–92.
Kenny Ailbhe. 2010. "Too Cool for School? Musicians as Partners in Education." *Irish Educational Studies*, 29 (2), 153–66.
Laurence, Felicity. 2008. "Music and Empathy." In *Music and Conflict Transformation: Harmonies and Dissonances in Geopolitics*, edited by Olivier Urbain, 13–25. London: I.B.Tauris.
Laycock, Jolyon, ed. 2008. *Enabling the Creators: Arts and Cultural Management and the Challenge of Social Inclusion*. Oxford: European Arts Management Project in Association with Oxford Brookes University.
Lehikoinen, Kai. 2013. "Qualification Framework for Artistic Interventions." In *Training Artists for New Contexts: Competencies for New Contexts*, edited by Joost Hiensius and Kai Lehikoinen, 49–65. Helsinki: Theater Academy of the University of the Arts.
Matarasso, Francois. 1997. "Use or Ornament? The Social Impact of Participation in the Arts." *Commedia*. Accessed May 12, 2011, www.comedia.org.uk/pages/pdf/downloads/use_or_ornament.pdf.
Miell, Dorothy, and Karen Littleton, eds. 2004. *Collaborative Creativity: Contemporary Perspectives*. London: Free Association Books.
Morgan, Sarah, and June Boyce-Tillman. 2016. *A River Rather than a Road: The Community Choir as Spiritual Experience*. Oxford: Peter Lang.
Ong, Walter. 1982. *Orality and Literacy: The Technologizing of the Word*. London: Methuen.
Pascale, Louise. 2005. "Dispelling the Myth of the Non-Singer—Embracing Two Aesthetics for Singing." *Philosophy of Music Education Review*, 13 (2), 165–75.

Reddington, Clare, 2015. "Enabling Collaboration, Some Thoughts from the Middle, iShed." Accessed April 22, 2015, www.interact.mmu.ac.uk/resources/EnablingCollaboration.

Schiuma, Giusy. 2009. *The Value of Arts-Based Initiatives: Mapping Arts-Based Initiatives*. London: Arts & Business. Accessed July 25, 2010, www.artsandbusiness.org.uk/Media%20library/Files/Research/Mapping%20ABIs% 20-%20Prof%20SchiumaFINAL.pdf.

Small, Christopher. 1998. *Musicking: The Meanings of Performing and Listening*. Middletown, CT: Wesleyan University Press.

Sonvilla-Weiss, Stefan. 2008. "Science and Education." In *Educating Artists for the Future: Learning at the Intersections of Art, Science, Technology and Culture*, edited by Mel Alexenberg. Chicago: University of Chicago Press.

Swanwick, Keith. 2008. "The 'Good-Enough' Music Teacher." *British Journal of Music Education*, 25 (1), 9–22.

Tillman, June B. 1976. *Exploring Sound*. London: Stainer & Bell.

Tillman, June B. 1983. *Forty Music Games to Make and Play*. Basingstoke: Macmillan.

Tillman, June B. 1990. *The Christmas Search*. Cambridge: Cambridge University Press.

Veblen, Kari K. 2012. "Adult Music Learning in Formal, Nonformal, and Informal Contexts." In *The Oxford Handbook of Music Education*, edited by Gary McPherson and Graham Welch, Vol. 2, 243–25. New York: Oxford University Press.

Vella-Burrows, Trish, and Grenville Hancox. 2012. *Singing and People with Parkinson's*. Canterbury: Canterbury Christchurch University.

Vygotsky, Lev S. 1962. *Thought and Language*. Cambridge, MA: Massachusetts Institute of Technology, Wiley.

Yeorgouli-Bourzoucos, Styliani. 2004. "Improvisation in the Curriculum of the Special Music Schools in Hellas." Unpublished PhD thesis, University College, Winchester.

Yinger, Olivia Swedborg. 2014. "Adapting Choral Singing Experiences for Older Adults: The Implications of Sensory, Perceptual and Cognitive Changes." *International Journal of Music Education*, 32 (2), 203–12.

11

An Urban Arts Partnership: Teaching Artists and the Classroom Teachers Who Collaborate with Them

HAROLD F. ABELES

Introduction

The work presented in this chapter is based on a five-year case study of one orchestra/school partnership in a large U.S. city. The chapter describes a comprehensive partnership in which a music-based interdisciplinary instructional program provided by a professional orchestra was used as a means to promote learning in music as well as in subjects outside of the music. It examines how collaborating in the partnership affected both the classroom teachers and teaching artists.[1]

Beginning in the 1990s, both in the United States and internationally, education policy prioritized student outcomes on year-end mastery tests as the primary indicator of school success (Dylan 2013). By adopting a "learning through the arts" focus, which promised an improvement in students' academic performance, arts organizations were in sync with this policy, and in addition, the approach helped them connect with additional funding sources from agencies and foundations interested in supporting student achievement beyond the arts. Current education policy continues to emphasize high-stakes test scores as the most important criterion for judging the effectiveness of schools.

The Orchestra/School Partnership

Steam Forward (SF)[2] was a program developed and centered in the education department of the *Metropolis Symphony Orchestra (MSO)*. The stated objectives of the program included the integration of arts-based learning at all grade levels throughout the curriculum; improved teaching of the arts; the strengthening of higher-order thinking skills in disciplines such as math, language arts, social studies, and science; increased parental involvement; and the exploration of cultural diversity through the arts. The National Endowment for the Arts, the state and Metropolis [fictional city name] area departments of education, and private foundations funded the program. These funds were raised by the MSO specifically to support SF and were used to pay for musician services, to hire music-in-education consultants to assist in the development of curriculum materials and design the workshop experiences for teachers and teaching artists, to hire additional MSO education staff to support the program, and to fund the assessment of the program.

SF was designed to supplement the existing music program in each of the participating schools. To participate in SF, schools in urban and suburban communities in or near Metropolis were invited to complete applications. The MSO required that the applications be endorsed by both the school principal and the school-based music specialist[3] to ensure their commitment to the project. Seven elementary schools (ages 5 to 11), three middle schools (ages 12 to 14), and three high schools (ages 15 to 18) were selected to participate in a five-year pilot implementation of the program. The 13 schools represented a diverse sample, including, (1) under-resourced urban schools—composed predominately of minority students; (2) better-resourced suburban schools with a more diverse population; and (3) well-resourced private schools, whose students were predominately European Americans. The curriculum materials were developed and implemented in stages so that in the first year of the SF, first grade, sixth grade, and ninth grade classrooms participated in the program. Each year, an additional three grades were added at each elementary, middle, and high school until all of the students at the thirteen schools were participating.

The components of the program included curriculum development workshops; arts-integrated grade-level curriculum guides with multiple instructional units; teaching artist/classroom teacher planning sessions; teaching artist training; teaching artist presentations; MSO concerts; and resource materials for each classroom, such as a selection of books and recordings to support the music-based interdisciplinary lessons. To prepare teachers for Steam Forward, music-in-education consultants organized both curriculum development and staff development workshops. The purpose of the curriculum development workshops was to have classroom teachers engage in the initial stages of the development of the units found in the Steam Forward Curriculum Guide. In these workshops, teachers identified and discussed common grade-level concepts and curriculum content, which served as the basis for the units. In addition to these workshops, teachers attended at least one professional development workshop. These were designed to assist classroom teachers in integrating the partnership's lessons into the core curricula of their classrooms and included both consultant demonstrations of instructional strategies from the units and teacher demonstrations of lessons they had tried in their classrooms. Teaching artists gave presentations in each of participating classrooms approximately six times a year. Students also attended an education concert at the MSO's performance hall.

Initially, twenty-five MSO musicians agreed to serve as teaching artists for SF. They also received training to help them prepare their presentations. Each musician was expected to prepare a presentation that would coordinate with a particular unit in the SF curriculum guide. Orchestra musicians typically chose a grade level that they would feel comfortable working with. Initially, the musicians received guidance from two music-in-education consultants to help them identify possible presentation connections to the curriculum. As they refined their presentation, they would also work with the orchestra's education staff. Once they began presenting in classrooms, the MSO education staff would often accompany them to assist them with logistics and to provide the musician/teaching artist with feedback regarding their presentations. In the third year of the program, a small group of eight professional musicians from Metropolis, who were not members of the MSO, were added to the pool of teaching artists. This was done because the MSO teaching artists were almost all European or Asian Americans and the students in the Metropolis schools were mostly African or Latino Americans. This was an effort by the MSO to better connect with the students SF was serving. The community musicians also added to the traditional classical repertoire of the orchestra musicians from other music genres, including jazz and Latin musical styles. These community musicians received the same training as the teaching artists from the MSO.

An important component of the program was the thirty-minute teaching artist/teacher planning sessions, which would typically occur two weeks before each of the teaching artist's classroom presentation. In some schools, the school-based music specialist would also attend these meetings. The intent of these sessions was to help the teaching artist and classroom teacher coordinate the instructional experiences around a unit in the SF Curriculum Guide.

A typical SF instructional experience would begin with a unit from the curriculum guide that was developed by a group of participating teachers and closely tied to the state and local curriculum goals. The classroom teacher and teaching artists would meet prior to the first instructional experience to plan how each would support certain aspects of the unit. The experience would typically begin with a lesson by the classroom teacher that fit easily into the fourth-grade science (e.g., solids, liquids, and gases) or other curriculum area. A few days later, the teaching artist's visit would provide another perspective of the science lesson. Finally, the classroom teacher might follow up with one or two more classes to reinforce the concepts that she presented earlier and to reinforce the teaching artist's presentation.

Approach to Assessment

A team from the Center for Arts Education Research (CAER)[4] was engaged to undertake an assessment of the program. The CAER's approach was to provide multiple perspectives of the program. Presenting multiple perspectives involved obtaining information about the program by using different data-gathering strategies, such as classroom observations; the review of student work; and interviews with students, teachers, teaching artists, and program staff. The SF assessment focused on (1) the effect of SF on students, (2) teachers' skill and interest in using the arts to provide interdisciplinary instructional experiences, (3) teachers' personal interest and value for music, (4) collaboration among teachers, (5) the effect of participating in the program on school-based music specialists, and (6) the effect of participating in the program on the teaching artists. The assessment also sought teachers' perspectives on different components of the program, such as curriculum materials, as well as their views on how participating in SF affected their students and themselves.

The data-gathering strategies for this project included (1) observations of workshops, classroom presentations by teaching artists, teacher presentations of related lesson materials, and MSO SF education concerts and (2) interviews with classroom teachers, school-based music specialists, orchestra-based teaching artists, community-based teaching artists, music-in-education consultants, MSO education staff, and annual surveys of classroom teachers.

During each of the first four years of the pilot program, the number of classroom teachers participating increased as grade levels were added. In the first year, twenty-four first-grade classroom teachers, eleven middle school subject teachers, and thirteen high school subject teachers participated. In the fifth year, there were 267 teachers participating, with 211 elementary school teachers (first through fifth grade), thirty-three middle school teachers, and twenty-three high school teachers. Most of the middle and high school subject teachers were in humanities and science areas. In the last year of the program, SF served approximately 7,000 students in the Metropolis area.

Results

Because this was a five-year pilot, challenges in the initial design of the project that were apparent in the early years were addressed in subsequent years. For example, during the first year or two of the program, many teachers and principals viewed SF as a very top-down partnership, where the MSO was mandating certain program expectations. Yet as the program progressed and the MSO and school personnel became more comfortable with each other, a perspective of a more mutual collaboration became dominant as teachers realized that they had a critical role to play in decision making about the curriculum and the specific lesson plans.

This change in perspective over time is also illustrated with the relationship between the teachers and the teaching artists. Early in the project, when we asked teachers about the planning sessions with the teaching artists, they would make comments like, "[T]hey [the planning sessions] really take a lot of time. Why am I giving up my ... time? I'm not getting paid for it, they [the musicians] are." And some of the teaching artists would say, "I felt that in a lot of cases, [the teachers] ... didn't have a whole lot of time, or didn't really know what I was doing there, but it needs to happen anyway . . . even if the teachers . . . don't really get why I'm there." Nearer the end of the five-year project, after working together on planning experiences for students over several years, we were more likely to hear from teachers comments like, "You're building a relationship with the musicians on a more personal level . . . even if you're not talking about music . . . so that both you and that person are more comfortable when they come into your classroom . . . It feels like there's someone you know coming in." This change of perspectives from both the teaching artists and the classroom teachers illustrates the importance of longer-term collaborations—that is, the building of relationships over time.

Teachers' Skill and Interest in Using the Arts to Provide Interdisciplinary Instruction

We surveyed all of the participating teachers each year during the five-year pilot with an average survey response rate of 62 percent. Teachers reported that SF had an effect on them professionally. Teachers generally agreed that in terms of their teaching, the program provided them with practical, arts-based instructional tools. Teachers also agreed that they became more interested in connections between subject areas as a result of their participation and that they developed professionally through the workshops and through their attempts to implement the SF curriculum. Several teachers commented that because of their previous lack of knowledge about music or because of their previous anxiety regarding their own music skills, they tended to avoid using music in their classrooms. Many of these teachers reported that SF changed that circumstance and that they were developing new ways to use music with their students.

The survey results were supported by our conversations with teachers and principals. As one teacher told us: "It's given me another exciting, concrete vehicle to use in the classroom to demonstrate the concepts we teach. It's so motivating. It has shown me ways to enhance other areas." Principals also noted changes in participating teachers. One principal stated, "I've seen growth in teachers in that they're exploring avenues which they didn't do before because now they have the equipment and materials and the lesson is right there that allows them to move in a new direction."

These perspectives reflect results from teachers who were engaged in the program near the end of the pilot, but not some of the challenges that were observed earlier in the pilot. For example, a typical grade-level curriculum guide contained approximately twenty units. In the second year of the pilot, some teachers used as many as ten units during the school year, but other teachers used only one or two of the units. The number of units used tended to increase over the period of the pilot, which appeared to be related to conversations among teachers at each school as they learned how their colleagues were using particular units.

At the end of the second year of the program we observed that given the diverse profiles of the partner schools, implementation varied across schools and between grade levels. In some schools, implementation of SF was mandated by the school administration. We found this approach received mixed feedback from teachers. Teachers who were enthusiastic about the program had no problems with this approach, whereas those teachers who were not yet actively involved perceived the mandate as a burden and were less likely to have positive feelings towards the program. Other schools supported SF implementation with strong liaison teachers[5] who provided leadership for other teachers within their grade or school. Additionally, some of the schools supported program implementation by expanding the role of school-based music specialists to further the process of SF curriculum integration. However, in some partnering schools, classroom teachers' integration of the program was minimal. It should also be noted that the majority of teachers interviewed at the end of the second year expressed a need for more SF implementation support from their administration.

In the Year Two Assessment Report, we described three groups of teachers. The first included teachers with minimal to no participation in the SF program. These teachers might be characterized as having one or two teaching artist presentations in their classroom and occasionally using resource materials, but may or may not have participated in planning sessions. These teachers would also occasionally use a lesson from the SF curriculum guide in preparation for musician presentations, but overall integration of the curriculum lessons or activities was minimal. A second group included teachers with limited-to-active participation. These teachers used the SF curriculum to prepare for or as follow-up to teaching artists' presentations. They were also likely to use the resource materials, prepare for planning meetings, write SF curriculum, and integrate SF activities and lessons. The third group included teachers who were not just active participants but whose roles also included advocacy of and leadership in the program. In year two, the majority of teachers fluctuated between the first two levels. The different levels of classroom teachers' involvement in SF appeared to be due to three factors: (1) the amount of pressure individual teachers felt regarding the need to prepare their students for the year-end mastery tests; (2) teachers' previous personal engagement with music, such as singing in a school or church choir; and (3) their interest in trying something new, either to invigorate their classroom's curriculum or themselves as teachers.

Collaboration among Teachers

Many of the approaches to school reform that emerged in the last two decades focused on collaborative planning among teachers, such as can be found in professional learning communities (Ronfeldt et al. 2015). We observed early in SF that the program seemed to encourage collaboration among classroom teachers. Consistently, principals told us that participating in the program contributed to team building among the teachers in their schools. One principal told us: "One of the nice things that has happened is just that by virtue of the fact that teachers are finding more reasons to talk, you begin to find more links between subjects which can only benefit students." Our interviews with teachers supported this perspective. As one teacher reported,

> There's more cooperation between teachers within my grade and across grades. I find myself talking to them about what they're doing with that part of the program, and sometimes it's just having the time to talk to them when we go to these meetings together.

In general, collaborative activities increased among classroom teachers who participated in SF. SF complemented, reinforced, and, in some schools, seemed to serve as a catalyst for these collaborations. The program appeared to have helped participating schools move towards school reform objectives that feature teacher collaboration as a key component.

Participation of School-Based Music Specialists

We observed the important role that school-based music specialists had in the SF program. In several schools, the school-based music specialist served as the liaison for the program and supported the interactions between the classroom teachers and the teaching artist. In most of the schools, the program placed the school-based music specialists in a new, more central position. Whereas some arts-in-education programs work independently from school-based music specialists, SF had strong commitments from the school-based music specialists, as they required them to be a central part of program planning right from the beginning. SF increased the number of opportunities for school-based music specialists and classroom teachers to collaboratively develop curriculum and plan instructional experiences by requiring collaborations in order to implement the program. The school-based music specialists played an important central planning role in each of the pilot schools, and the community/orchestra-based teaching artists played a pivotal supplemental instructional role in the classrooms. This team approach proved to be very successful.

We frequently heard from classroom teachers that they had more contact with school-based music specialists in their schools as a result of the SF program. As one teacher put it, "If I had questions, I would naturally go to her [music teacher], whereas before, maybe I wouldn't have."

Some music teachers noted that classroom teachers sought them out for advice more than in the past. As one school-based music specialist put it, "I think they started coming to me more and more saying, 'Oh, I see why I can use this, can you help me?'" One school-based music specialist told us that

SF had allowed her to work more closely with the classroom teachers in reading skills. For this music teacher, SF promoted value among the faculty for her insights and skills: "I don't think they realized that I had anything to offer and now they're coming more and more to me—I want to teach this story, I want to do this book, I want to do this play, how do I use sounds?"

During the fifth year, we conducted a case study of an experienced school-based music specialist at one participating elementary school. This music teacher had been a member of the school faculty for fifteen years and had developed good rapport with many of the experienced classroom teachers at the school. He had a broad background, which included not only undergraduate training in music but art experiences as well. Prior to SF the music teacher had occasionally undertaken some collaborative projects with the classroom teachers. SF provided this school-based music specialist and his classroom teacher colleagues with another reason to collaborate. He immediately saw the potential of SF at his school and participated in the development of his school's application to the program. Once the program was initiated, he served as liaison for his school. Throughout the program, the music teacher worked closely with several of the classroom teachers in planning instruction around SF lessons. Together, they parceled out certain lessons or parts of lessons, relying on each other's instructional strengths and expertise. In addition, the music teacher developed lessons that have been incorporated into the SF Curriculum Guide; he has also demonstrated lessons at staff development workshops. Classroom teachers at this school talked about how SF "just opened the doors for the way that everything inter-connects and inter-relates." In describing how the school-based music specialist worked with the program, they reported that

> [I]t's just amazing how he has been diving into all the disciplines and all the different grade levels, and taking a look at books and novels and different ways that music could be integrated with folk tales, with animals, with the seasons. Just tapping into more, into what we're doing and tying that directly into what he's doing. The kids see this whole big connected piece. They get so much more out of it, and teachers get more out of it working with him.

By the end of the program, many classroom teachers played an important role in the implementation of the SF program. They were active in selecting the appropriate resources provided by the program to achieve desired student experiences and outcomes. Without this active planning, the experiences would have been just isolated events, unable to support the links that students were encouraged to develop. By the fifth year, teachers felt comfortable with their abilities to effectively present the material and appeared to be committed to the idea of integrating the arts into the curriculum, as well as making the arts an enduring component of their teaching. They seem to have acquired skills and confidence in integrating the arts and other disciplines, and they were more likely to plan collaboratively with both their colleagues in classrooms and with school-based music specialists. In addition, their interest in music increased.

Skills and Understandings Developed by Teaching Artists

The evidence regarding teaching artists' skill in developing instructional presentations for students comes from seventeen classroom observations of teaching artists' presentations during the five-year project, approximately fifty interviews with teachers and principals, and the results of teaching artists' evaluations completed by 122 classroom teachers in years two and five of the program. In addition, twenty-three interviews were conducted with teaching artists in years two and five of the project.

During the initial years of the program teachers would occasionally comment about how a teaching artist was "developing" as a presenter; however, the teachers' overall perspective was that teaching artists' presentations were interesting to students and effective in supporting core learning outcomes.

As the pilot ended, we heard consistent praise for the musicians' presentations from teachers in elementary schools through high schools. For many teachers, this was the most valued part of the program. As the program became more established in each school, and as the teachers became more familiar with what the teaching artists' programs were like, the presentations became even more integrated into the ongoing classroom curriculum. We heard one high school science teacher talk about how well a musician's demonstration elaborated a physics unit on sound. This was the first year he had invited an SF musician into his classroom and was pleased with his students' eager responses and the number of questions that were generated by the presentation. Many teachers mentioned that the presentations illustrated a curriculum concept from a different perspective, which helped some students understand a concept for the first time. The different perspectives that enhanced students' understandings were typically achieved by relating musical concepts to concepts in other fields, for example, how the relationship between beat and meter parallels the mathematical concept of fractions. However, it should be noted that providing students with illustrations of concepts by professionals in another field, such as architecture, might equally enhance students' understandings.

When classroom teachers were asked to evaluate the teaching artists' presentations in the last year of the pilot, in general, they viewed the teaching artists as successful. Teachers felt that the teaching artists chose appropriate subject matter and were well prepared. Teachers indicated that the teaching artists allotted the appropriate amount of time for the lesson and were well organized, and most teachers thought the musicians' presentations enabled the children to feel successful at the end of the lesson. Teachers also described the teaching artists as having a style of presentation that engaged the students. They indicated that the teaching artists paced the lesson effectively, demonstrated the ability to deal with whole-group classroom management issues, answered questions in an appropriate manner, and were able to hold the students' attention and interest. Most of the teachers thought that the teaching artists' manner of delivery showed an understanding of the age group, were sensitive to individual differences of the children, and demonstrated the ability to deal with classroom management issues presented by individual children. All of the teachers described teaching artists as skilled performing artists, and a large percentage of the teachers felt that the children enjoyed the teaching artists' presentations.

We also explored the dimensions that contributed to the teaching artists' positive evaluations. It was clear from interviews with the teaching artists that they spent a considerable amount of time preparing, refining, and practicing their presentations. For example, one teaching artist told us:

> When I first began working on my presentation, I realized that I needed to read more about what the students were studying. So I talked with a teacher at the high school, and bought a couple of books he recommended. After reading them, I [spent] a few more hours, developing my ideas, and then I tried the presentation out with my husband and kids, both of whom are in high school. So, the first time I actually went into the classroom, I felt pretty comfortable.

Several teaching artists also commented about the assistance they received from the SF education staff and the consultants who were hired to help them develop their presentations. By the end of the pilot, the teaching artists who participated in SF appeared to develop a new repertoire of skills and understandings about presenting in classrooms. They appeared to be comfortable and effective in schools. One community artist reported that as a consequence of her work with SF she was being contacted by other arts-in-education organizations to work in their school programs.

Concluding Comments

Several key aspects contributed to the generally positive outcomes of Steam Forward at the end of the five-year pilot implementation. First, because it was identified as a pilot program, it was easier to address aspects that were less effective in the early years of implementation; that is, there was more flexibility in the design—the organizers were not wedded to the original configuration. Second, the program was implemented at each school over five years, allowing it to mature and providing opportunities for the relationship between classroom teachers, school-based music specialists, and teaching artists to develop. Third, SF was a learning *through* music program and thus was tied to the existing nonmusic curriculum, something that the classroom teachers already felt comfortable with and also giving the teaching artists and classroom teachers specific content areas to focus on where the classroom teachers had expertise. Fourth, the teachers were an integral part of developing the curriculum materials, and fifth, in many schools the school-based music specialists had an important role in the program.

In some ways, the results reported in this chapter differ from the results of some previous studies of arts-in-education partnerships. For example, Christophersen (2013), when describing a national program for arts and culture in Norwegian schools, *The Cultural Rucksack* (TCR), reported that "linking artists and students basically makes the teachers redundant as teacher (11)." However, the design and goals of TCR and SF differed considerably. The aim of TCR was more focused on giving "all children access to professional artistic and cultural productions of high quality (3)," whereas SF was focused on learning through music, where classroom teachers have a central role and their expertise is valued and critical to the effectiveness of the program.

Another aspect of SF that distinguishes it from some other arts-in-education programs is the extensive professional development component for both teachers and teaching artists. Both Kenny (2010, 14) and Wolf (2008, 90) underscore the importance of extended preparation for successful partnerships. In SF both the teaching artists and teachers had extensive professional development experiences during their initiation into the program, and in each of the following years additional professional development experiences were provided for all SF teachers by grade level across all of the participating schools. In addition, in several schools weekly grade-level planning meetings, which at times focused on SF units, provided opportunities for teachers to refine their instructional strategies.

Nevertheless, some aspects of SF were similar to previous work reported. As Bresler (2010) noted, when reporting on education performances in the Midwestern United States, SF classroom teachers also "emphasized good behavior and self-control" (141) during the MSO education performances at MSO Hall, which were often attended by more than 1,000 students.

A final important distinctive quality of SF is that it was a very well-funded program with resources that supported extensive professional development opportunities. Although both MSO administrators and school administrators viewed Steam Forward as a success, the program required such an extensive commitment of resources and time by both the MSO and the schools that the program was not sustainable. Fundraising efforts were eventually redirected to other MSO education areas. The MSO still offers educational programming, including traditional education performances at MSO Hall, as well as an El Sistema–inspired program, but Steam Forward is no longer a part of their educational offerings.

Notes

1 The full assessment of Steam Forward also included the effects of the program on the students it served.
2 Pseudonyms are used throughout this chapter to maintain the anonymity of the program and participants. STEAM is an acronym that includes the arts in a curriculum composed of science, technology, engineering, and math (STEM).
3 In a majority of U.S. schools, elementary schools (ages 5 to 11) have a full-time school-based music specialist teacher who typically focuses on general and choral music education. U.S. secondary schools typically offer instruction for at least one year in general music for all students and elective choral and instrumental ensembles.
4 The Center for Arts Education Research is an interdisciplinary group founded to stimulate and support basic and applied research in the arts, art education, and the arts in education located at Teachers College, Columbia University. Assessment teams are composed of both faculty members and doctoral students. The center has engaged in numerous arts-in-education assessment projects since its inception in 1993.
5 Each of the participating schools identified a school liaison for the project. In most schools it was the school-based music specialist, but in several of the middle or high schools it was an administrator, such as an assistant principal.

References

Bresler, Liora. 2010. "Teachers as Audiences: Exploring Educational and Music Values in Youth Performances." *Journal of New Music*, 39 (2), 135–45. Academic Search ed, EBSCO host. Accessed January 29, 2017.

Christophersen, Catharina. 2013. "Helper, Guard or Mediator? Teachers' Space for Action in The Cultural Rucksack, a Norwegian National Program for Arts and Culture in School." *International Journal of Education & the Arts*, 14 (SI 1.11), 1–17. Accessed January 15, 2017, www.ijea.org/v14si1/.

Dylan, Wiliam. 2013. "How Is Testing Supposed to Improve Schooling? Some Reflections." *Measurement: Interdisciplinary Research and Perspectives*, 11 (1–2), 55–9.

Kenny, Ailbhe. 2010. "Too Cool for School? Musicians as Partners in Education." *Irish Educational Studies*, 29 (2), 153–66.

Ronfeldt, Matthew, Susann Ownens Farmer, Kiel McQueen, and Jason A. Grissom. 2015. "Teacher Collaboration in Instructional Teams and Student Achievement." *American Educational Research Journal*, 52 (3), 475–514.

Wolf, Shelby, A. 2008. "The Mysteries of Creative Partnerships." *Journal of Teacher Education*, 59 (1), 89–102.

12
Dialogues between Teachers and Musicians in Creative Music-Making Collaborations

RANDI MARGRETHE EIDSAA

Introduction

This chapter addresses the interaction between musicians and teachers in creative music-making partnerships in schools. The collaborations referred to are supported by The Cultural Rucksack, a national Norwegian cultural program that facilitates concerts and performances by professional artists in schools. Most often, The Cultural Rucksack projects are organized as thirty-five- to forty-minute-long school concerts presented to relatively large audiences of children (www.kulturtanken.no). However, the program also includes *partnership projects*, collaborative projects lasting for more than one day. A partnership project is defined as:

> an entity in which two or more partners (e.g. schools, cultural institutions, universities, local arts agencies, libraries, senior citizen organizations, and other community groups) have agreed formally to collaborate for a specified duration, with financial support from a recognized agency or organization responsible for the partnership's administration and management.
>
> (Colley et al. 2012)

The cases referred to in this chapter were financed by The Cultural Rucksack and organized by local cultural institutions in collaboration with participating schools. The schools were chosen as project partners based on individual applications to the local Cultural Rucksack administration. Participating teachers had been involved in the application process and had taken part in similar collaborations previously. These teachers agreed to take part in the upcoming collaboration, either as organizers only or as organizers and workshop instructors, or even as organizers, workshops instructors, and performers together with the visiting professionals.

The term *creative music-making* could be applied "not to any particular kind of music activity but, rather, to an approach applicable to a great many or, perhaps, to all forms of musical activity" (Laycock 2005, 6). But even if process-oriented creative approaches are highlighted in school curriculum as well as in culture programs, both teachers and visiting professionals seem to aim for artistic excellence to some degree. School organizers and culture institution administrations, parents as well as the participating pupils' schoolmates, are expecting a musical result, a *product*. Creativity involves something *being made*. This is emphasized by Elliott (1995) who claims that "it is the tangible outcome or product that has priority on determinations of creativity" (Elliott 1995, 216).

Kenny and Christophersen (Chapter 1) present criticism of The Cultural Rucksack program. Others also have critically questioned musicians' ability to select suitable repertoires, to collaborate with teachers, and to communicate with young audiences (Holdhus and Espeland 2013; Breivik and Christophersen 2013; Christophersen et al. 2015; Borgen and Brandt 2007). Kenny and Christophersen underline that musician–teacher relationships need to be attended to and further investigated because the alliance between the two participant groups seems to be an essential criterion for success in collaborative projects. They argue that musicians need to possess certain skills to succeed in creative music-making projects. Even though this is evidently correct, findings from the research referred to in this chapter suggest that the *teachers'* experiences and skills also are equally necessary to achieve the desired aims.

The objective of this chapter is therefore to shed light upon how musicians and teachers communicated on how to compose pieces of music and to develop their musical pieces into a performance presented to an audience. An overall aim is to suggest which conditions are necessary to facilitate meaningful collaborative activities within partnerships that develop musical performances.

Background

This chapter builds on a reanalysis of data from a previous study of creative music-making projects (Eidsaa 2015), with a view to focusing on the dialogical interaction between musicians and teachers. The cases referred to mirrored different approaches to creative music-making in the classroom, such as the Write an Opera method, sound-oriented experimental concepts of composition, community music-inspired collaborations between symphony orchestras and school children, and the creation of easy-to-perform musicals or musical plays based on children's narratives. The musicians in the partnerships worked as freelance performers or were part-time employees of orchestras or local cultural schools, worked in universities, or as studio musicians. The teachers had been involved in previous partnerships and had various roles, such as organizer, workshop instructor, performer, project leader, and costume designer. The partnerships were supported by The Cultural Rucksack, local cultural institutions, and private sponsors. All collaborations were structured within practical workshops. The pupils worked in pairs, groups, or plenary sessions. After four days or more, the ensembles presented their musical performance either at school during the daytime or as an evening event.

In both cases that are referred to in this chapter, the Write an Opera method was selected as a framework for collaborations. This method emphasizes pupils' creative involvement in opera libretto writing, music composition, and theatrical staging. Professional performers, such as actors, dancers, and musicians, guide teachers and pupils through the creation of an opera performance.

The Cases

In Case One, *Opera Buffa*, forty seventh graders took part in the partnership. The project was organized by a classroom teacher and a music teacher, who both were involved in creative workshops during the partnership. The project lasted for thirteen days, and the outcome was a staged performance (duration: fifty minutes). The performance included a plot, dialogue, songs, musical intermezzos, and recitatives, altogether twenty-one musical pieces. Ten pupils were selected to compose the music, and the rest of the pupils were given other tasks. The music teacher and the professional musician worked closely together in the composition group.

Case Two, *Music Theatre*, lasted for three months and was organized in weekly three-hour sessions and daily intensive workshops during the last two weeks of the project. The ensemble included thirty-five children, a primary school teacher, a music teacher, a choreographer, a theater instructor, and three musicians. The primary school teacher organized the partnership, and in the following discussion she is referred to as *teacher and project leader*. She was also involved in an amateur theater group and a ballet studio, and she had extensive experience in staging school performances. The final presentation was a musical-like performance in a contemporary pop style that was presented at the local culture hall. Three professional musicians were also involved in the partnership during the last project week, where they functioned as musical arrangers and accompanists for the children throughout the performance.

Investigating Dialogues

Dialogues quickly emerge as an object of research when studying collaborative projects. Questions have been asked about *when* the dialogues take place, *which issues* are discussed, and *who* initiates the conversations. The dialogues referred to in this chapter are recognized as both formal and informal talks. *Formal* talk means information shared among the adults or instructions given to the pupils during sessions, whereas *informal* talk refers to conversations and "small talk" between teachers and musicians in meetings and during workshops. A pertinent question is "What characterizes the dialogues between musicians and teachers in creative music-making projects?"

It should be mentioned that continuous dialogues with the pupils ran in parallel to the communication between the adults. This means that there was a lot of talk going on during creative music-making projects. Still, the present study focuses on how musicians and teachers communicate through dialogue during creative music-making partnerships, from the introduction of musical ideas in the classroom to the presentation of the result of the collaboration.

O'Neill (2011) explains dialogues as *interaction in time and place*, on the one hand, to present narratives and stories and, on the other hand, to position oneself. In this study, the dialogues are investigated to identify musicians' and teachers' values. Mans (2009) explains *value* as "a continuum of which something is rated either high(er) or low(er), or somewhere between good and bad" (Mans 2009, 108). She further reflects on values in relation to musical performance: "Reflection will show that values guide every musical performance, whether in the grandest theatre or the most poverty-stricken home" (Mans 2009, 109). Verbal and nonverbal behavior convey teachers' values (2009, 110). The musicians and the other professional performers who participate in the projects, as well as the teachers, indirectly expose their aesthetic and didactic values or perspectives. *Aesthetic perspectives* signify the artistic or musical dimensions in the partnership (sound, concept, function, and meaning), whereas *didactic approaches* refer to the strategies and learning styles used during the collaborative workshops.

In the following section dialogues from the two cases will be discussed. A model of aesthetic learning processes by Austring and Sørensen (2006) was used as a tool for description and analysis of the data collected during the various phases of the creative process in the music-making partnerships. The seven phases of the model can be easily recognized in a wide range of art partnerships:

Phase 1 Motivation is the first step of the partnership when the adults meet for the first time to discuss their upcoming collaboration, and *Phase 2 Introduction* is the first encounter between pupils, teachers, and professionals. During *Phase 3 Experiments*, the ensemble explores melodic motifs, rhythmical patterns, ostinatos, dynamics, harmonies, and musical structures, and the process of selecting a repertoire for further rehearsals takes place during *Phase 4 Exchange of Musical Ideas*. When the ensemble reaches *Phase 5 Repertoire and Rehearsals*, the process will correspond to the rehearsals of a choir, a school band, or an orchestra before a traditional concert. *Phase 6 The Performance* is the artistic presentation of the collaborators' newly developed musical expressions, and the process and result are discussed during *Phase 7 Aesthetic Evaluation*. The identification of phases in creative music-making partnerships makes it easier to compare data collected in individual projects and clarifies the difference between creative music-making projects and projects with a scored repertoire, such as a cantata or a collection of standard jazz melodies.

This study focuses on verbal communication during these seven phases. In the following section examples of dialogues or talks from each case will be presented.

Examples: Dialogues in Creative Music-Making Projects

Phase 1, Motivation: Expectation

The visiting professionals and the teachers in both cases meet to discuss the framework of the upcoming project. The introductory dialogues are informal, almost like "small talk." They seem pleased with the Write an Opera concept, and no one suggests alternative musical concepts. To develop a unique musical performance seems to motivate both teachers and visiting professionals. During the first meeting the musicians and the teachers mainly exchange information, as shown in the following dialogue in Case One:

Music teacher:	I am very eager to see what ideas the children will suggest for the topic of the opera.
The musician:	Yes, it is always exciting on the first day. You never know what's coming up!
Music teacher:	Should we organize an audition for the opera characters the first week?
The musician:	I think we will need to have an audition on next Friday.

This dialogue is optimistic and task oriented. The musician's and the music teacher's curiosity for what will unfold during the next days is evident. The atmosphere seems to be relaxed even if they know that the project content doesn't exist yet and the musical repertoire and other aesthetic expressions have yet to be made. Their conversation mirrors a practical approach to the creative music-making process: We will create *something*.

Phase Two, Introduction: Ownership and Relevance

The teachers' and the pupils' motivation is based on their experience of relevance and ownership of the tasks given (Craft 2005). As soon as the children in Case One selected the keywords *mafia drama, robbery, Italy, hidden treasure, stolen diamonds*, the music teacher and the musician commented:

Musician:	It's great that the children have selected to work with this topic! I'll stop by a shop on my way home to get a book about Italy.
Music teacher:	I have an idea! Now I am going to create a video promoting Italy for a presentation before the performance! Tomorrow I'm going to choose a group of five pupils.

The adults left the meeting in good spirits, giving the impression that they evaluated the idea as relevant and motivating. Neither the classroom teacher nor the other visiting professionals (actor and designer) commented that producing a video could be considered out of context considering their performance should be based on the Write an Opera method.

Based on this example it seems that the musician and the music teacher already share a feeling of ownership, even on the very first day of the partnership. Their involvement created a "community feeling" or team spirit. In this situation, the pupils' keywords served as "a contact zone" among adults as well as among children. The term *contact zone* is used by O'Neill (2011), who discusses how the performing of music in an ensemble can function as a zone for understanding between collaborating partners. A contact zone is:

> a meeting point between cultural groups where meanings and practices of the contacting partners change as result of communication, understandings, and misunderstandings.
> (O'Neill 2011, 185)

The visiting professional and the teachers valued the children's keywords, which were created in the classroom with excitement during the very first workshop. During the conversation in meetings, the adult participants seemed to increase their expectations for the upcoming performance.

Phase Three, Experimentation: The Challenge of Music-Making Activities in the Classroom

In the following dialogue, the participating adults in *Case Two, Music Theater*, described their own roles throughout the process as creators and organizers:

The teacher (project leader):	During the first stage of the Write an Opera process, it is the pupils themselves who decide and vote for the plot, the opera characters, the title and the dialogues. It is almost like IDOL. However, when you continue the process, the teachers need to connect all things together.
Theatre instructor:	Yes, the pupils are often unrealistic about what we can manage to do in [a] performance. They suggested bringing a car on stage during the introduction of the performance. That couldn't work. All the time, I need to reduce and simplify their ideas.

In this dialogue the teacher (project leader) and the theater instructor shared the perspective on the children's ability to create musical expressions. Their understanding of the pupils' artistic capacity was that they lack *artistic overview*. The teacher (project leader) explains and defends her decision to hire professional musicians for the final phase of the performance:

The pupils need a lot of assistance in their process of creating music. Often only fragments of their ideas could be used, such as short choruses or single melodic phrases or their suggestion of chords. Therefore, at this school, we prefer to hire professional pop musicians to develop the pupils' ideas into new songs. The musicians create sing-back recordings for us to use in rehearsals, and sometimes they are also playing on stage together with the children. The children are proud of their ideas when they are presented in a new style on stage.

Even if the teacher's choice is controversial compared to creative composition concepts for classrooms, she openly expresses her belief in the standard pop song as the most suitable musical expression for the upcoming performance.

Phase Four, Exchange of Ideas: Belief in the Children's Competence

The musicians and the teachers in Case One talked informally every day during morning meetings, breaks, and afternoon meetings. The conversations included personal comments, such as:

The music teacher: I am not quite sure if this performance will ever be realized. Every day the presentation draws nearer. And today the pupils even started to invite the audience!
Visiting designer: I am sure there will be a performance! Because of the kids, they always manage!
The music teacher: But will this always be true? Are you sure?
Visiting designer: Yes, in fact, this always happens! I have experienced this many times before.

The music teacher's honest question came after a chaotic workshop on the fifth day of the partnership. His worries were easy to understand because the children at this stage didn't concentrate on the creative tasks and the situation had been chaotic most of the day. The pupils didn't succeed this day in presenting any musical material for the classmates who had created the lyrics.

Phase Five, Repertoire and Rehearsals: Challenges in Music-Making Activities

The following dialogue is between the teacher (project leader) and the music teacher in Case Two when they share reflections on composition activities based on the Write an Opera principles.

The music teacher: To compose music is the most difficult part of the Write an Opera method. Every time the children develop the opera

	plot and narrative, and as well as the creation of the opera characters, they are happy and cheerful. The moment we start to compose music, the problems appear.
The teacher (project leader):	Yes, every time we have prepared a Write an Opera project at our school, I was the one who connected the pupils' ideas and elements into the final performance. Very few children have the competence to do such things.

The conversation between the music teacher and project leader revealed that their aim for the music-making tasks was to create ordinary, melodic "songs" like popular hits. However, none of the teachers in Case Two had the necessary skills to scaffold creative music-making processes in the classroom. Aware of the fact, the project leader and the music teacher decided to involve three local professional musicians from outside the school. The children's musical sketches were then changed into catchy pop tunes by three professional pop musicians.

Phase Six, Performance: Disagreement on the Performance Concept

The musician, the actor, the designer, and the two teachers continued through the various phases of the collaborative project in Case One with a shared intensity. However, there were moments of tension, as mirrored in the following interview with the music teacher:

Music teacher:	Before the second presentation of the ensemble's final performance, I suggested to the actor, the project leader, that the most musically talented pupil in the class should be offered the position as a soloist in the school opera when the ensemble should present their musical result for the second time at the local concert hall. I argued that it would be favorable for the girl to perform in front of a new audience. I had been working on connecting a violin solo part into the opera libretto. The girl attended an advanced level group at cultural school, and my intention was to give the audience a pause from the solid sound of Orff instruments to the soft timbre of the violin. The actor didn't agree. I guess he didn't want anyone to be a star in this performance concept. His argument is that this performance is a Write an Opera project, and none of the pupils should be raised up above others.

This narrative reflects the teacher's and the musician's contrasting aesthetic perspective and didactic approach. The music teacher defended his choice and claimed that the sound of the violin in this context in particular would be meaningful to the audience. And a second dimension is that the young soloist herself is going to benefit from the presentation. The teacher's attitude seems rational from a didactic perspective. But he leaves the final decision on performance details to the visiting professional. This situation exemplifies the traditional understanding of roles, with the professional musician as superior to the teacher.

Phase Seven, Aesthetic Evaluation: A Music Teacher's Reflections on Creativity in the Classroom

The teacher's reflection referred to in Phase Three mirrors an uncertainty about the children's ability to compose music for the ensemble. The teacher honestly shares her opinion: "only fragments of ideas could be used." As shown in this quote, the music teacher claims that the children's raw musical material should be refined and developed before being presented on stage. To develop musical ideas from one phase into the next is described by Austring and Sørensen (2006) as demanding. However, the transition between Phase Four (exchange of ideas) and Phase Five (rehearsals and repertoire) is critical. At this point, the musician and the teacher in Case One succeeded in selecting the ideas and the musical components for the final performance, whereas the music teacher and the project leader in Case Two gave up the creative music-making process. The teacher left the principle of the Write an Opera method, which is to let the pupils create all parts of the performance, though assisted by the professionals' scaffolding. Elliott (1995) discusses the importance of the music teacher's (or musician's) scaffolding in music-making processes and refers to *modeling, coaching, mentoring, fading, reflection,* and *exploration* as important aspects of the creative process (Elliott 1995, 278).

In Case Two, *Music Theatre*, it was primarily the music teachers and the project leaders who were in need of scaffolding because they lacked competence in creating music by the step-by-step approach, a distinctive feature of the Write an Opera method. In their effort to create a "good" result that made the pupils feel "proud," they lean on a professional pop trio's contribution.

One of the findings of this study is that creative music-making processes are complex. The adult participants (teachers, musicians, or other professionals) are obliged to communicate with each other through all seven phases described earlier. Their ability to make decisions along the way is essential. Fautley and Savage (2007) underline that to conduct creative music-making processes in the classroom demands the ability *to understand direction, innovation, action, development, awareness of convention, being willing to take risks, and being imaginative* (Fautley and Savage 2007, 103). Therefore, it is easy to understand the decision made by the project leader in Case Two to let professionals complete the creative music-making process without involving the children. The further development of the two ensembles' performances takes its point of departure in the fixed repertoire. At this stage the communication pattern changes, and the talk will primarily be short, explicit instructive dialogues, addressing aesthetic details.

The analysis revealed that the professionals in the two musician–teacher teams used various aesthetic approaches in developing their ensemble's musical performance. In Case One, *Opera Buffa*, teachers and musicians were qualified to connect the children's contributions into coherent aesthetic expressions. Before the workshops, the musician and the music teacher discussed how to reduce possibilities or problem spaces in the composition processes (Sloboda 1985). In Case Two, *Music Theatre*, the music teacher and the project leader guided the pupils step by step on libretto writings, design, and choreography, and the music-making process was transferred to a professional ensemble.

What Characterizes the Dialogues between Musicians and Teachers in Collaborative Music-Making Projects?

The findings show that musicians and teachers exchange ideas and share opinions during the various stages of the creative process. Their ability to be flexible and open, to make decisions, and their willingness to take risks is essential to the success of the partnerships (Fautley and Savage 2007). To take part in a creative partnership could be compared to being on a voyage of discovery, such as described by Benson (2003). The discovery, Benson says, always "takes place within a specific context" (2003, 39f). The music-making process in the partnership project is a definite context in which discovery is possible for all participants. According to Hallam (2011), geographical or historical aspects will influence the situation. For the success of the partnership, it is necessary that the visiting musicians are familiar with the school's ethos and that they value local circumstances:

> While new initiatives may assume a blank canvas, in reality, there will be a history. Every successful local intervention has to be placed within the context of unique local circumstances.
>
> (Hallam 2011, 159)

Even if the projects referred to in this chapter were differently structured and the final presentations showed diversity in genre and style, musicians and teachers identified and defined their respective roles during early stages of the collaboration. For this reason, the ensemble in Case One chose to compose music in a modernistic recitative-like style, using minimalistic patterns and four tone scales, whereas the teacher and the music teacher in Case Two preferred to present traditional melodies based on pop music chord progressions as their own ensemble's expression. By communicating through dialogues from the very first day of the project, both ensembles managed to develop their own unique concept.

The audiences who attended each ensemble's final presentation seemed to value the result. The school administrators expressed their great admiration to the teachers and professionals who had assisted the children in their creative work, parents were moved, and the participating pupils' schoolmates were impressed. There were probably few individuals among the audience who could imagine the teachers' and musicians' intensive scaffolding from the very beginning to the conclusion of a partnership. The creative music-making processes in both cases appeared to be complicated because the eleven- and twelve-year-olds needed constant mentoring during all activities.

In creative collaborative partnerships, the participants share the uncertainty about the musical outcome. They must cope with the tensions caused by the unpredictability during the first four phases in creative music-making partnerships: *motivation, introduction, experiments,* and *exchange of ideas* (Austring and Sørensen 2006). Based on findings from this study, the lack of repertoire is stressful both for the musicians and the teachers during the first days of any collaborative project. To transfer children's musical ideas into tangible results far exceeds the effort it takes to prepare a fixed repertoire for an upcoming concert. Wiggins (2011) confirms the intensity in the classroom during composing activities:

> Even in the healthiest of learning situations, students and teachers find themselves in a constant state of negotiation, seeking a productive mutuality that will enable all parties to move forward toward their goals.
> (Wiggins 2011, 89)

Wiggins' reflections mirror that it is necessary for instructors to possess in-depth knowledge on composition techniques for classroom settings. From this researcher's perspective, relational aspects and organizational issues must also be taken into consideration. According to this study the participants' emotional stress seems to decrease parallel to the gradual release of the ensemble's new musical repertoire.

In both cases discussed in this chapter, the musician–teacher teams focused their attention on practical activities in the classroom. They were ambitious and determined to present a successful performance, and their dialogues were primarily focused on how to develop the aesthetic results. Musical styles and concepts were discussed, as well as the respective ensemble's limitations and potential. Few victory narratives were told during the collaboration, but occasionally, possible positive effects from participating in creative partnerships were mentioned in meetings between the teachers and the musicians. Both the visiting musicians and the teachers strived to balance artistic visions with what was possible to accomplish in the ensemble. In collaborative music-making projects, the adult participants will need to negotiate a realistic artistic concept (Wiggins 2011). Isaksen (2014) uses the metaphor of two ships navigating from one place to another, meeting each other on the open sea, when describing collaborative aesthetic processes (Isaksen 2014, 190).

The dialogues in creative music-making partnership continuously remind the partners about the upcoming result, the final product or *the music*. Although The Cultural Rucksack program describes creative partnerships as highly valuable for the children's aesthetic understanding and for developing their creative skills, the work in the classroom is characterized by a practical down-to-earth approach. The participants simply work on the task, step by step.

From the researcher's perspective, creative music-making partnerships become meaningful collaborations when the musicians and the teachers trust and respect each other. A criterion for the success in partnerships is to enjoy being in the contact zone between partners (O'Neill 2011) and to communicate with the partners through all phases of the creative process. Interaction and communication between musicians and teachers will bridge the participants' contributions together into meaningful aesthetic expressions, similar to how narrative film music creates a feeling of continuity in a movie.

References

Austring, Bennyé D., and Merete Sørensen. 2006. *Æstetik og læring: Grundbog om æstetiske læreprocesser*. København: Hans Reitzels Forlag.

Benson, Bruce Ellis. 2003. *The Improvisation of Musical Dialogue: A Phenomenology of Music*. Cambridge: Cambridge University Press.

Borgen, Jorunn S., and Synnøve S. Brandt. 2006. Ekstraordinært eller selvfølgelig? Evaluering av Den Kulturelle Skolesekken i grunnskolen. *NIFU STEP*, Rapport 5/2006.

Breivik, Jan-Kåre, and Catharina Christophersen. 2013. *Den Kulturelle Skolesekken*. Oslo: Kulturrådet.

Christophersen, Catharina, Jan-Kåre Breivik, Anne D. Homme, and Lise H. Rykkja. 2015. *The Cultural Rucksack: A National Program for Art and Culture in Norwegian Schools*. Oslo: Art Council Norway.

Colley, Bernadette, Randi Eidsaa, Ailbhe Kenny, and Bo-Wah Leung. 2012. "Music Education Partnerships in Practice." In *The Oxford Handbook of Music Education*, Vol. 1, edited by Gary McPherson and Graham F. Welch, 341–57. Oxford: Oxford University Press.

Craft, Anna. 2005. *Creativity in Schools: Tensions and Dilemmas*. London: Routledge/Falmer.

Eidsaa, Randi Margrethe. 2015. "Hvem skaper musikken? En studie av musikalsk skapende partnerskapsprosjekter i skolen utfra et estetisk og et didaktisk perspektiv." PhD diss., University of Aarhus. Accessed June 11, http://edu.au.dk/fileadmin/edu/phdafhandlinger/PhD-afhandling-Randi-Margrethe-Eidsaa.pdf.

Elliott, David. 1995. *Music Matters: A New Philosophy of Music Education*. Oxford: Oxford University Press.

Fautley, Martin, and Jonathan Savage. 2007. *Creativity in Secondary Education*. Exeter: Learning Matters.

Hallam, Richard. 2011. "Effective Partnership Working in Music Education: Principle and Practice." *International Journal of Music Education*, 29 (2), 155–71.

Holdhus, Kari, and Magne Espeland. 2013. The visiting artist in schools: Art based or school based practices? *International Journal of Education and the Arts*, 14 (S1.10) Accessed January 15, 2014 from http://www.ijea.org/v14si1/v14si1-10.pdf

Isaksen, Bjarne. 2014. "Kunstnerlæreren—mellom det kontinuerlige og det diskontinuerlige." In *Kunstner eller lærer: Profesjonsdilemmaer i musikk- og kunstpedagogisk utdanning*, edited by Elin Angelo and Signe Kalsnes, 184–94. Oslo: Cappelen Damm Akademisk.

Laycock, Jolyon. 2005. *The Changing Role of the Composer in Society a Study of the Historical Background and Current Methodologies of Creative Music-Making*. Bern: Peter Lang AG.

Mans, Minette. 2009. *Living in the Worlds of Music: A View on Education and Values*. Dordrecht, The Netherlands: Springer.
O'Neill, Susan. 2011. "Learning in and Through Music Performance: Understanding Cultural Diversity via Inquiry and Dialogue." In *A Cultural Psychology of Music Education*, edited by Margaret S. Barrett, 179–97. Oxford: Oxford University Press.
Østergaard, Edvin. 2004. "Hemmelige rom: Komponeringens slektskap med mysteriet." In *Musikk og mysterium: Fjorten essays om grensesprengende musikalsk erfaring*, edited by Erling Guldbrandsen and Øivind Varkøy, 91–110. Oslo: Cappelen Forlag.
Sloboda, John. 1985. *The Musical Mind: The Cognitive Psychology of Music*. Oxford: Oxford University Press.
Wiggins, Jackie. 2011. "When the Music Is Theirs: Scaffolding Young Songwriters." In *A Cultural Psychology of Music Education*, edited by Margaret S. Barrett, 83–114. Oxford: Oxford University Press.

13
Abigail's Story: The Perspective of the Professor/iPadist/Teaching Artist

CLINT RANDLES

Tragedy

On May 21, 2010, Abigail was hit by a car while crossing the street. She was rushed to the hospital with numerous injuries, including a broken left leg, a broken back, a broken neck, and most critically a collapsed lung and severe traumatic brain injury. For the next eight months she was in a coma, and for the years since coming out of it up to the writing of this chapter she has battled every challenge that has been put in front of her, including eight major life-threatening surgeries. She is a survivor. Abigail's mom, Robin, has been with her through it all, providing a constant source of support during her recovery process.

I am a music education professor, performing guitarist, and iPadist in the Tampa Bay, Florida, region of the United States and VSA (International Organization on Arts and Disability) Teaching Artist. It is my role as a performing musician that brought the people who work for VSA into my life and led to my becoming a VSA Teaching Artist. I have worked now in this role for four years, becoming a national expert on how the iPad can be used as a musical instrument with students with disabilities. Relating to the themes of this book, I am both the musician and the teacher in this collaboration.

This chapter is the telling of the story of Abigail's reconnecting to music, something that she loved before her accident, and something that she had longed to have back in her life after the accident. It is a story of a student with special needs being reconnected to music through a teacher's use of technology (Randles 2015). Although the literature in this area suggests a connection to the use of technology in enhancing the well-being of students with special needs (Kern et al. 2007; Patterson 2003; Pellitteri 2000; Wilson and McCrary 1996) and the use of music in therapeutic applications to remedy patients' cognitive functioning (Besson and Frederique 1995; Capodieci et al. 2010; Sakamoto et al. 2013), few stories provide a window into what technology can do to reconnect students with their lost identity as musicians. Because removing myself from this story would be impossible and counterproductive to sharing as I am the teacher, the scholar, and the musician in my classroom, I choose to utilize an autoethnographic approach (Chang 2008). I shall begin by providing some context to this story by way of both the students with special needs literature in and outside of music education and the literature on the use of iPad technology in music teaching and learning.

Teaching Artists, the iPad as an Instrument, and Community Arts Education Partnerships

I am a VSA Teaching Artist. Notice that both "teaching" and "artist" are mentioned in my title. I am a musician in the real world,[1] and I teach my students how to be similarly musical. My connection with VSA (Very Special Artists, now more commonly referred to as the International Organization for Arts and Disability) began in the summer of 2013. Wendy Finklea, the Director of Programs for VSA Florida (which is housed at my university) attended a concert by Touch, the iPad band that I am a part of at the University of South Florida, and recruited me to begin a program for students with disability, ages eight to twenty-eight, with the assistance of a team of paraprofessionals and volunteer helpers once a week. That program expanded to include summer camp experiences and various webinar teaching sessions where I have shared ideas with colleagues from around the country with Teaching Artists in Florida. I have been a music teacher in both tertiary and collegiate settings in the United States for sixteen years as of the writing of this chapter and have had experience teaching students with special needs at all levels. However, few teaching endeavors before becoming a VSA Teaching Artist have stretched my patience, tested my resolve, or made me feel more human than the past years that I have spent using the iPad as a musical instrument with students who for various reasons have been distanced from performance-based, creativity-centered, music-making experiences.

As I have described in previous work, I am an iPadist (Randles 2013b). I mention this here because iPadists are still not all that common in the world of musicians. My iPad is not *like* an instrument; my iPad *is* an instrument (Williams 2014). It took my being an iPadist, in conjunction with years of experience working with special needs populations, to recognize the utility of what my unique instrument could mean for disadvantaged (physically, socially, emotionally) students. Although all of the instruments that have existed up until this point in history will most likely be valuable in the future to some extent, the development of tablet technology is likely to create new spaces for musical performance that were not previously given consideration.

The literature on students with disabilities and musical engagement is more developed in the areas of art therapy, occupational therapy, music therapy, medicine, education (Pellitteri 2000), and psychology (Kern et al. 2007) than in music education (Patterson 2003; Wilson and McCrary 1996). Art therapists, who use music in their sessions, have been examining how to better analyze the interactions between teacher and participants during teaching sessions (Ball 2002). Occupational therapists have been studying how computer systems have allowed students with little mobility to play and create music (Tam et al. 2007). Music therapists have examined the role of technology in working with students with special needs and music, defining seven categories, where one uses "adapted musical instruments" (Crowe and Rio 2004, 291–2). Crowe and Rio suggest that all manner of adaptations be made for students with special needs, which might include the use of iPads as instruments. This chapter and related research are necessary to develop a better understanding of technology's role in providing students with disabilities opportunities to engage meaningfully with music in new and interesting ways. Because these "adapted musical instruments" (Crowe and Rio 2004, 291–2) are relatively new, few studies have looked at how these technologies affect the lives of students with special needs.

The iPad itself, as a technology that can enhance music instruction, has received some attention in the music education literature in recent years. Elliott has listed iPad orchestras in his vision of music education as/for artistic citizenship (2012). Some music educators suggest that music and education would be wise to embrace technologies such as the iPad as a means of staying relevant in the context of a world culture that utilizes and embraces these and other ubiquitous technologies (Peluso 2012; Williams 2014). Colleagues in Singapore have presented their vision of classrooms where the iPad plays a central role in teaching composition, listening, and performance (Zhou et al. 2011). Riley (2013) uses and advocates for the use of the iPad and other tablet technologies in all manner of music teaching and learning. Randles et al. (in press) write specifically about how the iPad can create performance and creative experiences in the emerging modern band curricular area for students with special needs in North America. In summation, the iPad is a technology that a growing number of practitioners and scholars/researchers have implemented in practice, sometimes with harsh criticism by proponents of solely traditional musical instruments (Randles 2013a). It was this technology that brought the world of Teaching Artists into both my practical and research worlds.

Teaching Artists are performing musicians who also teach, typically in community settings (Lee 2013). They represent individuals who are both musicians and teachers, and they embody a form of school–community–university partnership in action (Moon 2016). As a university professor, I represent the university where I teach. I live in the greater Tampa area and am therefore a member of the community. I work in local schools with students with special needs as a Teaching Artist. All of these roles work together to describe what Bringle and Hatcher (2002) call campus–community partnership for the common good, where resources including knowledge and expertise are leveraged for the betterment of peoples' lives. Abigail was struck by a car at the same time that we were starting an iPad band at my university. This was an opportunity for me as a Teaching Artist to address what Bringle and Hatcher (2002) call critical issues—in this case, a young woman who desired to make music once again.

Abigail's Story

Serendipity

I met Abigail in the spring of 2014 when she enrolled in the VSA class that I taught that met once a week at a rehabilitation/community center/school in Tampa, Florida. Robin, Abigail's mother, heard about the VSA program through her physical therapist, and so on a warm February day in Florida, Robin rolled Abigail's wheelchair in. It is then that I met the twenty-two-year-old former musician in person. Her acute sense of witty humor was the first quality that I noticed about her—she had a better command of comedy than most people I know, not a person who I would have expected to have been through as much trauma as she had been. The other students and parents in the group welcomed them without reservation. Robin told me quickly about the accident and how before all of that Abigail was a very fine flute player in her school band, one of the best at her high school. Tragedy had taken that away, but Abigail (and Robin) where curious to see how she might be reconnected to her former musician self.

As I took in the enormity of what I was being told about the accident, I dialed up one of the iPads to produce flute sounds via an app that we frequently used called *ThumbJam*. As I made the first sounds on the iPad that reproduced the sounds of the flute, I could see that Robin and Abigail were optimistic about the extent to which a program such as the one that I taught could be beneficial to her recovery process. As was typical in most of the classes that I taught for VSA during that time, I set her iPad to play within a key—G minor blues—so that all of the students could play together and sound good as a group (at least there would be fewer notes that would sound wrong for what we were trying to accomplish together). I handed Robin the iPad to hold for Abigail (yet another instance where she had been an advocate for her daughter's well-being), and as Abigail played those first notes I could see hope and joy in their faces. It was real joy, the kind that very few things in all of life can provide a person, joy in musical sound form, joy in notes, motion, and sound waves.

At that moment I saw clearly in a way that I had not very many times in my entire career as a music teacher the healing, almost spiritual, quality of music. Musicians know it well. It is what keeps us coming back time and time again. It gives the unencumbered, free-spirited, flute-playing 17-year-old girl wings as much as it does the wheelchair-bound 22-year-old iPadist. Music gives us voice and something to say. We can take it for granted if we are not careful. That feeling that we get when we are a part of something bigger than ourselves is one of the benefits that music provides. Abigail had lost it through her adversity and that night found it again. There is not a better thing that any Teaching Artist (or music teacher for that matter) can do for a person than to give someone back the gift of being able to make music that was lost. Someone had returned to music-making, with all of the benefits that so doing entails.

Being an iPadist

The first encounter with using the iPad as a musical instrument with Abigail in the class mentioned previously led to more of the same and to more instances where I tried to replicate that sense of joy in as many ways as I could. The social cohesion of the class helped in that there were other students who had found their own unique ways into a class that utilized the iPad as an instrument. They each had their own reason for being there. One student, Michael, was an accomplished self-published (via *SoundCloud*) composer of mostly video game music. In the class he had found a vehicle for being musical with other people and not just with his computer (Randles 2015). Zachary, the student with Down syndrome, found an instrument in the app *Cosmovox*, one that did not require him to press down, hold, or position his fingers over keys; rather, he simply needed to tilt the iPad in either direction to articulate the performance of melodic content. Asani, another student, found a source of joy in the wash of musical sounds that he created by fixating on a pattern of notes and repeating them over and over and over again. For all of these students the iPad was not like a musical instrument; the iPad was a musical instrument (Williams 2014), a way into a musical performance world where they could sound good from the beginning (Randles et al. in press). With the iPad as an instrument my students performed for the public, their peers, and their families.

Improvisation

There is something special that is hard to describe about making good in musical performance. Abigail improvised a solo on the iPad flute in the presence of hundreds of people at the University of South Florida's School of Music, her performance forever linked to the experiences of everyone in attendance. With her performance, Abigail provided an example of how she has continued on despite her circumstances and adversities. Although her improvisation that night was a public performance, the special aspect of this sort of music-making was consistently present in each of the weekly classes that I taught as a Teaching Artist.

Improvising was and has always been a powerful entryway into meaningful music-making for myself and my students (not only my students with special needs). My work as a VSA Teaching Artist would not have been possible if it were not for the power and interest-sustaining potential of musical improvisation. We improvise in every session. I structure lessons and progressions of lessons based on grooves from the music that students enjoy listening to. This tends to be based on some aspect of popular or contemporary music. Abigail has limited mobility in her left arm that often necessitated her mother holding her iPad for her as she played. Over a number of hour-long sessions, she learned how to improvise with an iPad.

Making good in musical performance is for everyone. What I did as a Teaching Artist in this way, facilitating improvisation, overlaps nicely with the field of music therapy (Kern and Humpal 2014). That night Abigail showed all in attendance that she would not be limited by her physical disabilities, that she can—like she did before her accident—perform music with other people on a stage. Music can continue to move us when our bodies have been changed, when we have experienced hardship, when we feel like giving up, when no one thinks that we have a chance to survive.

Back to Notation

I have found myself being an advocate in Abigail's case for reading and performing from standard Western classical notation. I have only recently come to realize what Abigail needs most of all from the iPad as a musical instrument class. Robin's main goals for Abigail as she began using the iPad as a musical instrument were (1) better left/right brain connectivity and strengthened left brain, (2) memory connection, and (3) being out on a regular basis for more than just therapy appointments.

It seemed that my primary strategy for most of the students, that of creating situations where musicians of very different cognitive and physical functioning could jump in and contribute to the group sound through singing and instrumental improvisation, although still beneficial, might fall short of giving Abigail the left brain help that comes more from decoding notation and performing something that is supposed to sound more or less a certain way. So I purchased a music stand and some flute books for her, one that included some songs from the Harry Potter movies, as I remembered that she had performed a Harry Potter show in marching band before her accident. As of the writing of this chapter, Abigail is reconnecting with the read-from-notation side of music-making and experiencing some positive results that her physicians and Robin have noticed. This example points to my dual competence as both a teacher and a musician/artist, responding in the moment and over time to the personal needs of my students, having empathy, and working as best I can to present the best of what music can offer.

I have learned more than anything about the therapeutic power of music to achieve multiple beneficial qualities for human beings by being a Teaching Artist in this school–community–university partnership (Moon 2016). All of the ways that music is made seem to contribute to different areas of benefit. My groove-making, improvisation-centered approach to teaching is great for most students most of the time, but it is not the end-all-be-all for all students all of the time. As a Teaching Artist I must look at all of the diverse ways that people engage with music so that I can effectively use all of the strategies that are available to help my students.

With Abigail my strategy has been to access the part of her brain that organizes and makes logical the translation of written notation into musical sounds, with the goal in mind of helping her with the areas that her mother and physicians would like to see improved. Joy will always be my primary goal in my teaching, but these secondary goals (primary goals for her doctors) have also been important to me as I desire to bring to Abigail the best of what music, my field of expertise, has to offer. We know that the benefits of music are many and that they touch on the many ways that humans exist and thrive in the world (Bowman 1998; Elliott and Silverman 2015; Mark and Gary 2007). I have to now think more about the role of musical processes as medicine for her brain, for her overall well-being. I am hopeful that doing this will also have the potential to be fun for her.

Discussion

As I reflect on Abigail's story where the iPad is concerned, I see (1) a connection of my work with her to what Crowe and Rio (2004) have call "adapted musical instruments" and (2) the process of my work with her as an illustration of my theory of change in music education (Randles 2013b). I wonder how life stories such as this one can help the music education profession critique and challenge assumptions about the value of technology in current music teaching and learning settings. It took me being an iPadist to recognize the value of a tablet being something that could be used as an instrument. It takes my continual reflection on Abigail's needs to decide which of the benefits of music I should focus my attention on as I provide experiences for her in a classroom music setting. My work with her borders on the work that music therapists do in a clinical setting (Crowe and Rio 2004), but is clearly music education in that I work with her in a classroom setting where public performances tailored to the students' needs are a constant expectation.

A VSA Teaching Artist must necessarily be a different variety of Teaching Artist than the kind typically mentioned in the arts education literature (Beveridge 2010; Graham and Zwirn 2010). Teaching Artists tend to be different from regular classroom arts teachers in that they are still practicing artists in addition to fulfilling their teaching roles. VSA Teaching Artists meet those requirements as well. However, students with special needs further require levels of patience and pedagogical strategy, and so require a different kind of teacher, one sensitive to their specific needs. Furthermore, I would not be able to be a Teaching Artist for VSA if I were not also a musician/artist with a tablet. I inspire my students by being a musician they can emulate, and I use my expertise to bring out the best in them.

In many circumstances, teacher and musician competence reside in two different people, and there could be tensions. However, this may not always be the case. Some of the best teachers that I know and work with function well as both teachers and artists. Certain teaching roles in music education require a higher degree of the coexistence of these two roles. An applied lessons teacher must be an excellent practicing musician in order to teach people daily to be excellent practicing musicians. An ensemble director might be able to hide the fact that they are not excellent performers currently by going about the business of making an ensemble sound better—never picking up an instrument, composing, or improvising. As a VSA Teaching Artist, my musicianship must make its way into my daily practice in order to have any semblance of success. I must demonstrate for and constantly be thinking of ways to improve the experience of my students to maximize their learning.

Abigail's story points to a process that a music teacher must work through as she seeks to understand her specific context and plan for meaningful music-making for all—students, parents, colleagues, and community—in her unique setting. Stauffer's (2012) notions of place-conscious music education are particularly relevant to this discussion. Teachers like "Jim" (Stauffer 2012, 447) who suggests to teachers, "Open your eyes. Open your ears. Look where you are, and create what needs to be there," are the kind of teacher who is required if technologies are to be incorporated successfully into teaching practice. Each student with special needs has such a wide array of difficulties that can make interaction and functioning within their worlds (that include a music classroom) at times profoundly difficult. However, as I have suggested in other work, students with special needs, being an outlier population of students, point us in unique ways to the needs of all humanity (Randles et al. in press), and community programs such as VSA Florida can help us see what might be possible in our school music programs (Haroutounian 1998). Who does not deserve a customizable music education? Technology can allow music teachers to turn things that would not generally function in musical ways (Crowe and Rio 2004) into primary pathways for musical meaning making, if they are open to new possibilities.

Multiple motivations for what music can do for Abigail were a part of this story, and part of most stories where the incorporation of a new technology is involved. At first, the motivation was to (1) use the iPad to function as a flute by using *ThumbJam*, an app where a musician can touch the note of the scale on the screen and hear a close approximation of authentic sounds produced, and (2) use improvisation in a particular style as a safe place to play around with sound. This method was successful in that she is now able to play in a band and not worry about being wrong. Moving from there to logical/sequential note reading from notation satisfied her mother's desire to more directly address the memory-recall portions of her brain that she was struggling with, as advised by her physicians who saw Abigail's return to the form of music that she was enjoying before her accident—playing flute from notation—as a way of reinvigorating parts of her brain that were having to relearn certain processes after the accident. Multiple motivations are normal, expected, and philosophically justifiable.

This autoethnographical work (Chang 2008) is primarily the telling of Abigail's story, of being separated from music and then reconnected to it in an albeit different way through a music teacher's innovative (Randles 2013b) use of a particular technology. It is a story that is particularly meaningful to me, someone who is daily a performing musician, music teacher, and scholar/researcher. This story would not have happened if I was not all of these things rolled into one. Although I can certainly see how in many cases the artist cannot also be the teacher, in this case, the result would not have been possible if the artist were not also the teacher. I must therefore question the dualistic notion of the artist being separate from the teacher. In some cases these two roles must be inseparable.

Note

1 http://clintrandles.com/?page_id=2.

References

Ball, Barbara. 2002. "Moments of Change in the Art Therapy Process." *The Arts in Psychotherapy*, 29 (2), 79–92.
Besson, Mireille, and Frederique Faita. 1995. "An Event-Related Potential (ERP) Study of Musical Expectancy: Comparison of Musicians with Nonmusicians." *Journal of Experimental Psychology: Human Perception and Performance*, 21 (6), 1278–96.
Beveridge, Tina. 2010. "No Child Left Behind and Fine Arts Classes." *Arts Education Policy Review*, 11 (1), 4–7.
Bowman, Wayne. 1998. *Philosophical Perspectives on Music*. New York: Oxford University Press.
Bringle, Robert G., and Julie A. Hatcher. 2002. "Campus-Community Partnerships: The Terms of Engagement." *Journal of Social Issues*, 58 (3), 503–16.
Capodieci, Salvatore, Pietro Pinelli, Daniela Zara, Luciano Gamberini, and Giuseppe Riva. 2010. "Music-Enhanced Immersive Virtual Reality in the Rehabilitation of Memory Related Cognitive Processes and Functional Abilities: A Case Report." *Presence*, 10 (4), 450–62.
Chang, Heewon. 2008. *Autoethnography as Method (Developing Qualitative Inquiry)*. Walnut Creek, CA: Left Coast Press.
Crowe, Barbara, and Robin Rio. 2004. "Implications of Technology in Music Therapy Practice and Research for Music Therapy Education: A Review of Literature." *Journal of Music Therapy*, 41 (4), 282–320.
Elliott, David. 2012. "Another Perspective: Music Education as/for Artistic Citizenship." *Music Educators Journal*, 99 (21), 21–7.
Elliott, David, and Marissa Silvermann. 2015. *Music Matters: A Philosophy of Music Education*. New York: Oxford University Press.
Graham, Mark A., and Susan G. Zwirn. 2010. "How Being a Teaching Artist Can Influence K-12 Art Education." *Studies in Art Education: A Journal of Issues and Research*, 51 (3), 219–32.
Haroutounian, Joanne. 1998. "Drop the Hurdles and Open the Doors: Fostering Talent Development Through School and Community Collaboration." *Arts Education Policy Review*, 99 (6), 15–25.
Kern, Petra, and Marcia Humpal. 2014. *Early Childhood Music Therapy and Autism Spectrum Disorders: Developing Potential in Young Children and Their Families*. Philadelphia, PA: Jessica Kingsley Publishers.

Kern, Petra, Mark Wolery, and David Aldridge. 2007. "Use of Songs to Promote Independence in Morning Greeting Routines for Young Children with Autism." *Journal of Autism and Developmental Disorders*, 37 (7), 1264–71.

Lee, Bridget. 2013. "The Process of Developing a Partnership Between Teaching Artists and Teachers." *Teaching Artist Journal*, 11 (1), 26–34.

Mark, Michael, and Charles Gary. 2007. *A History of American Music Education* (2nd ed.). Lanham, MD: Rowman & Littlefield Publishing.

Moon, Seungho. 2016. "'Active Citizenship Is an Awesome Party!' Creating in-Between Spaces for the School-Community-University Partnership." *Teaching Artist Journal*, 14 (3), 145–53.

Patterson, Allyson. 2003. "Music Teachers and Music Therapists: Helping Children Together." *Music Educators Journal*, 89 (4), 35–8.

Pellitteri, John. 2000. "The Consultant's Corner: 'Music Therapy in the Special Education Setting.'" *Journal of Educational and Psychological Consultation*, 11 (3&4), 379–91.

Peluso, Deanna. 2012. "The Fast-Paced iPad Revolution: Can Educators Stay Up to Date and Relevant About These Ubiquitous Devices?" *British Journal of Educational Technology*, 43 (4): E125–E127.

Randles, Clint. 2013a. "Being an iPadist." *General Music Today*, 27 (1), 48–51.

Randles, Clint. 2013b. "A Theory of Change in Music Education." *Music Education Research*, 15 (4), 471–85.

Randles, Clint. 2015. "Opening Doors: iPad Musical Creativity and the Student with Special Needs." In *Music and Media Infused Lives: Music Education in a Digital Age*, edited by Susan O'Neill, 73–88. Montreal, QC: CMEA.

Randles, Clint, Kevin Droe, and Adam Goldberg. In Press. "Creating a Customizable Music Education Through Popular Music." *Music Educators Journal*.

Riley, Patricia. 2013. "Teaching, Learning, and Living with iPads." *Music Educators Journal*, 100 (1), 81–86.

Sakamoto, Mayumi, Hiroshi Ando, and Akimitsu Tsutou. 2013. "Comparing the Effects of Different Individualized Music Interventions for Elderly Individuals with Sever Dementia." *International Psychogeriatrics*, 25 (5), 775–84.

Stauffer, Sandra. 2012. "Place, Music Education, and the Practice and Pedagogy of Philosophy." In *The Oxford Handbook of Philosophy in Music Education*, edited by Wayne Bowman and Ana Lucia Frega, 434–52. New York: Oxford University Press.

Tam, Cynthia, Heidi Schwellnus, Ceilidh Eaton, Yani Hamdani, Andrea Lamont, and Tom Chau. 2007. "Movement-to-Music Computer Technology: A Developmental Play Experience for Children with Severe Physical Disabilities." *Occupational Therapy International*, 14 (2), 99–112.

Williams, David A. 2014. "The iPad Is a REAL Musical Instrument." *Music Educators Journal*, 101 (1), 93–8.

Wilson, Brian, and Jan McCrary. 1996. "The Effect of Instruction on Music Educators' Attitudes Toward Students with Disabilities." *Journal of Research in Music Education*, 44 (1), 26–33.

Zhou, Yinsheng, Graham Percival, Xinxi Wang, Ye Wang, and Shengdong Zhao. 2011. "MOGLASS: Evaluation of a Collaborative System of Mobile Devices for Classroom Music Education of Young Children." In *Proceedings of the SIGCHI Conference on Human Factors in Computing Systems*, edited by Ed Chi and Kristina Hook, 523–32. Vancouver, BC, Canada. Accessed June 12, 2017, doi: 10.1145/1978942.1979016

Part III
Working Towards Partnership

14

"Ideal Relationships": Reconceptualizing Partnership in the Music Classroom Using the Smallian Theory of Musicking

JULIA PARTINGTON

Introduction

In the context of primary music education, a range of international research literature confirms low levels of "generalist" teacher musical confidence (Mills 1989; Gifford 1993; Jeanneret 1997; Hennessey 2000; Conway and Finney 2003; Glover and Ward 2004; Holden and Button 2006; Ruismaki and Tereska 2006; Wiggins and Wiggins 2008; Russell-Bowie 2009, 2010; Welch and Henley 2014). Musician-teacher collaborations in which the musician displays technical skills and expertise are often fraught with hierarchy, and I propose that this can potentially further undermine teachers' musical self-perception and deepen feelings of musical inadequacy.

It is my contention that the predominant model of musician-teacher "partnership" adopted in the United Kingdom in which the musician actively leads and the teacher passively participates, observes, or is actually absent cannot constitute an equal or effective partnership. Furthermore, I would argue that this approach to music teaching is a potential threat to an inclusive music education in that it perpetuates socially constructed notions about musicality being for the "gifted" few in the minds of both teachers *and* children.

In this chapter, I will draw upon Christopher Small's theory of what it means to "music" in relation to my own study of musician-teacher collaboration in the classroom. What follows is a conceptual exploration of how Small's work can inform and revitalize a critical debate about partnerships and collaboration, while also providing a theoretical basis from which to explore an alternative model of musician-teacher collaboration.

Problematizing Partnership

The term "partnership" is highly problematic. As Goodlad asserts:

> Partnering is another of those vanilla-flavored ideas to which we commonly nod our heads in unthinking approval. But good partnering—as

in a good marriage—is hard work. Ideally, each partner has something the other lacks or needs and a willingness to contribute to the other's needs. In other words, there is a potentially powerful positive symbiosis.

(Goodlad 2004, 37–8)

Goodlad's description of partnership as a "vanilla-flavored" concept suggests it is broadly considered to be innocuous. In recent decades partnership has arguably become a fashionable educational concept, model of working, and "buzz-word." In response, researchers have increasingly begun to examine and discuss the nature, potential importance, and possible pitfalls of partnership. For example, Pugh and De'Ath pose the crucial question: "Does partnership really exist or is it simply empty rhetoric?" (1989, 1).

Indeed, trying to ascertain one clear definition of the meaning of partnership proves challenging upon examination of the literature, as attested by Todd (2000), who asserts that partnership is often assumed to be "both an accepted and an unproblematic relationship" (2000, 48). She makes the point that any definition of partnership cannot take into account the complexity of specific relationships, their underlying foundations, and inherent, but perhaps not transparent, hierarchies, particularly where professional expertise is a significant factor.

Thus it is clear that although the term "partnership" may be applied within educational contexts and within educational policy and rhetoric, what is happening in classrooms might not necessarily represent partnership in its truest *implicit* sense.

Background: A Classroom-Based Research Study into Musician–Teacher Partnership

I recently conducted my own seven-month study of a program of collegial classroom "musicking" (Small 1998b), in which I was the visiting musician collaborating with three Key Stage One[1] class teachers with varying low levels of musical confidence. The purpose of the study was to interrogate the nature of the ubiquitous (presently in the United Kingdom) primary school musician–teacher partnership. My research strongly indicated that partnerships in this context are often inadequate in terms of raising both the "musical self-esteem" (Mills 1994, 6) of class teachers and the quality of music teaching and learning at the primary level (Partington 2016). This being so, I sought to identify *another* kind of partnership, one that would disrupt accepted notions of who "can" and "should" teach music and that would enable teachers to become musicians in their own classrooms and their own self-perception.

I began with a strong sense that it was the *relationships* between teachers and musicians that held the most interest for further enquiry and the most potential for gaining a clearer understanding of how a more equal model of partnership in this context might be founded. One participating teacher indicated in an interview at the end of the study that from her perspective, the strength of the human relationships between us as colleagues was of crucial importance and a new experience for her in the context of an in-school music education project. In the interview she commented, "It's not just about the singing. It's about the *people*."

Within the more common model of music education, a musician in the classroom is there to teach music, and the teachers (if present at all) are usually passive participants or serve as mere "assistants to artists" (Christophersen et al. 2015, 43). The prime relationship seen as relevant in this context is that between musician and children, rather than that between musician, teacher, and children altogether. Although the teachers in my study felt this kind of musical experience to be beneficial for *children's* musical learning, they reported that their own musical skills and self-perceptions were not positively developed by this model, nor that it constituted a partnership or relationship in which they felt able, or even permitted, to contribute or collaborate.

Two of the teachers also had experience of a different model of music teaching "partnership" in which a visiting pianist, sent by a local authority music service, accompanied the children singing for thirty minutes each week in the school hall. In this arrangement, the teachers *were* expected to take the lead, choosing the repertoire and actively leading the children as they sang along to the piano accompaniment. Although quite different an experience from one in which the musician takes control in both leadership and selection of repertoire, both teachers told me in an interview that this experience of working with a musician was worst of all in terms of eroding their already fragile musical confidence.

Thus, we see clearly how such models potentially reinforce for children *and* teachers the image of music as being about expertise and only to be taught by those who "know about music" in order to be able to "do it" (Small 1996, 203). My study aimed to move towards a relationship in which music teaching and collaborative experiences of making music together were *shared* between teacher and musician in order that a more reciprocal exchange of what Christophersen et al. refer to as the "broad competency" of teachers and the specialized "narrower sphere" of musicians might occur (Christophersen et al. 2015, 31).

In order to begin establishing relationships that might provide an effective means of altering the deficit way in which the teachers felt about music, their own musical identities, and music teaching, I applied Small's theory of musicking (1998b) to both the implementation and analysis of the study, using it to develop an alternative model of musician–teacher collaboration that does not serve to diminish the musical confidence of teachers.

My findings show that through the establishment of relationships between musicians and teachers that included opportunities for enjoyable musicking, as Small suggests, "in the present" (1996, 211) (including collaborative classroom-based musicking, joint music teaching, and a musician–teacher ukulele band) that afforded teachers, musicians, and children equal creative agency and was rooted in ongoing, honest dialogue, the teachers gradually became receptive to the possibility of repositioning themselves as "musical" and could conceive of their own wider professional expertise as artistically valid and on a par with that of a visiting musician. Such a repositioning of attitudes within the primary classroom, filtered as they are to children who Mills calls "the teachers of tomorrow" (Mills 1994, 6), has potential for the wider disruption of dominant cultural assumptions of what it means to be musical and who has the right to music.

Applying a Smallian Perspective to the Concept of Partnership

I propose that the pursuit of a musician–teacher partnership relationship that operates without hierarchy can be viewed in terms of Christopher Small's extended thesis of musicking in which the notion of relationship is pivotal (1998b).

In what follows, I will discuss how the development of "ideal relationships" (Small 1998b) through collaborative musicking between musicians and teachers might diminish hierarchies relating to musical knowledge and expertise and allow new possibilities of more equal, dialogic relationships to emerge.

A brief, collective view of Small's work enables themes and ideas that are pertinent to the issue of musician–teacher partnership to emerge for discussion. The main body of his work consists of three books, *Music, Society, Education* ([1977] 1996); *Music of the Common Tongue* ([1987] 1998a); and *Musicking* (1998b), along with numerous chapters and articles in music education volumes, journals, and online publications. The trajectory of Small's philosophies contained in these works includes conceiving of children as creative artists rather than as consumers of packaged education; universal musicality or musicality as an innate human trait; the meanings of music itself; and the culminating theory that gained him the most notoriety, his theory of musicking, Small's idea that "[t]he fundamental nature and meaning of music lie not in objects, not in musical works at all, but in action, in what people do" (Small 1998b, 8).

In definition of this concept he writes:

> The act of musicking establishes in the place where it is happening a set of relationships, and it is in those relationships that the meaning of the act lies. They are to be found not only between those organized sounds which are conventionally thought of as being the stuff of musical meaning but also between the people who are taking part, in whatever capacity, in the performance.
>
> (Small 1998b, 13)

It is the attention Small gives to human *relationships* and the potential and, in fact, the very *function*, of musicking to "explore, affirm and celebrate" those relationships (Small 1998b, 183) that is of particular importance to my exploration of the concept of partnership. If, through the act of musicking and the attached exploration of ideal relationships, identities can be constructed, altered, and affirmed and individuals can be empowered in terms of how they situate and perceive themselves in the world, Small's theory might be brought to bear upon the development of a model of *real* and equal partnership between teacher and musician in which the musical, artistic, and pedagogical potential of both partners might be realized *through* collaborative classroom musicking.

Small's specific use of the word "ideal" might be interpreted as a suggestion that some relationships explored and established through musicking are inherently better than others. However, just as I have argued that the term "partnership" in the educational context is generally assumed to infer positive equality, musicking can "celebrate relationships of hierarchy, power and alienation" just as effectively as it can "promote inclusion and peace" (Laurence 2010, 248). On this matter, Small himself tells us, "Musicking is not necessarily a unifying force at all: on the contrary, it can articulate and even exacerbate social divisions" (Small 1998a, 71).

The reason for this potential division lies in the differing values and tastes of individual participants. When the musicking affirms one's values, he tells us:

> In empowering us to explore and affirm our values, taking part in an act of musicking leaves us with a feeling of being more completely ourselves, more in tune with the world and our fellows [. . .] In short, it leaves the participants feeling good. It is thus an instrument of celebration.
> (Small 2007, 212)

However, as Small puts it, "what would be heaven for one might be hell for another" (1998a, 71), suggesting that experiences of musicking do not have to be necessarily positive or meaningful for all taking part in order to be considered valid. With this point, he challenges the "enthusiastic rhetoric" or "goodness discourse" (Christophersen et al. 2015, 56) that permeates commonly held societal attitudes towards music and arts education, the idea that "learning music makes for a better and more rounded human being" (Philpott 2012, 49). If the musicking does not have meaning or relevance to a participant, as we have seen in the examples given earlier of musician–teacher collaborations in which teachers are passive or potentially disempowered within and by the musicking, alienation may occur (Small 2001, 345), and this alienation can be potentially detrimental to the development of one's ideal relationships and exploration of identity.

The idea of musicking enabling individuals to try "relationships on to see how they fit" (Small 1998b, 63) and the potential of these relationships to facilitate the alteration of identities, musical and otherwise, is of crucial significance within this discussion of musician–teacher collaboration.

In much the same way in which Small argued that musicking opportunities and the attendant explorations of identities can potentially transform children into creative artists and constructors of knowledge for themselves, as opposed to passive consumers of an education handed down to them (Small 1996, 216), my contention is that it is through the *relationships* explored and affirmed in collaborative musicking between musicians and teachers that a teacher's own sense of musicality and musical agency might be found and realized. Additionally, it was through the analysis of such relationships within my own research that the essence of a more equal "partnership"—ontologically speaking—could be identified.

We do not have to accept experiences of musicking in which the teacher or the musician is absent or passive, where dialogue is absent, experiences in which one partner is alienated by the musicking, or is cast as dependent "consumer" (Small 1996, 182) beholden to the other. The concept of musicking functions as a tool to imagine *other* sorts of musicking relationships and "dualisms" of identity (Kenny et al. 2015, 161) that can provide a frame for a new understanding of musician–teacher partnerships that are mutually meaningful and enable all participants (including children) to explore, affirm, and celebrate their own musical artistry.

The Model of Dialogic Relationship: An Alternative Approach to Musician–Teacher Partnership

Taking the collected writings of Small as a theoretical lens, I propose that reconceiving of partnership as a dialogic[2] relationship in which equal credence is given to the professional expertise, musical backgrounds, creative ideas, and collective vulnerabilities (Neimeyer and Tschudi 2003) of *both* teacher and musician might lead to a more egalitarian model of collaboration.

I would argue that such an approach can potentially encourage teachers who have previously identified as musically unconfident to reconceptualize their own musicality and music teaching capabilities, while also disrupting the continuing cycle of low musical confidence among primary teachers, their dependency as consumers of music curriculum packages and on visiting musicians doing things *for* as opposed to *with* them.

My proposed model of dialogic relationship through musicking is represented in Figure 14.1. It depicts the "flow" of collaborative musicking of teachers and musicians, through which ideal relationships, both sound relationships and human relationships, can be explored. Small describes these relationships as "a complex web" (Small 2001, 345). He posits that at the center of the web are the musical sound relationships from which the interpersonal relationships between the performers and listeners radiate out and feed back (ibid).

"Ideal Relationships" • 165

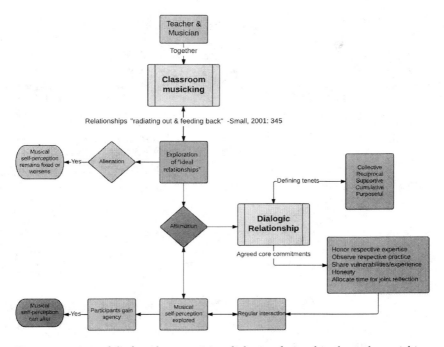

Figure 14.1 A model of teacher–musician dialogic relationship through musicking (Partington 2016)

The diagram shows that if the relationships explored are found to be alienating, the musical self-perception of the individual musicker either remains fixed or can potentially worsen. Conversely, however, if the musicking is found to be affirming, then musical self-perception and self-definition *can* be explored and potentially enhanced. In Smallian terms, through musicking interactions, musical identities can also be explored and potentially *transformed*. Also possible in instances of affirmation through musicking is the creation of the dialogic relationship.

The model conceives of dialogic relationship between teacher and musician as being linked to the five tenets of dialogic interaction outlined by Alexander (2006, see endnote 2). To the diagram I have also added key points of learning from my research that inform the model itself. These are core commitments that I suggest must be made in agreement between teacher and musician *before* any musicking begins and are derived from Pugh and De'Ath's definition of partnership, which they describe as:

> A working relationship that is characterised by a shared sense of purpose, mutual respect and the willingness to negotiate. This implies a sharing of information, responsibility, skills, decision-making and accountability.
> (Pugh and De'Ath 1989, 33)

My own suggested core commitments for dialogic relationship influenced by this definition include:

The honoring of respective expertise—Irrespective of role or title, both parties must recognize the professional skills and expertise of the other as being of fundamental significance in the pursuit of dialogic relationship.

Observe respective practice—I suggest that observing the teachers teach in general terms in their own classrooms on the part of the musician and the teachers then observing the musician lead musicking at the outset of any collaborative endeavor would mutually inform both parties about the other's pedagogy, while providing scope to identify ways to begin collaborating and to understand commonalities as well as differences within each other's work and role.

Share vulnerabilities and experience—The sharing of musical "histories," fears, concerns, and areas of self-identified musical or more general pedagogical strengths and weaknesses within my research study provided a basis for the active redressing of inherent power balances within the musician–teacher relationship.

Honesty—Cited by all teachers participating within my research as integral to our relationships, this must be a key feature of the dialogic relationship. Being freely and constructively critical without fear of causing offense appears to be integral to teachers' sense of agency within the dialogic musician–teacher relationship.

Allocate time for joint reflection—Regular dialogue and joint reflection about classroom musicking (both reviewing activity that has occurred and planning together for future musicking) were found to be crucial in the establishment of mutually satisfactory partner relationships. Linking back to the Smallian lens of musicking, these discussions can be considered legitimate aspects of musicking. Although they are not musical "acts" as such, they support the development of relationships that ultimately inform the musical activity. Through these dialogues, teachers and musicians can explicitly and implicitly negotiate and recognize their ideal relationship with one another, making the musicking partnership both meaningful and mutually beneficial.

In addition to these five initial core commitments, the potential success of the model depends on the time allocated to developing the relationship and the regularity of the musicking interactions. Testing of the model to date suggests that knowledge of one another built over time and regular interaction between musicians and teachers are crucial to establishing the hallmarks of dialogic relationship contained in the diagram. A weekly, or at least fortnightly, frequency of musician–teacher musicking interaction in the classroom over two academic terms, although time intensive, is suggested to be optimal for the development of dialogic relationships within which equality, familiarity, cordial feeling, honesty, and trust can flourish. Once relationships are established, this frequency may then potentially be reduced.

Outstanding Tensions

I turn now to address outstanding tensions arising from the discussion contained within this chapter and also from my own research in order to indicate how the Smallian perspective I have offered might inform the current debate on musician–teacher collaboration.

Roles, Titles, and Musical Expertise

Small's theory of musicking offers all participants, regardless of their musical history, opportunities to explore and recognize their own musical artistry. However, as the teachers involved in my research pointed out, although collaborative musicking increased their musical confidence and self-perceptions, along with their confidence to teach music in class more confidently, they could not accurately replicate my musical skill and singing technique. Nor did they feel able to describe themselves as "musicians," all preferring to articulate the alteration in their musical self-perception as being "a little more of a musical person now" or "on my way to *becoming* a musician." Although they recognized the children they taught as being innately musical and musical artists or "musicians" in their own right, the teachers remained uncomfortable claiming those same titles for themselves.

I make specific note of this to illuminate the entrenched nature of attitudes in primary music education towards the ways in which visiting musicians and teachers are expected and, indeed, often *expect themselves* to work alongside one another. It is an undoubtedly complex feat for musicians and teachers to work *together* in an equal and collaborative way as a result of the different roles they are required to fulfill. For example, musicians being paid to work at what Christophersen et al. describe as "the interface between art and schools" (2015, 43) are expected to "earn their keep" by supporting already busy teachers with musical provision. Children, class teachers, and head teachers expect (often both tacitly and overtly) that musicians will display their musical skill by performing both musically and professionally for everyone's enjoyment. Musicians are therefore often inextricably bound by their title and its attendant expectations. They cannot avoid displaying their technical skill, which can serve to alienate unconfident teachers and further lessen the potential for effective collaboration. Teachers meanwhile may be cast in a delicate "balancing act" of "subject positions" (idem, 35) within the music or arts education collaboration. As Christophersen et al. propose, depending on the needs of the project and the expectation or requirement of the collaborating artist, teachers may be required to shift the role as "helpers, guards or mediators" who "transmit" or "translate" between the visiting artist and the participating students (Christophersen et al. 2015, 29–34). Due to these challenges of role and expectation, Small suggests that musicians and teachers are "imprisoned" in and by the traditions and social connotations of the "luxurious concert hall" and at risk of "losing out" on the possibilities of working and musicking in new and different ways (Small 1998a, 11). I would suggest that awareness of the limiting potential of these issues is essential on the part of both musicians and teachers when embarking on collaborative work.

Small's Call for Music to Be Removed from School

Having used Small's work heavily to inform and interpret my work, I must address his call towards the end of his life that to take music out of the school curriculum "would do more good than harm to the pupils' experience" (Small 2010, 287), counter as this is to what is presented within this chapter. Given the advocacy for the importance of music in children's lives threaded throughout his work and particularly within *Music, Society, Education* (1996), such a statement is perhaps in response to the persistence of the consumer model of education over the forty-year period in which Small wrote his critiques.

I cannot support the removal of music entirely from school, however. As a music educator I meet many children for whom musicking out of school is confined by economic, cultural, and geographic factors and is often limited to the music of TV, radio, CDs, computer games, and toys. Although in Smallian terms listening to or interacting with these are indeed instances of musicking, they do not necessarily involve interaction with other people. Such circumstances make the perpetuation of learning about and making music as only for the "musical" (and, therefore, read "affluent") all the more likely and limiting to children's potential. As previously cited Small himself describes how these messages are passed on to children (1998a, 120) and the cyclical myth of musicality continues on.

Although it may first appear that my work (based as it is within the school) and ontological stance are at odds with his statement, I find congruence in Small's use of the word "curriculum" in this instance. I agree with him that all too often, we allow "experts" to dictate *what* and *how* we teach and learn and to do our thinking and our feeling for us:

> Music is too important to be left to the musicians, and in recognizing this fact we strike a blow at the experts' domination, not only of music but also of our very lives.
>
> (Small 1996, 214)

However, as explicated earlier, my research and the resulting model of dialogic relationship can inform both the debate on and the actual practice of musician–teacher collaboration in music by *subverting* the power of the curriculum through the resituating of teachers and children as agentic, competent, and creative musickers in their own right. Disruption of notions of expertise and musical talent, coupled with a teacher who feels competent with regard to their own musical skill and creative agency, leads to a relocation of power and far less reliance on curriculum as expressed in the pre-prepared musical material with which schools are inundated and to the domination of "packaged," "consumerist" educational approaches to which Small was opposed (Small 1996, 182). What is of prime importance is that children are offered continuous opportunities to explore, affirm, and celebrate their own identities and ideal relationships through musicking by teachers who are confident and able to, as Small says, "do the best they can with what they have" (2006, 14).

In conclusion, it is not enough for teachers and musicians to simply enter into a benign, well-meant relationship in the pursuit of partnership. I propose that successful dialogic relationships between musician and teacher will always require both a fundamental understanding and recognition of the embedded nature of hierarchy in that relationship and continuous effort to reallocate power and expertise more equally. This is therefore not a simple task, but I suggest that for musicians, music educators, and teachers, an exploration of dialogic relationships through musicking will serve the interests of reclaiming the musicality of teachers and children—that is, of remusicalizing teachers and ensuring that children are *never* demusicalized by school music. As Small tells us, our "job as music teachers is to treasure and encourage that creativity and that musicality which is part of the universal human birthright" (Small 1990, 5).

Notes

1 Key Stage One is the National Curriculum learning stage for children aged 5 to 7 years in the United Kingdom.
2 The central tenets of dialogic teaching, according to Alexander (2006) are as follows: *Collective*: teachers and children address learning tasks together, whether as a group or as a class; *Reciprocal*: teachers and children listen to each other, share ideas, and consider alternative viewpoints; *Supportive*; children articulate their ideas freely, without fear of embarrassment over "wrong" answers, and they help each other to reach common understandings; *Cumulative*: teachers and children build on their own and each other's ideas and chain them into coherent lines of thinking and enquiry; *Purposeful*: teachers plan and steer classroom talk with specific educational goals in view (Alexander 2006, 38).

References

Alexander, Robin. 2006. *Towards Dialogic Teaching: Rethinking Classroom Talk*. York: Dialogos.
Christophersen, Catharina, Jan-Kåre Breivik, Anne Homme, and Lise Rykkja. 2015. *The Cultural Rucksack: A National Programme for Arts and Culture in Norwegian Schools*. Bergen: Fagbokforlaget.
Conway, Hannah, and John Finney. 2003. "Musical Enchantment in the Early Years." *Teacher Development*, 7 (1), 121–9.
Gifford, Edward. 1993. "The Musical Training of Primary Teachers: Old Problems, New Insights and Possible Solutions." *British Journal of Music Education*, 10 (1), 33–46.

Glover, Joanna, and Stephen Ward. 2004. *Teaching Music in the Primary School*. London: Continuum.
Goodlad, John, I. 2004. "A Guiding Mission." In *The Teaching Career*, edited by John Goodlad and Timothy McMannon, 19–46. New York: Teachers College Press.
Hennessey, Sarah. 2000. "Overcoming the Red-Feeling: The Development of Confidence to Teach Music in Primary School Amongst Student Teachers." *British Journal of Music Education*, 17 (2), 183–96.
Holden, Hilary, and Stuart Button. 2006. "The Teaching of Music in the Primary School by the Non-Music Specialist." *British Journal of Music Education*, 23 (1), 23–38.
Jeanneret, Neryl. 1997. "Developing Confidence to Teach Music: A Model for Pre-Service Teaching." *Bulletin for the Council for Research in Music Education*, 133, 37–44.
Kenny, Ailbhe, Michael Finneran, and Eamonn Mitchell. 2015. "Becoming and Educator in and Through the Arts: Forming and Informing Emerging Teachers' Professional Identity." *Teaching and Teacher Education*, 49, 159–67.
Laurence, Felicity. 2010. "Listening to Children." In *Sociology and Music Education*, edited by Ruth Wright, 243–62. Farnham: Ashgate.
Mills, Janet. 1989. "The Generalist Primary Teacher of Music: A Problem of Confidence." *British Journal of Music Education*, 6 (2), 125–38.
Mills, Janet. 1994. *Music in the Primary School*. Cambridge: Cambridge University Press.
Neimeyer, Robert A., and Finn Tschudi. 2003. "Community and Coherence: Narrative Contributions to the Psychology of Conflict and Loss." In *Narrative and Consciousness: Literature, Psychology and the Brain*, edited by Gary D. Fireman, Ted E. McVay, and Owen J. Flanagan, 166–94. New York: Oxford University Press.
Partington, Julia S. 2016. "The Problematics of Partnership Between the Primary Class Teacher and the Visiting Musician: Power and Hierarchy in the Pursuit of Dialogic Relationship." PhD diss., Newcastle University.
Philpott, Chris. 2012. "Assessment for Self-Directed Learning in Music Education." In *Debates in Music Teaching*, edited by Chris Philpott, and Gary Spruce, 153–68. Abingdon: Routledge.
Pugh, Gillian, and Erica De'Ath. 1989. *Working Towards Partnership in the Early Years*. London: National Children's Bureau.
Ruismaki, Heikki, and Tarja Tereska. 2006. "Early Childhood Musical Experiences: Contributing to Pre-Service Elementary Teachers' Self Concept and Success in Music Teaching (During Student Age)." *European Early Childhood Education Research Journal*, 14 (1), 113–30.
Russell-Bowie, Deirdre. 2009. "What Me? Teach Music to My Primary Class? Challenges to Music Teaching in Primary Schools in Five Countries." *Music Education Research*, 11 (1), 23–36.
Russell-Bowie, Deirdre. 2010. "Cross-National Comparisons of Background and Confidence in Visual Arts and Music Education of Pre-Service Primary Teachers." *Australian Journal of Teacher Education*, 35 (4), 65–78.
Small, Christopher. 1990. "Whose Music Do We Teach Anyway?" Online article www.musekids.org/whose.html
Small, Christopher. 1996. *Music, Society, Education*. Hanover, NH: Wesleyan University Press.
Small, Christopher. 1998a. *Music of the Common Tongue: Survival and Celebration in African American Music*. Hanover, NH: Wesleyan University Press.
Small, Christopher. 1998b. *Musicking: The Meanings of Performing and Listening*. Middletown, CT: Wesleyan University Press.
Small, Christopher. 2001. "Why Doesn't the Whole World Love Chamber Music?" *American Music*, 19 (3), 340–59.
Small, Christopher. 2006. "Article for Quodlibet." Unpublished article.
Small, Christopher. 2007. "Seven Aphorisms and Six Commentaries." In *The Christopher Small Reader*, edited by Robert Walser, 2016. Middletown, CT: Wesleyan University Press.
Small, Christopher. 2010. "Afterword." In *Sociology and Music Education*, edited by Ruth Wright, 283–90. Farnham: Ashgate.
Todd, Elisabeth S. 2000. "The Problematic of Partnership in the Assessment of Special Educational Needs." PhD diss., Newcastle University.
Welch, Graham F., and Jennie Henley. 2014. "Addressing the Challenges of Teaching Music by Generalist Primary Teachers." *Revista da ABEM*, 22 (32). www.abemeducacaomusical.com.br/revistas/revistaabem/index.php/revistaabem/article/view/459
Wiggins, Robert A., and Jackie Wiggins. 2008. "Primary Music Education in the Absence of Specialists." *International Journal of Education and the Arts*, 9 (12). www.ijea.org/v9n12/v9n12.pdf

15
Nurturing on the Go? A Story of Nomadic Partnership

KATHARINE KRESEK

Bringing professional performing musicians into schools to carry out the educational missions of nonprofit cultural organizations is an undertaking that has created new and often beneficial reciprocal learning opportunities for both the performers (in this chapter, referred to as teaching artists) and the schools partnering with the organization (Abeles and Hafeli 2012; Booth 2009; Csikszentmihalyi 1997; Hunter et al. 2014; Myers 2005). Schools and classroom teachers often gain exposure and experiences with the art of music through creative, imaginative, and aesthetic pathways that invigorate learning and enrich school musical culture (Booth 2009; Greene 2001; Holzer 2009; Fowler 1996; Frawley 2013; Jaffe et al. 2013). But as teaching artist presence in the schools increases and sometimes may represent the only arts learning that occurs within a particular school, tensions exist surrounding the most effective ways to prepare teaching artists for working in school environments (Myers 2005; Kaschub and Smith 2014; Reeder 2009; Wolf 2000). Additionally, with interest in musical careers on the rise but full-time orchestral performance employment offerings in decline (VanWaeyenberghe 2013) and the increasing cultural phenomenon of the rise of the freelance workforce, many teaching artists find themselves working for multiple nonprofit organizations with highly specific musical and pedagogical missions and therefore attempting to nurture and develop multiple partnerships simultaneously. Serving even one organization as a teaching artist already represents a hybrid career in which movement between performance (or art making) and pedagogy is a large part (Booth 2009; Jaffe et al. 2013; Graham and Zwirn 2010). When a teaching artist works for multiple organizations, they find themselves working in what can be called *nomadic conditions*, meaning that they are itinerant not only within their freelance performance careers, but also as they move between the differing environments of cultural organizations, school environments, and performance settings. Although their work is grounded in beliefs and perceptions about performance and pedagogy as individuals and as part of the organizations for which they serve, the cumulative impact of their itinerancy (both physical and conceptual) and their status as outsiders and part-timers may intersect with their attitudes and beliefs about their roles in the schools and the organizations in which they partner.

Research has shown that music and arts specialists are far more likely to be itinerant than teachers of other subjects and therefore tend to experience higher rates of burnout, turnover, and attrition (Gardner 2010; McLain 2005). Although music teachers tend to show a higher ability to overcome burnout than teachers of other subjects, environmental factors such as feeling outside of the school community and feeling a lack of community support can lead to emotional exhaustion and depersonalization (Hedden 2005; McLain 2005). Additional research in the field of positive organizational scholarship has also shown that mobile workers can still be highly committed to the organizations for whom they work (Pittinsky and Shih 2004); therefore, teaching artists may find themselves fully committed to their work, yet experiencing tension with expectations surrounding how to develop their partnerships with schools writ large while also negotiating personal relationships with their partnering teachers in addition to the work they do with students. Through personal reflection this chapter will explore a teaching artist perspective on expectations, attitudes, and experiences with a classroom teacher partnership in the hopes of contributing to a larger conversation about music teaching artists and their place in schools.

In *The Music Teaching Artist's Bible*, Booth defines the term "teaching artist" as "an artist who chooses to include artfully educating others, beyond the technique of the art form, as an active part of a career" (2009, 3). A more recent definition has evolved to the following:

> A teaching artist is an active artist who embodies and further develops the complementary skills, curiosities, and habits of an educator, in order to achieve a wide variety of learning goals in, through, and about the arts, with a wide range of learners.
>
> (2014, 7)

The resulting definition is purposefully broad and not necessarily distinctive from the role of classroom arts teachers with full- or part-time employment in schools, as they may be quite active as artists and yet primarily making a living from their teaching. Therefore, for the purpose of this chapter, I define a nomadic music teaching artist as *an active freelance performer who also teaches in multiple schools through nonprofit cultural organizations*, distinguishing the role from that of a music teacher who is employed full-time by one school or school district, and from that of a full-time performing musician involved in outreach or other involvement in schools, and further still from artists who present in schools independently.

By definition, a nomad is one without a permanent home. The nomadic condition is one in which the teaching artist works for multiple institutions, teaches multiple grade levels, is not provided with permanent or designated office or classroom space, visits multiple teaching sites within the space of a month, and is without a full-time position as a performer. For a nomadic teaching artist, itinerancy is more than a complex schedule of balancing multiple teaching obligations with their performance obligations. It is also a condition that begs investigation: When nomadic music teaching artists are moving between varied performance and teaching roles across multiple employers, how do they negotiate their relationships to multiple classroom teachers across their varied teaching?

To make the case for the distinction between teaching artist and nomadic teaching artist, it is necessary to offer a personal testimony about my own experience. I teach for four in-school partnering programs for nonprofit cultural organizations in New York City. I visit an average of sixty to seventy-five individual classrooms annually, working with approximately 2,000 students and approximately seventy-five to one hundred teachers. Partnership is emphasized only in the schools in which I am visiting more than once, though good interactions and relationships are encouraged all around. My largest partnering commitment is working in an orchestral program in order to design lessons that educate public school students between the ages of seven and eleven creatively in performance, perception, and composition. I typically come to each partnering classroom two to three times a month, depending on the schedule of the school, for an average of about twenty lessons in each classroom, sixty lesson plans across three grades, 300 class sessions this school year. Partnership has always been a core tenet of the program's mission. The idea is straightforward: teaching artists serve as the facilitators of participatory musical experiences codesigned with the teachers of each class. For the purposes of this chapter, I will focus on one unique partnership that has occupied my mind of late. Here is that story:

At 5:45 p.m. on a Thursday evening, I am on the train heading to play a 7 p.m. show. As we pass 14th Street, there is a brief but lifesaving area of full mobile phone reception where I can connect with the world above. I check my email and see an address in my inbox that has never been there before. I think immediately that it must be spam, and as my thumb begins to swipe to the left and cast it permanently into the trash, my eye catches the first sentence: "great lesson today."

I open the full body of the text, but there is no more. I think over my day, where I was, what lesson I taught, and it feels years and miles away. Who was I with today? What did I teach? In the back of my mind, I remember the long day of teaching at the elementary school I visit weekly. At the front of my mind is getting through the subway ride without any problems, arriving early enough to navigate the crowds. What's on my mind is dinner. I am thinking about which of my favorite spots in the area meet the criteria: nearby, no line, under $10.00, delicious. No line is of critical importance. I don't have time to wait. My show has a curtain-up time of 7:05 p.m., and there are several steps that need to happen well before that. I must be dressed in the appropriate regulation black, my instrument tuned, my microphones correctly placed, well hydrated, fed, caffeinated, having reviewed several difficult solo passages, and I need to be in my chair at least five minutes before the regular players come in. Do not upset the regulars.

The journey to tonight's show represents part of my career. When I'm not teaching, I work as a professional violinist. I play in orchestras, with rock and folk bands; I make recordings of music that other people have written; I tour; I play in the pits of musicals. Tonight I am a substitute in a show, meaning I only play the show when the regular player is out and I'm fortunate enough to have gotten the call and to have been available. This is why my thoughts echo those of a guest in someone else's house. The rules for subs, written and otherwise, are different than for the regulars. As a guest in the show for the night, I am relied on heavily to have prepared in such a manner that nobody would know I'm dropping in; that I don't play the show every night. I need to get along well with my colleagues. I need to either be genuinely comfortable and confident or fake it with every ounce of performing experience I can muster. The conductor and the contractor have to like me too, or this could be my last time on the gig. To say that there is an element of pressure would be an understatement. This is not at all unlike another part of my career: my job as a teaching artist.

I return to that email and check the sender's address, hoping to distract myself from my perceived travel dramas. I am jolted away from reviewing my pre-show routine and back into my teaching life. It hits me that I've written to this sender dozens of times but never received a response, which is why it feels so worthy of attention. It's from one of the fourth-grade teachers with whom I partner. I will call him Mr. C.

The importance of the moment begins to sink in. I first took note of Mr. C at a large planning meeting held with the fifteen teachers in the school with whom I partner for the academic year. Although late and occasionally distracted, he still had a great deal to say. He appreciated that the students had the opportunity to study music through the lens of the orchestra and expressed the desire to make curricular connections between that of the program and his own. His interest and eagerness stood out, but what also became clear was that despite a willingness and enthusiasm, there was a lack of concrete suggestions as to how it would all work.

In my program, the word "partnership" is heavily imbued with expectations. A teaching artist's entrée into the faculty means becoming familiar with inspiring examples of collaboration with classroom elementary school teachers that result in meaningful student work. We are given a teaching artist handbook that outlines these expectations, which supports the notion of our partner teachers as our most important allies in our work in the schools. The guidelines also stipulate that we are to hold planning meetings with our teachers during a prep or during the teachers' lunch hour. Professional development in the form of several after-school meetings is held throughout the year to assist with classroom teachers' comfort levels with working in music. We help them gain familiarity with the program, the music, and through the time allotted we are encouraged to nurture these relationships in support of the work we do. However, it is important to note that we cannot force our partners to come to these meetings. Teachers do not self-select to participate in the program.

Over many years, my relationships with partner teachers have brought about meaningful teaching experiences I could never have anticipated. I learn from their expertise as teachers and as the conduits for getting to know my students and the school culture more quickly and efficiently. Because I have extremely limited time with my kids, their support helps me to better speak their language, ultimately creating greater clarity for the children. Together we've created projects ranging in topic from The Silk Road to American football players to the Arab Spring, to abolition, just to name a few. Gauging a new partner teacher's interest and enthusiasm often reminds me of playing a new piece for an audience for the first time—I have high hopes, but no idea how they're going to react to what I bring to the table.

As our year together began, the enthusiasm I sensed from Mr. C in the first meeting began to wane. When I came in, I made efforts to appeal to him for involvement. If I asked a question to the students, I would often invite him to give his thoughts. I would ask in front of the class if there was a better way to explain things (even when students were already displaying comprehension). He kept his head down for the most part and said I was doing fine. I didn't sense that he disliked how I was teaching; I just don't think he felt it necessary to become involved.

Then in midwinter, we arrived at a study of musical myths and legends in preparation for a concert experience. The day of the lesson, I approached his desk to give him a quick overview of the plan. We hadn't had time to meet in weeks. Teachers are entitled to a duty-free lunch, and there is no common prep period on the day that I go in, so I get by with talking to the teachers for a few minutes before and after the lesson period, through emails, and by small drop-in visits and brief but succinct text messages. In these few moments while the students were transitioning, I indicated to Mr. C that part of preparing the kids to see the performance would include a discussion of the differences between myths and legends, and he sat straight up. "That's what we're doing this week!" he exclaimed energetically. He told me that they had just spent the previous day reading a legend in class.

As the lesson began, I asked if we could first share what we knew about legends, and Mr. C jumped in with reminders from the work they had done yesterday, referencing a legend they had read together and helping the class make the connection to my activity. The students nodded, and suddenly they were off creating stories. Hands flew up. Kids were jumping up and down and calling out unable to wait their turn. Within minutes we had a range of possibilities for creating music inspired by the story. We had a momentum that was new, ignited by a moment of collaboration. The students were set in motion by his participation. They wanted him to know they understood, and they wanted to share their music-making with him. As he saw that the students made music from the springboard of his contributions, I got the sense that he found the work genuinely meaningful.

I received confirmation of this that night on the subway, on the way to my show at 5:45 p.m. Although I usually do send some kind of recap of the day's events to keep myself on track as much as my partner teachers, I hadn't had time that day. I finished teaching and had to drive home, find parking, go grocery shopping, plan my lessons for the next day, and practice before leaving enough time to travel to my performance. As I read the unsolicited words of acknowledgement that we had done something good, the sense of reward was quickly replaced with the question: "Why did this moment take so long to achieve?"

I thought back to our first meeting and his initial enthusiasm over making connections. He had shown motivation and excitement, but it was like a seed planted in the ground that needed a nurturing neither of us yet knew how to give. He had an opportunity to authentically use his expertise, to help his class deepen their understanding of a topic through modalities I don't think he realized could be used for such a purpose. However, I had to also realize that the alignment of our curriculum had been coincidental. Without a consistent opportunity to plan, and with his being new to the process, how could I have expected him to know how important he was?

As the year continued, I used that day of myths and legends as fuel to further every interaction we had. Each lesson I checked in about what he was teaching, and each time he would say "Can you do something to match up with that?" Although his involvement increased, I realized that I couldn't completely reorder the entire curriculum to align with his. I was still obligated to fulfill the work of my program, but without sufficient time, how could we really develop? I could reach out to explore the ways in which my curriculum could be relevant to him, but would that keep him engaged? And the question loomed, "Why had this one fleeting moment taken so long?" Perhaps my perceptions and expectations of the speed of partnership were what had been misaligned. Perhaps some classroom teachers underestimate just how critical their involvement might be. My questions were speculative, but I couldn't help but marvel at how responsive the students were when Mr. C became the facilitator for helping students make the connections to their curriculum. And I couldn't ignore how much it freed me to concentrate on making music with the students.

That is one story of many stories I could share about my partnerships with classroom teachers; however, this one stands out because of the extreme swing of the pendulum from passivity to activity, indifference to engagement. It also remains salient because it represents one of nine partnerships I maintain in the school over the course of a year. Through a variety of methods and within our limitations, Mr. C and I were able to find a way to work together, but as I consider the scope and range of my partnerships, I cannot help but feel overwhelmed at the need for individualized approaches for each and every classroom teacher with whom I work.

A critical question looms for the future: How can individual partnerships between teaching artists and classroom teachers be enhanced and developed within the larger organizational partnerships between nonprofit cultural institutions and schools? Although both schools and arts organizations can attend to these issues, the question is further complicated by the fact that teaching artists negotiate their teaching and performing work to extraordinary degrees. They are guests in the schools by virtue of their visiting status. The depth and richness of experience in their music-making enhance the cultural life of the school and benefit the students, but to what extent are they, or can they be, members of the school community? And when teaching artists have multiple communities in which to invest, what impact might that have on their relationships with their collaborators?

A severe limitation of the perspective put forth in this chapter is the absence of the classroom teacher voice on the very same issues of expectations, time constraints, and the nature of the teaching artist as guest. What are their expectations for partnering with teaching artists? How does the teaching artist partnership affect their teaching, if at all? How many outside partners are they expected to collaborate with in the course of their school year? What impact does that have on them? What else are they negotiating? If teaching artists are to become successful partners, they must make the effort to understand their school culture, administration, and challenges that each partner teacher may be facing, both professionally and in their relationships to areas outside of their professional comfort zone.

I often find myself returning to the question that had been provoked by my partnership with Mr. C over why it had not sparked until months into the school year. As I try to respond to it, I think about the intersection of time and place for teaching artists who are constantly shifting between environments. Booth (2009) has referred to time as the *hardest currency of schools*. Every teacher of subjects not considered core must figure out how to make their time with students count. When the collaborative aspect of classroom teacher partnering is added to the expectation, it can represent both possibility and peril, depending on the scope of a teaching artist's activities in and outside the school and how much time and motivation they have to invest. The question becomes, how can we shift the many kaleidoscopic details, the many moving parts, to present an image of a high standard of work imbued with reasonable and fair expectations for all involved? To what extent can cultural organizations support their teaching artists as they navigate complex environments over sustained yet fragmented encounters with their schools? If nomadic music teaching artists are to create partnerships that thrive on behalf of the cultural institution, then perhaps a first step to understanding how we nurture our relationships with teachers is through understanding and acknowledging the complexities of the conditions in which we perform, teach, and partner and addressing expectations along the way.

References

Abeles, Harold, and Mary Hafeli. 2012. "Seeking Professional Fulfillment: US Symphony Orchestra Members in Schools." *Psychology of Music*, 42 (1), 35–50.

Booth, Eric. 2009. *The Music Teaching Artist's Bible: Becoming a Virtuoso Educator*. New York: Oxford University Press.

Booth, Eric. 2014. "New Times for TAs: A Growth Spurt for Teaching Artistry." *National Guild for Community Arts Education, Guild Notes*, 3, 1–9.

Csikszentmihalyi, Mihalyi. 1997. "Assessing Aesthetic Education: Measuring the Ability to 'Ward off Chaos.'" *Arts Education Policy Review*, 99 (1), 33–8.

Edelman Berlind. 2014. "Freelancing in America: A National Survey of the New Workforce." Accessed June 12, 2017, www.freelancersunion.org/blog/dispatches/2014/09/04/53million/

Fowler, Charles. 1996. *Strong Arts, Strong Schools: The Promising Potential and Shortsighted Disregard of the Arts in American Schooling*. New York: Oxford University Press.

Frawley, Timothy. 2013. "Aesthetic Education: Its Place in Teacher Training." *Art Education*, 66 (3), 22–8.

Gardner, Robert D. 2010. "Should I Stay or Should I Go? Factors that Influence the Retention, Turnover, and Attrition of K-12 Music Teachers in the United States." *Arts Education Policy Review*, 111 (3), 112–21.

Graham, Mark A., and Susan Goetz Zwirn. 2010. "How Being a Teaching Artist Can Influence K-12 Arts Education." *Studies in Art Education*, 51 (3), 219–32.

Greene, Maxine. 2001. *Variations on a Blue Guitar: The Lincoln Center Institute Lectures on Aesthetic Education*. New York: Teachers College Press.

Hedden, Debra Gordon. 2005. "A Study of Stress and its Manifestations Among Music Educators." *Bulletin of the Council for Research in Music Education*, 166 (Fall), 57–67.

Holzer, Madeline Fuchs. 2009. "The Arts and Elementary Education: Shifting the Paradigm." *Teacher and Teaching: Theory and Practice*, 15 (3), 377–89.

Hunter, Mary Ann, William Baker, and Di Nailon. 2014. "Generating Cultural Capital? Impacts of Artists-in-Residence on Teacher Professional Learning." *Australian Journal of Teacher Education*, 39 (6), 75–88.

Jaffe, Nick, Rebecca Barniskis, and Barbara Hackett Cox. 2013. *Teaching Artist Handbook*, 1st edition. Chicago: Columbia College Chicago Press.

Kaschub, Michele, and Janice Smith. 2014. *Promising Practices in 21st Century Music Teacher Education*, 1st edition. New York: Oxford University Press.

McLain, Barbara Payne. 2005. "Environmental Support and Music Teacher Burnout." *Bulletin of the Council for Research in Music Education*, 164 (Spring), 71–84.

Myers, David E. 2005. "Preparing Performers and Composers for Effective Educational Work with Children." *Arts Education Policy Review*, 106 (6), 31–8.

Pittinsky, Todd L., and Margaret J. Shih. 2004. "Knowledge Nomads: Organizational Commitment and Worker Mobility in Positive Perspective." *American Behavioral Scientist*, 47 (6), 791–807.

Reeder, Laura. 2009. "Hurry Up and Wait: A National Scan of Teaching Artist Research and Professional Development." *Teaching Artist Journal*, 7 (1), 14–22.

VanWaeyenberghe, Brandon. 2013. "Musical Chairs: A 28-Year Study of the Supply and Demand of Orchestra Musicians in America." Accessed June 12, 2017, http://ssrn.com/abstract=2361771

Wolf, Dennie Palmer. 2000. "Beyond Outsourcing: Creating Corridors of Arts Opportunity." *Arts Education Policy Review*, 101 (3), 23–4.

16

Musician–Teacher Collaborations in Composing Contemporary Music in Secondary Schools

VICTORIA KINSELLA, MARTIN FAUTLEY, AND NANCY EVANS

Introduction

This chapter describes the *Resolution* composing project, a partnership between Birmingham Contemporary Music Group and the Rheumatology Research Group based at the Institute of Biomedical Research at the University of Birmingham, along with researchers from Birmingham City University. This composing project involved pupils aged fourteen and fifteen years old from three local secondary schools creating their own compositions from a specific set of stimuli. It was funded by The Wellcome Trust and involved biomedical scientists and composers working with classroom music teachers and young people to create new music around the theme of autoimmune disease. The title *Resolution* comes from a terminology connected with rheumatoid arthritis and, of course, music.

The English Context

In order to understand the collaborations described in this chapter, we begin with a description of music in the English National Curriculum (NC). At the time of this research, music was a statutory subject for all pupils up to the age of fourteen years. The NC itself can be considered generalist music education. It involves three main activities: composing, performing, and listening. This makes it different from music education in some other jurisdictions in that it does not employ a primarily ensemble performance–based modality. Instead, what takes place is that pupils learn to perform using classroom instruments, such as tuned and untuned percussion, guitars, keyboards, and music technology. Pupils who play instruments other than these often bring them into the class too. Composing normally takes place directly into sound; it does not need to involve stave notation, although it can. The *Resolution* project was designed to help the participating schools with the composing aspect of their National Curriculum work. It is important to note that pedagogies for composing are sometimes considered an area that teachers struggle with (Berkley 2001; Fautley 2014; Kenny 2014).

Historical Background: Composers Working in Schools in England

Since the early 1980s, professional composers and orchestral musicians have worked in schools delivering composition projects as part of orchestral education programs. In England, the London Sinfonietta was one of the first orchestras to employ an Education Officer, Gillian Moore, in 1983. Their very first project involved composer George Benjamin and former London Philharmonic Orchestra flautist Richard McNicol working with twenty teachers from the Inner London Education Authority. The focus of the project was to prepare a group of children and their teachers for attendance at a concert of music by Ravel and Varese and involved the young people creating their own Varese pastiche compositions (Ruffer 1988). This type of repertoire project, with the aim to prepare children for listening to the featured music in an upcoming concert, has been the backbone of orchestral education programs for many years and, concomitantly, of composers working in schools. More recent developments in orchestral repertoire projects tend to have a wider reach than "bums on seats" and "audiences of the future" projects of the past, and orchestras now employ composers to work in schools on a wide range of composition projects.

The *Resolution* Composing Project

Birmingham Contemporary Music Group (BCMG), the musical organization at the heart of this project, specializes in contemporary classical music and offers a broad range of composing projects as well as repertoire-based projects. These focus on offering young people the techniques of featured composers and their works (where applicable) and more general composing strategies to support their development as composers.

The participants were young people aged fourteen to sixteen, teachers of the young people, experienced professional composers, what were termed "emerging" professional composers (Sawyer 2003b), and PhD-level graduate student scientists. Three secondary schools in Birmingham, UK, were participants, differing in type, size, cohort, cultural background, and socioeconomic status. There was a comprehensive single-sex girls school, a selective academy single-sex girls school, and a comprehensive academy mixed school.

The aim of the project was to generate greater understanding around inflammation, an important area of biomedical science, and to explore differences and commonalities of artistic and scientific practices. The intention was to compose, create, and perform new music based on the medical theme of inflammation. All music by both emerging composers and the young people involved was presented in a public performance at the CBSO Centre in Birmingham, a major performance venue in the heart of England's second largest city. It is important to note that the project was not primarily performance led, however, but the final performance did offer the young people and the composers an opportunity to demonstrate and celebrate music-making and learning in front of a wider audience. It was important for this work that the performance was carefully planned in the overall structure of the project so that it did not take precedence over composing pedagogy and creative composing processes. It was not until the final stages of the project that the performance was made a feature of activity. It was seen therefore as a celebration of collaboration and process, rather than solely of final outcome. This runs counter to the ideology sometimes espoused in collaborative projects, which can be of the "let's put on a show" variety. In this work, it was the *processes* of composing and researching these processes that were deemed to be the most important. This accords with Sawyer's (2003a) description:

> [a] shift in creativity research from a focus on creative products to a focus on the creative process that generates them . . . in group creativity, the process is the essence of the genre, and it must be the central focus of any scientific study.
>
> (Sawyer 2003a, 6)

Project Activity

In-school activity stages of *Resolution* took the form of a series of workshops in which the focus shifted as the phases of the composing developed:

> Initial phase: One workshop in which music was used to present the scientific aspects of the project.
>
> Clarification phase: Two workshops aimed primarily at the composing work undertaken by the emerging composers, where most of the activity involved rehearsal and getting feedback on new works they had composed for participants.
>
> Main Workshop phase: This consisted of eight workshops in each school. This is clearly where the bulk of the composing work for the pupils took place. In these workshops the young people worked with the scientists before composing music for an ensemble of themselves and a BCMG professional musician. To achieve this, the young people used identified scientific content as stimuli for their composing. Workshops were partly led by the established composers and partly led by the emerging composers. What made this project differ from some other artist-in-schools work was that two additional forms of activity were scheduled from the outset. These were (1) structured reflection sessions for all the adults involved in the project and (2) continuing professional development (CPD) sessions for emerging composers.
>
> Reflection phase: One issue identified at the outset was that of planning. We know, often anecdotally, that some projects in schools are not as effective

as they might otherwise be due to a mismatch between the wants of the artist and the needs of the school (Christophersen 2015; Fautley 2014). In order to address this, three formal planning and reflection sessions took place throughout the year, alongside informal ones at the end of workshops in schools. Then at the end of the project was a final reflection session for all the participating adults.

Continuing Professional Development (CPD) phase: Alongside the reflection phase, eight CPD sessions were provided for participating emerging composers. These covered a range of aspects important for those working with young people in schools, including planning for composing with young people, the National Curriculum, and introductions to classroom practice and pedagogic strategies.

Reflection phase: The final performance was followed by a public discussion and Q&A session exploring commonalities and differences of artistic and scientific practices. Discussion provided valuable insights into actions and intentions of the partners, impact of the project, and ways in which these collaborations could continue in the future.

Roles and Responsibilities

Conceptualizations of collaborative learning are often predicated on the social construction of knowledge (Lave and Wenger 1991; Wenger 1998) and notions of distributed cognition (Salomon 1993; Nardi 1996). In the case of *Resolution*, it was taken for granted that all pupils could work collaboratively on a composing task; this was not for the special few, but for all young people in regular classes.

An issue raised by this project was *professional knowledge*. Shulman (1986) describes two types of knowledge that are relevant here, *content knowledge*, knowledge about the subject domain and its contents, and *pedagogical content knowledge* (PCK), knowledge concerning ways in which the subject is taught:

> the most useful forms of representation of those ideas, the most powerful analogies, illustrations, examples, explanations, and demonstrations—in a word, the ways of representing and formulating the subject that make it comprehensible to others.
> (Shulman 1986, 6)

Professional knowledge is not, however, a unified construct. Eraut (1994), for example, describes a range of dichotomies:

> theory and practice, public knowledge and personal knowledge, propositional knowledge and process knowledge, analytic and intuitive thinking.
> (Eraut 1994, 19)

All of these dichotomies found their outworking at some point during the *Resolution* project. In order to investigate this more closely, we turn to describing roles played by the key stakeholders.

The Composers

The composers working on *Resolution* fell into two distinct categories. Established composers had experience working with pupils in a range of schools, building relationships with teachers, and enabling project delivery. Their role in the project was to support pupils through a series of workshops, developing compositions on the scientific theme. This included demonstrating and modeling how scientific starting points could be used to generate, develop, and structure musical material. The composers also mentored emerging composers in the development of their compositions for the class.

The Emerging Composers

The emerging composers' role was twofold: first, to compose a new piece of music for the class to perform and second, to support the composer in delivering workshops. They were asked not just to produce a new composition working alone, but to involve pupils in the composing process, for example, by trying out ideas and getting feedback. A key aspect of the project was for the emerging composers to compose their own piece so that the pupils could observe a parallel model of how they might go about composing from an extra-musical starting point.

A priority for the emerging composers' professional development was to foster an understanding of classroom composing. They were offered opportunities to observe teaching and learning led by established composers and teachers and to look at interactions with pupils. There were also opportunities to develop knowledge of content, pedagogy, and curriculum. It is noteworthy that emerging composers were not just seen as "apprentices," but as composers with significant knowledge. Their specialized understanding of composing processes was drawn on by all participants. Knowledge transfer was not one way, but remained fluid between all the collaborators.

The Teachers

Resolution required teachers and composers to align composing with teaching and learning in a number of meaningful ways. For example, the composers had little personal experience of working with examination specifications and systems. Doing this required an integration of curriculum, as seen from the teacher's perspective, with the composer's practice. The teachers played a central role in aligning composer knowledge with exam specifications, and it is important not to downplay this centrality (Kenny 2010; Christophersen 2013).

For teachers, linking developing composerly thinking in their learners with increased student understanding was important. The teacher has ultimate responsibility for providing evidence of student learning and for maintaining academic progress of the pupils. Therefore the composer's knowledge and skills had to work with, and be developed alongside, exam specifications and outcomes. Sharing responsibility through cocreated sessions was important. In this project the teachers supported composers to evaluate teaching and learning, to better help pupils and ultimately reach outcomes required for examination. Likewise, the teachers were also offered the opportunity to expand their practice through observing the composers.

We know from the work of Ball (2003) that the performativity agenda currently rife in schools in England and elsewhere creates pressures on teachers to conform. This emphasis on accountability and performativity has had an impact on pedagogies of creativity in schools, especially at GCSE (see for example Fautley et al. 2011). Therefore, working with the composers opened up possibilities and encouraged new approaches and outlooks on composing for the teachers concerned.

Learning and Doing

One aspect of professional knowledge that was important in *Resolution* was with regard to the provision of *intended learning* statements, a common requirement for English schools, where the teacher has to inform the class at the outset of a lesson what they will be learning. The composers were not always able to clearly articulate the intended learning that the pupils would be undertaking. This is not so much an issue of competence, but of practice and awareness. The teachers, all of whom are music graduates, were well used to doing this from the strictures of their daily lives. The importance of PCK has already been noted, and it became clear during the course of *Resolution* that this distinguished teachers from composers. As Bowman observes:

> a music education professional . . . is not simply a musician with pedagogical training. Music education professionals are not mere music specialists (musicians) who happen to teach.
> (Bowman 2007, 114)

This is an important conceptualization. At some point in their education teachers and composers would have rubbed shoulders in the university or in the conservatoire; it is what happened next and their professional induction into their various *communities of practice* (Lave and Wenger 1991; Kenny 2016) that make a difference to their respective professional knowledge. This is not to say that composers lacked aspects of PCK—far from it—but having to deal with it did not form part of their everyday work. By way of exemplification, for composers, meaning often emerges from a process of doing, and then learning follows. For schools, this is not the way learning is conceptualized. At the beginning of the project, the notion of prespecifying learning was resisted by some of the composers, "I don't know in advance what they are going to learn," one said. However, once exploration of this had taken place in reflection sessions, this often turned out not to be the case. The composers did know, but they were unused to having to specify in advance, especially utilizing formats that schools would recognize. One teacher articulated their concerns in this regard:

> I think the role of the teacher needs thinking through, as in all composing projects, especially in terms of recording the musical learning that is taking place. Workshops should not become tick box exercises for the national curriculum, but they would not get past the senior management in schools if there was no musical progress demonstrated.
> (project teacher, interview data)

The key phrase here is "would not get past the senior management in schools if there was no musical progress demonstrated." This is central to the ways schools operate in a performativity-driven, results-based culture. Indeed, as Christophersen observes:

> Everyone can serve as a source of learning to others, but only teachers are teachers. Teachers are professionals, and teaching in school is teaching within a formal context that has a cultural and societal mandate.
> (Christophersen 2015, 371)

When learning needs to be legislated for in educational settings, then this has to happen. Due to accountability and performativity pressures, the teachers and composers needed to consider what was being *learned* and therefore what was being evaluated. Swanwick (1999, 74) states: "any valid and reliable assessment has to take account of two dimensions: what pupils are doing and what they are learning." Music learning has to be evidenced in achievement, and understanding comes about from this. This means that learning and doing are intertwined, and these two aspects need to be considered concurrently. Throughout their planning teachers consider the learning that will be taking place and the progression of knowledge longitudinally over time. However, with artists in schools, the possibility can exist for activity to be mistaken for learning; indeed, planning for *activity* is often easier than planning for *learning*. This is not to say that there is not a place for active learning, but it does mean that young people should be engaged in musical learning during such activity. The main issue for work practices involving music is that they involve an interplay between doing—in other words, making music—and learning. The teachers understood this; the composers grew to understand it, but began by thinking about doing, and then retrospectively grafting on learning from this.

Although the main area of expertise of the composers was clearly composing, they also brought other related and potentially transferable aspects of their working practices to the project. These included ways in which creativity, especially creative ideas, could be nurtured, fostered, and developed. The composers had considerable expertise in taking original creative musical ideas, working on and with them, and developing them to fruition, something that was often lacking in many of the learners. We know that for many pupils sticking with an idea at the early stages of composing is not something they are used to (Fautley 2014). By focusing on what might be termed "micro-aspects" of composing, taking small ideas and sticking with them, teachers gained insights into the composing process they could develop with their own pupils. As one of the participating teachers observed:

> They [learners] are being more creative with their ideas; they are composing music that is more imaginative . . . they are more confident and resilient with their ideas.
> (project teacher, interview data)

The professional knowledge of the teachers in terms of defining learning has already been explained. Christophersen (2013, 1) posits that teachers in such projects often become positioned as "artists' helpers, students' guards, or as mediators between artists and students." It is useful, therefore, to consider the various types of learning that were taking place during the course of the *Resolution* project and the implications of these.

The Centrality of Learning

A key issue for music education we have already discussed from the perspectives of the stakeholders in this work are the differences between *learning* and *doing*. But we also know from, among others, the work of Hattie (2009, 2012) that making learning visible is no straightforward process. Professional knowledge, as we have described it, was evidenced, but so was professional learning. After all,

> if learning occurs from and with others, as members of communities, the assumption is that within musician-teacher collaborations, collective knowledge through dialogic practice will be key to transformative practice.
> (Kenny and Christophersen, this volume, 15)

This was the case with this project. Indeed, in order to make sure that the necessary facilitating conditions (Torrance 1987) were in place for this, the project set aside time for reflection. Schön (1983) has noted that reflection *in* and *on* practice is an important part of the professionalism of teachers. Teacher pedagogy often involves careful planning, action, and reflection in and on teaching and learning. Within the reflection sessions both teachers and composers had to recognize distinct but overlapping perspectives of composing pedagogy. As the project involved exam group–aged pupils, workshops had to work within examination specifications. This required collaborative reflections between the teachers and composers on teaching and learning where a shared language was fostered. This cultural mediation involved a number of aspects: the composers learning about the school context, the curriculum, exam expectations, performativity, and targeted ways to engage young people. Equally important, the teachers explored composerly thinking and creative processes and how they could develop these when working solo after the composers had left. For the teachers, the composers offered a way in to altered perceptions of practice. Music teachers were exposed to new ways of working, of approaching composing. One teacher noted:

> it produced exciting, innovative performances; pupils grappled with some pretty advanced science, and understood enough of it to translate into music; it was a refreshing and challenging project for all concerned—and those ones tend to be the ones that spark further ideas.
> (project teacher, interview data)

Significantly, the CPD and reflection sessions that were offered for the composers were important for developing an educational perspective of composing in schools and establishing the scene for what was going to take place. By including time for reflection, composers critiqued, questioned, and planned for a continuum of learning. The learning–doing dichotomy was again evidenced here, in that although some of the activities were concerned with doing, such as rehearsing composed pieces, learning was linked to knowledge. Sfard (1998) explores this in her two metaphors for learning: the acquisition and participation metaphors. In the acquisition metaphor the main focus is gaining knowledge, which Sfard observes "brings to mind the activity of accumulating material goods" (1998, 5). Knowledge is developed, meaning is created, and this is owned by the individual. On the other hand, the participatory metaphor involves moving from acquisition to participation: "the permanence of having, gives way to the constant flux of doing" (1998, 6). The composers and teachers planned for learning by evoking both metaphors—through knowledge acquisition, learning about music, but also participation and learning by making music together.

Discussion

One of the significant factors that has emerged from this research is the notion of professional knowledge. What we see at play in this project is knowledge existing in three principal domains, those of what might be termed (1) composerly thinking knowledge, which, using Sfard's (1998) terminologies, is, by and large, owned and participated in by the composers; (2) pedagogical content knowledge, which is, again by and large, the property of the teachers; and (3) lying at the intersection of the two, what might be called subject domain knowledge. Figure 16.1 gives a graphical representation of this overlap.

Although it may seem the case that these represent relatively finely graded delineations of the three knowledge types, nonetheless in the context of partnership working, they are significant. After all, as Bowman observes:

> Professional knowledge and expertise are things that are not easily or casually come by. As such, they designate capacities that are not shared by members of society at large; but they also and more particularly designate skills, knowledge, and capacities not shared by individuals in fields of endeavor that might, to the casual observer, seem closely related.
> (Bowman 2007, 114)

It is important, too, that the *Resolution* project is not seen as an example of a "victory narrative" (see Chapter 1). The *Resolution* project was a success, in that it altered thinking, gave young people powerful experiences, and, importantly, produced worthwhile learning for composers and teachers, but it was because of the recognition of domains of expertise and the in-built reflection sessions that this took place. We know that in some instances partnership working can be problematic:

> lack of agreement about the purpose of the partnership, together with a sense of confusion about the roles of the numerous partners, were identified as principal inhibitors to working together.
> (Pinkus 2005, 185)

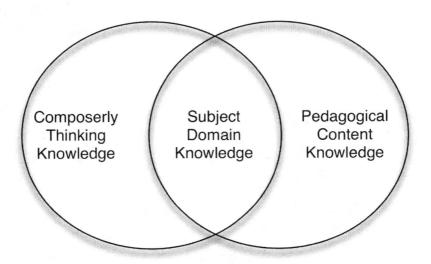

Figure 16.1 Overlapping domains of professional knowledge

This project recognized this from the outset, and one of the significant pieces of learning from this work is the notion of actively facilitating, and then building on, reflection time for key stakeholders. These also need integration into funding bids.

The learning of the pupils, although important and significant, was not the only learning in this project. Indeed, from the outset this was conceived as a knowledge exchange project for the key stakeholders. Structured reflection, guided by a critical friend, gave this project an impetus, which meant that the professional knowledge of all parties was both respected and enabled. For the hosting organization, BCMG, this meant that there was a developmental relationship with the composers, which meant that their own professional learning was recognized. The teachers learned composing pedagogical techniques that they employ with other classes. In *Resolution*, reflection sessions were facilitated by researchers. This meant that conversations of the "that was okay" variety were challenged. Reflection needs to be deeper than the "what went well/even better if" variety common in English schools today. Deep reflection is difficult and challenging, and observations that start and end with enjoyment (however important that may be thought) of participants may not be enough. Challenging questions force stakeholders to really think about what they are doing and why they were doing it. These were not generic prescribed questions, but arose from the actuality of the individual sessions. Examples include:

"Why did you accept some ideas but not others from the pupils?"
"Why did you intervene in that group at the back?"
"Why did you stop the group working when they seemed to be getting on well?"
"What was the purpose of stopping everyone after a few minutes?"
"Who do you think did the most work this session: the children, the teacher, or the composer?"

These questions made the participants really think, and using what in psychological research are referred to as "think aloud protocols" (inter alia Sloboda 1985), made the stakeholders share their thoughts in the safe arena of joint reflection sessions.

Success in this project was not measured by a glittering end concert, but by the learning of participants. As examples, a composer observed:

Working around school music lessons (on a two week timetable) is limiting, I hadn't realized that's how music lessons worked in schools, or that this was why we were working like this, or that how difficult it was to try to get time for this work in school timetables.

(research interview data)

One of the teachers said:

As the teacher I wanted to be a participating performer and along the way I picked up interesting things about my teaching.

(research interview data)

Another teacher noted:

I have felt supported and learnt new ideas to bring back into the classroom.

(research interview data)

These observations may seem superficial, but they are significant in being examples of the ways in which professional learning for teachers about composing and performing and for composers about school structures took place. This developed the professional learning of each group and has hopefully had an important function in terms of what they would do next in their respective professional capacities.

Conclusion

This chapter has described a partnership project focused on composing in schools involving composers and teachers in England. It has unpicked key aspects of professional learning that occurred, outlined both successes and problems, and drawn out some of this learning for an international audience. We hope that the points we have outlined in this chapter are not only of interest to those working in artist–teacher partnerships, in whatever jurisdiction they are taking place, but that some of the observations we have made will be helpful for those embarking on such work too. In times of austerity and budget cuts in many jurisdictions, we owe it to our young people to ensure that they are having the best exposure to multiple ways of working that we can provide for them. Anything else is a disservice to schools, composers, and music education.

References

Ball, Stephen J. 2003. "The Teacher's Soul and the Terrors of Performativity." *Journal of Education Policy*, 18 (2), 215–28.
Berkley, Rebecca. 2001. "Why Is Teaching Composing So Challenging? A Survey of Classroom Observation and Teachers' Opinions." *British Journal of Music Education*, 18 (2), 119–38.
Bowman, Wayne. 2007. "Who Is the "We"? Rethinking Professionalism in Music Education." *Action, Criticism, and Theory for Music Education*, 6 (4), 109–31.
Christophersen, Catharina. 2013. "Helper, Guard or Mediator? Teachers' Space for Action in The Cultural Rucksack, a Norwegian National Program for Arts and Culture in School. *International Journal of Education & The Arts*, 14 (SI. 1.11). Accessed June 12, 2017, www.ijea.org/v14si1/.
Christophersen, Catharina. 2015. "Changes and Challenges in Music Education: Reflections on a Norwegian Arts-in-Education Programme." *Music Education Research*, 17 (4), 365–80.

Eraut, Michael. 1994. *Developing Professional Knowledge and Competence*. London: RoutledgeFalmer.
Fautley, Martin. 2014. *Listen, Imagine, Compose—Research Report*. London: Sound and Music.
Fautley, Martin, Richard Hatcher, and Elaine Millard. 2011. *Remaking the Curriculum: Re-Engaging Young People in Secondary School*. Stoke-on-Trent: Trentham.
Hattie, John. 2009. *Visible Learning: A Synthesis of over 800 Meta-Analyses Related to Achievement*. New York: Routledge.
Hattie, John. 2012. *Visible Learning for Teachers—Maximizing Impact on Learning*. Abingdon: Routledge.
Kenny, Ailbhe. 2010. "Too Cool for School? Musicians as Partners in Education." *Irish Educational Studies*, 29 (2), 153–66.
Kenny, Ailbhe. 2014. "Sound Connections for Institutional Practice: Cultivating 'Collaborative Creativity' Through Group Composition." In *Developing Creativities in Higher Music Education: International Perspectives and Practices*, edited by Pamela Burnard, 469–93. Abingdon: Routledge.
Kenny, Ailbhe. 2016. *Communities of Musical Practice*. Abingdon: Routledge.
Lave, Jean, and Etienne Wenger. 1991. *Situated Learning: Legitimate Peripheral Participation*. Cambridge: Cambridge University Press.
Nardi, Bonnie. 1996. "Studying Context: A Ccomparison of Activity Theory, Situated Action Models, and Distributed Cognition." In *Context and Consciousness: Activity Theory and Human-Computer Interaction*, edited by Bonnie Nardi, 69–102. Cambridge, MA: MIT Press.
Pinkus, Susanna. 2005. "Bridging the Gap Between Policy and Practice: Adopting a Strategic Vision for Partnership Working in Special Education." *British Journal of Special Education*, 32 (4), 184–7.
Ruffer, David. 1988. "The London Sinfonietta Education Programme—an Analysis of an Interface Between the Professional Artist and Music in Education." *British Journal of Music Education*, 5 (1), 45–54.
Salomon, Gavriel, ed. 1993. *Distributed Cognitions*. Cambridge: Cambridge University Press.
Sawyer, R. Keith. 2003a. *Group Creativity. Music, Theater, Collaboration*. Mahwah, NJ: Lawrence Erlbaum.
Sawyer, R. Keith. 2003b. "Emergence in Creativity and Development." In *Creativity and Development*, edited by R. Keith Sawyer, Vera John-Steiner, Seanna Moran, Robert. J., Sternberg, David Henry Feldman, Jeanne Nakamura, and Mihaly Csikszentmihalyi, 12–60. New York: Oxford University Press.
Schön, Donald. (1983) *The Reflective Practitioner*. Aldershot: Academic Publishing.
Sfard, Anna. (1998) "On Two Metaphors for Learning and the Dangers of Choosing Just One." *Educational Researcher*, 27(2), 4–13.
Shulman, Lee. 1986. "Those Who Understand: Knowledge Growth in Teaching." *Educational Researcher*, 15 (2), 4–14.
Sloboda, John. 1985. *The Musical Mind*. Oxford: Oxford University Press.
Swanwick, Keith. 1999. *Teaching Music Musically*. London: Routledge.
Torrance, E. Paul. 1987. "Teaching for Creativity." In *Frontiers of Creativity Research: Beyond the Basics*, edited by Scott G. Isaksen, 189–215. Buffalo, NY: Bearly Limited.
Wenger, Etienne. 1998. *Communities of Practice: Learning, Meaning, and Identity*. Cambridge: Cambridge University Press.

17

"I'm Just the Bass Player in Their Band": Dissolving Artistic and Educational Dichotomies in Music Education

LARS BRINCK

Introduction

It seems to be a quite established fact that art in schools has a positive impact on students' general development and well-being (Bamford 2006), a notion that internationally has led to a vast number of initiatives strengthening the presence of art in school, very often operated as visiting artists and as artist-teacher collaborative models (cf. the introductory chapter of this book). However, such initiatives are not without built-in problems (Buckingham and Jones 2001; Bresler 2002; Laycock 2008; Angelo and Kalsnes 2014; Bennett and Stanberg 2008; Kenny 2010; Kenny et al. 2015), especially with regard to the roles and mutual expectations in musician–teacher collaborations. Within music education the general discourse seems, for instance, to somehow dichotomize musicians as fair teachers and music teachers as fair musicians (Christophersen 2015; Rønningen 2014; Varkøy 2014), opposing two deeply interrelated and entwined domains within music education, namely music performance and *learning* to perform music.

My point here is that such dichotomies are problematic for the quality and hence the impact of music education in general and that widening our analytical perspective of what constitutes learning in the music classroom may prove a viable way to resolve this predicament—in practice. In this chapter I take the specific perspective of the pop/jazz musician developing his or her teaching skills in the context of the music academy, hoping this will add to a discussion of the parallel significance of the teacher's artistic practice in school. This hopefully will contribute to dissolving the dichotomies indicated earlier. In other words: How can we discuss the "collaboration of artist and teacher" within the artist/teacher herself without dichotomizing artistic and pedagogical skills and experiences?

In the chapter I will argue for a social practice theoretical offset in analyzing learning in schools' musical practices as situated in everyday practices. By analyzing learning as changing participation in changing practice (Lave and

Wenger 1991; Lave 2011), I aim at providing a conceptual space for recognizing musicians' (already present) pedagogical resources *as well as* the significance of the music teachers' (already present) artistic resources.

Analyzing Learning as Changing Participation in Changing Practice

To unfold my argument I will describe and analyze how two popular music academy students of mine engaged in teaching a rock band of five youths and what everyone involved seemed to learn from that endeavor. Applying situated learning theory in an explicit social practice theoretical perspective (Lave 1996, 2011, draft), I analyze examples of the two music students' and their rock band pupils' changing participation in and across their changing artistic and educational practices as learning.

Participant observation (Atkinson and Hammersley 1994) of the students teaching their rock band has been documented through field notes and semi-structured interviews (Kvale and Brinkmann 2009) addressing possible connections between the students' own artistic practice in their different bands and teaching the rock band at the academy[1] have been transcribed verbatim for subsequent analysis. I aim at unfolding details of the moments and persons by offering "thick descriptions" (Geertz 1973) of the historically, didactically construed practices and participants.

Now let me commence my argument by revisiting the analytic theory of situated learning from a social practice theoretical perspective.[2] First of all, clarifying situated learning theory's philosophical grounds, Lave (1996) states how

> [t]he region of social theory that seems richest in clues for how to conceive of learning in social terms, in my view, is that of historical, dialectical, social practice theory. Such a theoretical perspective takes learning to be an aspect of participation in socially situated practices.
> (150)

A social practice theoretical ontological and epistemological foundation to situate learning theory's analytic concepts appears to provide a solid and consistent take on how to detect and talk about learning as situated in and inseparable from human practice; as changing relations between persons and the world in historically informed ways.

A pivotal situated learning theoretical perspective is the idea of learning not to be regarded as a *condition* for taking part in a practice, but rather as "an evolving form of membership" (Lave and Wenger 1991, 53). Defining learning as a process of change makes it necessary to investigate each person's changing "participation" in practice, and even to regard the changing participation as deeply entwined with the changing practice itself—in reciprocal ways: Practice changes, but practice also changes people's participation, and this dialectic relational complex can be analyzed as an arena where processes of learning unfold.

In this chapter I choose specifically to focus on how situated learning theory's analytic concept of "participation" enables us to grasp "[t]he importance of *access* to the learning potential of given settings" (42, my italics), in other words whether what practice is *about* (Brinck 2012, 2014; In Press) is evident and appears meaningful and transparent to the participants. Lave and Wenger argue to analyze whether participants have broad access to "arenas of mature practice" (110). The ongoing changing participation in the changing practice could be analyzed as "situated opportunities for the improvisational development of new practice" (Lave 1989 in Lave 1991, 97) as "practice itself is in motion" (Lave and Wenger 1991, 116). In a situated learning theoretical analysis we consequently ask how different ways of participation enable newcomers as well as old-timers to learn more about what a practice is about and how to participate in it—through the development of practice itself.

Analyzing participants' changing participation in changing practices in historical, dialectical terms requires us to be "decentering" our analytic perspective. Lave (draft) suggests that the object of analysis should be "a textured landscape of participation" (4), questioning common and conventional notions of teaching, of pedagogy, of who's the master of what, and ultimately of learning. This involves shifting our analytic binoculars from the individual learner to the notion of changing participation in and through changing practice.

Educating Musicians as Teachers

Coherent with the idea of a decentered situated learning theoretical analysis, let me briefly introduce the educational context within which the students' teaching project that we are about to describe and analyze takes place.

The students are third-year Bachelor of Music students, and we have known each other for more than two years, engaging in many interesting discussions and shared practices on aspects of learning and subsequently teaching. This has included theoretical discussions on social practice theory, situated learning theory, the relations between individual and collective artistic work processes, and between their artistic endeavors and their pedagogical engagement in future generations' passion for music. And it has included different specific musical and teaching practices, including the one presented later in this chapter.

At the academy we share an ambition to provide our students with tools to bridge developing their own musical practices with skills to *teach* others to engage in such practices. First of all, we try to nourish the music students' sprouting interest in learning through in-depth analyses of their own and their peers' historical as well as ongoing artistic development. In Haug's (2000) unfolding of Gramsci's ideas of a "philosophy of praxis" he suggests with Hegel to "banish from history the destructive moment and transform contradictions into differences" (3). Such an explicitly historical (and productive) developmental perspective on persons' iteratively changing of being in the world appears to be a very productive and tangible handle when aiming to bridge artistic development with educational.

In effect, through an entwined theoretical and practical approach, the students write essays on learning from the perspective of their own upbringing with a focus on significant moments of realizing what kinds of emotions and sensations different musical and educational experiences entail. In other words, we ask the students to unfold their "biography of participation" (Lave 2011), then share these historically informed insights into their peers' and their own educational heritage towards a deeper understanding of what constitutes learning and consequently teaching. And we then bridge their discovery of such significant moments with an in-depth analysis of how and why that might constitute moments of learning, moments of change.

This overall approach to developing the musicians' educational interest and knowledgeability (Lave 2011) highlights how musicians, through their daily artistic work (especially within popular music and jazz), are used to being highly dependent on—and therefore competent within—a detailed orientation towards other persons' perspectives, skills, and aspirations (Berliner 1994; Green 2001; Kenny 2014, 2016; Brinck 2011, 2014, 2017). Working in pop, jazz, and rock bands—often with a high degree of collective creative processes writing and arranging the music together—provides the musician with a set of highly advanced skills and competences related to, on one hand, generating ideas and suggestions and, on the other hand, negotiating such notions with the other musicians in delicate processes of trial, critique, and decision making.[3] As we shall see later, revealing such resources becomes pivotal for the students' emerging teaching practice "experiments." Insofar as the students trust their skills as musicians and collective art process specialists, they initially trust their approach to teaching the rock band as "a composite band with members of different levels of expertise and experience." Let me now tell a little about the teaching project at hand.

"I'm Just the Bass Player in Their Band"

The children's rock band is now called Wibamara.[4] In the beginning it wasn't even a band (or a name). Just four kids twelve to thirteen years of age signing up for the music academy's teaching practice. None of the kids knew each other beforehand. The academy students Ida (bass) and Daniel (guitar) wanted song writing to be at the core of their teaching practice, and the pupils signing up knew this. The students also play together in a professional rock band composing and performing their own songs, where the musicians work collectively from the first sketches towards the final version and arrangement. The students' pedagogical aims and challenges were initially formulated along the lines of: How can our experiences from writing and playing our own songs in our different bands translate into a music pedagogy of collective song writing and band playing? How can we as musicians help younger musicians to become a band writing *their* own songs and perform them?[5]

It's Monday again.[6]

This particular Monday Daniel is absent. And Ida is the teacher responsible for today's session. Ida plays the electric bass, as the band does not have a bass player.

— Why don't we start by repeating the song that we started writing last Monday? Ida asks.

Last week the band put together a sequence of chords, a groove and a melodic line for an A- and a B-part. The chords were randomly selected by tossing dice, each number representing a specific chord. The randomly constructed chord sequence was subsequently adjusted by the band until it finally represented something that everybody liked. No lyrics were developed, only a sketch of a melodic line for each section.

Ida and the band agree that the two singers go outside to come up with some nice lyrics for the melodic line already composed, while the rest of the band rehearse the two song parts.

— You do the count-in, Ida suggests to the drummer, who takes the lead:
— One, two, one, two, three, four.

The band sounds fine. Ida's bass playing of course sticks out as being on a professional level.[7]

The rhythm section rehearses. In particular, bridging the two parts represents a challenge, as the two parts are built on quite different grooves. They try again, Ida investigating different approaches through her bass playing. Ida also tries to stand at different positions in relation to the drummer, moving her body with the pulse while producing a very subdivided bass line. Ida faces him, smiling and grooving, and at the same time nods at Ra on guitar, being more on top of things in this song, shifting between playing chords and melodic lines. A rhythm section is rehearsing.

At one natural pause in the rehearsal Ida takes off the bass:

— Can you rehearse without me for a while? I need to go and check on the girls.

Ida leaves the room. And the drummer and the guitarist start to rehearse. The drummer knows how to count in, and the two kids give another go at the two sections and the intro. No bass line to support but the groove seems

to linger in the air. Now the guitarist stands facing the drummer, just like Ida stood before. A rhythm section in a rock band is rehearsing.
(based on author's field notes, my transl.)

Analysis

Access

Situated learning theoretical analysis can be conducted in numerous ways, providing a careful focus on persons' changing participation and changing relations to each other and the (historically constructed and construing) social world in which they are a part. From an arts and musical practice educational perspective, the perspective coined as *access* appears to be very helpful when analyzing *how*, *when*, and *through which* changing practice learning seems to take place. Analyzing the earlier empirical example as a "textured landscape of participation" with respect to *access* reveals a number of interesting aspects of learning taking place.

I want to point to the fact that newcomers as well as old-timers (Lave and Wenger 1991) are in fact participating as musicians. The concepts of teacher versus pupil seem somehow evaporated. The kids' participation in the band rehearsal room becomes legitimate insofar as Ida does not talk to them or act towards them as pupils but rather as band members. At the same time their participation at some point is peripheral in the sense that Ida's bass playing is of a professional quality that clearly circumscribes what the musical groove is about. Ida provides *access* to the musical sound and groove through her playing. And the quality of the music appears transparent to the pupils.

At one point during the interviews with Daniel and Ida, we talked about the impact of playing with the kids, being a member of the band rather than taking on the role as an observing, directing teacher/verbal instructor. Ida states: "It's quite simple, really. I'm just the bass player in their band" (personal communication, Oct. 26, 2016). Of course, this is not entirely so. As already touched upon, Ida, of course, is not "just" the bass player. Being the more experienced musician she would—based on years of experience with band playing—adjust her playing, but also be strictly aware of the immediate relevance of her playing. Her decisions would be based along the lines of: What do I need to play to provide and secure everyone's *access* to the actual music in this actual moment? As an example of such "adjusted participation" on her behalf, I observed Ida on many occasions playing a more subdivided bass role than probably would be called for in a professional band in order to support the young drummer's sense and playing of subdivisions, strengthening the overall groove. Such adjusted teacher participation in practice provided access to everyone's participation in a strong and well-connected groove.

Ida also provides access to other sides of band life, when she at one point changes her role from being the bass player to "wanting to check out how far the girls are with the lyrics in the other room." But she keeps this decision (to leave the rhythm section rehearsal) within the band discourse by asking the two remaining kids in the band room to keep on practicing without her. This situation provides access to "how do bands rehearse?" and "how do we engage in improving the music (without a teacher telling us what to do)?"

The moment when Ida leaves the room and the two kids start rehearsing on their own indeed is a moment of changing participation: The context changes and their participation changes suddenly to become less peripheral in relation to the more experienced bass player and becoming increasingly legitimate as band rhythm section musicians rehearsing. The band is also a band without Ida—of course. This would be a nice example of what Lave (draft) calls "changing linguistic usage" (p. 7). Language is not a practice of "teacher-instructs-students" but rather a practice of "band-members-are-communicating."

Being Distinct and Making Things Clear

Two other examples from the rock band project are worth mentioning here:

In one of her essays on learning to become a musician[8] Ida writes about what constitutes pivotal aspects of the (musical and oral) communication between the professional musician visiting the class and herself. Ida states how "you can do a whole lot by just showing the kind of communication you want" in the band room. "I often experience how you in the band room invent your own language to communicate the music and use [musical] sounds and your body to show, what you want with the music" (Ida, personal communication). It becomes clear how Ida's experiences from the band reflect her own ambition as teacher to be distinct in her communication and in ways that are adequate for the band context. Her professional experiences with participation in her own bands (and what is helpful in terms of communicating in order to get access to the best possible music) immediately affect what she finds relevant to teach.

Daniel also states, how "we have this sort of mantra, where the kids' ideas should be allowed to evolve without us interfering too much" (Daniel, personal communication), referring to how Wibamara, for instance, were struggling with two sections of a song fitting together. Daniel allowed them to address this challenge by talking about it and trying out different solutions. In a situated learning theoretical analytical perspective Daniel here seemed to provide access to the band members' participation in a collective process involving "how a band collectively identifies and addresses musical, creative challenges and subsequently overcomes them without the authoritative interference of a teacher or a (seemingly) more experienced instructor."

Generally, in a situated learning theoretical analysis, clarity through the more experienced musicians' participation in the collective musical and other communication arguably seems to translate into access. Ida communicates clarity regarding the groove through bodily and musical gestures, and both Daniel and Ida try to be clear and distinct in the way they talk, and in fact through their participation in the collective practice address the many little challenges connected to working collectively with creative production of material. Through participating in such work processes in a number of legitimate peripheral ways, the pupils develop an increasingly detailed knowledge regarding what constitutes working in a band. Ida and Daniel maintain a focus on their own participation in the collective practice to represent clearly and distinctly what they "know" from their own band practice, which appears to represent a productive and ethical teacher's and musician's approach to such intricate collective work processes.

Discussion

Musician–teacher and artist–pedagogue dichotomies appear to be difficult to dispose of. However, the situated learning theoretical analyses offered here seem to provide a somewhat coherent argument for at least one way to reconcile this predicament.

Taking the music educational institutional perspective of the musician learning to teach, the analyses seem to offer important pedagogical resources in consciously bridging the musician's own artistic practice with that of teaching others, as well as suggestions as to how such educational ideas may *in practice* be operated in terms of actual pedagogical encounters with young bands.

However, such an argument seems to be closely connected to a conception of learning to be a matter of changing relations in changing practice and for such processes to be historically and contextually informed. To accept such a coherence implies teaching to involve many forms of participation on behalf of everyone involved, and it implies putting the musical practice itself at the core of activities—to provide access to what music is and does. Here I find situated learning theory helpful in detecting such coherence when looking at the academy students' changing practice *and* when looking at the rock band pupils' changing practice in Wibamara.

In the introduction to this chapter I claim to examine the musician–teacher collaboration "within" the musician–teacher herself. Does this prove helpful to the overall discussion of such collaborative challenges? I think it does! By reinforcing the importance of the music teacher's participation as artist and by reinforcing the musician's participation as teacher through a situated learning analysis, we come to see how dichotomies do not necessarily need to be as cemented into our artistic educational practices as we might sometimes find ourselves doing. The music teacher *is* an artist and should let this show in everyday school practices—providing access for the pupils to the music. And the musician *is* a teacher with crucial pedagogical resources at hand—providing access to the music in other *and* in similar ways.

Notes

1. I performed one collective semi-structured interview with Ida and Daniel on Wednesday, October 26, 2016. The framework for the interview was the following three questions that I mailed to Ida and Daniel in advance: How does you playing in a professional band hold consequences for your teaching the youth band here at the academy? Which differences and similarities do you see between playing in your own band and playing with your pupils? Can you as a musician learn anything from teaching a band of less experienced musicians/pupils? (my transl.). The interview was performed in Danish. Analytically interesting excerpts were subsequently translated into English for this chapter.
2. Having introduced the (now) monumental book *Situated Learning. Legitimate Peripheral Participation* in 1991, Jean Lave's and her then student Etienne Wenger's paths seem to have been headed in quite different directions in terms of how their mutually developed theory of learning as situated could and should be applied: Wenger seems over the years to have taken a quite prescriptive approach, suggesting ways to design and improve "communities of practice." In *Cultivating Communities of Practice. A Guide to Managing Knowledge* from 2002, Wenger et al. set off by stating how to "organize systematically to leverage knowledge remains a challenge" and that "cultivating communities of practice is a keystone of an effective knowledge strategy" (cover leaf). Please cf. Brinck and Tanggaard 2016 for an extensive review on especially leadership research, where you will find illustrative examples of situated learning theoretical misfits between analytic intentions and prescriptive applications.
3. Please cf. Brinck 2011 (in Danish) for an in-depth account for how the collective band work enhances such competences related to collegiate supervision towards developing the collective teaching environment.
4. A name constructed by taking the first two letters of each of the four children's names and putting the syllables together. Right at the beginning of the year band project teachers Ida and Daniel wanted—through naming the band—to help the kids develop a sensation of community, of togetherness: We're a band, we have a name, we talk about our collective thing with a short recognizable term that we collectively developed. In terms of the band project also providing empirical data for the present research project, the two academy students Ida and Daniel, as well as the kids in the band Wibamara (represented by their parents), have provided their informed consent to be a part of this small research inquiry in a nonanonymous manner. The final chapter has been offered to academy students and parents for approval in terms of quotes and examples utilized.
5. These two questions generally constitute the didactical "problematic" for Ida and Daniel to investigate as formulated by them at the beginning of the spring semester, having met and discussed this with the pupils over some time. Ida, Daniel, and Wibamara quite soon agreed on forming a band that was to write their own material and perform it. Ida and Daniel also interviewed the pupils from time to time on their experience with playing and song writing. The pupils appeared to have *very* different experiences, some having tried song writing and performing before and others completely new to the field.
6. Monday nights throughout the spring and the fall semester the members of Wibamara met with Ida and Daniel to write songs and play them. Wibamara is Wi on drums, Ba on piano and vocals, Ma on lead vocals, and Ra on guitar.
7. Ida later in her interview discusses whether she plays differently in Wibamara than she would with professional peers. Please cf. analysis in this chapter.
8. The educational aim of the project initiating this essay is to have the students experience working closely together with a professional musician in a band context, subsequently reflecting on different aspects of these work processes in an overall learning perspective.

References

Angelo, Elin, and Signe Kalsnes, Eds. 2014. *Kunstner eller lærer? Profesjonsdilemmaer i musikk- og kunstpedagogisk utdanning* [Artist or Teacher? Occupational Dilemmas in Music and Art Educational Programs]. Oslo: Cappelen Damm.

Atkinson, Paul, and Martyn Hammersley. 1994. "Ethnography and Participant Observation." In *Handbook of Qualitative Research*, edited by Norman Denzin and Yvonna Lincoln, 110–37. London: Sage Publications.
Bamford, Ann. 2006. *The Wow Factor: Global Research Compendium on the Impact of the Arts in Education*. New York: Waxmann Munster.
Bennett, Dawn, and Andrea Stanberg. 2008. "Musicians as Teachers: Fostering a Positive View." In *Inside, Outside, Downside Up: Conservatoire Training and Musicians' Work*, edited by Dawn Bennett and Michael F. Hannan, 11–22. Perth, WA: Black Swan Press.
Berliner, Paul. 1994. *Thinking in Jazz: The Infinite Art of Improvisation*. Chicago: The University of Chicago Press.
Brinck, Lars. 2011. "Kollegial supervision med en kunstnerisk tilgang" [Collegiate Supervision from an Artistic Approach]. In *Kollegial supervision som udviklingsredskab i undervisningskulturer* [Collegiate Supervision as a Developmental Tool in Teaching Environments], edited by Hanne Leth Andersen and Lene Tortzen Bager, 89–96. Aarhus: Aarhus University Press
Brinck, Lars. 2012. "Bringing Drumsticks to Funerals: Jamming as Learning." *Nordiske Udkast (Outlines)*, 40 (2), 16–30.
Brinck, Lars. 2014. "Ways of the Jam. Collective and Improvisational Perspectives on Learning." PhD diss., Aalborg University, Department of Communication and Psychology, Denmark.
Brinck, Lars. 2017. "Jamming and Learning: Analyzing Changing Collective Practice of Changing Participation." *Music Education Research*, 19 (2), 214–25. Accessed June 13, 2017, http://dx.doi.org/10.1080/14613808.2016.1257592
Brinck, Lars. In Press. "Funk Jamming in New Orleans: Musical Communication in Practice and Theory." *International Journal of Music Education*.
Brinck, Lars, and Lene Tanggaard. 2016. "Embracing the Unpredictable: Leadership, Learning, Changing Practice." *Human Resource Development International*, 19 (5), 374–87.
Bresler, Liora. 2002. "Out of the Trenches: The Joys (and Risks) of Cross-Disciplinary Collaborations." *Bulletin of the Council for Research in Music Education*, 152 (Spring), 17–39. Chicago, IL: University of Chicago Press.
Buckingham, David, and Ken Jones. 2001. "New Labour's Cultural Turn: Some Tensions in Contemporary Educational and Cultural Policy." *Journal of Education Policy*, 16 (1), 1–14.
Christophersen, Catharina. 2015. "Changes and Challenges in Music Education: Reflections on a Norwegian Arts-in-Education Programme." *Music Education Research*, 17 (4), 364–80.
Geertz, Clifford. 1973. *The Interpretation of Cultures*. New York: Harper Collins.
Green, Lucy. 2001. *How do Popular Musicians Learn? A Way Ahead for Music Education*. London: Ashgate Press.
Haug, Wolfgang F. 2000. "Gramsci's Philosophy of Praxis: Camouflage or Refoundation of Marxist Thought." *Socialism and Democracy*, 14 (1), 1–25.
Kenny, Ailbhe. 2010. "Too Cool for School? Musicians as Partners in Education." *Irish Educational Studies*, 29 (2), 153–66.
Kenny, Ailbhe. 2014. "'Collaborative Creativity' Within a Jazz Ensemble as a Musical and Social Practice." *Thinking Skills and Creativity*, 13, 1–8. Accessed June 13, 2017, www.sciencedirect.com/science/article/pii/S1871187114000078.
Kenny, Ailbhe. 2016. *Communities of Musical Practice*. New York: Routledge.
Kenny, Ailbhe, Michael Finneran, and Eamonn Mitchell. 2015. "Becoming an Educator in and Through the Arts: Forming and Informing Emerging Teachers' Professional Identity." *Teaching and Teacher Education*, 49, 159–67.
Kvale, Steinar, and Svend Brinkmann. 2009. *InterViews: Learning the Craft of Qualitative Research Interviewing*, 2nd edition. Thousand Oaks, CA: Sage.
Lave, Jean. 1996. "Teaching, as Learning, in Practice." *Mind, Culture, and Activity*, 3 (3), 149–64.
Lave, Jean. 2011. *Apprenticeship in Critical Ethnographic Practice*. Chicago, IL: The University of Chicago Press.
Lave, Jean (draft, 2017). *Situated Learning: Historical Process and Practice*.
Lave, Jean, and Etienne Wenger. 1991. *Situated Learning: Legitimate Peripheral Participation*. Cambridge: Cambridge University Press.
Laycock, Jolyon, ed. 2008. *Enabling the Creators: Arts and Cultural Management and the Challenge of Social Inclusion*. Oxford: European Arts Management Project in Association with Oxford Brookes University.

Rønningen, Anders. 2014. "Den skal tidlig krøkes som god konstruksjon skal bli." In *Kunstner eller lærer? Profesjonsdilemmaer i musikk- og kunstpedagogisk utdanning*, edited by Elin Angelo and Signe Kalsnes, 218–32. Oslo: Cappelen Damm.

Varkøy, Øivind. 2014. "Mellem relevans og frihet: Om kunsttenkning og profesjonstenkning." [Between Relevans and Freedom: On Art Thought and Occupational Thought]. In *Kunstner eller lærer? Profesjonsdilemmaer i musikk- og kunstpedagogisk utdanning*, edited by Elin Angelo and Signe Kalsnes, 172–83. Oslo: Cappelen Damm.

Wenger, Etienne, Richard McDermott, and William M. Snyder. 2002. *Cultivating Communities of Practice: A Guide to Managing Knowledge*. Boston, MA: Harward Business School Press.

18
Small Composers: Creating Musical Meaning in a Community of Practice

SVEN-ERIK HOLGERSEN, PETER BRUUN,
AND METTE TJAGVAD

Introduction

The present chapter discusses roles and responsibilities of the collaborating partners in a creative music workshop called *Small Composers*.[1] It is a pedagogic platform provided by the Copenhagen-based classical music ensemble FIGURA. *Small Composers* has been developed over ten years through collaboration with a number of Danish primary schools, and as such the workshop represents the tradition of "visiting artists" in schools. As stated in the introductory chapter of this book, musician–teacher collaboration in a school context often implies participants' dichotomized approaches to music as a school subject, especially when the collaboration is part of a compulsory program (Christophersen 2013). In particular, the lack of school ownership is considered a general problem in visiting artist studies (Holdhus and Espeland 2013). This problem is very often related to the different professional backgrounds of the collaborating partners (Holst 2013). Thus, a point of departure for the present study was that "[q]uestions of music's nature and value are questions of personal and professional identity" (Bowman 2007). Following this line of thinking, genuine collaboration depends on the extent to which the collaborating partners share musical values and beliefs about music as a school subject.

In the present case, the collaborating partners very easily could be described in a dichotomized way, namely as a class teacher (music classes being only part of her duties) collaborating with two artists with no formal training in classroom teaching: a composer of avant-garde classical music and a professional clarinetist playing in an ensemble specializing in contemporary music. The present chapter aims to be attentive to a number of potential alterations implicated by the collaborating partners' different backgrounds. The following questions guided the study: What expectations do the class teacher and the professional musicians have to the creative practice, that is, to the collaboration and to the musical outcome? To which extent do the collaborating partners share a common understanding of the aim, content, and method of the workshop? How do the roles and responsibilities of the collaborating partners become visible through the practice? How do the professional identities of the teacher and the musicians become visible, and what are the implications for the workshop as a musical community of practice?

Background

Drawing on a previous case study (Bruun and Tjagvad 2016), a point of departure for the present case study was that collaboration between professional musicians and a class teacher can provide a productive field of tension between artistic and pedagogical intentions. The previous study explored group composition processes in a *Small Composers* workshop with another third-grade class and the same composer as in the present case. In the previous study the primary focus was on the creative process rather than on teacher–artist collaboration, but it appeared that the teacher played a crucial role in the process. The teacher's empathy and understanding of the children's ideas and intentions, as well as her familiarity with the pupils' social backgrounds and relations in the group, provided a secure space for artistic expression and exploration. Furthermore, the creative situation relied on a shared understanding of "music" encompassing interactive and collaborative aspects. Bruun and Tjagvad (2016, 29) concluded that musical creativity implies a "social ear." Social discourse and music as discourse are connected and influence each other in the compositional process (Espeland 2006). In *Small Composers*, social and musical aspects are inseparably connected through an ethical obligation to acknowledge musical otherness.

The present study investigates a workshop similar to the previous one (Bruun and Tjagvad 2016) and in some respects, it also relates to other studies: Wiggins (2011) developed a pedagogic design for songwriting through an interpretive collaboration with pupils scaffolding their musical ideas. Espeland (2006) used short text as a starting point for musical creativity and investigated children's composition processes between musical and social discourses in the classroom. In the present case study, the pupils made up a short tale as a narrative frame for the composition. Visiting artist studies inspired Espeland's cases, whereas in *Small Composers* a professional musician and a composer acted as visiting collaborative partners together with the class teacher throughout the workshop.

Eidsaa (2014) investigated partnerships where composers and professional musicians played a major role in the process, whereas the teachers played a minor role. Eidsaa reported cases in different genres representing explorative studies rather than a single well-tried format—as in the case of *Small Composers*. In a study of interactions and communication between pupils and their teachers working with composition in classrooms, Fautley (2004) concluded that teachers tended to talk or explain a great deal and with a main focus on the end product rather than on the compositional process. In the present study, particular attention was paid to communication (linguistic, bodily, and musical) in order to understand the notions and beliefs of music and music teaching guiding the teacher, the workshop leader, and the musician, respectively.

Small Composers: A Creative Workshop

Small Composers is based upon the work of the FIGURA Ensemble in avant-garde classical music. Introducing the workshop to first- through fifth-grade pupils and teachers, it is imperative to explain that the study title—*Small Composers*—has nothing to do with size or age; it is not child composers as opposed to adult composers. *Small Composers* only means composers who are not "great composers" like Beethoven or Mozart. A small composer could be anybody who can make music—which includes everyone.

The governing musical idea in *Small Composers* is that no particular sounds are privileged in music; only participants perform sounds (and silence) intentionally.

Small narratives provide the artistic and pedagogic framework for an animated structure of sound events: through a process of negotiation, the participants make a short tale and try to imagine how it can be told using no words but only sounds from instruments, artifacts, voice, body, etc. Creating the music is a matter of bringing the story to life using sounds that the participants perceive as meaningful for the purpose. The pupils are encouraged to bring their own sound sources from home; it may be manufactured or homemade musical instruments, toy instruments, kitchenware, or other artifacts suitable for sound production. The piece of music may include tonal material and even already existing material ("musical quotation"). The music is ready to perform when the tale has been transformed into a structured sound sequence that makes sense to the participants and that they are able to play, remember, repeat, and recognize. The pupils create, rehearse, and refine the pieces of music facilitated by the musicians and the teacher, culminating with a performance where parents are invited.

FIGURA Ensemble has developed slightly different formats of the workshop (one day with a composer or two days with a composer and a musician), and it distinguishes itself through a clear progression in the creative musical process (Bruun and Tjagvad 2016, 12–13). Participating in the present workshop were a third-grade class (twenty-four pupils aged between nine and ten years), their classroom teacher, a composer, and a clarinetist. The workshop was conducted over two days in a normal classroom setting. Based on the discovery of the teacher's crucial role in the previous case study, the teacher–artist collaboration was emphasized.

Preparation

1. The school made practical arrangements with FIGURA Ensemble about the workshop. The teacher received a short written introduction to the workshop, guidelines for listening exercises to be performed

prior to the workshop, and examples of sound sources that pupils were encouraged to bring.

Day One in the Classroom
2. Introduction: Meeting between pupils, teacher, and workshop leader (composer). Introductory music-making exercises.
3. Guided composition with the whole group of pupils: Transforming a small narrative into music with application of graphic notation.
4. Compositions in groups of four to five pupils: Working in separate rooms, each group created their own narrative and started composing music.

On day one the teacher was instructed to take an active part in the class exercises, both as an instructor and as a participant together with the pupils.

Day Two in the Classroom
On day two the teacher was asked to facilitate the creative processes in the groups on the same conditions as the musicians. Thus the teacher was encouraged to engage in musical collaboration and not only the social interaction in the groups.

5. Presentation of musician from FIGURA (in this case a clarinetist).
6. Continued composition in groups assisted by workshop leader, teacher, and musician.
7. Dress rehearsal with pupils and musicians where final decisions about the pieces and the performances are made.
8. Performance for an invited audience of parents/family.
9. Evaluation of the workshop.

Framing the Study
The main aim of the present case study was to understand how a classroom music teacher and professional musicians engage in collaboration in order to encourage and facilitate pupils' creative musical processes. The study, therefore, calls for theoretical perspectives on collaborative practices and teacher and musician identity, as well as on music as a teaching subject.

Theoretical Points of Departure
Members of the research team—which included the workshop leader—shared the belief that pedagogical understanding relies on informed reflection based on

sensitive listening and observing (van Manen 2016). This general approach implicates a certain openness to "music" as a phenomenon, for example, that music may become meaningful in many ways and that "improvisation" is involved in all musical activities—listening, playing, composing, etc. (Benson 2003). Benson emphasizes that music becomes meaningful in a continued dialogue between subjects and "[s]ince music making is something that we inevitably do with others (whether they are present or not), musical dialogue is fundamentally ethical in nature" (Benson 2003, 164). Bowman extends the intersubjective argument to account for a radical notion of music and music education building on "we-ness" as the most profound core value (Bowman 2007).

Referring to the open approach in creative music activities, the research team shared the belief that "[b]ecoming good at something involves developing specialized sensitivities, an aesthetic sense, and refined perceptions that are brought to bear on making judgments about the qualities of a product or an action" (Wenger 1998, 81).

Throughout the processes of collecting and analyzing data, a particular focus therefore was on whether and how "[n]egotiating a joint enterprise gives rise to relations of mutual accountability among those involved" (Wenger 1998, 81). The questions guiding the study (see introduction) reflect this concern. The case study is concerned with how participants contribute to create meaning through musical action and communication, that is, in a community of musical practice (Kenny 2016).

The professional identities of the teacher and the musicians are seen as products of their different educational and personal backgrounds (Holgersen and Holst 2013; Holst 2013), and a particular focus therefore is on the professional musicians' artistic background as well as on the class teacher's pedagogical professionalism.

Research Design and Methodology

The research group included three persons: Peter Bruun, composer and leader of the workshop *Small Composers*, was acting as insider, yet at the same time contributing as a researcher of his own practice. Mette Tjagvad, the second researcher, was trained as a schoolteacher and had a decade of teaching experience, thus representing the insider in the school context. Furthermore, Bruun and Tjagvad both held master's degrees in music education. Sven-Erik Holgersen represents an outsider's perspective as researcher in music education, including classroom research.

The combination of insider-outsider perspectives (Kvernbekk 2005; Fink-Jensen 2013) was considered productive for understanding values at stake in the creative musical practice, and the research team was intentionally formed this way in order to carry out triangulation through the data analysis. Different qualitative methods based on a phenomenological approach were applied. Inspired by Fink-Jensen (2013) pre-interviews and observations were combined with stimulated recall interviews (Lyle 2003):

- Pre-interview with the classroom teacher and the composer
- Participant as well as nonparticipant observation using video (two cameras) during the creative processes, the performance, and the evaluation
- Stimulated recall interviews with teacher, composer, and clarinetist

The analyses took place as "collaborative interpretation" (van Manen 1990) in which participants' lived experiences were described in thematic form and validated through triangulation of video and interview.

Towards a Musical Community of Practice

In the following, results from the analysis are highlighted in order to answer the research questions.

The Teacher's and the Musicians' Expectations to the Creative Collaboration

The teacher had previously participated in a similar workshop, mainly in the role of a pedagogical assistant rather as an instructor on equal terms with the musicians. Evaluations of visiting artist projects emphasize this kind of asynchrony as a major problem (cf Christophersen 2013). On the workshop leader's suggestion, the teacher in the pre-interview agreed to participate on equal terms with the musicians both in the introductory exercises and in the compositional process.

In his own words, the composer and workshop leader distinguished between being "accepted," being "welcomed," and being "met" in the school. If the composer and musician were merely accepted, negotiating a joint enterprise (Wenger 1998) would be difficult, if even possible. The workshop leader argued that the level of preparation on both sides of the partnership was crucial for the outcome of the workshop. A short meeting or even a phone conversation between the workshop leader and the teacher prior to the workshop could make a big difference for cooperation in the classroom. It mattered if the teacher has had just a little time together with the pupils to engage in the preparatory material. In the present case, the composer and musician were confident they would be genuinely "met" by the teacher and the school, yet it should be noted that the partners had one previous experience working together in a similar workshop.

The clarinetist explained that she saw the workshop as an opportunity to show the pupils what it is like to be a musician and be able to make all kinds of sounds with the instrument. Her approach as a professional musician to the workshop as well as to the pupils was playful and yet serious. As the clarinetist should only participate on day two, she expected the pupils to already be "attuned" to work as small composers.

The class teacher was an experienced and dedicated music teacher and occasionally she played the trumpet in amateur ensembles outside the school, but she had no training in composing music. When the workshop leader suggested the teacher should have a more autonomous role in the compositional process together with the pupils, she immediately accepted; however, in the pre-interview the teacher repeatedly referred to her own role as a mediator or supporter of the situation. Obviously, this was due to her humble approach to the composer. The teacher in the pre-interview also explained, "Other ensembles visiting the school do not have the same pedagogical approach to the children as in the case of *Small Composers*."

Composing music is mandatory according to the syllabus for music as a school subject.[2] Complying with the syllabus, the teacher explained, she had tried to include composing in the music class, despite the difficulty in doing so with a class of twenty-four pupils. Activities tend to generate a lot of noise, and being alone with the class separating the pupils into smaller groups may not be an option. The teacher expected the workshop to be a positive experience, not only because she had a previous positive experience with *Small Composers*, but also because some pupils already had some experience writing texts and music as a leisure time activity. "Composing music promotes their self-esteem because it gives them the feeling that everything is possible for them" (teacher in pre-interview).

Common Understanding of the Aim, Content, and Method of the Workshop

The aim of the workshop is not that the compositions should meet any standards outside of the classroom. The teacher, supported by the composer, explained the aim of composing music to the pupils: "The music composed in the workshop can never sound wrong, because it is your decision how it should sound!"

The teacher, in the pre-interview, pointed to the paradox that "some pupils tend to view music as a recreational subject in school, but at the same time the pupils do not realize how much they learn in the music class, even knowledge referring to other school subjects . . . Many of the pupils learn music very quickly, if they learn it in a musical way," she said. "Learning music is not only about specific musical skills, rather composition is as much about how pupils use their senses, listen to each other, and experience the joy of learning in a creative activity."

The composer and the clarinetist shared years of experience developing the ideas of the workshop, and therefore they did not need to discuss details about the aim, content, and method. Corresponding to findings in Kenny (2016), the musicians' shared history turned out to be of great value for the community of musical practice as a whole. During the dress rehearsal, a situation in which the clarinetist interrupted the composer occurred, yet in the stimulated recall interview, they explained that none of them experienced this as an interruption. Rather the communication in the workshop was similar to playing music together. The shared understanding between the two musicians reached far beyond the situation as such. It was reminiscent of musical meanings, of their identities as musicians, of the intimacy between colleagues—a certain kind of "we-ness" (Bowman 2007) seemed to guide this situation.

When all instructors were together at a rehearsal, they first of all paid close attention to the music rather than to the pupils as individuals—the joint focus gave rise to relations of mutual accountability between teacher, composer, clarinetist, and pupil-musicians (Wenger 1998).

Roles and Responsibilities

The teacher, unlike the musicians, in some situations addressed the pupils in a more assertive way, for example, in plenum sessions if some of the pupils took too long to sit down or to stop talking after an intermission. This is how schoolteachers are supposed to act, but surprisingly, the teacher was never assertive in the role as instructor. When the pupils negotiated how to play and combine sounds, a lot of time was spent listening to or waiting for each other, and these situations were always very quiet.

During a rehearsal, one of the boys experienced a problem playing a bell with a built-in feather. He had difficulties making the sound exactly on time, because the bell produced two sounds at each strike. The boy tried to explain the problem in different ways, for example, when to strike the bell or how it should sound in relation to other sounds, etc. In the situation he might have talked for a long time if the teacher had not acted. In the stimulated recall interview, the teacher talked about the situation in terms of classroom management, but in the situation she explained the problem to the pupil in a *musical* way so that the rehearsal could continue. In the interview, the teacher explained that she still considered the composer the real authority in the situation. On the other hand, the composer felt supported musically as well as pedagogically.

The teacher and the composer were both aware of their roles, yet they both were unsure whether they had acted appropriately in the situation. From an outsider's position, action was taken, and in the situation, teacher and composer mutually seemed to recognize each other for acting according to their professional role and responsibility (Honneth 2004).

In the stimulated recall interview with the clarinetist, she explained her role in the process of composing as that of a playmaker. By showing the pupils what they could pay attention to, she offered musical knowledge and in this way delegated musical responsibility rather than managed the compositional process.

During the concert, the teacher, the composer, and the clarinetist had different roles. The video showed how they contributed to the musical unity from different positions: The composer pointed at the blackboard (the graphic notation) with one hand and conducted the orchestra with the other hand. The clarinetist sat in the orchestra together with the pupils expressing her attention to the music and the other members of the orchestra through her body language and her musical contributions playing the clarinet. The teacher sat in the audience paying close attention the orchestra and being a role model for the audience—and then all of a sudden she took on the role of the conductor. The distributed as well as mutual responsibilities described here were the rationale of the musical community of practice, where the product—the musical performance—relied entirely on collaboration (Kenny 2016).

Professional Identities in a Musical Community of Practice

Despite the teacher's explanation in the pre-interview that her primary role is to provide pedagogical support for the visiting artists, the videos from the rehearsal and the concert witness full participation (Lave and Wenger 1991) as the teacher takes responsibility for the musical situation. In the course of the workshop, the teacher, the composer, and the musician worked autonomously with separate groups.

At the concert the teacher introduced *Small Composers* to the audience, carefully explaining the role of the musicians as professional leaders. Just before the conclusion of one piece of music, however, the teacher suddenly took over conducting the conclusion of the music while sitting on the floor—totally in control of the situation and having all the pupils' attention. It was very clear at this point that the initial hierarchy between the professional musicians and the teacher no longer existed; rather they appeared to be companions in a community of *musical* practice (Kenny 2016).

Initially, the composer was granted the musical authority because the teacher presented him as a *professional* composer. *Small Composers*, however, reflects the idea that everyone can compose music, and the composer appeared to incarnate this idea as he presented the concept. He is unimpressed with his own status and identity as a professional composer and invited everyone to contribute. Rather than being a learning process mediated by the composer (responsible for the outcome) and the teacher (responsible for pedagogy and classroom management), the workshop turned into a community of practice, including equal partners sharing a focus on composition as a collaborative process (Wenger 1998).

Finally, the clarinetist was observed working with a small group and again when she played the clarinet at the press rehearsal and the concert performance. She was intensely attentive and she tried to communicate her understanding of the music and the community of practice through bodily as well as musical gestures and facial expressions. She explained her perceived musical identity as an authentic musician having fun playing the clarinet. At the same time she experienced that her authenticity and genuine interest in the pupils' musical ideas was key to being part of the group and having access to pupils' social space.

Discussion

Participants in a pedagogical practice tend to experience any deviation from the didactic plan as a didactic irritation (Rønholt 2003) calling for pedagogical reflection. Both teacher and musicians mentioned pedagogical reflection (van Manen 2016) and mutual recognition (Honneth 2004) as preconditions for collaboration in the school-based workshop. Yet the need for pedagogical reflection may be interpreted in different ways. Teachers and other adult participants tend to interpret noise or trouble among the pupils as a didactic irritation (Rønholt 2003). In this kind of situation visiting musicians usually see the problem as belonging to the teacher's pedagogical domain. In the example with bells noted earlier, however, the teacher interpreted the didactic irritation as belonging to the musical domain and therefore chose to offer a musical explanation to the pupil rather than act as classroom manager. The different roles and perspectives of the teacher, the musician, the composer, and the pupils may be illustrated by two figures, one forming the didactic triangle (Figure 18.1) and another forming a multidimensional field of tension (Figure 18.2).

The didactic triangle encompassing the teacher, the pupils, and the teaching subject may not capture the complexity at play in the composition workshop, which also included visiting artists. The professional knowledge of the classroom teacher relies on teacher training, teaching experience, and personal experience. If two or more classroom teachers were present, the situation would, of course, get more complex but still rely on the same kinds of

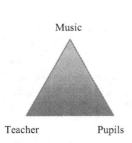

Figure 18.1 The didactic triangle

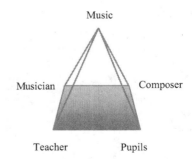

Figure 18.2 The multidimensional field of tension

knowledge. When professional musicians enter the room, they contribute a different kind of musical identity adding to the complexity of the situation. Therefore, we suggest the idea of a multidimensional field of tension including composer, musician, teacher, and pupils and their different ways of engaging in music and composition.

Composition is basically a matter of musical creativeness and improvisation (Benson 2003), which in the present case entirely relies on negotiation between all participants in a community of musical practice. The pupils' voices, therefore, are equally important as the teacher's and the musicians'. In the evaluation, several pupils commented that they "would appreciate access to more instruments" and that "it would have been easier with more time" to compose; furthermore they needed "more time for rehearsal" and "more time to perform." These comments reflect the pupils' engagement on the one hand, and on the other they represent a relevant critique not only of *Small Composers* but also of the way music as a school subject is usually organized. Despite the teacher assuming that many pupils view music as a recreational subject in school, the pupils were very serious about the work and conscious about how time consuming learning music is.

Collaboration in *Small Composers* very much relies on the participants' ownership of the workshop. The case study offered insight into the reflections of the teacher and visiting musicians, and they all tend to agree that personal and professional engagement—from both a pedagogical and an artistic perspective—is a precondition for ownership. For the teacher, it was important to participate with a musical responsibility. At the same time it was important for her to show solidarity with the pupils—for example, she could ask questions on behalf of the pupils in order to further their understanding. The clarinetist emphasized how important it was for her to convey her personal experience as a musician and thus her musical identity.

In the school context, the workshop was legitimized because composition was part of the syllabus and visiting artists are suggested in the regulations. Furthermore, many children have personal experiences composing music on instruments or iPads. All participants, however, initially saw the composer as the "owner" of the workshop, because composing was his profession. The case could have developed in quite a different way if the workshop had been introduced as an imitation of the composer's practice rather than as the pupils' own practice, including classroom as well as home activities (choosing or manufacturing instruments). The composer's fundamental view was that everyone is a potential composer. In other words, access to music relies on the fact that everyone is musically intertwined in a certain kind of "we-ness" (Bowman 2007).

Another precondition for the study as a whole was to accept that composing music needs the kind of energy that comes from tension—as suggested in Figure 18.2. A general tension was identified between artistic and pedagogical intentions (Bruun and Tjagvad 2016), for example, didactic irritations as described earlier or the question of how the idea of *Small Composers* fit (or does not fit) into specific learning objectives. It is a well-known truth that the creative moment in composing music lies between free imagination and constraints. Certainly, this applies to professional composers as well as third-grade pupils doing their first attempt in composition. In the case of *Small Composers* creative energies were related to negotiations between the pupils first about writing a story and next about composing music. Creative energies also depended on constraints related to the classroom that was poorly equipped and in which pupils struggled to handle instruments and other sound sources in their collaborative production of a soundscape that would be appropriate for a small concert.

In *Small Composers*, the professional practices of the composer, the musician, and the teacher tend to blend into a third kind of creative musical practice that encompasses different legitimate learning trajectories. The professionals all described themselves as learners in the workshop. Thus, the most important result of the case study may be that a precondition for professional collaboration, including pedagogical and artistic knowledge, is that participants be mutually committed to the continued development of the community of musical practice.

Notes

1 Small Composers' website: www.figura.dk/small_composers_workshop
2 According to the national Danish syllabus "Forenklede Fælles Mål," the pupils should learn how to create musical sound illustrations and compose and improvise music with their voice, body, and simple instruments: www.emu.dk/omraade/gsk-l%C3%A6rer/ffm/musik/3-4-klasse/musikalsk-skaben

References

Benson, Bruce Ellis. 2003. *The Improvisation of Musical Dialogue: A Phenomenology of Music*. Cambridge: Cambridge University Press.
Bowman, Wayne. 2007. "Who Is the 'We'? Rethinking Professionalism in Music Education" *Action, Criticism, and Theory for Music Education*, 6 (4), 109–31.
Bruun, Peter, and Mette Tjagvad. 2016. "Små Komponister—At mærke at være sammen [Small Composers—to sense togetherness]." Unpublished Master thesis, DPU, Aarhus University.
Christophersen, Catharina. 2013. "Helper, Guard or Mediator? Teachers' Space for Action in The Cultural Rucksack, a Norwegian National Program for Arts and Culture in School." *International Journal of Education & the Arts*, 14 (SI 1.11). Accessed February 3, 2017, www.ijea.org/v14si1/v14si1-11.pdf
Eidsaa, Randi Margrethe. 2014. "Hvem skaper musikken? En studie av musikalsk skapende partnerskapsprosjekter i skolen ut fra et estetisk og didaktisk perspektiv." PhD diss., The Danish University of Education, DPU, Aarhus University.
Espeland, Magne. 2006. "Compositional Process as Discourse and Interaction—a Study of Small Group Music Composition Processes in a School Context." PhD diss., The Danish University of Education, DPU, Aarhus University.
Fautley, Martin. 2004. "Teacher Intervention Strategies in the Composing Processes of Lower Secondary School Students." *International Journal of Music Education*, 22 (3), 201–18.

Fink-Jensen, Kirsten. 2013. "Astonishing Practices: A Teaching Strategy in Music Teacher Education." In *Professional Knowledge in Music Teacher Education*, edited by Eva Georgii-Hemming, Pamela Burnard, and Sven-Erik Holgersen, 139–55. Farnham: Ashgate.
Holdhus, Kari, and Magne Espeland. 2013. The Visiting Artist in Schools: Arts Based or School Based Practices?. *International Journal of Education & the Arts, 14*.
Holgersen, Sven-Erik, and Finn Holst. 2013. Knowledge and Professionalism in Music Teacher Education. In *Professional Knowledge in Music Teacher Education*, edited by Eva Georgii-Hemming, Pamela Burnard, and Sven-Erik Holgersen, 51–71. Farnham: Ashgate.
Holst, Finn. 2013. "Professionel musiklærerpraksis [Professional Music Teacher Practice]." PhD diss., The Danish University of Education, DPU, Aarhus University.
Honneth, Axel. 2004. "Recognition and Justice: Outline of a Plural Theory of Justice." *Acta Sociologica*, 47 (4), 351–64.
Kenny, Ailbhe. 2016. *Communities of Musical Practice*. Abingdon: Routledge.
Kvernbekk, Tove. 2005. *Pedagogisk teoridannelse: insidere, teoriformer og praksis*. Bergen: Fagbokforlaget.
Lave, Jean, and Etienne Wenger. 1991. *Situated Learning. Legitimate Peripheral Participation*. Cambridge: Cambridge University Press.
Lyle, John. 2003. "Stimulated Recall: A Report in Its Use in Naturalistic Research." *British Educational Research Journal*, 29 (6), 861–78.
Rønholt, Helle. 2003. "Didaktiske irritationer." In *Video i pædagogisk forskning—krop og udtryk i bevægelse*, edited by Helle Rønholt, Sven-Erik Holgersen, Kirsten Fink-Jensen, and Anne Maj Nielsen,106–53. Københavns Universitet: Forlaget Hovedland og Institut for Idræt.
Van Manen, Max. 1990. *Researching Lived Experience*. New York: Suny Press.
Van Manen, Max. 2016. *The Tact of Teaching: The Meaning of Pedagogical Thoughtfulness*. London and New York: Routledge.
Wenger, Etienne. 1998. *Communities of Practice: Learning, Meaning, and Identity*. Cambridge: Cambridge University Press.
Wiggins, Jackie. 2011. "When the Music Is Theirs: Scaffolding Young Songwriters." In *A Cultural Psychology of Music Education*, edited by Margaret S. Barrett, 83–113. New York: Oxford University Press.

19
Equal Temperament: Coteaching as a Mechanism for Musician–Teacher Collaboration

MARITA KERIN AND COLETTE MURPHY

Introduction

Previous chapters in this book have highlighted the need for collaboration between musicians and teachers and the challenges in developing successful collaboration. This chapter presents coteaching, a collaborative practice based on sharing expertise and working together in planning, practice, and evaluation of practice in the context of musician–teacher collaboration. Our metaphor for the ideal musician–teacher collaboration via coteaching is the concept of "equal temperament," which refers to the tuning system that divides the octave into equal parts, representing the notion of individuals collaborating as part of a whole, playing equal but different roles, each depending on the other for overall success. Our coteaching research comprises musician and teacher coplanning, coteaching, and coevaluating. This chapter outlines the philosophical basis, the theory, and the practice of coteaching; discusses factors leading to successful and less successful collaboration; and reveals how the musician–teacher collaboration developed. Findings from our three studies involving undergraduate music students coteaching in the role of musician expose two significant interpersonal or temperament themes, *harmony* and *commitment*, concepts familiar to all musicians but now emerging as crucial in developing successful collaborative partnerships. The chapter traces these themes in the context of the development of a reciprocally enriched musician–teacher partnership built on the philosophical and structural dimensions of coteaching. Our findings identify the essential elements of ideal musician–teacher collaboration via coteaching. We conclude by suggesting ways that coteaching can support musician–teacher collaboration wherever it takes place.

Philosophical and Theoretical Underpinnings of Coteaching

Coteaching implies synergy (Sommer 1996). Sommer argues that synergy includes a set of individuals who interact. Each member brings their particular character to its interactions in the synergy. Synergy in coteaching is underpinned by shared expertise between two or more professionals from the same or different disciplines in professional contexts (Murphy and Beggs 2010) and embraces collaboration as coteachers work together within a framework comprising three equal, interdependent elements: coplanning, copractice, and coreflecting (see Figure 19.1).

Coplanning accommodates conversations that expose different perspectives and passions, copractice reveals the professional refinement of each area of expertise, and coreflection provides the space to consolidate professional friendships and to make sense of the learning (Carlisle 2008).

Although coteaching is based on the principles of sharing expertise, simply asking two or more practitioners to work together may not always lead to successful coteaching. A catalyst or spark is essential to stimulate individual and/or collective "a-ha" moments that inspire coteachers as they interact to move towards developing successful partnerships (Murphy 2016). The Russian educator, psychologist, and theater critic Lev Semenovich Vygotsky (1896–1934) proposed that learning occurs from the social to the individual, in the opposite direction to that suggested by the dominant psychology at the time (Vygotsky 1978). Vygotsky developed a mechanism for how learning is passed to individuals. His idea was termed "kategoria," an expression used chiefly in Russian theater and film meaning a *dramatic collision*, which describes an inner tension causing a change in interest, motive, or emotion leading to change in behavior. For Vygotsky, a dramatic collision must be experienced for the development of higher-order thinking skills, such as reflection (Veresov 2004). In coteaching, we use the idea of a dramatic collision to represent the "sparks" that occur between engaged coteachers, in this case, between musician and teacher, that lead to reciprocal professional learning.

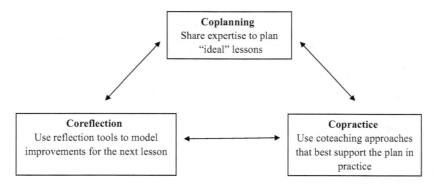

Figure 19.1 Coteaching framework comprising the three interdependent elements of coteaching
(Murphy 2016)

Criticisms of Coteaching

Three main concerns have been voiced about coteaching:

1. Coteachers may have difficulty "going it alone" after such close collaboration (Murphy et al. 2009).Research has shown the opposite; the experience of coteaching fosters a willingness and confidence to work with others (Juck et al. 2010).
2. Coteaching could result in poorer practice in the case of a less effective yet more dominant coteacher. Enculturation into poor practice is unlikely to occur if the coteaching is focused on shared expertise (Murphy and Beggs 2006) and/or corespect (Scantlebury et al. 2008).
3. Adverse consequences may ensue if coteachers do not get along (Murphy 2016). The relationship issue is the most challenging aspect when participants initially engage with the coteaching model. Coteaching program leaders acknowledge this and find ways to support new coteachers before and in the early stages of coteaching. The model of developing coteaching illustrated in Figure 19.2 has been a very useful heuristic for coteachers to reflect on (Kerin, data not yet published). Indeed, a less-than-perfect coteaching relationship can also spark deep learning. Carambo, an in-service coteacher, and Stickney argue that:

[D]ifference (pedagogical, epistemological, philosophical disagreements) between coteachers is (under the right circumstances) a powerful motive for self-examination and change. Difference achieves this because it does not allow for the reinforcement of the acceptable or the familiar, rather it provokes the examination of one's assumptions, and challenges our orthodox, habituated thoughts . . . the more difficult coteaching events

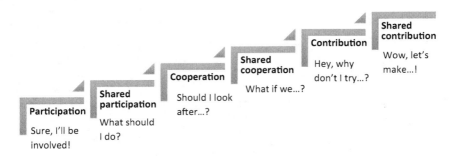

Figure 19.2 Stepwise development of coteaching from participation to shared contribution
(Kerin and Murphy 2015, adapted)

forced me [Carambo] to reexamine my perspectives in light of those represented by my coteachers.

(Carambo and Stickney 2009, 435)

Developing Coteaching from First Experiences

The theoretical premise we use to explain how coteachers develop is based on Vygotsky's cultural historical theory, which provides a model for how cognition develops *between*, and later, *within*, individuals (Murphy and Carlisle 2008). In coteaching we are aiming to improve learning for all participants—musician, teacher, and students—with the potential to transform classrooms to become more collaborative. Such potential is increased as coteachers develop from early stages, where they start participating in the process, to the later mature stage where they are consciously sharing their contributions as coteachers (Murphy and Carlisle 2008). The model, which shows progression through six stages, is illustrated in Figure 19.2.

The first level of coteaching is characterized as *participation* in the process. At this initial stage, a musician might have a more theoretical conception of music teaching, whereas a teacher's focus might be the here and now of the specific classroom. Recognizing and bringing these together characterizes the next stage of *active participation*, which can lead to the third, *cooperation* stage, as each coteacher develops aspects of their own pedagogical content knowledge (PCK) (Shulman 1986). Developing joint PCK represents the fourth phase, *shared cooperation*. By this stage partners should realize that, like any development, coteaching does not improve in a "straight line" and that it takes time. This recognition should sensitize each to the other and to the process, as they each focus on their contribution to coplanning, copractice, and coreflection (fifth stage). Recognizing what they can create *together* is the apogee of coteaching, as it results in a synergy between the coteachers that is greater than either could produce alone. This defines the final, sixth stage of coteaching development.

Coteaching has been shown to provide expanded opportunities for transformative action through shared contribution, collective responsibility, and the active promotion of each other's agency (Murphy 2016). The following section describes some of our empirical research on coteaching between musician and teacher.

Coteaching as a Mechanism for Musician-Teacher Collaboration

In exploring the impact of coteaching as a mechanism for supporting musician–teacher collaboration, we draw on three discrete music coteaching studies:

1. An interdisciplinary music and science program, *Quavers to Quadratics*, involving undergraduate music students in the role of musician and physics students in the role of scientist collaborating with teachers and

orchestral musicians to develop and deliver a STEAM[1] program to over 300 primary school children, embracing the principles of coteaching.
2. First-year, undergraduate music students in the role of musician coteaching music with primary school teachers in one school for one day per week over fourteen weeks.
3. Third-year undergraduate music students in the role of musician partnering with post-primary music teachers during a sixteen-week block placement.

Two strong themes that we describe as *commitment* and *harmony* emerged from the interview data from all three settings. Our research explores the relationship between the development of these two interpersonal themes and coteaching in the context of musician–teacher collaboration.

Commitment

In each of our studies, we identified varying levels of commitment, from the lowest, which we termed *resistance*, most frequently observed in the earliest days of the collaboration; to *compliance*, in which coteachers spoke of finding their feet; to the highest level of commitment, which was reflected as *trust* and we observed how the principles of coplanning, copractice, and coreflection as well as sharing expertise helped to develop commitment as partners progressed from the unstable initial participation phase, to the cooperation phase, and, for some, to the more advanced phase of co-contribution to practice.

Resistance

Expressions of resistance at the start of each of the three coteaching music projects emanated from uncertainty, confidence deficits, and feelings of insecurity (Kerin and Murphy 2015). The primary school teachers claimed to be less confident teaching music than teaching any other subject. The post-primary music teachers, whose identities were strongly linked to stellar choral, orchestral, and curricular music programs, were dubious about the notion of sharing their practice with an undergraduate musician. The interdisciplinary cohort of musicians and physicists expressed a level of incredulity at the prospect of blending two very different subjects. For some, designing a program with members of another discipline presented huge challenges, but when the coplanning stage offered opportunities for sharing passion and expertise, the synergy was palpable:

> Let's teach the Galaxy Song from Monty Python. The lyrics support the material we are going to cover and the children will really like performing it—we could make a backing track for the teacher and some lyric sheets.
> (Musician)

> Good idea but the information in the lyrics is not accurate—would it be possible for us to compose new lyrics?
>
> (Physicist)

> Absolutely—OK, let's jam, what do you want the kids to know about the galaxy?
>
> (Musician)

The participant's initial concerns were assuaged by providing sufficient time for coplanning and facilitating individual voices. Eventually everyone supported the project, agreeing to share their expertise to collaborate as musician and teacher. Time spent on coplanning fostered mutual understanding and the development of confidence, paving the way towards the next level of commitment, compliance.

Compliance

We characterize compliance as openness to the suggestions of the other and a willingness to accommodate ideas and requests of the other. At this level, teachers began to negotiate their roles and to make space for the other as relationships developed. Coplanning partnerships, which identified mutual benefit, thrived. The prospect of hosting a weekly *in situ* musician and learning to play the ukulele was very attractive for the primary teacher, whereas the centrality of the child and observing how the teacher planned lessons from the perspective of the child were hugely emancipatory for the musician, challenging them to question their conceptions of teaching and learning as fixed.

Coplanning provided opportunities for teachers to become familiar with each other, to communicate with each other, and to develop mutual commitment. Connections were made, networks were formed, and plans were hatched in relation to who would be doing what. Coteachers found codrafting and cosubmitting weekly lesson templates and reflections helpful as Anna, a primary teacher, recalls:

> I loved the idea of the musician drafting the initial lesson-plan and sending it to me for comment and/or development. I committed to reviewing, adding some ideas for integration and e-mailing it back by Wednesday evening so both of us could prepare for the lesson on Monday.

The coreflection element presented further opportunities for the growth of professional intimacy between coteachers. Although the coreflection template served simply to capture a summary of the post-lesson discussion, Carol, a post-primary teacher, spoke of her initial misgivings:

> Although my coteacher and I communicated very well, I was nervous of (submitting) the reflections but the template which asked me to describe

what I learned from my coteacher and to say how I learned it, was very specific and helpful. It forced me to be alert to the occasions for learning and to maximize the opportunities for learning during the following lessons.

Partners initially interpreted coteaching as a content transaction, but in enacting the process they gained insights into important dimensions of collaboration, tuning into their partner's temperament, to the interpersonal skills that are so fundamental to successful relationships, in new and nuanced ways. They were encouraged to embrace a progressive pathway towards ideal coteaching, which was characterized as *co-contribution to practice*. The systematic developmental model (see Figure 19.2) provided a progression route that helped to accelerate the process of collaboration. Even for those partners who did not progress beyond this stage, a certain level of synergy was experienced in mutual collaboration. However, most of the benefits accrued to those who progressed to the next stage, to the highest level of commitment—trust.

Trust

In coteaching, we suggest that trust is built on mutual affirmation and reliability. Although each partner is learning to appropriate a set of skills from the other, each is aware that they are exchanging expertise and experience rather than simply imitating the other. Respect and admiration for the expertise of one's coteacher is important in building trust. Aine, a musician, noted:

> It's important to trust your coteacher and do as he asks even if you don't think it's important. You might be wrong! In fact, I would go so far as to say, it's important not simply to do what your coteacher asks but to do it to the best of your ability!

Such a sentiment resonates with a philosophy of collaboration expressed recently by the great musician and collaborator, Yo-Yo Ma (Beard 2016). Trust was built on solid foundations developed during coplanning and coreflecting. With the development of trust, lessons became more creative and spontaneous, and coteachers wove with confidence their own area of expertise and unique experience into the fabric of the lesson. They recalled these lessons as being dynamic and energetic, with partners describing how yielding to the other during copractice often triggered a deeper engagement, both with their own area of expertise and with that of their partner. This is exciting, as suggested by Martin, a musician coteacher, on the interdisciplinary study:

> If you have a room with a projector or white board, possess knowledge of your subject, relegate egos to outside the classroom, and are willing to revel in the expertise of the other, the learning opportunities for everyone involved are phenomenal.

Later, Martin tried to explain why this was "one of my greatest moments in a classroom," describing the reciprocity and trust that he and his coteacher shared as a team. They were:

both focused on the other, both receptive to the other, each triggering yet another amazing insight in the other.

And John, also a musician, said that in some strange way:

I discovered while working with Helen, whom I hardly knew beforehand, that I was better than I thought I was. I was surprised at how natural it came to me, how willing I was to share—she made it easy—she gave me space and trust. She trusted me so I was duty bound to give that trust back.

He later added that mutual trust allowed them to simply sketch the lesson outline; the remainder they filled in spontaneously and creatively on the day. He summarized the result as follows:

We had no fixed roadmap but the journey was a blast . . . between us we lit a fire!

John's coteacher Helen used the same language recalling her experience. She used the verb "trigger" several times to explain how she was sparked to a deeper engagement with the pedagogy of own subject, physics, because of the trust and empathy her coteacher exerted during copractice. Achieving trust depended upon developing a high level of mutual commitment.

The second theme that emerged from this research is *harmony*, and the next section outlines the challenges associated with developing harmonious relationships in the coteaching context.

Harmony

Participants in coteaching studies allude strongly to the importance of developing harmonious relationships with their collaborators (Carlisle 2008). We identified three degrees of consonance in our coteaching studies of musician-teacher collaboration. Borrowing the common parlance for texture in music, we have categorized these relationships as monophonic,[2] homophonic,[3] and polyphonic,[4] as discussed next.

Monophonic

Harmonious relationships lay the foundation for *sharing expertise*, a cornerstone of a flourishing coteaching collaboration (Carlisle 2008). Monophonic relationships were experienced in situations where one of the partners dominated during coplanning and copractice and in so doing, diminished the possibilities for cocreation of new ideas and professional development. During the interdisciplinary project, there was less evidence of dominance, but incidences of monophonic-style collaborations did occur where certain individuals guarded aspects of the knowledge as theirs, confining their partner to their own subject, as George recalls:

> I felt a distinct "back off, you're in my territory now" attitude as I proceeded to demonstrate the tuning fork in water experiment which I had practised.

In the primary school setting, one of the teachers described a situation that continued throughout the project despite his efforts week after week to negotiate a rich partnership:

> My (musician) coteacher never sent the lesson plan beforehand (the excuses became more ridiculous each week) so opportunities for me to collaborate and to advance my own teaching of music were lost.

Efforts to negotiate a partnership were ignored even after the teacher showed the musician a video recording in which she was dominating the lesson while the teacher stood on the sidelines, unable to participate as he had not been included in the planning.

At the post-primary level, incidences of one partner controlling the lesson also were reported:

> I am constantly reminded by the teacher that the ultimate responsibility for student examination scores is hers and so I am forced to adopt her (theoretical) approach rather than developing an approach based on practical music-making.

Where dissonance was experienced between musician and teacher, coplanning, copractice, and coreflection provided opportunities for remediation (Christophersen 2013). Whereas the lack of real harmony was experienced as angst for some, for others, dialogue during coplanning and coreflection provided opportunities for resolution which in turn propelled the pair forward towards a more collaborative, homophonic stage.

Homophonic

A homophonic relationship was characterized as an attempt to form a relationship that offered support for the other, but in a situation where freedom was limited. Such defined and confined arrangements manifested themselves in interviews with partners in all three coteaching studies. Primary teachers who eagerly supported the coteaching music project were disappointed in some instances when the musician coteacher failed to consult them or to seek their opinions, as Conor (a primary teacher) recalls:

> I know the songs the girls enjoy so I would have liked to discuss this with my coteacher. Unfortunately, she had decided on the programme in advance so there was little room for my opinion. While I understand that she is an expert musician, I like to integrate opportunities for learning across the curriculum so I was hoping that the exploration of pitch, pulse and rhythm could have taken place in the context of songs about feelings and identity. It was an opportunity lost in my view.

Musician coteachers, even if they felt welcome in the classroom, would have appreciated opportunities to arrange the furniture differently during lunch breaks or to have access to the interactive whiteboard, but not without an invitation to do so. There were some other problems also as one musician reported:

> It is difficult to cooperate with a teacher who doesn't reply to my e-mails. I would love to have more feedback in terms of how I'm doing but my coteacher said that she rarely uses e-mail. I have sent her text messages but I haven't heard anything back all term but she is lovely and very helpful while I'm there.

Equal voice and mutual support were considered essential if relationships were to develop harmoniously, as deficits here were sometimes interpreted as disinterest. Musicians who reported overcoming such situations demonstrated strong commitment and determination. One such musician reported:

> My coteacher while happy to have me come and teach the children tended to fade into the background. I heard (during co planning) that he used to play bass guitar when he was in school so I added a line on the score for him and invited him to bring in his instrument. He is now completely immersed in the lesson and invested in learning.

Occasions for encountering multiple philosophical perspectives during coplanning and coreflection presented opportunities for expanded worldviews. Teachers indicated, however, that the time needed to communicate as coteachers is not always available. Difficulties in finding time to dialogue during the school day were resolved by using e-mail, Skype, and WhatsApp, and where partners were willing, coteaching provided a framework for supporting them towards a truly democratic or polyphonic partnership.

Polyphonic

Of the three coteaching settings, partners from the interdisciplinary coteaching setting reported the most opportunity for polyphonic relationships, characterized by the valuing of individual voice within the collective. Sharing expertise such that the integrity of each subject was observed, preserved, and valued by the other proved exciting and energizing.

> I couldn't believe how excited the physicists were at the prospect of composing and performing with us. Most hadn't played music since school and they were really into how we might blend music and physics for the kids.

Musicians were also fascinated by the interdisciplinary coteacher dialogue that challenged taken-for-granted assumptions about school music. Questions from scientists like "Why not teach the theremin instead of the recorder?" heralded lively debate on identity, for example, "Is a theremin player a scientist or a musician?" Such lively discourse served not only to weave individual voice into corporate enterprise, but also to promote harmonious relationships and remove barriers between disciplines and, according to one physicist "provided the kind of conversations I remembered wishing I could have about being a musician and a scientist when I was about 11 years old."

Coteaching with a physicist was, in Martin's opinion, "absolutely amazing." He goes on to describe their polyphonic relationship during coteaching as follows: "we were flexible and remained attuned to the knowledge, skills, and intentions of the other, choreographing their parts intuitively as they cotaught with 'ears for each other.'" Musician participants in primary schools also identified experiences of polyphony characterized by the teacher affirmation of the musician's contribution to the lesson and later reciprocating by mentoring them in pedagogic maneuvers, communicating fluently and spontaneously during the coplanning, copractice, and coreflection aspects of the lesson. One musician was so struck by the impact of her coteacher's recently developed passion for music that she realized for the first time the resource that is the primary teacher in garnering the audiences for musicians of the future.

Not all participants experienced polyphonic relationships, but for those who did, subsequent feelings of affirmation, well-being, and engagement contributed to the formation of deeply synergetic relationships evidenced in co-contribution to practice. There were many examples. A school which, prior to coteaching, did not have a music program now boasts an entire staff who feel confident teaching music. One duo produced a text, a music listening resource for primary school teachers, called *Travelling around the World in Search of Musical Concepts*. Another pair staged a public performance of school children and university music students with an international musician of repute. The interdisciplinary team designed and delivered a program, *Quavers to Quadratics*, which is currently in its third iteration. Partners were adamant that these developments were codependent on sharing expertise.

Discussion

Collaboration is strongly recommended in music education (Bamford 2006; Shehan Campbell 2008; Kenny 2014). The research presented in this chapter aimed to explore mechanisms through which collaboration could be enacted. Findings from three empirical studies, in line with international research in arts collaboration (De Wachter 2017) seem to indicate that such collaboration is a complex, elusive, mercurial process that has human temperament at its core and requires the fine-tuning of interpersonal skills if it is to have a significant, rather than a superficial, impact.

We suggest that coteaching provides a solid framework based on synergy, sharing expertise, and mutual respect for supporting musician–teacher collaboration. The coteaching architecture comprises the three interdependent elements of coplanning, copractice, and coevaluation (Figure 19.1) and an incremental progression route to support coteachers to proceed from the earliest experience as "participant" in the process towards mature coteaching in which partners share contributions to practice, thereby improving learning for themselves as well as for their students (Figure 19.2). We also introduced the concept of "kategoria," or "dramatic collision" (Veresov 2004), as an indicator of how learning passes from the social to the individual in collaboration. Awareness of dramatic collisions prompts us to reflect deeply on our own behavior within a collaboration and perhaps change our behavior accordingly. In addition, our data revealed the two themes of *commitment* and *harmony* which provide insight into how participants (coteachers) interact with each other to develop successful collaborations.

Where coteaching reached the highest level, participants spoke of rich relationships, infused with mutual energy and dynamism. Participants who invested in the development of commitment and harmony reported reaching the apogee of coteaching, co-contribution to practice. At that point many experienced expanded or transformed perspectives.

The focus on collaboration as development is based on Vygotsky's concept of development, which includes "not just evolutionary, but also revolutionary changes, regression, gaps, zigzags, and conflicts" (Vygotsky 1931/1997, 221). Such a complex, exciting, and visceral idea of development encourages collaborators to remain confident, particularly in the early stages, when coteaching is not straightforward and the participants are vulnerable as they develop a new relationship.

This chapter has presented coteaching as a mechanism for developing and enacting musician–teacher collaboration. Coteaching research has shown that the framework of coplanning, copractice, and coevaluation (Murphy and Beggs 2010); the stepwise direction for development (Kerin and Murphy 2015); harnessing the emotional element of learning (Murphy 2016); and the importance of commitment and harmony, when taken together, provides scaffolding for developing successful collaboration in several contexts.

Results from these three musician–teacher partnerships have been truly rewarding. We believe that coteaching has the potential to dramatically affect music teaching in the classroom.

Our intention is for readers to appreciate that successful collaboration is achievable through hard work and commitment with professional support throughout the early stages. We hope that this chapter not only provides an insight into the theoretical concepts and practical experiences of the participants in our studies from novice to expert collaborators, but that coteaching may inspire the implementation of many more deep, meaningful, productive, and enjoyable collaborations for both musician and teacher.

Notes

1 Science, technology, engineering, arts, and maths.
2 Monophonic refers to one solo unsupported melody in music.
3 Homophonic refers to one dominant or main melody with harmonic support.
4 Polyphonic refers to two or more melodies, each contributing equally.

References

Bamford, Anne. 2006. *The Wow Factor: Global Research Compendium on the Impact of the Arts in Education*. New York: Waxmann Munster.
Beard, Alison. 2006. "Yo-Yo Ma on Successful Collaborations." *HBR Ideacast*. https://hbr.org/ideacast/2016/05/yo-yo-ma-on-successful-creative-collaboration.html.
Carambo, Cristobal, and Clare Tracy Stickney. 2009. "Coteaching Praxis and Professional Service: Facilitating the Transition of Beliefs and Practices." *Cultural Studies of Science Education*, 4 (2), 433–41.
Carlisle, Karen. 2008. "An Examination of Coteaching in Initial Teacher Education." PhD diss., Queen's University Belfast.
Christophersen, Catharina. 2013. "Helper, Guard or Mediator? Teachers' Space for Action in The Cultural Rucksack, a Norwegian National Program for Arts and Culture in Schools." *International Journal of Education and the Arts*, 14 (SI 1.11). Accessed June 14, 2017, www.ijea.org/v14si1/
De Wachter, Ellen. 2017. *Co-Art: Artists on Creative Collaboration*. London: Phaidon.
Juck, Matthew, Kathryn Scantlebury, and Jennifer Gallo-Fox. 2010. "Now It's Time to Go Solo: First Year Teaching." In *Coteaching in International Contexts: Research and Practice*, edited by Colette Murphy and Kathryn Scantlebury, 241–61. New York: Springer Publishing.
Kenny, Ailbhe. 2014. "Practice Through Partnership: Examining the Theoretical Framework and Development of a 'Community of Musical Practice.'" *International Journal of Music Education*, 32 (4), 396–408.
Kerin, Marita. In preparation. "Primary Teacher Experiences of Coteaching Music in Ireland". PhD diss., Trinity College Dublin.
Kerin, Marita, and Colette Murphy. 2015. "Exploring the Impact of Coteaching on Pre-Service Music Teachers." *Asia-Pacific Journal of Teacher Education*, 43 (4), 309–23.
Murphy, Colette. 2016. *Coteaching in Teacher Education: Innovative Pedagogy for Excellence*. St. Albans: Critical Publishing.

Murphy, Colette, and Jim Beggs. 2006. "Addressing Ethical Dilemmas in Implementing Coteaching." *Forum Qualitative Sozialforschung/Forum: Qualitative Social Research*, 7 (4), Art. 20. Accessed June 13, 2017, www.qualitative-research.net/fqs-texte/4-06/06-4-20-e.htm.

Murphy, Colette, and Jim Beggs. 2010. "A Five-Year Systematic Study of Coteaching Science in 120 Primary Schools." In *Coteaching in International Contexts: Research and Practice*, edited by Colette Murphy and Kathryn Scantlebury, 11–34. The Netherlands: Springer Publishing.

Murphy, Colette, and Karen Carlisle. 2008. "Situating Relational Ontology and Transformative Activist Stance within the 'Everyday'Practice of Coteaching And Cogenerative Dialogue." *Cultural Studies of Science Education* 3 (2), 493–506.

Murphy, Colette, Karen Carlisle, and Jim Beggs. 2009. "Can They Go It Alone? Addressing Criticisms of Coteaching." *Cultural Studies of Science Education*, 4 (2), 461–75. Scantlebury, Kathryn, Jennifer Gallo-Fox, and Beth Wassell. 2008. "Coteaching as a Model for Preservice Secondary Science Teacher Education." *Teaching and Teacher Education*, 24, 967–81.

Scantlebury, Kathryn, Jennifer Gallo-Fox, and Beth Wassell. 2008. "Coteaching as a Model for Preservice Secondary Science Teacher Education." *Teaching and Teacher Education*, 24, 967–981.

Shehan Campbell, Patricia. 2008. *Musician and Teacher: An Orientation to Music Education*. New York: Norton.

Shulman, Lee. 1986. "Those Who Understand: Knowledge and Growth in Teaching." *Educational Researcher*, 15 (2), 4–14.

Sommer, Eric. 1996. "Synergy." An introduction chapter in *The Mind of the Steward: Inquiry-Based Philosophy for the 21st Century*. Accessed June 13, 2017, www.newciv.org/ISSS_Primer/seminzk.html

Veresov, Nikolai. 2004. "Zone of Proximal Development (ZPD): The Hidden Dimension?" In *Language as Culture Tensions in Time and Space*, edited by Anna-Lena Østern and Ria Heila-Ylikallio, 1: 13–30. Vasa: ÅBO Akademi.

Vygotsky, Lev. Semenovich. 1931/1997. *The History of the Development of Higher Mental Functions*, translated by Marie J. Hall in The Collected Works of L. S. Vygotsky, Volume 4: *The History of the Development of Higher Mental Functions*, 1–251, edited by Robert W. Rieber. New York: Plenum Press.

Vygotsky, Lev. Semenovich. 1978. *Mind in Society: The Development of Higher Psychological Processes*, edited by Michael Cole, Vera John-Steiner, Sylvia Scribner, & Ellen Souberman. Cambridge, MA: Harvard University Press.

Conclusion

20
Alteration, Disruption, or Reharmonization? Pathways for Musician–Teacher Collaborations

CATHARINA CHRISTOPHERSEN AND AILBHE KENNY

Introduction

Although there are obvious benefits to musician–teacher collaborations within educational settings, it is also clear that collaborations could have problematic dimensions, such as assymetrical power relations, opposing ideologies, and competing discourses connected to professional expertise, identity, and traditions. These issues will need to be further addressed by policy makers, by practitioners, and by researchers. In this volume, authors from ten countries contribute valuable input to this discussion: from chapters questioning the purposes and agendas of collaboration, thus highlighting issues of power and discourse, to chapters discussing professional relationships emphasizing reciprocity and dialogue.

The chord alteration as a metaphor for musician–teacher collaborations enables a critical exploration of the dynamics of collaborations: Like the new note changes the dynamics of the chord, the musician who enters an educational setting somehow changes the dynamics of that space. How? What does he or she add? What tensions or new possibilities are created, and what could come from such collaborative endeavors? This concluding chapter will draw upon insights from previous chapters to highlight critical issues within musician–teacher collaborations to discuss the dynamics of such collaborations, as well as prerequisites for effective partnerships.

What and Whom Is It Good For?

There seems to be widespread acclaim and enthusiasm for collaborations and partnership programs. When something is perceived as valuable and "good" by so many, critical voices may be difficult to raise. A discourse of "goodness" implies that there is something "good" that many agree upon (Loga 2003, 75), and will thus ascribe power and define legitimate and illegitimate speaking positions. Speakers and doers of "good" possess unassailable power, and opposing positions could be ridiculed, rejected, ignored, or even attacked (Christophersen et al. 2015, 40). Thus, there could be mechanisms in the field actively protecting the idea of the "good" nature of partnerships. Still, previous research (Bresler 2010; Christophersen 2013; Griffiths and Woolf 2009; Kenny 2010) pinpoints tensions and conflicts connected to ideologies, identities, roles, and responsibilites surrounding partnerships. Challenging the goodness discourse and recognizing the potential of tension and conflict seem to be a precondition for a working musician–teacher partnership practice, as well as efforts to critically explore and discuss partnerships and collaborations.

Authors in this volume question the inherent "goodness" and address power relations, agendas, and dominant ideologies that could be integral parts of collaborations. According to Benedict (Chapter 6) it is not sufficient to accept collaborations as beneficial per se; one should also ask who they are beneficial *for*, thus indirectly pointing to agendas in the field. This stance resonates closely with Froehlich's (Chapter 2) framework for analyzing agendas and stakes in collaborations. Although collaborative practices may intend to enrich children's lives by enabling musical experiences, musicians' involvement in educational settings are not only altruistic. Economic interests are surely a driving force behind many collaborations and partnerships, either directly and short term in terms of salaries or in a more long-term perspective in terms of so-called "audience development," that is, building long-term relationship with an audience, thereby countering trends of shrinking and aging audiences (Sigurjonsson 2010, 276). From a consumer perspective, outreach programs and school concerts could be inexpensive and quite effective with regard to reaching large and diverse audiences (Kemp and Poole 2016, 60). For example, as pointed out by Holdhus (Chapter 3), a Norwegian organization for visiting concerts in schools generates over a million "tickets" each year, thus making schools significant arts venues.

Although school–community partnerships are generally encouraged as a means for creating links between schools and the outer world, one could still question the curricular impact of introducing outreach programs with obvious economic interest into schools (Partti and Väkevä Chapter 7). Educational institutions may attract artists and artists organizations; however, "education" could still in some cases be perceived as a dirty word. Tensions relating to perceptions of arts as different from education has been reported in previous research. For example, education may be described as something "other" than aesthetic experience: as rigid, intellectual, moralistic, rule-driven, and restricted. Arts, on the other hand, may often evoke connotations of emotions, freedom, flexibility, and groundbreaking or even transformational experiences (Holdhus and Espeland 2013; Laycock 2008; Kenny 2010).

The previous chapters also refer to such differences between the fields of art and education. Rolle et al. (Chapter 5) describe art and education as disparate communicative systems ruled by different logics, thus causing discursive tensions within collaborations. Such discursive tensions could manifest as disgreements on what actions are appropriate and how to relate to curricular goals and the concept of learning (Kinsella et al. Chapter 16). Discursive tensions could thus be identified in very practical situations within collaborations, but are still connected to belief systems that govern actions and speech. Rolle et al. (Chapter 5) invoke well-known debates about art's autonomy, including arguments of how such autonomy could be unattainable in schools, thus resulting in "school art" (see also Bresler 2003). School art could then refer to children's inventions that may resemble art but that could hardly be recognized as art because, being produced within an educational frame, they are motivated from pedagogy rather than from art itself. Holdhus (Chapter 3) traces these beliefs to the Kantian genius-aesthetic views in which both music and genius are provided by God, thus rendering education unnecessary. Consequently, musicians, when in educational settings, may first and foremost perceive of themselves as artists, protecting music from educational intervention.

Clearly, what is at stake is also certain musical beliefs and traditions. Bowman, by contending that music's value is always value *for* (Bowman 2004, 44), points to music's cultural and contextual character. He thereby also indirectly refers to the well-known distinction between intrinsic and extrinsic values of music, which from a music education perspective could refer to the distinction between aesthetic/musical values and educational benefits (Westerlund 2008). From this perspective, the claim that music is something "other" than education is an ideological claim that will serve certain interests and not others.

Within collaborations, then, there is obviously potential for tensions, even conflicts, with regard to values, beliefs, and motivations. A pertinent question is how such tensions are handled. A *normative* approach would be to strive for equal value, and thus equally distributed power for all stakeholders (Froehlich Chapter 2). However, within an *instrumental* approach some stakes are ascribed more value than others, thus possibly nullifying the idea of collaboration itself (Fineberg 1994). Although many agree that the idea of collaboration implies some sort of equity and reciprocity, research suggests that this is not always the case. Artists and arts organizations may assume, or are granted, the lead and possibly also the power of definition, thus leaving the teacher or the school to take on a more passive and supportive role. Moreover, this hierarchy may be accepted, or even set up, by schools (Christophersen 2013; Kenny and Morrissey 2016; Snook and Buck 2014). However, in order to create equal partnerships, it would seem necessary to strengthen the schools' and teachers' positions (see also Holdhus Chapter 3, Partington Chapter 14, Kresek Chapter 15).

Relationships, Reciprocity, and Respect

As argued earlier, a questioning of collaborations in educational settings should take as a starting point that the "good" intentions of partnerships and collaborations may not be obvious to all stakeholders and thus should be questioned and discussed. Indeed, even the term "collaboration" may contain conflicting interpretations and hold different meanings.

It could denote a joint and intimate effort between partners, but it could also refer to a more distanced, even forced, cooperation with an agency one does not belong to or even connect to.[1] The editors' previous research studies of artist-teacher collaborations in Norway and Ireland (see Chapter 1) represent two extremes. In the case of Ireland, pairs of musicians and teachers worked closely together for a long time, thus defining collaboration as a personal partnership practice with a joint responsibility for the outcome (Kenny and Morrissey 2016). The study of the Norwegian Cultural Rucksack program showed, on the other hand, a politically intended collaboration where the organization ascribed power of definition to the artists and artists' organizations, thus in effect defining schools' and teachers' collaboration as being of service to the artists (Christophersen et al. 2015). It is probably obvious to the reader that the Irish example is collaborative. However, it is more uncertain if the Norwegian initiative qualifies as collaboration; it may be closer to what could be called a "service program" (Fineberg 1994). While acknowledging that provider–client services could be beneficial to schools, Fineberg contends that such relationships are often falsely identified as collaborations. Collaborations, on the other hand, "set off a different set of dynamics that have farther-reaching and longer-lasting results" (Fineberg 1994, 9).

According to Myers, collaborations "suggest a mutually beneficial relationship based on the contributions of individuals to a whole that is greater than the sum of the parts" (2003, 7). Authors of this volume, too, contend that collaboration is a relational concept that signals reciprocity, dialogue, and equality, and the need to foster relationships runs like a golden thread through many of the chapters. Partington (Chapter 14) draws upon Small's concepts of "musicking" and "ideal relationships" to suggest a model for collaboration that could enable teachers and musicians to engage in mutually beneficial relationships that afford mutual respect, shared experiences, and constructive criticism. Kresek (Chapter 15) narrates a visiting artist's struggle to establish a relationship with the seemingly disengaged teacher. Eidsaa (Chapter 11) underlines the importance of communication and respect within creative partnerships, as well as the partners' enjoying each other's professional company. Boyce-Tillman (Chapter 10) argues that the ability to establish dialogue, build trust, and negotiate outcomes with educational institutions and teachers are necessary qualifications for professional musicians and thus should be part of their training. Kerin and Murphy (Chapter 19) apply the concept of coteaching to explore different dimensions of musician–teacher relationships and how these may or may not play out in a collaboration. As showed by Leung (Chapter 8), there may be different modes of collaboration, meaning that teachers and musicians may need to step back or forward and take turns assisting each other, depending on the situation. A working partnership between musician and teacher should thus entail equality, mutual respect, trust, dialogue, and room for negotiation as well as for constructive criticism. An effective partnership is thus hard to envisage as long as only one is granted power of definition, and thus a more prominent position, than the other.

The authors of this volume highlight two aspects that could make or break collaborations—the perceptions of expertise and time. Both are discussed here.

Reconceptualizing Expertise

Even if mutual recognition and respect are preconditions for effective partnership, many collaborations entail a sense of hierarchy, where the musician is discursively positioned as "the expert" and consequently granted power of definition. As pointed out by several authors in this volume, such hierarchies could be maintained by both teachers and musicians (see for example Holgersen, Bruun and Tjagvad Chapter 18). This hierarchy could be viewed in terms of domination and violence (Holdhus Chapter 3), in which neither the dominator nor the dominated are aware of the symbolic violence or the dominant culture (Benedict Chapter 6) that legitimizes it.

However, if viewed from a role theory perspective, another interpretation is possible. Rolle et al. (Chapter 5) show that "musician" and "teacher" are not just individuals, they are social roles that come with expectations and assignments. For example, a musician may be hired into the educational setting because of his or her particular expertise; however, this expertise could disempower and alienate the teacher, who then takes it upon himself or herself to function in a more subordinate role, thus reinforcing the notion of the artist as an expert. If we shift the perspective from role and back to person, we can see that collaboration could be confusing and difficult for musicians as well as for teachers. Kresek's description of the nomadic teaching artist (Chapter 15) who is constantly trying to fulfill expectations and negotiate relationships in different settings is a good example of the challenges and demands a musician must face in collaborations.

The different descriptions and explanations of hierarchies highlight the role of discourse when it comes to producing and maintaining hierarchies in collaboration. An underestimation of teacher competence (even from teachers themselves) aligns with a common discourse surrounding collaborations in educational settings in which artists are often mentioned positively for their competence and contributions, whereas teachers are not (Christophersen 2013). Despite a boost in awareness of the performative elements of teaching (Prendergast 2008), teachers' artistic competence may not be recognized. For example, although it is a common perception that musicians have dual competences, including performing *and* teaching (Bowman 2007; Zeserson 2012; see also Smith Chapter 4), the same goodwill is not always granted to teachers,

"We glibly refer to artsts who teach as *Teaching Artists*; where is the language for teachers who are artists? What do we call them?" (Burnaford 2003, 168).

Music education research shows that teachers' confidence with regard to their own artistic skills may be low, especially among generalist teachers (Hallam et al. 2009; Kenny 2017; Partington 2016; Russell-Bowie 2009; Welch and Henley 2014). In fact, even obviously competent music teachers report low levels of confidence (Wiggins and Wiggins 2008). As described in Kenny and Morrissey's study of artist-teacher partnerships, a music teacher who conducted the school choir "claimed that she had no musical knowledge or skills: 'she said I don't really conduct, I just wave!'" (Kenny and Morrissey 2016, 39). A lack of music teacher confidence will represent a challenge for developing dialogic relationships within collaborations, because both teachers and musicians will need recognition and respect as equal and competent partners in a collaborative endeavor. A necessary step would be to acknowledge the different competencies that both musician and teacher bring to the collaboration. According to Kinsella et al. (Chapter 16), musicians and teachers have distinct professional knowledge, developed in their respective communities of practice. The musician brings a specialized, but still complex, competence of artistic expressions, communication, materials, and processes (see Boyce-Tillman Chapter 10). Teachers' professional knowledge is equally complex, but could be quite broad, especially among generalist teachers (Christophersen 2013). Teachers are often expected to demonstrate knowledge of educational research, philosophy, policies, and history, as well as a general insight into theories of upbringing, socialization, development, learning, and classroom management in their planning and teaching, in addition to content knowledge of the school subjects they teach. The difference in background will inevitably color musicians' and teachers' interpretations of educational situations, as well as their preferred actions and strategies, as exemplified by several authors (see Rolle et al. Chapter 5; Kinsella et al. Chapter 16).

Furthermore, acknowledging distinct competences accentuates the need for mutual exchange and learning so that the involved parties can learn from each other. Learning, as pointed out by Brinck (Chapter 17), is not a product, but a process of changing participation and evolving membership in a community. Thus, shifting from professional knowledge to professional learning and development means to set something in motion. This shift could also be characterized as a shift from an individualistic to a collaborative, community-oriented culture (Wolf 2008, 92). Kerin and Murphy (Chapter 19) describe this distinction between an individualistic and a collaborative approach with the musical terms *monophonic* (individualistic) and *homophonic* (synergetic relationship with shared expertise), respectively.

As pointed out by Smith (Chapter 4), Randles (Chapter 13), and Brinck (Chapter 17), a sharp distinction between musician and teacher may not be helpful. In some cases, competences will reside within one person, thus making exchange and negotiations between different competences and roles effortless. For example, as in the case of the VSA[2] Teaching Artist (Randles Chapter 13), the interchanging artistic, educational, and special education competencies are necessary to create and adapt a music education strategy for students with special needs. However, in most cases of partnerships and collaborations, the exchange and flow of competence will occur between two different individuals with different backgrounds. Even if both musicians and teachers have a dual competence to some extent, there will be different strengths and weaknesses, thus actualizing needs for mutual professional exchange and development (Kenny and Morrissey 2016; Myers 2003; Wolf 2008). A mutual exchange of this kind thus represents an opportunity for the collaborators to enter each other's professional space, thus changing the dynamics of the collaboration. We could also call this "altering the chord" (Chapter 1), or with Kerin and Murphy's words (Chapter 19), forming a "polyphonic relationship."

Time Is of the Essence

It should be obvious by now that a musician within a classroom does not in itself constitute collaboration. Furthermore, if relationships are indeed central to collaboration, developing collaborations means developing the musician–teacher relationship (Myers 2003; Snook and Buck 2014; Wolf 2008). As noted by Kenny and Morrissey (2016, 26), an effective partnership requires long-term, sustained working relationships between teachers and artists. In other words, developing relationships that allow for trust, vulnerability, risk taking, discussion, negotiation, and a sense of collegiality is hard work, and it will take time.

Time is identified as a crucial factor in several of the chapters, for example, connected to joint planning, preparation, and reflection (see Partti and Väkevä Chapter 7; Hultberg Chapter 9; Abeles Chapter 12; Kinsella, Fautley and Evans Chapter 16). Holgersen, Bruun and Tjagvad (Chapter 18) describe a community of practice between a teacher and a musician that contains an intimate mutual understanding of each other and a sense of an "us," both of which have taken a very long time to develop. Consequently, shorter projects or once-off happenings are less likely to provide necessary conditions for developing sustainable partnerships than long-term efforts. Indeed, achieving a sense of mutual understanding and engagement between a musician and a teacher could even be very difficult within sustained relationships (Kresek Chapter 15), due to lack of time for joint planning and discussion.

This preference for long-term arts involvement instead of once-off happenings or short-term projects will again challenge the pervasive idea of arts exposure, that is, the belief that mere exposure to or experience with arts may affect children's lives. This belief has been met with skepticism from scholars. Myers (2003), for example, claims that a lasting effect of the arts takes more than brief encounters and haphazard instruction, and Hanley (2003) states that "[m]eaningful learning in any discipline occurs over time. Exposure to the arts is just that—exposure" (Hanley 2003, 14).

The idea of arts exposure is closely connected to the previously mentioned Western perception of art's autonomy and the hierarchies between musicians and teachers enabled by such perception (Holdhus Chapter 3; Rolle et al. Chapter 5; Partington Chapter 14). In addition, the idea of arts exposure is in some cases connected to economic agendas (see for example Borgen 2011; Christophersen et al. 2015). Bumgarner-Gee (2002) connects such agendas directly to a manipulation of the concept of time. Following an analysis of arts advocacy literature from various arts service and funding organizations, Bumgarner-Gee claims that arts organizations willfully confuse "learning outcomes associated with years of regular arts study with intermittent arts 'experiences and exposure'" (2002, 5) in order to gain political influence and economic support. This claim, although radical, is related to issues of stakes, interests, and purposes, as put forward by Froehlich (Chapter 2) and Benedict (Chapter 6).

Consequently, time seems to be of the essence, both with regard to the quality of musician–teacher collaboration and with regard to the perceived outcome for the students, who are usually the targets for the good intentions of collaborations. The inclusion of time as a crucial factor for collaboration, then, again actualizes the critical question of who collaborations are good for.

Warranting Multiple Perspectives

The aim of this book has been to critically question and discuss musician–teacher collaborations in educational settings, thus challenging the policies and practices of such collaborations. Up to this point, we have sought common characteristics and unity by extrapolating critical issues across the nineteen previous chapters.

The authors have challenged the so-called "goodness discourse" that so often is invoked in these collaborations by asking what and whom is it good for. They have challenged the concept of collaboration by emphasizing that it takes more than the physical presence of one or more musicians for collaboration to take place. The authors describe collaboration as a personal relationship that takes hard work and quite some time to develop. In so doing, the authors have also implicitly challenged the idea of arts exposure. It is contended, and even questionable, that short arts encounters/exposures have any lasting or transforming effects. Seen from a collaboration perspective, ad hoc or once-off performances do not promote reciprocal relationships between musicians and teachers. Consequently, the authors of this volume also challenge the idea of the expert as a custodian of professional knowledge. The idea of collaboration as a reciprocal relationship between musician and teacher thus promotes joint professional learning and development rather than an individualized notion of knowledge.

However, as we approach the end of this book, it is time to also emphasize nuances and differences. The chapters have been written from different points of view, thus producing different perspectives on musician–teacher collaborations, again providing different insights and triggering different critical questions about the issues at stake in these collaborations.

First, the chapters demonstrate cultural and national variations with regard to collaborative initiatives and their foundations within educational policy contexts. For example, collaborations in Hong Kong schools are used to empower certain cultural expressions as part of building a national identity through music in schools (Leung Chapter 8). The Scandinavian countries have strong social-democratic traditions, in which it is the state's perceived duty to supply welfare, culture, and education for all citizens. Thus, not surprisingly, outreach initiatives have been organized into state programs available for all schools and students (see Hultberg Chapter 9; Eidsaa Chapter 12). Within the United States, there is a great deal of local and regional variation with regard to educational programs in the arts. An obvious consequence, then, is that outreach initiatives and visiting artists represent the only arts education alternatives for some U.S. students (Kresek Chapter 15; Abeles Chapter 11). Insight into national or regional education and cultural policy issues, as well as knowledge about the place of the arts in education, school cultures, etc., provide frameworks for interpretation, understanding, and discussion of specific collaborations within the classroom.

Second, there are differences between the chapters with regard to their degree of criticality. The authors have met the editors' call for a critical discussion of musician–teacher collaborations differently: Some underline differences, tension, and conflicts, whereas others seek common ground, dialogue, and communication. There should be room for several of such basic positions within a critical approach. The advantage of a critical approach is the will to ask questions, including those that could be disturbing or even offensive. The questions may be very interesting, but could in the end turn out to be just noise unless they contribute constructive suggestions. On the other hand, too much emphasis on consensus and harmony may overlook tensions and conflicts, thus repressing possibly productive disruptions.

Finally, the chapters vary with regard to their proximity to the practices of collaborations. Most chapters have empirical foundations, whereas others are more theoretically or philosophically oriented. With regard to the latter, for example, both Holdhus (Chapter 3) and Benedict (Chapter 6) draw upon philosophical perspectives to enable the questioning of epistemic and discursive constructions within collaborations. Such perspectives propel critical questions of ideological foundations and implications of collaborations. Other chapters are closer to the action. Kresek's narrative (Chapter 15) of a visiting artist's struggle to reach out and understand the aloof Mr. C is a compelling and personal story that provides the reader with close experience and understanding for individual actions and thoughts, as well as dilemmas and tensions in the hullabaloo of everyday life. The sociological approaches provided by Froehlich (Chapter 2) and Rolle et al. (Chapter 5), on the other hand, provide overarching theoretical frameworks that connect individual actions within collaborations with systems and policies, as well as ideologies and discourses.

To gain a deeper understanding of collaborations within educational settings, having different perspectives is necessary. If collaborations are part of larger programs, these programs are likely to be initiated on a meso (institutional) or macro (societal or national) level. Still, their implementation will always involve the micro level, that is, the people, their relationships, and their actions. Vice versa, even if collaborations are realized through interpersonal relationships, various professional identities, organizational agendas, or educational policy discourses are likely to influence negotiations on "the floor." For example, the personal collaboration between teacher and musician in an opera project was affected negatively by the organizer's refusal to allow time for joint planning (Hultberg Chapter 9). In the case of the Birmingham composition project (Kinsella et al. Chapter 16), the teachers' and musicians' colliding perspectives on classroom actions and the epistemological significance of these were formed by backgrounds and professional identities, as well as discourses within the field. This goes to show that multiple perspectives are beneficial when collaborations are discussed, acted out, or researched. The practical, the structural, and the ideological dimensions of collaborations are connected. Isolated actions that are not situated within a structural context or that lack connection to an ideological foundation may appear flat or detached. Descriptions of structures without connections to people or actions could be obsolete and bland, whereas isolated philosophical considerations could appear abstract and intellectualistic. Thus, different approaches provide different perspectives that may inform and give depth to each other.

Coda

As implied by the title of the book, as well as the heading of this chapter, there is a dynamic to collaboration as well as to a musical chord. Adding a note to a chord alters the sound of the chord, and this alteration subsequently alters the dynamics of the chord. The new note may bring a new dimension to the already existing sound, allowing us to hear something new and interesting. It may create surprise, even tension, that will make other notes move in other directions, thus eventually forming a new harmony. Or maybe the new note neither fits the chord nor adds much else than an uncomfortable dissonance. A musician entering an educational setting represents a similar alteration. This alteration may produce tensions and disruptions, new harmonies or insights, or maybe not much at all. Ideally, as has been suggested in this book, interesting (though not necessarily good) things could happen when musicians and teachers enter each other's professional spaces with the intention to learn from each other.

Notes

1 According to the Oxford English Dictionary, "collaboration" could mean 1) United labour, co-operation, especially in literary, artistic or intellectual work; 2) Traitorous cooperation with the enemy.
2 Very Special Arts.

References

Borgen, Jorunn Spord. 2011. "The Cultural Rucksack in Norway: Does the National Model Entail a Programme for Educational Change?" In *The Routledge International Handbook of Creative Learning*, edited by Julian Sefton-Green, Pat Thomson, Ken Jones, and Liora Bresler, 374–82. Oxon: Routledge.

Bowman, Wayne. 2004. "Pop Goes? Taking Popular Music Seriously." In *Bridging the Gap: Popular Music and Music Edudaction*, edited by Carlos Rodriguez, 29–50. Reston: MENC.

Bowman, Wayne. 2007. "Who is the 'We'? Rethinking Professionalism in Music Education." *Action, Criticism and Theory for Music Education*, 6 (4), 109–131.

Bresler, Liora. 2003. "School Art as Hybrid Genre: Institutional Contexts for Art Curriculum." In *The Arts in Children's Lives: Context, Culture and Curriculum*, edited by Liora Bresler, and Christine Marmé Thompson, 169–183. Dordrecht: Kluwer Academic Publishers.

Bresler, Liora. 2010. "Teachers as Audiences: Exploring Educational and Musical Values in Youth Performances." *Journal of New Music Research*, 39 (2), 135–145.

Bumgarner-Gee, Constance. 2002. "The 'Use and Abuse' of Arts Advocacy and Consequences for Music Education." *Arts Education Policy Review*, 103 (4), 3–21.

Burnaford, Gail. 2003."Language Matters: Clarifying Partnerships Between Teachers and Artists." *Teaching Artis Journal*, 1 (3), 168–71.

Christophersen, Catharina. 2013. "Helper, Guard or Mediator? Teachers' Space for Action in The Cultural Rucksack, a Norwegian National Program for Arts and Culture in School." *International Journal of Education and the Arts*, 14 (SI 1.11). Accessed June 13, 2017, www.ijea.org/v14si1/.

Christophersen, Catharina, Jan-Kåre Breivik, Anne Homme, and Lise Rykkja. 2015. *The Cultural Rucksack*. Oslo/Bergen: Norsk kulturråd/Fagbokforlaget.

Fineberg, Carol. 1994. "Collaborations and the Conundrums They Breed: Introduction to the Symposium on Community Resources." *Arts Education Policy Review*, 95 (5), 9–11.

Griffiths, Morwenna, and Felicity Woolf. 2009. "The Nottingham Apprenticeship Model: Schools in Partnership with Artists and Creative Practitioners." *British Educational Research Journal*, 35 (4), 557–574.

Hallam, Susan, Pamela Burnard, Anne Robertson, Chris Saleh, Valerie Davies, Lynne Rogers, and Dimitra Kakatsaki. 2009. "Trainee Primary-school Teachers' Perceptions of Their Effectiveness in Teaching Music." *Music Education Research*, 11 (2), 221–240.

Hanley, Betty. 2003. "The Good, the Bad and the Ugly—Arts Partnerships in Canadian Elementary Schools." *Arts Education Policy Review*, 104 (6), 11–20.

Holdhus, Kari, and Magne Espeland. 2013. "The Visiting Artist in Schools: Arts Based or School Based Practices?" *International Journal of Education & the Arts*, 14 (SI. 1.10). Accessed June 13, 2017, www.ijea.org/v14si1/

Kemp, Elyria, and Sonja Martin Poole. 2016. "Arts Audiences: Establishing a Gateway to Audience Development and Engagement." *The Journal of Arts Management, Law, and Society*, 46 (2), 53–62.

Kenny, Ailbhe. 2010. "Too Cool for School? Musicians as Partners in Education." *Irish Educational Studies*, 29 (3), 153–66.

Kenny, Ailbhe. 2017. "Beginning a Journey with Music Education: Voices from Pre-Service Primary Teachers." *Music Education Research*, 19 (2), 111–122.

Kenny, Ailbhe, and Dorothy Morrissey. 2016. *Exploring Teacher-Artist Partnership as a Model of CPD for Supporting & Enhancing Arts Education in Ireland: A Research Report*. Dublin: Association of Teachers/Education Centres in Ireland, Department of Education and Skills, Department of Arts, Heritage and Gaeltacht.

Laycock, Jolyon. 2008. *Enabling the Creators: Arts and Cultural Management and the Challenge of Social Inclusion*. Oxford: European Arts Mangement Project in Association with Oxford Brookes University.

Loga, Jill M. 2003. "Godhetsdiskursen." In *Maktens Tekster*, edited by Kjell Lars Berge, Siri Meyer, and Tom Are Trippestad, 62–81. Oslo: Gyldendal Akademisk.

Myers, David E. 2003. "Quest for Excellence: The Transforming Role of University-Community Collaboration in Music Teaching and Learning." *Arts Education Policy Review*, 105 (1), 5–12.

Partington, Julia. 2016. "The Problematics of Partnership Between the Primary Class, Teacher and the Visiting Musician: Power and Hierarchy in the Pursuit of Dialogic Relationship." PhD dissertation, University of Newcastle, Newcastle.

Prendergast, Monica. 2008. "Teacher as Performer: Unpacking a Metaphor in Performance Theory and Critical Performative Pedagogy." *International Journal of Education and the Arts*, 9 (2). Accessed June 13, 2017, www.ijea.org/v9n2/

Russell-Bowie, Deirdre. 2009. "What Me? Teach Music to My Primary Class? Challenges to Music Teaching in Primary Schools in Five Countries." *Music Education Research*, 11 (1), 23–36.

Sigurjonsson, Njordur. 2010. "Orchestra Audience Development and the Aesthetics of 'Customer Comfort.'" *The Journal of Arts Management, Law, and Society*, 40 (4), 255–78.

Snook, Barbara, and Ralph Buck. 2014. "Artists in Schools: 'Kick Starting' or 'Kicking Out' Dance from New Zealand Classrooms." *Journal of Dance Education*, 14 (1), 18–26.

Welch, Graham, and Jennie Henley. 2014. "Addressing the Challenges of Teaching Music by Generalist Primary Teachers." *Revista da ABEM*, 22 (32), 12–38.

Westerlund, Heidi. 2008. "Justifying Music Education: A View from Here-and-Now Value Experience." *Philosophy of Music Education Review*, 16 (1), 79–95.

Wiggins, Robert, and Jackie Wiggins. 2008. "Primary Music Education in the Absence of Specialists." *International Journal of Education and the Arts*, 9 (12). Accessed June 13, 2017, www.ijea.org/v9n12/.

Wolf, Shelby. 2008. "The Mysteries of Creative Partnerships." *Journal of Teacher Education*, 59 (1), 89–102.

Zeserson, Catherine. 2012. "Partnerships in Music Education." In *Debates in Music Teaching*, edited by Chris Philpott and Gary Spruce, 209–220. Oxon: Routledge.

Contributors

Harold F. Abeles, Professor of Music and Music Education, Teachers College, Columbia University, New York City (USA)

Cathy Benedict, Director of Research, Don Wright Faculty of Music, Western University (Canada)

June Boyce-Tillman, Professor of Applied Music, University of Winchester (UK), Artistic Convenor of the Winchester Centre for the Arts as Wellbeing and Extraordinary (UK), Convenor of Tavener Centre for Music and Spirituality, Professor at North West University, Potchefstroom (South Africa)

Liora Bresler, Professor at the Department of Curriculum and Instruction, College of Education, Professor at the School of Art and Design, and Affiliate Professor at the School of Music, University of Illinois at Urbana Champaign (USA)

Lars Brinck, Associate Professor and Head of Research and Development, Rhythmic Music Conservatory, Copenhagen (Denmark)

Peter Bruun, Freelance Composer and Music Teacher (Denmark)

Catharina Christophersen, Professor of Music Education, Western-Norway University of the Applied Sciences, Bergen (Norway)

Randi Margrethe Eidsaa, Associate Professor, University of Agder (Norway)

Nancy Evans, Director of Learning and Participation, Birmingham Contemporary Music Group (UK)

Martin Fautley, Professor and Director of Research in Education, Birmingham City University (UK)

Hildegard C. Froehlich, Professor Emeritus, College of Music, University of North Texas, Denton (USA)

Kari Holdhus, Associate Professor of Music Education, Western Norway University of Applied Sciences, Stord (Norway)

Contributors

Sven-Erik Holgersen, Associate Professor Danish School of Education, Aarhus University (Denmark)

Cecilia K. Hultberg, Professor Emeritus, Department of Music Education, The Royal College of Music, Stockholm (Sweden)

Ailbhe Kenny, Lecturer in Music Education, Mary Immaculate College, University of Limerick (Ireland)

Marita Kerin, Assistant Professor in Music Education, School of Education, Trinity College, Dublin (Ireland)

Victoria Kinsella, Research Fellow in Education, Birmingham City University (UK)

Katharine Kresek, Freelance Music Teaching Artist and Adjunct Faculty, St. John's University, New York (USA)

Bo-Wah Leung, Professor and Head of Department of Cultural and Creative Arts, Education University of Hong Kong (China)

Colette Murphy, Associate Professor in Science Education, School of Education, Trinity College, Dublin (Ireland)

Julia Partington, Music Education Researcher, based at Newcastle University (UK)

Heidi Partti, Acting Professor, Faculty of Music Education, Jazz, and Folk Music, Sibelius Academy, University of the Arts Helsinki (Finland)

Clint Randles, Associate Professor and Coordinator of Music Education, Center for Music Education Research, University of South Florida (USA)

Christian Rolle, Professor of Music Education, Cologne University (Germany)

Matthias Schlothfeldt, Professor, Folkwang University of the Arts (Germany)

Gareth Dylan Smith, Visiting Research Professor, New York University and Manager of Program Effectivenss, Little Kids Rock (USA)

Mette Tjagvad, Teacher at Nathalie Zahle's Seminary School, Research Assistant, Danish School of Education, Aarhus University (Denmark)

Lauri Väkevä, Vice Rector, University of the Arts Helsinki. Professor, Faculty of Music Education, Jazz, and Folk Music, Sibelius Academy, University of the Arts Helsinki (Finland)

Julia Weber, PhD student, Cologne University (Germany)

Verena Weidner, Professor of Music Education, University of Music, Freiburg (Germany)

Index

Note: Page numbers in *italics* denote references to Figures.

active participation 220
activity vs. learning 186
adjusted participation 198
aesthetics: autonomy-aesthetic art 33–4; creative music-making partnerships and 141; experiences 98, 99; heteronomy-aesthetic approach to art 33–4; learning processes 136; perspectives 136; products 97; relational 31
agenda 31, 33, 43, 79, 185
Alexander, Robin 165
altered chord, as a metaphor 3, 22–3, 233
anarchism 44, 46
Arendt, Hannah 64, 69
art/arts: arts-in-education 4, 127, 130–1; exposure to 239–40; therapists 147–8
Arthur, Michael B. 41
artists: as ethnographer 35; as friends 93; music teacher's participation as 200; qualification framework for 108–10; reservations to pedagogical programs 53–4; role of 58, 88; student's relationship with 92–3; as temporary teaching assistant 92; *see also* musicians; teaching artists; visiting artists
artist/teacher dichotomy 58
art of school vs. school of art 56
Austring, Bennyé D. 136, 141
audience development 234
audience/s: artist collaboration with 30–1, 36n4; building long-term relationships with 234; creating a community 36n3; developing 51; manipulating 33; nurturing future 91; participating 30, 97, 103–4; teacher's participation with 99–100
authority: in the classroom 93; of collaborations 64–5, 69; of composer 211–2; natural 66; of normativity 69; pedagogical 45–6
autonomy 56, 235, 240
autonomy-aesthetic art 33–4

Bakhtin, Mikail xi
Ball, Stephen J. 185
Barretta, Scott 16
Bateson, Gregory 18
beliefs: about the audience 31; artists' 31; authority and 64; in compositional pedagogy 53; disciplinary 68; punk pedagogies and 43–4; teachers' 8; teamwork effectiveness and 58–9; *see also* epistemological beliefs; personal epistemology
Benjamin, George 181
Benson, Bruce Ellis 142, 208
Biesta, Gert 66–7, 69
Bildung 19, 34, 36n5, 60n6
Bishop, Claire 33
Booth, Eric 35, 172, 177
Bourdieu, Pierre 29
Bourriaud, Nicolas 31
Bowman, Wayne 185, 189, 235
Bresler, Liora 6, 34
Bringle, Robert G. 148–9
Broncano, Fernando 68
Buber, Martin 35
Buckingham, David 5
Bumgarner-Gee, Constance 240
Burnard, Pamela 74

249

campus-community partnership 148–9
Carambo, Cristobal 219–20
Cartwright, Phillip A. 41–2
Carvalho, Sara 65
challenge: to aesthetic practices 33; to artistic beliefs 31; authority and 64; to authority of normativity 69; of composing projects 60–4, 79–80; coplanning stage 221; in coteaching context 224; creative approach to 98; cultural experiences and 98; in developing successful collaboration 217; to existing artistic conventions 117; facilitating participation for students 101, 103–4; for musicians as teachers 43–5; of music-making activities 138–40; music teacher confidence 238; of opera project 91–3; of professional composers to school music lessons 81; in teacher education programs 40; of technology 152
changing linguistic usage 199
changing participation 194–5, 199, 238
chord alterations, as a metaphor 3, 22–3, 233
Christophersen, Catharina xiii, 6, 10, 58, 100, 131, 134, 186
classroom-based musicking 161–3, 166
classroom/classroom settings: artistic creation in 74; composing in 77, 184, 205–7; coteaching 220–1; disruptions in 54; introducing professional into 73; managing 92–3, 130, 211–12, 238; music-making activities in 138–41, 143–44; nomadic music teaching artists in 173; participating artists in 92–4; as safe community of learners 35; working conditions 58; see also teachers
cognitive diversity 67–8
collaborative interpretation 209
collaborative moderation 103–5
collaborative mode with parallel participation 90
collaborative musicking 162–4; see also musicking

commitment: demonstrating 226; development of 228; for dialogic relationship 63–4, 165–66; levels of 221–24; of school-based music specialists 106, 122, 127
common sense 64, 69
communicative action and rationality theory 21
communities of practice 5, 185, 212–13
competencies: cognitive strand of 117; ethical strand of 109, 117; functional strand of 109, 115; personal strand of 108–9; for teaching artists 108–10
composer/composing: ambiguous role definitions 58–9; appreciating students' works 55; challenges with 50–2; composer-student relations in 53–7; composer-teacher relations in 57–8; delivering composition projects 181; developmental relationship with 190; educational perspective of 188; emerging 184; in Finnish basic education 73; first step in 77–8; as mandatory in music class 210; as matter of musical creativeness 214; micro-aspects of 187; open-mindedness and flexibility in 79–81; pedagogy 54, 75; prespecifying learning 186; process of 77–9; quality criteria 82; of *Resolution* composing project 184; transparency, importance of 79
composer/teacher teams 79–9
composition workshop 210–11
conflict within collaborations 7, 9, 23, 109, 228, 234–6 *see also* role conflicts
consensus building 21–2, 32–3
contact zone 138
content knowledge 183
contextual competencies 108, 111–14
conventional art 31
coplanning: commitment to 221–2; compliance and 222; definition of 218; harmony during 224–5; as interdependent element to coteaching

218, 228–9; philosophical perspectives encounters during 226; remediation opportunities in 225; trust-building during 223
coteaching: commitment to 221–4; compliance and 222–3; as content transaction 223; criticisms of 219–20; development of 219–21, *219*; dramatic collision and 218; harmony 224–8; homophonic relationships in 225–6; interdisciplinary dialogue 227; monophonic relationships in 224–5; polyphonic relationships in 227–8; resistance, expressions of 221–2; synergy in 217–18, 228; for transformative action 220; trust and 223–4
creative collaboration 209–10
creative competencies 109, 116–17
creative music-making *see* music-making
creative music-making partnerships: aesthetic evaluations 141; dialogues in 142–4; exchange of ideas 139; experimentation 138–9; introduction 137–8; motivation 137; participants' emotional stress in 143; performances 140–1; repertoire and rehearsals 139–40; unpredictability during 143
creativity 74–5, 97
Crowe, Barbara 148, 152
cultural experiences 98
cultural historical theory 220
Cultural Rucksack program 4, 6, 133–5, 236
curriculum *see* school curriculum

data-gathering techniques 76, 123–24, 136, 208
De'Ath, Erica 160, 165
de-institutionalizing space 44
descriptive stakeholder analysis 21, 23
Dewey, John 98
dialogic art 30–4
dialogic relationship, core commitments for 166
dialogic relationship model 164–9
dialogic teaching 98, 169n2

dialogues: characterizing collaborative music-making projects 142–3; in creative music-making projects 137–42; formal talks 135; informal talks 135; as interaction in time and place 136; investigating 135–6
didactic approaches 136
didactic triangle 213–14, *213*
Didaktik 19
digital arts 74
Dines, Michael 44
Dirks, Kurt T. 34
disciplinary beliefs 68
discursive tensions 50, 234–5
diversity 67, 110, 121, 142
drama, use of 115
dramatic collision 218, 228
Drotner, Kirsten 97
Duarte, Eduardo M. 69

economic growth 20
economics: driving collaborations 234; outreach programs and 234; value and 109; value of musicians 42
education: art vs. 234–5; orchestras and 65–6; purpose of 62, 64; *see also* higher music education; music education; school curriculum
elitism 114
Elliott, David 134, 141, 148
emancipatory education 66–7, 69
empowerment 43–6, 65–6, 79, 102, 115, 163 *see also* power/power structure
epistemic responsibility 62, 69–70
epistemological beliefs 64, 66–8
epistemology: epistemological premises 66–8; personal 63–4; social 68–9
equality: dialogic relationship model and 166–7; in Greek project 115; musicians' mixed experiences and 100; between participants 32; social 97; on stage 99; through improvisational workshops 114; *see also* partnership
equal temperament 217
Eraut, Michael 183

Espeland, Magne 58, 205
essentially contested concepts 19
ethics 112
ethnography, performance 31
event preparation 102–3
expectancy-value theory 86
experience-based learning 98, 102
experiences, exchanging 103–6
exposure to arts 171, 191, 239–40
externalization 105

Fink-Jensen, Kirsten 209
Finklea, Wendy 147
flexibility 116–17
formal education settings 7
formal talks 135
Foster, Hal 30–1, 35
frame analysis 18–20, 23
frame breaks 19
frame disputes 19–20
frame fabrication 19
framing capacity 65
Freire, Paulo 63
funding 16, 17, 111, 121–22

Gallie, Walter 19
Geertz, Clifford xi
gender issues 96, 99, 100, 104
Georgii-Hemming, Eva 97
Gergen, Kenneth xi
Goffman, Erving 17, 18
Gómez de la Iglesia, Roberto 110
Goodlad, John I. 159–60
goodness discourse 233–5
governments, mobilizing arts 4–5
Greene, Maxine 6

Habermas, Jürgen 21
Hallam, Richard 142
Hanley, Betty 92
harmony, in coteaching studies 224–8
Hatcher, Julie A. 148–9
Hattie, John 187
Haug, Wolfgang F. 195–6
Hechtle, Markus 53–4

hegemonic macrostructures 46
Henze, Hans Werner 51
heteronomy-aesthetic approach to art 33–4
Hewison, Robert 41
Hickey, Maud 55
Hiensius, Joost 108
hierarchical relations 237
Higgins, Lee 65
higher education, de-institutionalizing space 44
higher music education 40, 43–4, 46; *see also* music education
Hofer, Barbara K. 63
homophonic relationships 225–6, 238

improvisatory activities 114–15, 150–1, 153, 214
improvising, as freedom 114
informal talks 135
innovation 110
in-school activity stages 182–3
in-service training in composing pedagogy (SÄPE) 83n4
insider-outsider perspectives 208–9
instrumental approach to collaborations 235
instrumental knowledge 68
instrumental stakeholder 21–2, 23
intended learning statements 185
interactionism: 8, 18, 23, 62; *see also* frame analysis; relational aesthetics; social interactions
interactions: dialogic 165; between musician and teachers 127, 134, 166–67; process of 110; with special needs students 153; between teacher and participants 147–48, 205–6; in time and space 136; *see also* musicking interactions; social interactions
interdisciplinary instruction 125–26
interdisciplinary knowledge 35
internalization 97, 105
intranalization 97, 105
iPad, as musical instrument 146–50

iPadists 147
Isaksen, Bjarne 143–4

John-Steiner, Vera 6
Jones, Ken 5

Kaltefleiter, Caroline K. 44
Kaplan, Andy 6
kategoria 218, 228
Kennon, Nicole 21
Kenny, Ailbhe 10, 40, 100, 131, 134, 238, 239
Kester, Grant H. 31–2
keying 18–19
Kind, Sylvia 7–8
Kitcher, Phillip 67
Klangnetze 51
knowledge: description of 238; dichotomies 183–4; instrumental 68; intended learning statements in 185; principal domains of 188–9, *189*; types of 183–4
knowledge transfer 184
Kostova, Tatiana 34
Kvarnhall, Victor 97

Langer, Susanne xi
Lave, Jean 194, 195, 199, 201n2
Laycock, Jolyon 7
learners/learning: activity vs. 186; centrality of 187–8; content 87; definition of 194–5; epistemological premises for 66; evidenced in achievement 186; experience-based 98, 102; interactive character of 97; from one's own upbringing perspective 196; as process of change 194–5, 238; scaffolding approach to 5, 104; from social to the individual 218; through social interaction 5; unidirectional movement and 8; *see also* situated learning
learning-doing dichotomy 188
"learning through the arts" 121
Lehikoinen, Kai 108

Leung, Eddie C. K. 86
Liebau, Eckart 56
Lipscomb, Scott D. 55
Luhmann, Niklas 52

Malatesta, Erico 44
Malmberg, Isolde 59n3
Malone, Mark 16
Mans, Minette 136
Mantie, Roger 42
marketing competencies 110
McNicol, Richard 51, 181
Menger, Pierre Michel 41
misframing 19
monophonic relationships 224–5, 238
Moody, Howard 111
Moore, Gillian 51, 181
Moran, Seana 6
Morrissey, Dorothy 239
Muldoon, Ryan 67
multidimensional field of tension *213*, 214–15
multiple creativities 74–5
music: as discourse 205; in English National Curriculum (NC) 180; interactions 114; literacy 67–8; as recreational subject 210; in therapeutic applications 146, 151–2; "we-ness" of 208
musical agora 113
musical events *see* school concerts
music education 161, 208; *see also* higher music education; school curriculum
musicians: acknowledging teacher's work 45; as collaborative entrepreneurs 44; educating as teachers 195–6; opposing objectives of 51; on pupils/students 29; romantic notion of 42; self-employed 41; serious leisure of 42; as teachers 39–40, 43–5, 161; teachers and 41–3; teachers vs. 39–41; training as school music teachers 42; view of school concert visits 28–9; *see also* artists; teaching artists
musician/teacher dichotomies 7–8

music industry 43–4
music-in-education programs 5
musicking: definition of 24n2, 162; dialogic relationship through 164–5, 165; exacerbating social divisions 163; instances of 168; relationships development in 162–4; theory of 34, 161–2, 236
musicking interactions 165, 166–67
music-making 42–3, 77–8, 134, 136, 214; see also composer/composing; creative music-making partnerships
music teacher see teachers
music teacher education program 85, 93–4, 110, 153
mutuality, importance of 116
Myers, David E. 236, 239–40

natural authority 66
negotiations 143, 206, 214–5, 237, 242
neoliberalism 41
Niknafs, Nasim 43, 44
Nocella, Athnoy J., II 44
nomadic music teaching artists: conditions of 171; definition of 172; description of 237; itinerancy 173; partnership story of 173–7; teaching artists vs. 173; see also teaching artists
normative stakeholder 22
normative stakeholder analysis 21
normativity 68–9, 235

observation: as data-gathering strategy 124; nonparticipant method of 87, 111; participant 190–1, 194
occupational therapists 148
Ojala, Juha 75
O'Neill, Susan 136, 138
orchestration 41–2; see also composer/composing

Parkinson, Tom 43, 46
participants: experiences of 99–101; observation 194

participation: access 198–9; adjusted 198; changing 194–5, 199; in collective process 199–200; as a concept 195
participatory art 30, 31
partnership: definition of 160, 165; good nature of 233–5; personal 236; problematic 159–60, 189–90; Smallian perspective of 162–4
partnership dance 35
partnership program, definition of 133
partnership teaching 86–8
Passeron, Jean-Claude 45
pedagogical authority 45–6
pedagogical content knowledge (PCK) 183, 185–6, 220
pedagogic competencies 109, 114–16
performance ethnography 31
performativity 31, 185–6, 188
performances 99–101
personal epistemology 63–4
personal partnership 236
Philpott, Chris 163
Pierce, Jon L. 34
Pintrich, Paul R. 63
place-conscious music education 153
policy/policy makers 19, 22–3, 43, 121, 160, 241
politically correct performance 101
polyphonic relationships 227–8, 239
popular music pedagogy 75
power of definition 235–37
power/power structure: among stakeholders 20–2, 235; artists holding 27; balance of 34–5, 169; in collaborative settings 16, 42–3, 105; of dialogic artwork 32; hierarchies 17; of music 150–51; symbolic violence and 29; see also empowerment
power relations 234
prespecifying learning 186
professional development: after-school meetings as 175; for composers 184; partnerships highlighting importance

of 6–7; for professional artists 111; Steam Forward (SF) program 131; for teachers 93–4, 115–16; teaching artists and 92
professional identities in musical communities of practice 212–13
professional knowledge *see* knowledge
professional learning *see* learners/learning
professional musicians *see* musicians
project management competencies 110
Przbylski, Liz 43, 44
psychological ownership 34–5
Pugh, Gillian 160, 165
punk pedagogies 43–6
purpose, notion of 64, 66

Rabkin, Nick 35
radical musical inclusion 112, 116
Ranciére, Jean-Jacques 33
Rasmussen, Bjørn 33–4
reflection/reflective stage 166, 182–3, 186–90
rehearsal 114, 136, 139, 182, 198, 211–2
relational aesthetics 31
repertoire 22, 68, 123, 134–6, 161
representation, in stakeholder analysis 20–1
research competencies 110, 117–18
research design 208–9
resistance, expressions of 221–2
resistance culture 44
resonance problems of social functional systems 53–4
rights and duties 66, 68–9
Riley, Patricia 148
Rio, Robin 148, 152
Rock band project: analysis of 198–200; communication between musician and class 199; participant observation 194; rehearsal 196–8
role conflicts 50, 52 *see also* conflict within collaborations
role models 63

Savage, Jonathan 141
Sawyer, R. Keith 182
scaffolding 5, 101, 141, 143, 205, 229
Schleswig-Holstein Musik Festival 51
Schön, Donald 187
school-based music specialists 127–9
school concerts: engaging teachers in 30; as heteronomic 34; musician sender-receiver relationship in 29–30; musicians view of 28–9; psychological ownership of 34–5
school curriculum: arts-based learning 121–2; budget cuts affecting 16; Cantonese opera in 85, 86; core element of 86; curriculum guide 128; group-based composing 73; Mississippi Blues Trail Curriculum 16–17; music education role in 109; musicians connecting with 35; music lessons in 91; National Core Curriculum for Basic Education 75, 82; process oriented creative approaches in 134; removal of music in 168; *Resolution* composing project 184; solidifying music in 16; Steam Forward (SF) program 122–6; subverting power of 168–9; updating 92
school kits 102
school of art vs. art of school 56
schools: as artistic venue 31; educational mission of 97
self-employed musicians 41
Sfard, Anna 188–9
Shulman, Lee 183
situated learning: in social practice theoretical perspective 194; theoretical analysis of 198, 200; *see also* learners/learning
situated perspectives 17
situated work orientation 101, 106
Small, Christopher 34, 161–2
social competencies 110
social discourse 205
social epistemology 68–9

social interactions 74, 110, 207
socially interactive model of art practice 31–2, *32*
social roles 237
sociological systems theory 52
Sommer, Eric 217
Sørensen, Merete 136, 141
special-interest groups 16
stakeholder analysis 18, 20–2
Stauffer, Sandra 153
Stickney, Clare Tracy 219–20
Stirner, Max 44
Strozzi, Barbara 102
structured reflection 190
students, perception of their teacher 59
students with disabilities, musical engagement and 147
subjects of teaching 66
subordinate roles 237
sustainability of projects 92, 116
Swanwick, Keith 112, 186
symbolic interactionism 8, 18
symbolic violence 29, 41, 237
synergy 217–8
systematic developmental model *219*, 223

teacher-as-student mode of teaching 90–1
teacher-centered with artist as assistant modes in teaching 88–9
teacher competence 237–8
teacher education programs 40
teacher/musician relationship: collaborative modes 88–91; as symbolic violence 29
teachers: burnout 172; collaboration among 126–7; competency of 161; educating musicians as 195–6; as failed professionals 39; lack of interest in participation 100; level of respect for 93; musical expertise of 167–8; musicians and 41–3; musician's participation as 200; musicians vs. 39–41; as nonartistic supporters 58; as passive participants 161; professional development for 115–16; professionalism of 187–8; role of 57, 87–8, 167–8, 205; social journey of 80–1; student's perception of 59; training of 110
teaching, performative elements of 237–8
teaching artists: competencies for 108–10; as a concept 92; definition of 172; description of 148; developing as a presenter 129; evaluating 129–30; facilitating improvisation 150–1; nomadic teaching artist vs. 173; orchestra musicians as 122–3; power balance and 34–5; preparing for school environments 171; skills development 129–30; for Steam Forward program 122–3; VSA (Very Special Artists) 152; working for multiple organizations 171; *see also* artists; nomadic music teaching artists; visiting artists
technology 146, 148–9, 153
tension: ambiguous role definitions 58; in arts-in-education initiatives 4; authority and 65; within collaborations 17, 33, 167–9, 234–5; composing projects and 214–5; in creative music-making projects 140–1, 143; discursive 50, 235; with expectations 172; inner 218; multidimensional field of 213–4, *213*; relaxation and 98; in student creativity and teacher education programs 40
therapy 147–8, 151, 152
thinking beyond the bubbles 17
time: as hardest currency of schools 177, 239–40; making music and 42
Todd, Elisabeth S. 160
Torrez, Estrella 44
transformative practice zones 6
trust 223–4

value 35, 112, 116, 136, 163, 235
Veloso, Ana Luísa 65

venue demands 113
victory narratives 3, 143, 189
visiting artists 4; *see also* artists; teaching artists
Vitale, John L. 93
VSA (Very Special Artists) 147, 152, 239
Vygotsky, Lev S. 5, 98, 101, 218, 220, 228

Wacquant, Loïc J. D. 29
Wenger, Etienne 35, 195, 201n2

Wiggins, Jackie 143, 205
Williamson, John 44
Winnicott, Donald 98
Wolf, Shelby A. 7, 131

Yeorgouli-Bourzoucos, Styliani 113

Ziehe, Thomas 97, 106
zone of proximal development (ZPD) 98, 101, 106